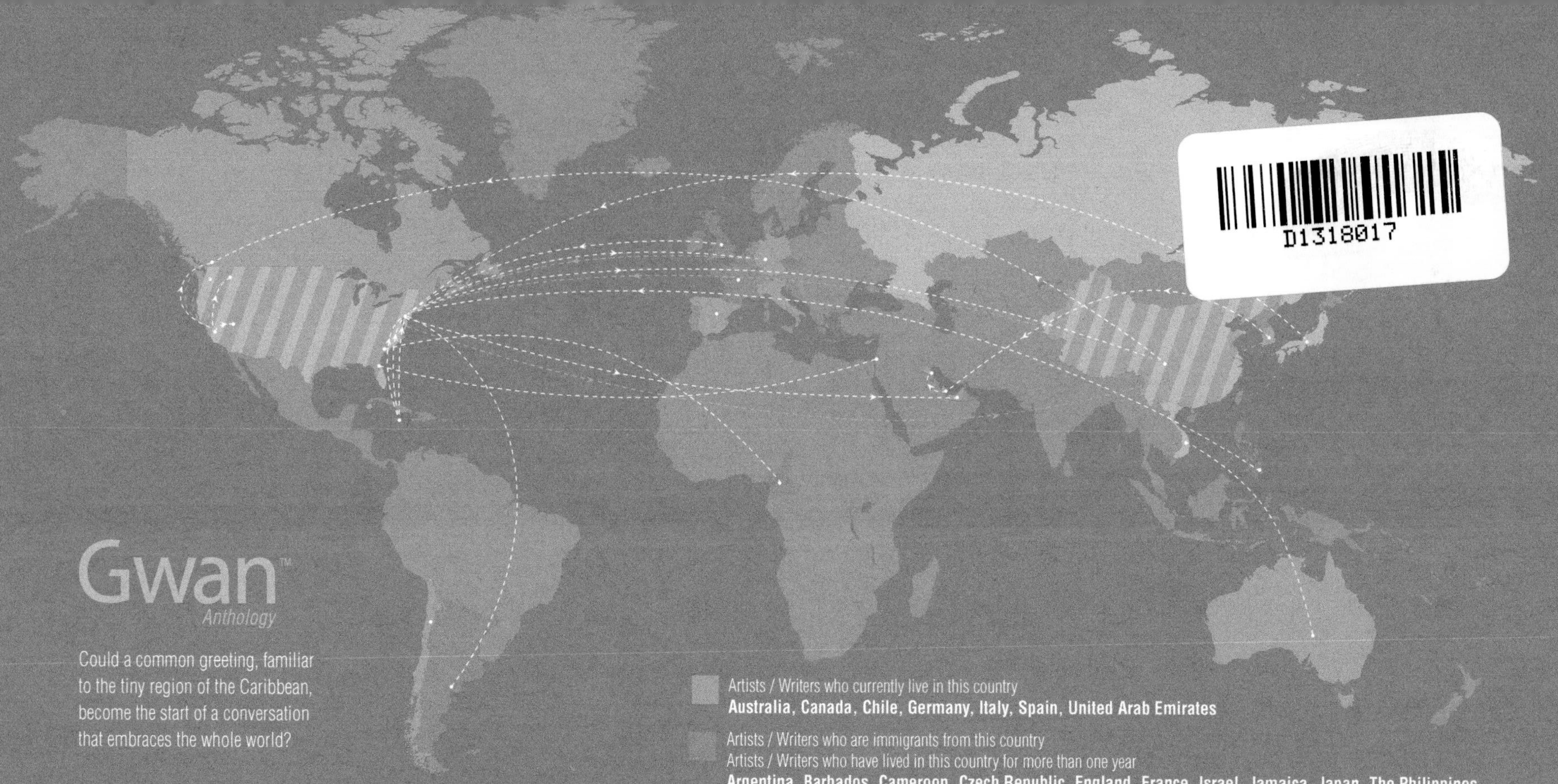

Gwan™
Anthology

Could a common greeting, familiar to the tiny region of the Caribbean, become the start of a conversation that embraces the whole world?

30+ Artists / 15 Countries / 5 Continents / 1 Book

FORWARD COMIX®

Artists / Writers who currently live in this country
Australia, Canada, Chile, Germany, Italy, Spain, United Arab Emirates

Artists / Writers who are immigrants from this country
Artists / Writers who have lived in this country for more than one year
Argentina, Barbados, Cameroon, Czech Republic, England, France, Israel, Jamaica, Japan, The Philippines

Artists / Writers who have based their story on experiences of a loved one from this country
Artists / Writers who have close family from this country
Japan, Russia, St. Kitts, Vietnam

Artists / Writers who are expats from this country and other artists / writers who currently living in this country
China, United States

International supporters of the Gwan Anthology project who live in this country
Cyprus, Kuwait, Qatar, South Korea

Table of Contents

*Based on a true story

The human story is one of migration.
We are connected by a common
thread, a bond across many paths on
a seemingly endless journey in the
search for "home."

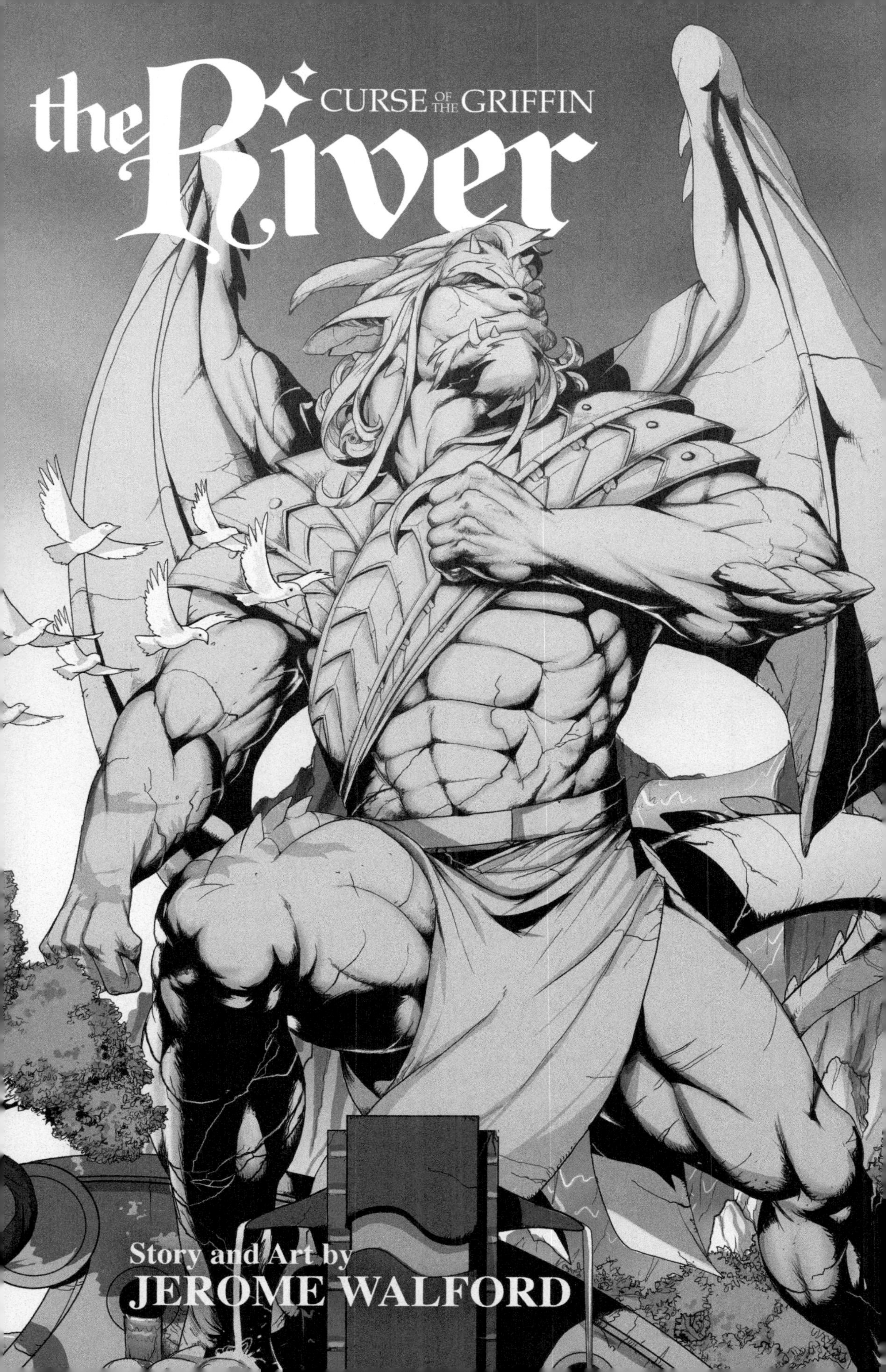
the River
CURSE OF THE GRIFFIN
Story and Art by
JEROME WALFORD

Jerome Walford, Writer/Artist

Jamaica / United States

Jerome Walford is an award-winning writer and illustrator, as well as the founder of Forward Comix. Jerome is best known for his graphic novel series *Nowhere Man* – winner of the Glyph Comics Award for Best Male Character, and Urban Action Showcase & Expo (UASE) Urban Action Comic Honoree. He is also the creator/writer/illustrator for *Freeing Violet, Effect, Rambun-shialon-ctious, Moon's Ostrich* and *The Scientist*. Jerome is also the author of the literary young adult series *Curse of the Griffin*. Jerome continues to publish under Forward Comix and collaborate on projects that align with his belief that unique stories have the power to impact one's personal journey and encourage positive cultural movement.

Nowhere Man

Curse of the Griffin: Daniel's Pride

Moon's Ostrich

The Scientist

Freeing Violet

Effect

forwardcomix.com

FROM THE EPIC, MYSTICAL SAGA

CURSE OF THE GRIFFIN

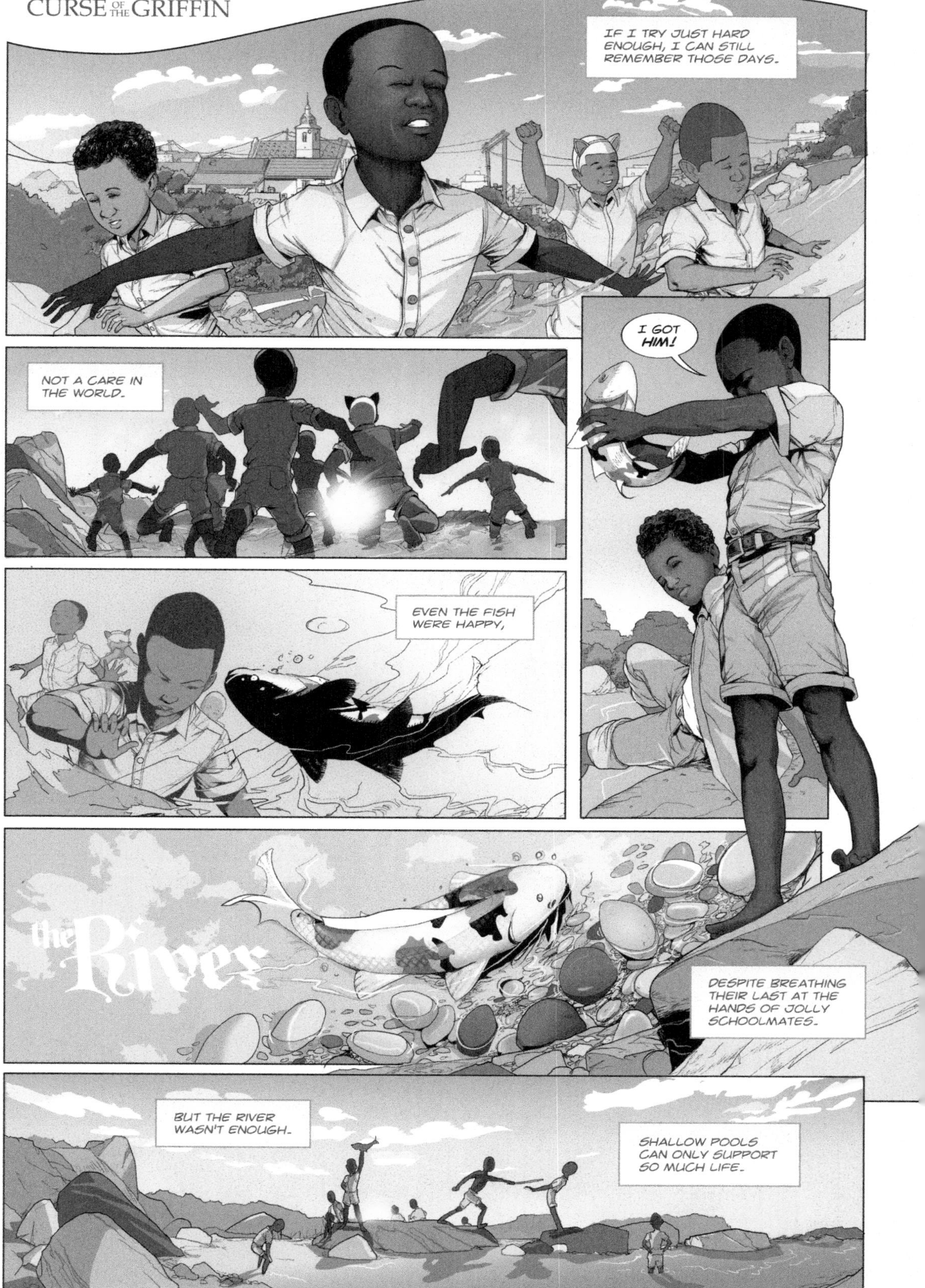
IF I TRY JUST HARD ENOUGH, I CAN STILL REMEMBER THOSE DAYS.
NOT A CARE IN THE WORLD.
I GOT HIM!
EVEN THE FISH WERE HAPPY,
the River
DESPITE BREATHING THEIR LAST AT THE HANDS OF JOLLY SCHOOLMATES.
BUT THE RIVER WASN'T ENOUGH.
SHALLOW POOLS CAN ONLY SUPPORT SO MUCH LIFE.

SIGH—

I DON'T WANT TO MOVE. I LIKE OUR HOUSE.

I LIKE MY SCHOOL, AND THE RIVER.

THERE CAME NEWS OF A MYSTICAL REGION, FILLED WITH OPPORTUNITY.

WE EMBARKED ON THE JOURNEY, LED BY FAMILY MORE CONCERNED ABOUT OUR FUTURE THAN THEIR PRESENT COMFORT.

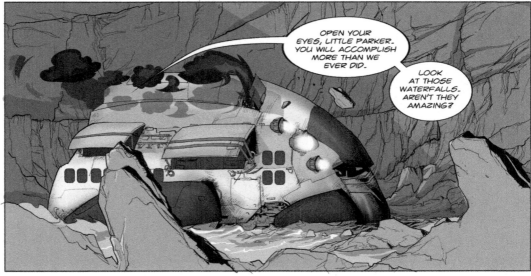

OPEN YOUR EYES, LITTLE PARKER. YOU WILL ACCOMPLISH MORE THAN WE EVER DID.

LOOK AT THOSE WATERFALLS. AREN'T THEY AMAZING?

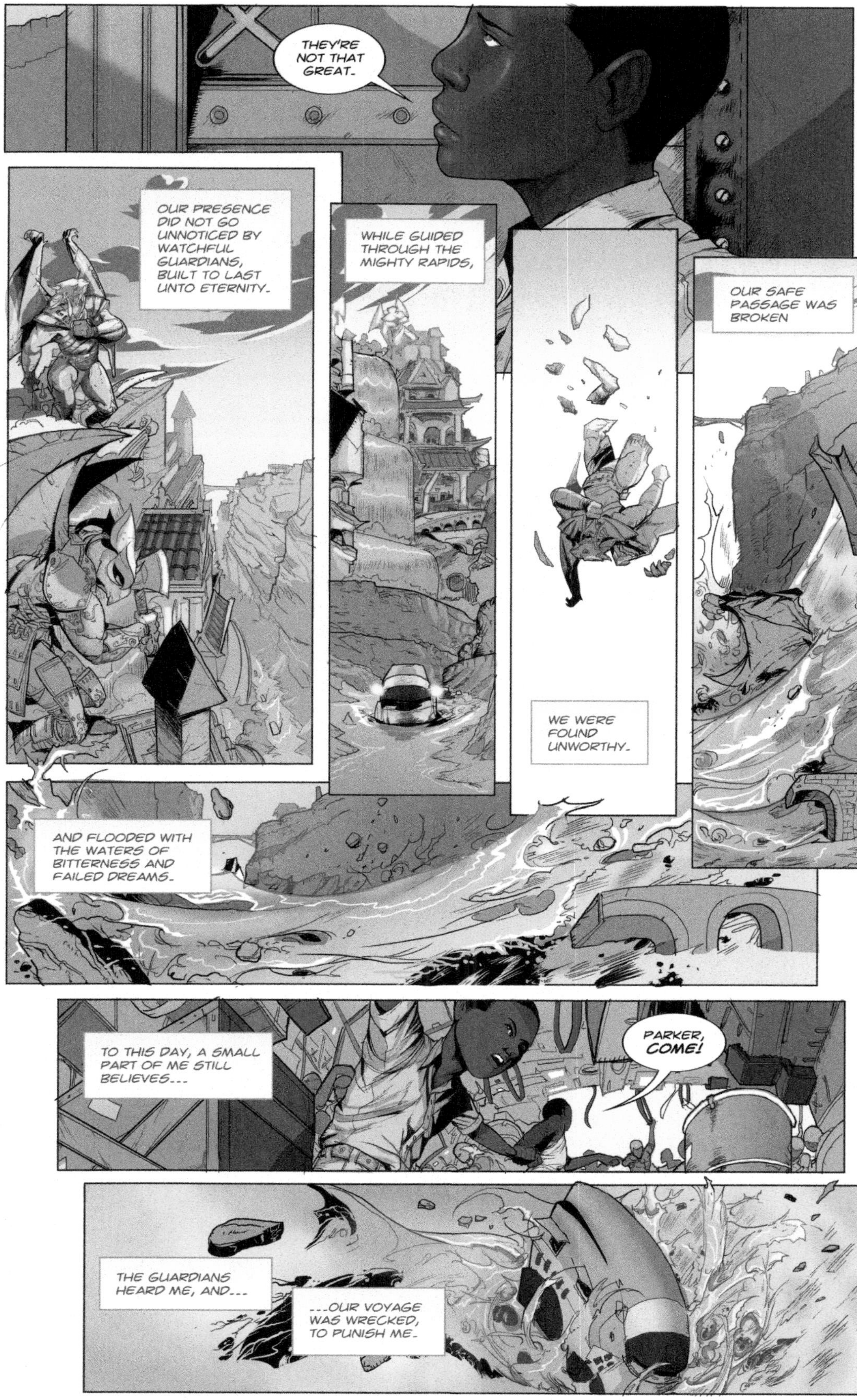
THEY'RE NOT THAT GREAT.
OUR PRESENCE DID NOT GO UNNOTICED BY WATCHFUL GUARDIANS, BUILT TO LAST UNTO ETERNITY.
WHILE GUIDED THROUGH THE MIGHTY RAPIDS,
WE WERE FOUND UNWORTHY.
OUR SAFE PASSAGE WAS BROKEN
AND FLOODED WITH THE WATERS OF BITTERNESS AND FAILED DREAMS.
TO THIS DAY, A SMALL PART OF ME STILL BELIEVES...
PARKER, COME!
THE GUARDIANS HEARD ME, AND...
...OUR VOYAGE WAS WRECKED, TO PUNISH ME.

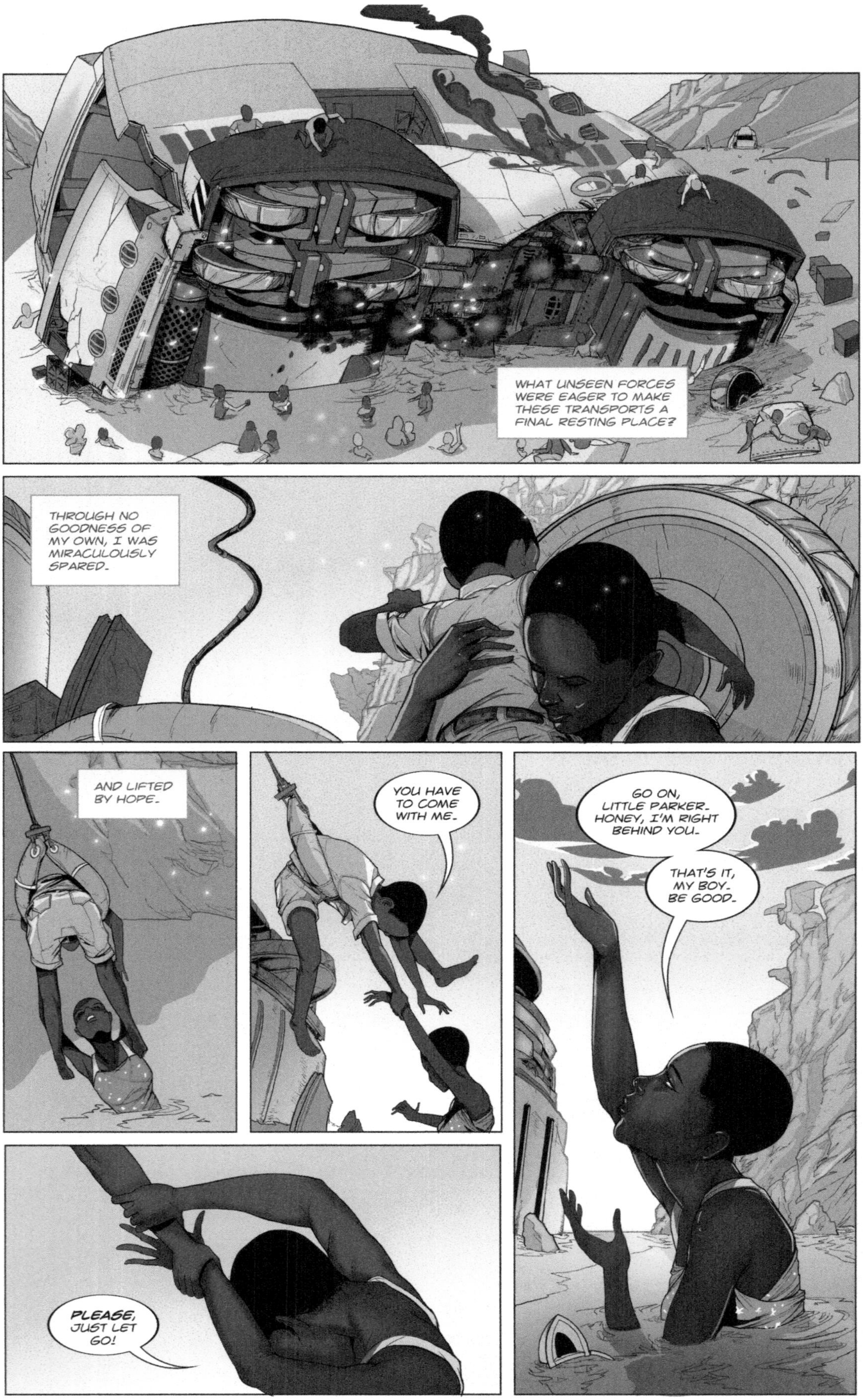
WHAT UNSEEN FORCES WERE EAGER TO MAKE THESE TRANSPORTS A FINAL RESTING PLACE?
THROUGH NO GOODNESS OF MY OWN, I WAS MIRACULOUSLY SPARED.
AND LIFTED BY HOPE.
YOU HAVE TO COME WITH ME.
GO ON, LITTLE PARKER. HONEY, I'M RIGHT BEHIND YOU.
THAT'S IT, MY BOY. BE GOOD.
PLEASE, JUST LET GO!

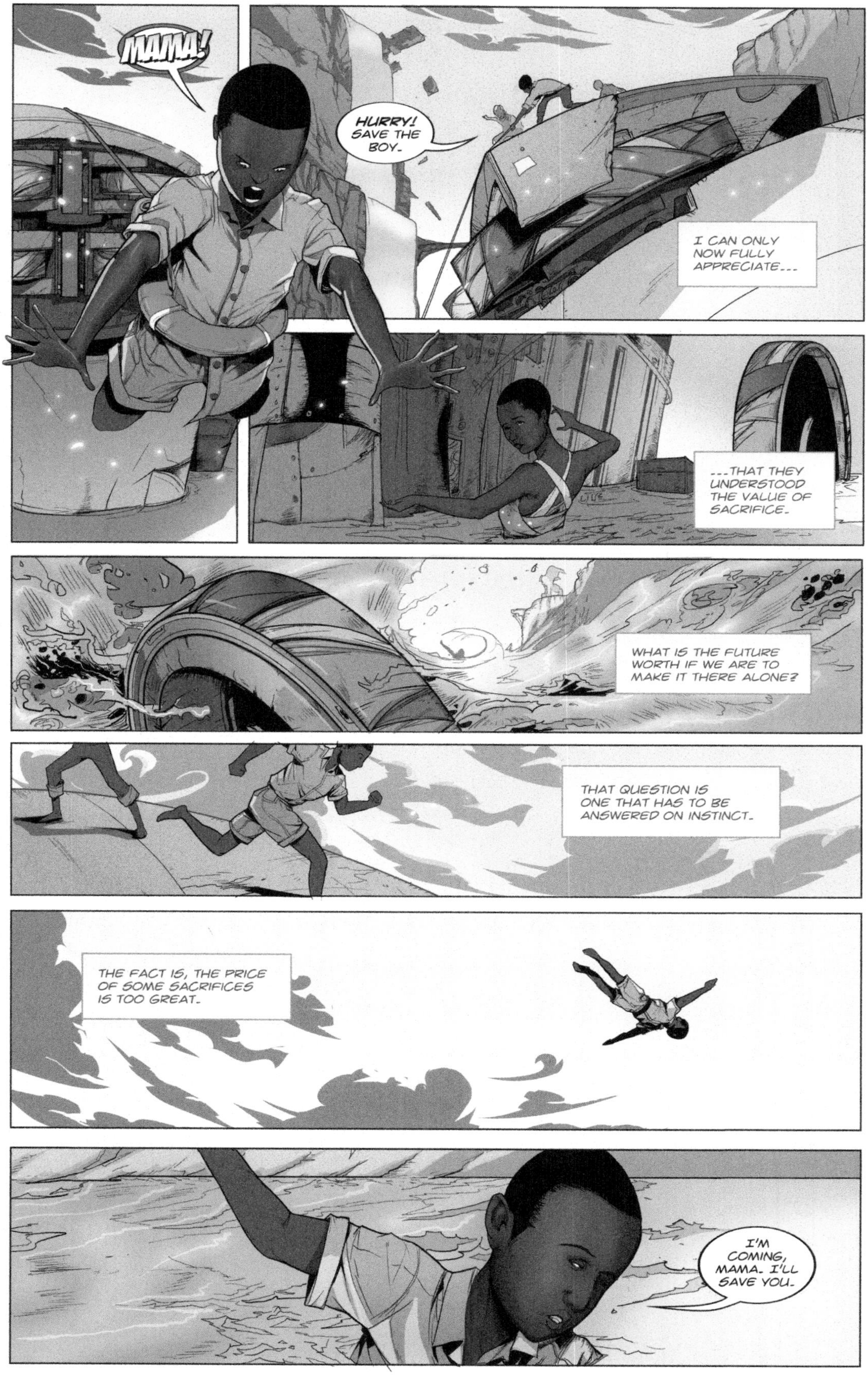
MAMA!
HURRY! SAVE THE BOY.
I CAN ONLY NOW FULLY APPRECIATE...
...THAT THEY UNDERSTOOD THE VALUE OF SACRIFICE.
WHAT IS THE FUTURE WORTH IF WE ARE TO MAKE IT THERE ALONE?
THAT QUESTION IS ONE THAT HAS TO BE ANSWERED ON INSTINCT.
THE FACT IS, THE PRICE OF SOME SACRIFICES IS TOO GREAT.
I'M COMING, MAMA. I'LL SAVE YOU.

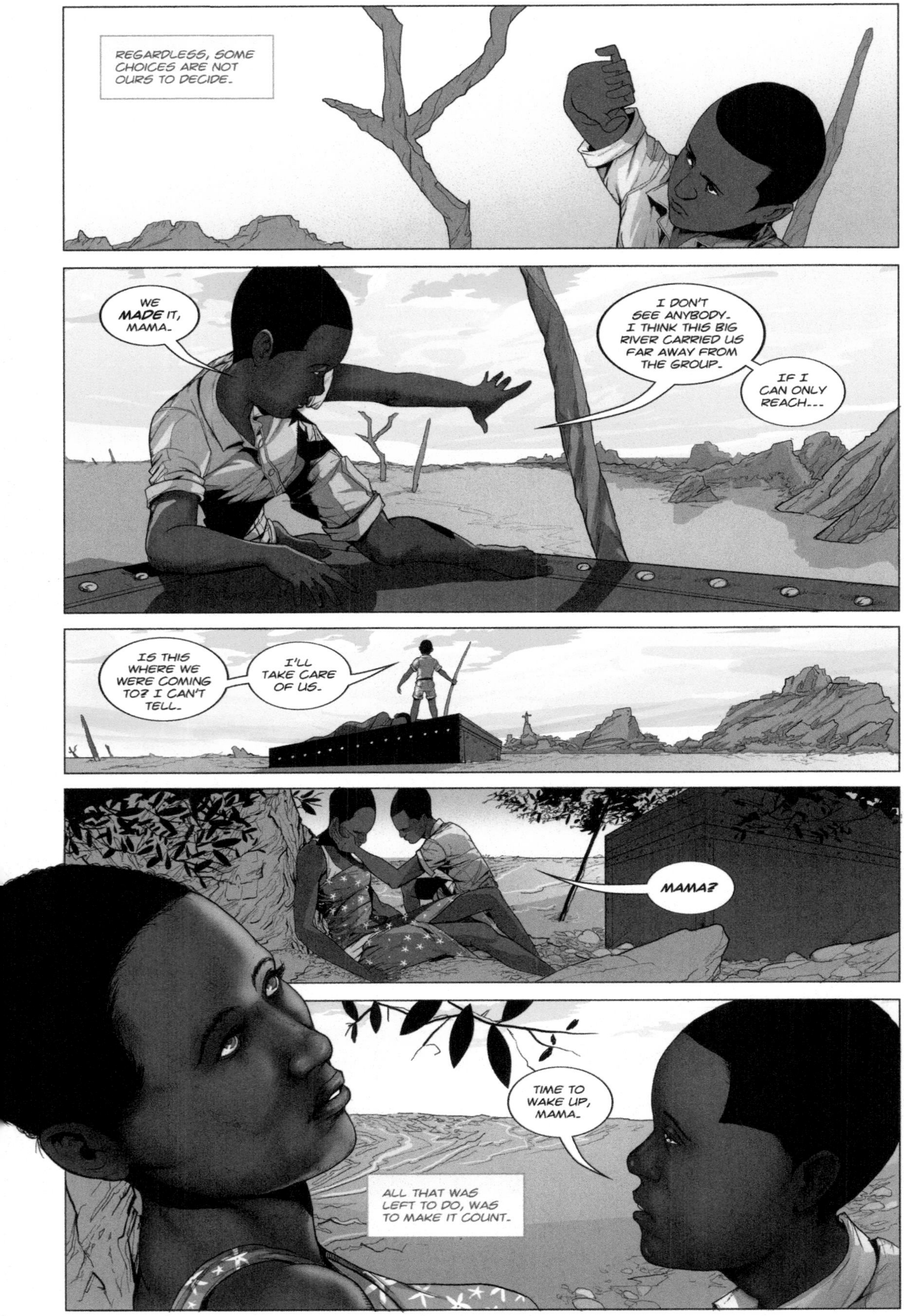
REGARDLESS, SOME CHOICES ARE NOT OURS TO DECIDE.
WE MADE IT, MAMA.
I DON'T SEE ANYBODY. I THINK THIS BIG RIVER CARRIED US FAR AWAY FROM THE GROUP.
IF I CAN ONLY REACH...
IS THIS WHERE WE WERE COMING TO? I CAN'T TELL.
I'LL TAKE CARE OF US.
MAMA?
TIME TO WAKE UP, MAMA.
ALL THAT WAS LEFT TO DO, WAS TO MAKE IT COUNT.

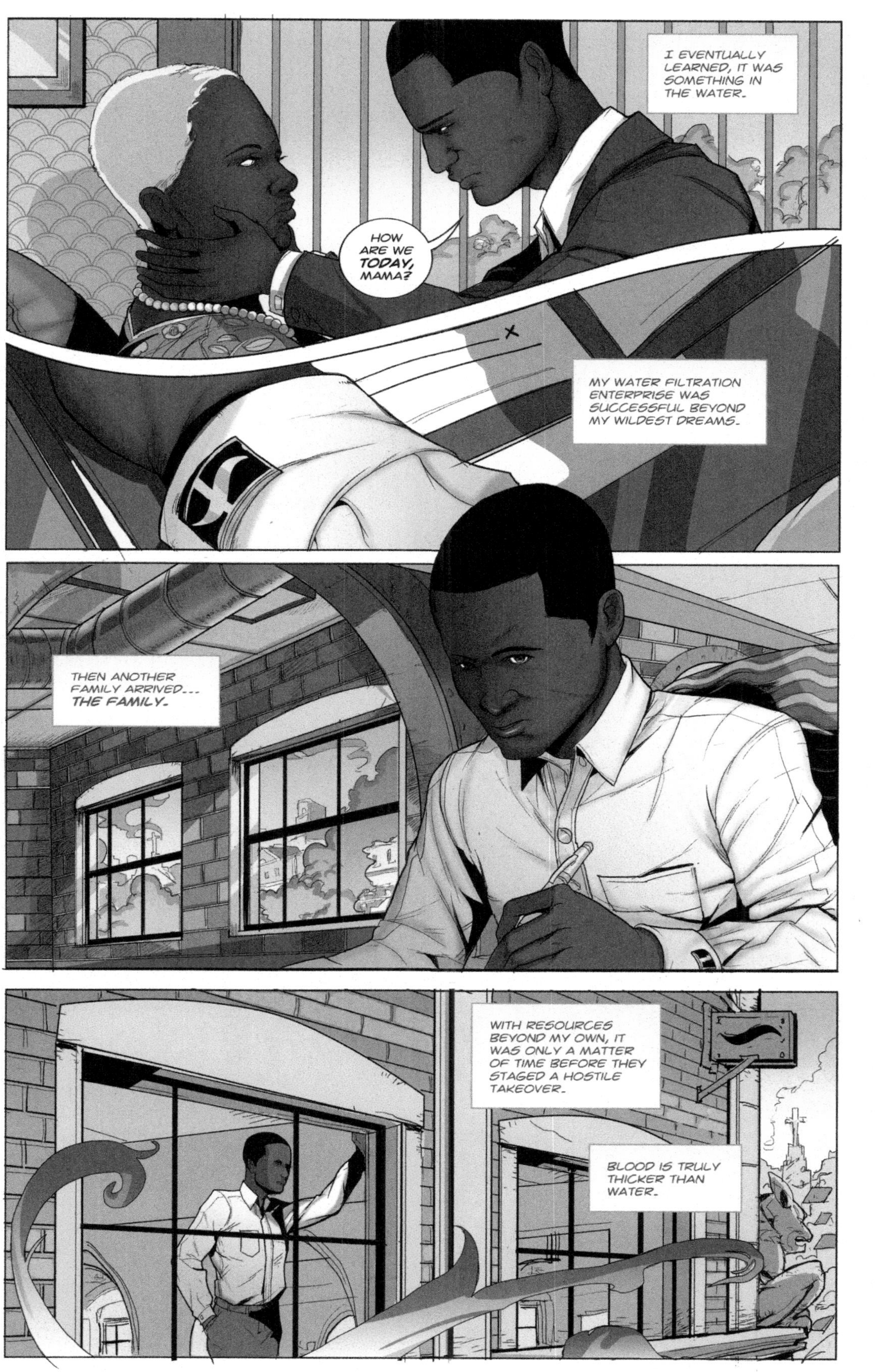
I EVENTUALLY LEARNED, IT WAS SOMETHING IN THE WATER.
HOW ARE WE TODAY, MAMA?
MY WATER FILTRATION ENTERPRISE WAS SUCCESSFUL BEYOND MY WILDEST DREAMS.
THEN ANOTHER FAMILY ARRIVED... THE FAMILY.
WITH RESOURCES BEYOND MY OWN, IT WAS ONLY A MATTER OF TIME BEFORE THEY STAGED A HOSTILE TAKEOVER.
BLOOD IS TRULY THICKER THAN WATER.

I DO WONDER, IF IT WAS ALL WORTH IT.

SIR, COMMONERS ARE ADVISED TO WEAR PROPER OUTERCOATS.

THANK YOU, DRONE OFFICER.

DID I MAKE IT COUNT?

THE LAST FILTRATION PLANT WILL CLOSE TODAY. WHO KNOWS WHAT THEY WILL BE CONVERTED INTO.

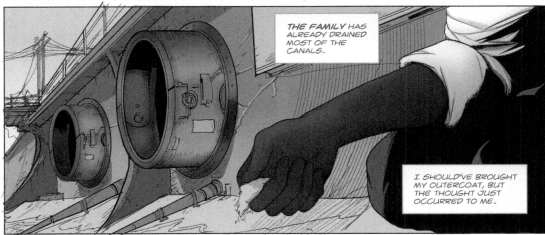

THE FAMILY HAS ALREADY DRAINED MOST OF THE CANALS.

I SHOULD'VE BROUGHT MY OUTERCOAT, BUT THE THOUGHT JUST OCCURRED TO ME.

THERE IS A SMALL STREAM AT THE EDGE OF THE DISTRICT, JUST OUT OF SIGHT.

I WONDER, IF I CULTIVATED IT WELL ENOUGH, WOULD THE FISH RETURN?

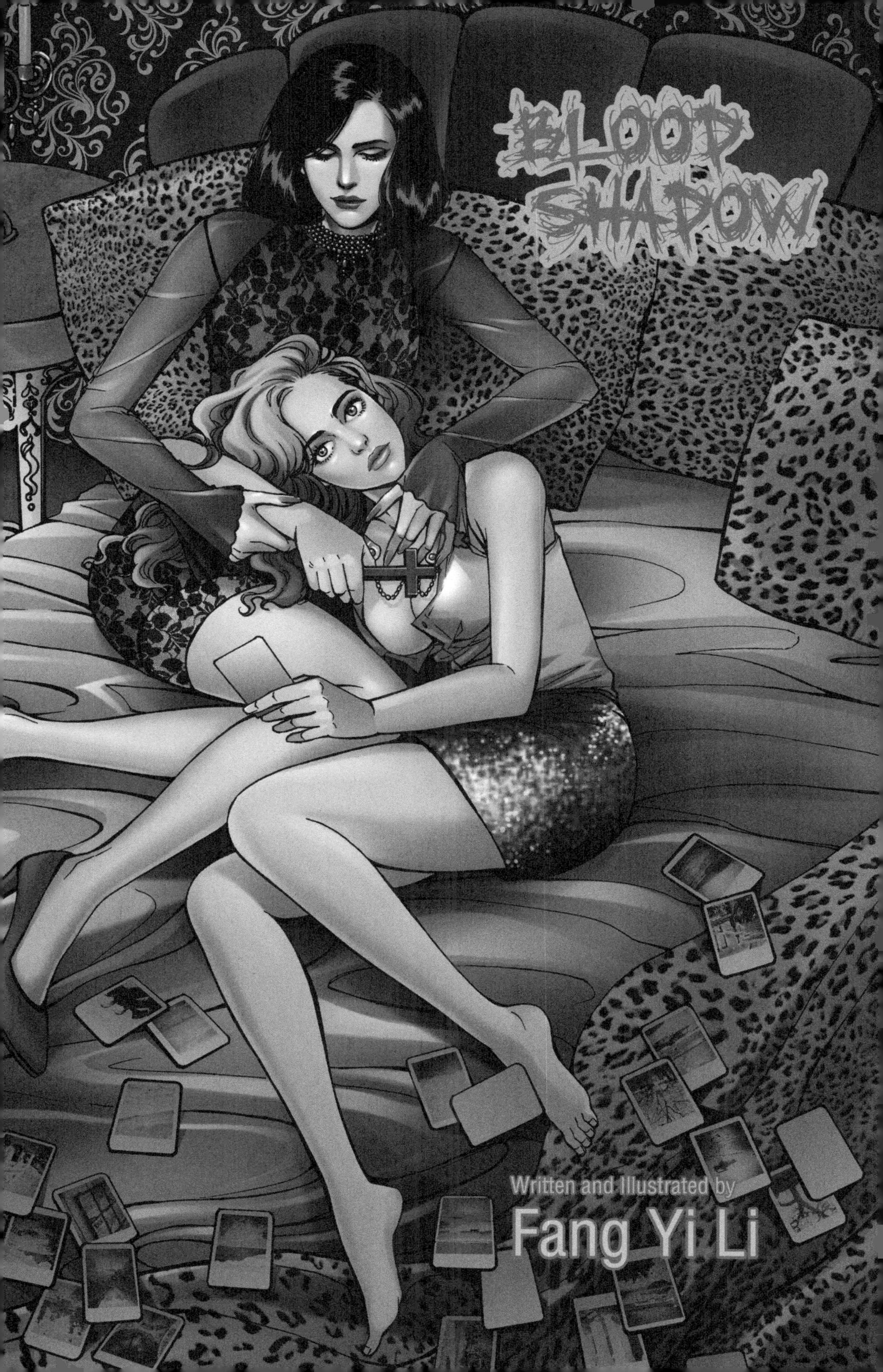

BLOOD SHADOW
Written and Illustrated by
Fang Yi Li

Fang Yi Li, Writer/Artist

China

My name is Fang Yi Li, but my friends call me Fang Fang. I was born in Sichuan, China, home of pandas and possibly the spiciest Chinese food. My favorite kinds of stories are Sci-fi and horror, like Star Wars, Watchmen, and AHS.

As a child I studied traditional Chinese painting, but as I grew up, I fell in love with American comics, and manga too!

I have written and drawn a few creator-owned comics. A few years ago, I was fortunate enough to start working with a French publisher. It was then that my style began to take on other influences.

I love American pop culture and I hope to work more in America. I'm hoping to connect with writers and editors who like my style and would like to collaborate.

fangfangyili.com

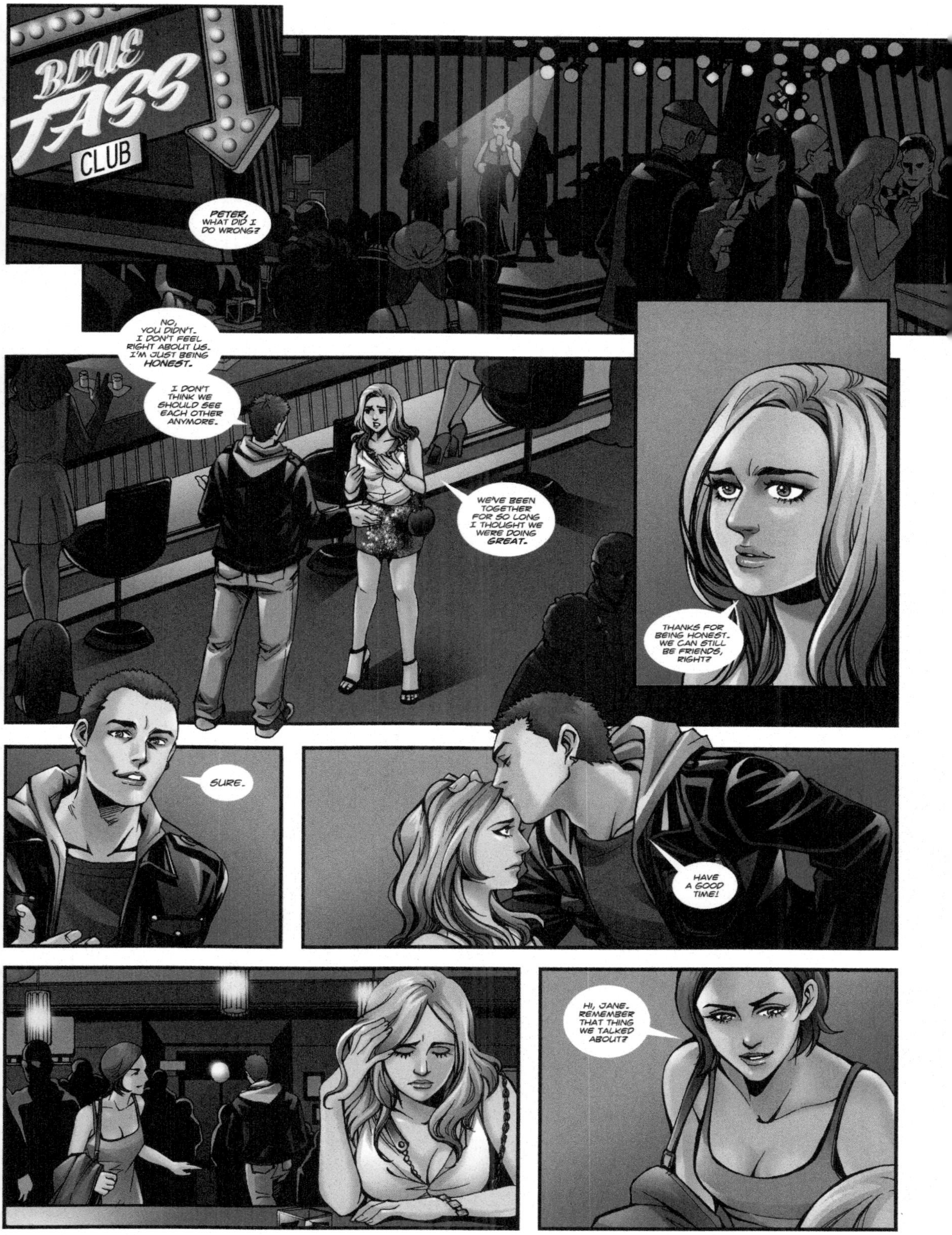
BLUE JASS
CLUB
PETER, WHAT DID I DO WRONG?
NO, YOU DIDN'T. I DON'T FEEL RIGHT ABOUT US. I'M JUST BEING HONEST.
I DON'T THINK WE SHOULD SEE EACH OTHER ANYMORE.
WE'VE BEEN TOGETHER FOR SO LONG I THOUGHT WE WERE DOING GREAT.
THANKS FOR BEING HONEST. WE CAN STILL BE FRIENDS, RIGHT?
SURE.
HAVE A GOOD TIME!
HI, JANE. REMEMBER THAT THING WE TALKED ABOUT?

NOT NOW, PETER AND I JUST...

DO I HAVE TO MOVE OUT SO *SOON?*

I *REALLY* DON'T WANT YOU TO MOVE OUT... BUT MY MUM MOVES IN NEXT WEEK.

MY MUM IS A VERY NEUROTIC PERSON. SHE CAN'T SLEEP IF SHE HEARS THE SLIGHTEST NOISE. I DON'T HAVE ANY CHOICE.

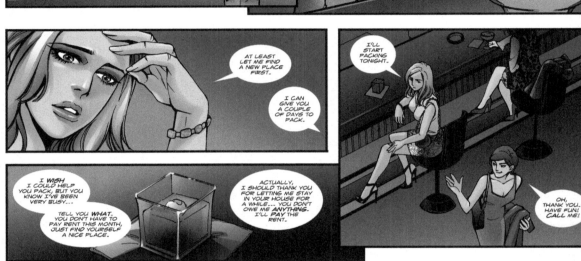

AT LEAST LET ME FIND A NEW PLACE FIRST.

I CAN GIVE YOU A COUPLE OF DAYS TO PACK.

I'LL START PACKING TONIGHT.

OH, THANK YOU, HAVE FUN! CALL ME!

I *WISH* I COULD HELP YOU PACK, BUT YOU KNOW I'VE BEEN VERY BUSY...

TELL YOU *WHAT.* YOU DON'T HAVE TO PAY RENT THIS MONTH, JUST FIND YOURSELF A NICE PLACE.

ACTUALLY, I SHOULD THANK YOU FOR LETTING ME STAY IN YOUR HOUSE FOR A WHILE... YOU DON'T OWE ME *ANYTHING.* I'LL *PAY* THE RENT.

DO YOU REALLY THINK THAT WAS A COINCIDENCE?

SORRY, I OVERHEARD YOUR UNFORTUNATE CONVERSATION.

HUH? WHAT DO YOU MEAN?

EVEN AN OUTSIDER CAN EASILY SEE...

I NOTICED THE LIPSTICK ON HIS WINE GLASS WHEN I WALKED IN, AND I WASN'T SURPRISED...

MAYBE THEY ARE RIGHT FOR EACH OTHER.

I'M NOT USED TO THE LIFE IN THIS CITY ANYWAY...

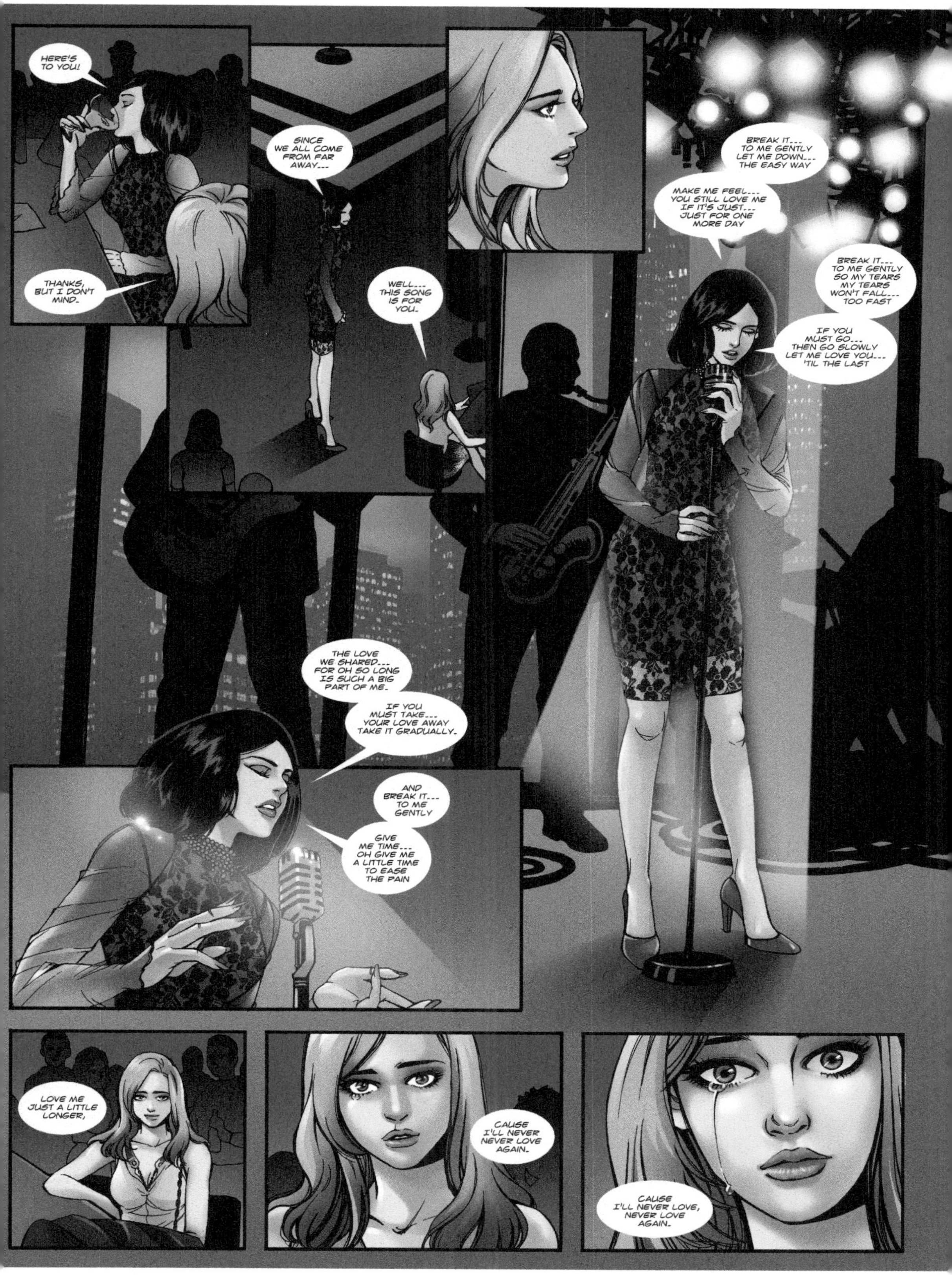
HERE'S TO YOU!
THANKS, BUT I DON'T MIND.
SINCE WE ALL COME FROM FAR AWAY...
WELL... THIS SONG IS FOR YOU.
BREAK IT... TO ME GENTLY LET ME DOWN... THE EASY WAY
MAKE ME FEEL... YOU STILL LOVE ME IF IT'S JUST... JUST FOR ONE MORE DAY
BREAK IT... TO ME GENTLY SO MY TEARS WON'T FALL... TOO FAST
IF YOU MUST GO... THEN GO SLOWLY LET ME LOVE YOU... 'TIL THE LAST
THE LOVE WE SHARED... FOR OH SO LONG IS SUCH A BIG PART OF ME.
IF YOU MUST TAKE... YOUR LOVE AWAY TAKE IT GRADUALLY.
AND BREAK IT... TO ME GENTLY
GIVE ME TIME... OH GIVE ME A LITTLE TIME TO EASE THE PAIN
LOVE ME JUST A LITTLE LONGER,
CAUSE I'LL NEVER NEVER LOVE AGAIN.
CAUSE I'LL NEVER LOVE, NEVER LOVE AGAIN.

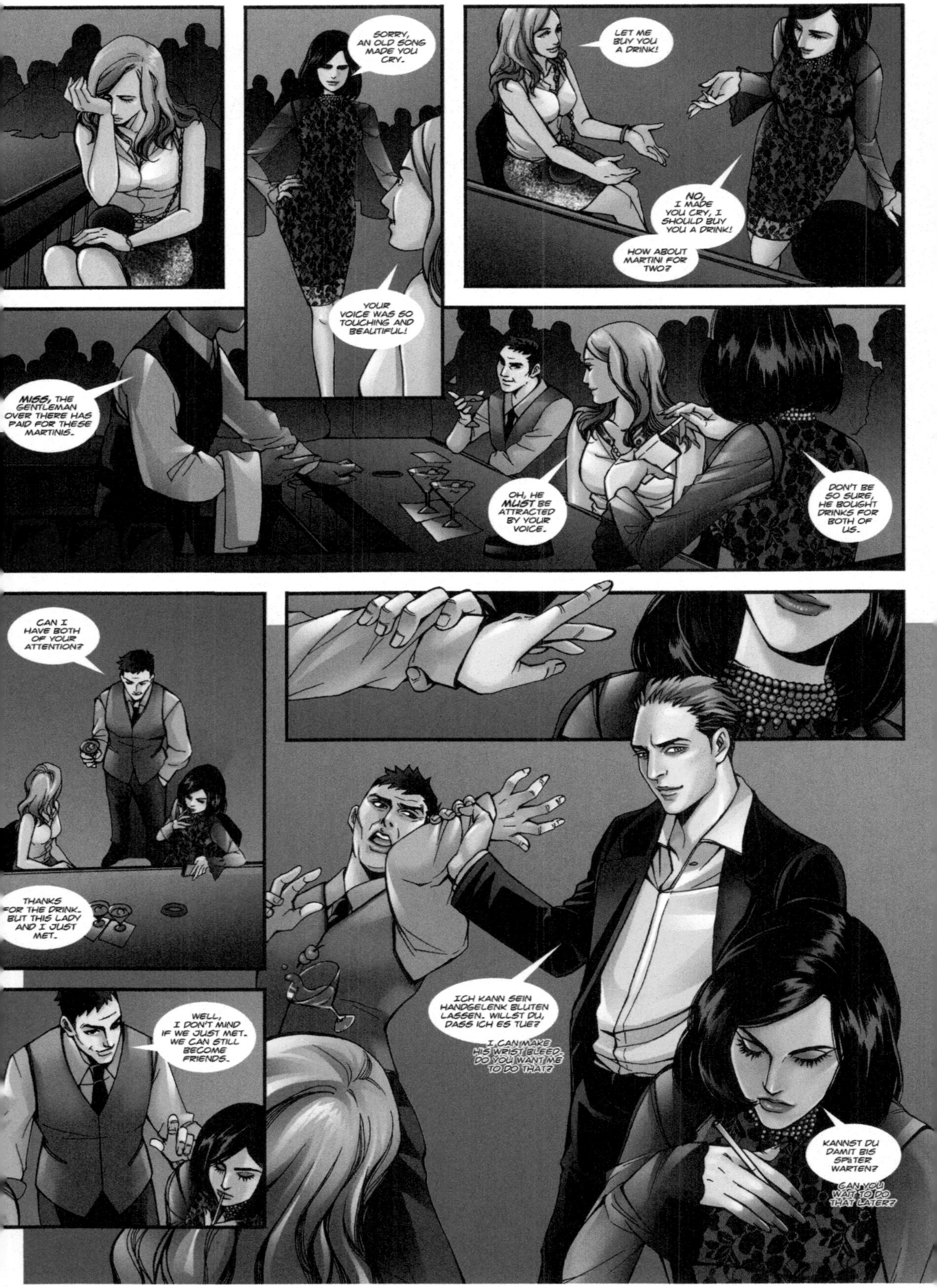
SORRY, AN OLD SONG MADE YOU CRY.
YOUR VOICE WAS SO TOUCHING AND BEAUTIFUL!
LET ME BUY YOU A DRINK!
NO, I MADE YOU CRY, I SHOULD BUY YOU A DRINK!
HOW ABOUT MARTINI FOR TWO?
MISS, THE GENTLEMAN OVER THERE HAS PAID FOR THESE MARTINIS.
OH, HE MUST BE ATTRACTED BY YOUR VOICE.
DON'T BE SO SURE, HE BOUGHT DRINKS FOR BOTH OF US.
CAN I HAVE BOTH OF YOUR ATTENTION?
THANKS FOR THE DRINK. BUT THIS LADY AND I JUST MET.
WELL, I DON'T MIND IF WE JUST MET. WE CAN STILL BECOME FRIENDS.
ICH KANN SEIN HANDGELENK BLUTEN LASSEN. WILLST DU, DASS ICH ES TUE?
I CAN MAKE HIS WRIST BLEED. DO YOU WANT ME TO DO THAT?
KANNST DU DAMIT BIS SPäTER WARTEN?
CAN YOU WAIT TO DO THAT LATER?

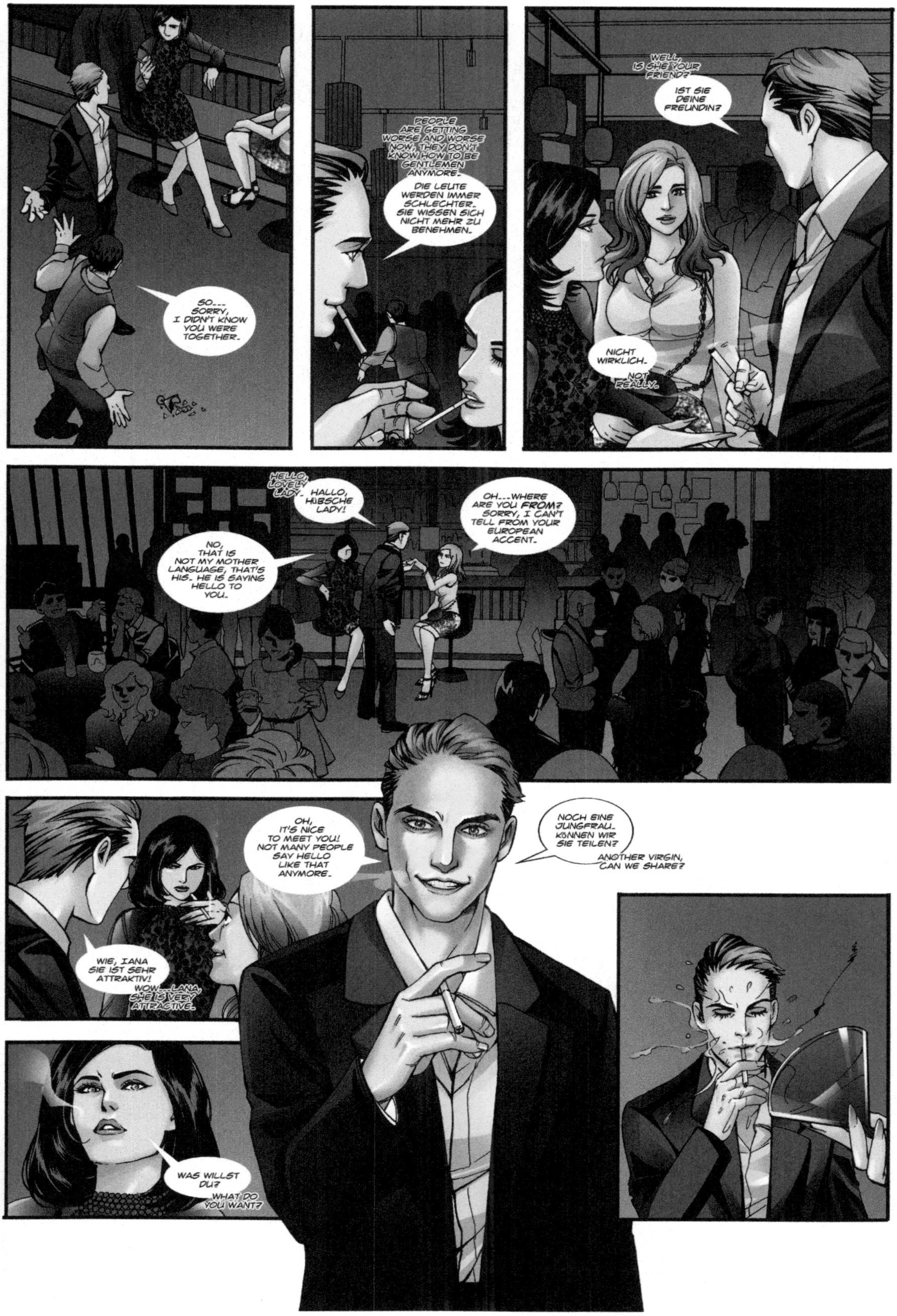
SO... SORRY, I DIDN'T KNOW YOU WERE TOGETHER.
PEOPLE ARE GETTING WORSE AND WORSE NOW, THEY DON'T KNOW HOW TO BE GENTLEMEN ANYMORE.
DIE LEUTE WERDEN IMMER SCHLECHTER. SIE WISSEN SICH NICHT MEHR ZU BENEHMEN.
WELL, IS SHE YOUR FRIEND?
IST SIE DEINE FREUNDIN?
NICHT WIRKLICH.
NOT REALLY.
HELLO, LOVELY LADY.
HALLO, HÜBSCHE LADY!
OH... WHERE ARE YOU FROM? SORRY, I CAN'T TELL FROM YOUR EUROPEAN ACCENT.
NO, THAT IS NOT MY MOTHER LANGUAGE, THAT'S HIS. HE IS SAYING HELLO TO YOU.
WIE, IANA SIE IST SEHR ATTRAKTIV!
WOW... LANA, SHE IS VERY ATTRACTIVE.
OH, IT'S NICE TO MEET YOU! NOT MANY PEOPLE SAY HELLO LIKE THAT ANYMORE.
NOCH EINE JUNGFRAU. KÖNNEN WIR SIE TEILEN?
ANOTHER VIRGIN, CAN WE SHARE?
WAS WILLST DU?
WHAT DO YOU WANT?

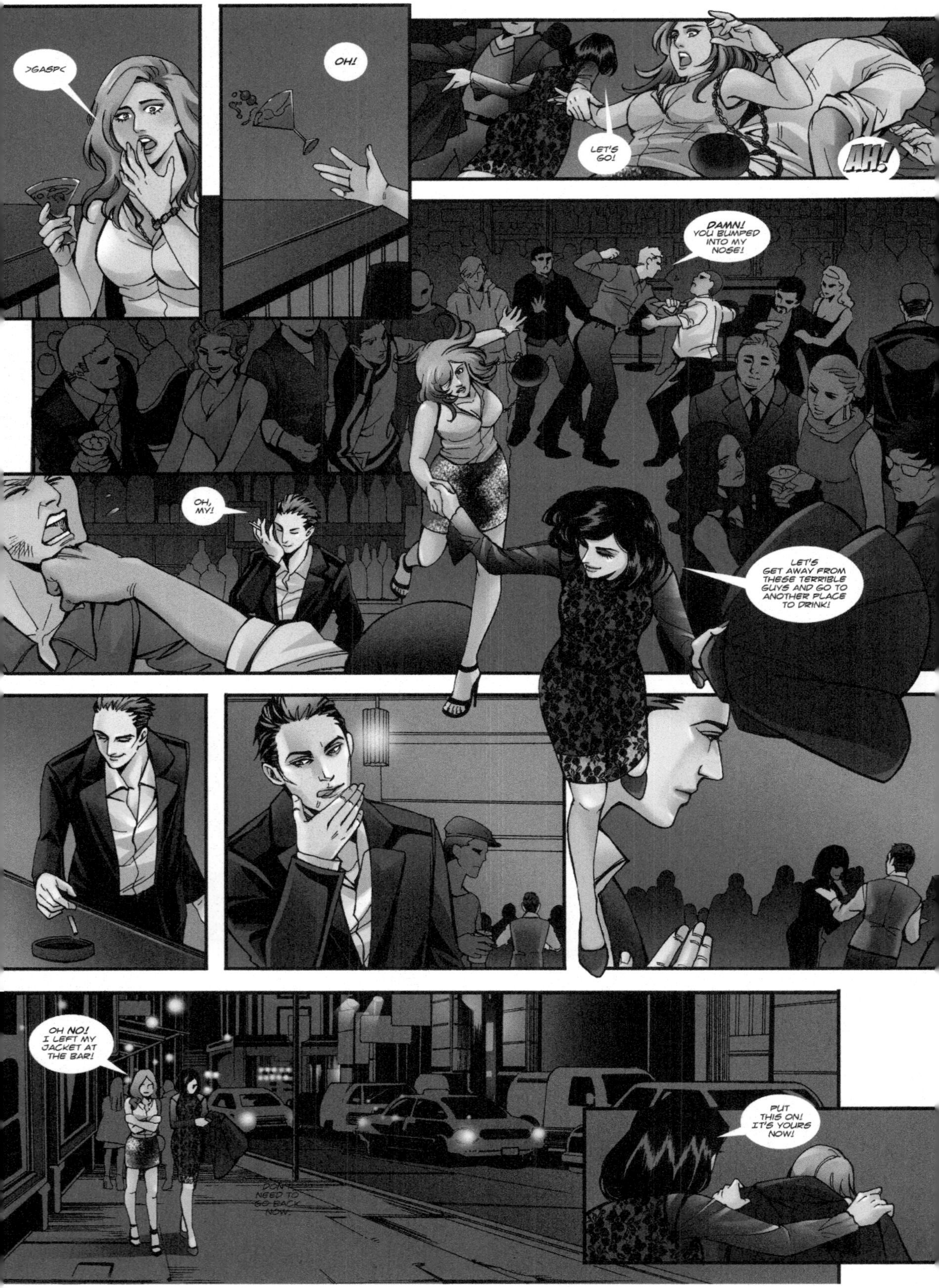

>GASP<
OH!
LET'S GO!
AH!
DAMN! YOU BUMPED INTO MY NOSE!
OH, MY!
LET'S GET AWAY FROM THESE TERRIBLE GUYS AND GO TO ANOTHER PLACE TO DRINK!
OH NO! I LEFT MY JACKET AT THE BAR!
DON'T NEED TO GO BACK NOW.
PUT THIS ON! IT'S YOURS NOW!

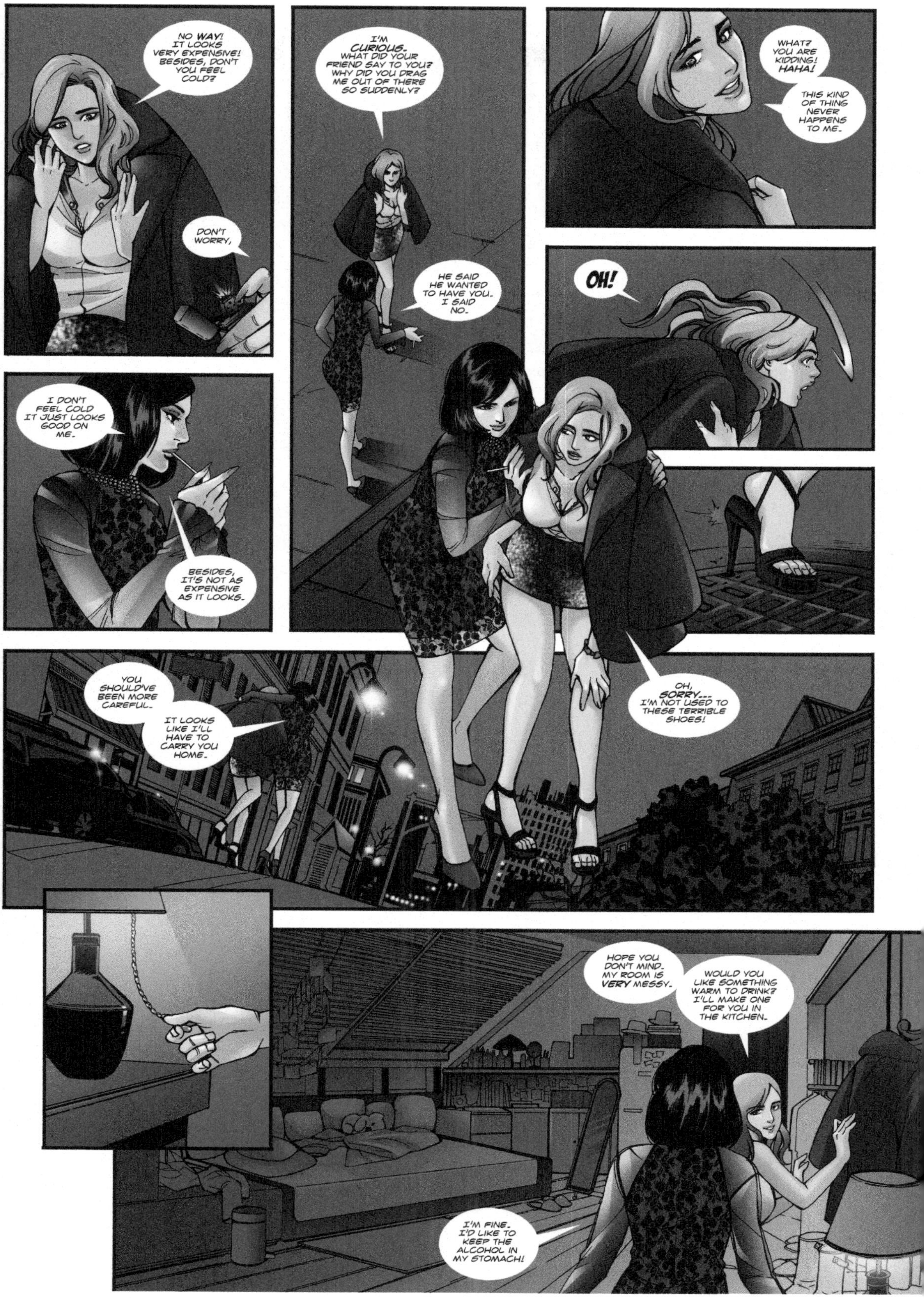
NO WAY! IT LOOKS VERY EXPENSIVE! BESIDES, DON'T YOU FEEL COLD?
DON'T WORRY,
I DON'T FEEL COLD IT JUST LOOKS GOOD ON ME.
BESIDES, IT'S NOT AS EXPENSIVE AS IT LOOKS.
I'M CURIOUS. WHAT DID YOUR FRIEND SAY TO YOU? WHY DID YOU DRAG ME OUT OF THERE SO SUDDENLY?
HE SAID HE WANTED TO HAVE YOU. I SAID NO.
WHAT? YOU ARE KIDDING! HAHA!
THIS KIND OF THING NEVER HAPPENS TO ME.
OH!
OH, SORRY... I'M NOT USED TO THESE TERRIBLE SHOES!
YOU SHOULD'VE BEEN MORE CAREFUL.
IT LOOKS LIKE I'LL HAVE TO CARRY YOU HOME.
HOPE YOU DON'T MIND. MY ROOM IS VERY MESSY.
WOULD YOU LIKE SOMETHING WARM TO DRINK? I'LL MAKE ONE FOR YOU IN THE KITCHEN.
I'M FINE. I'D LIKE TO KEEP THE ALCOHOL IN MY STOMACH!

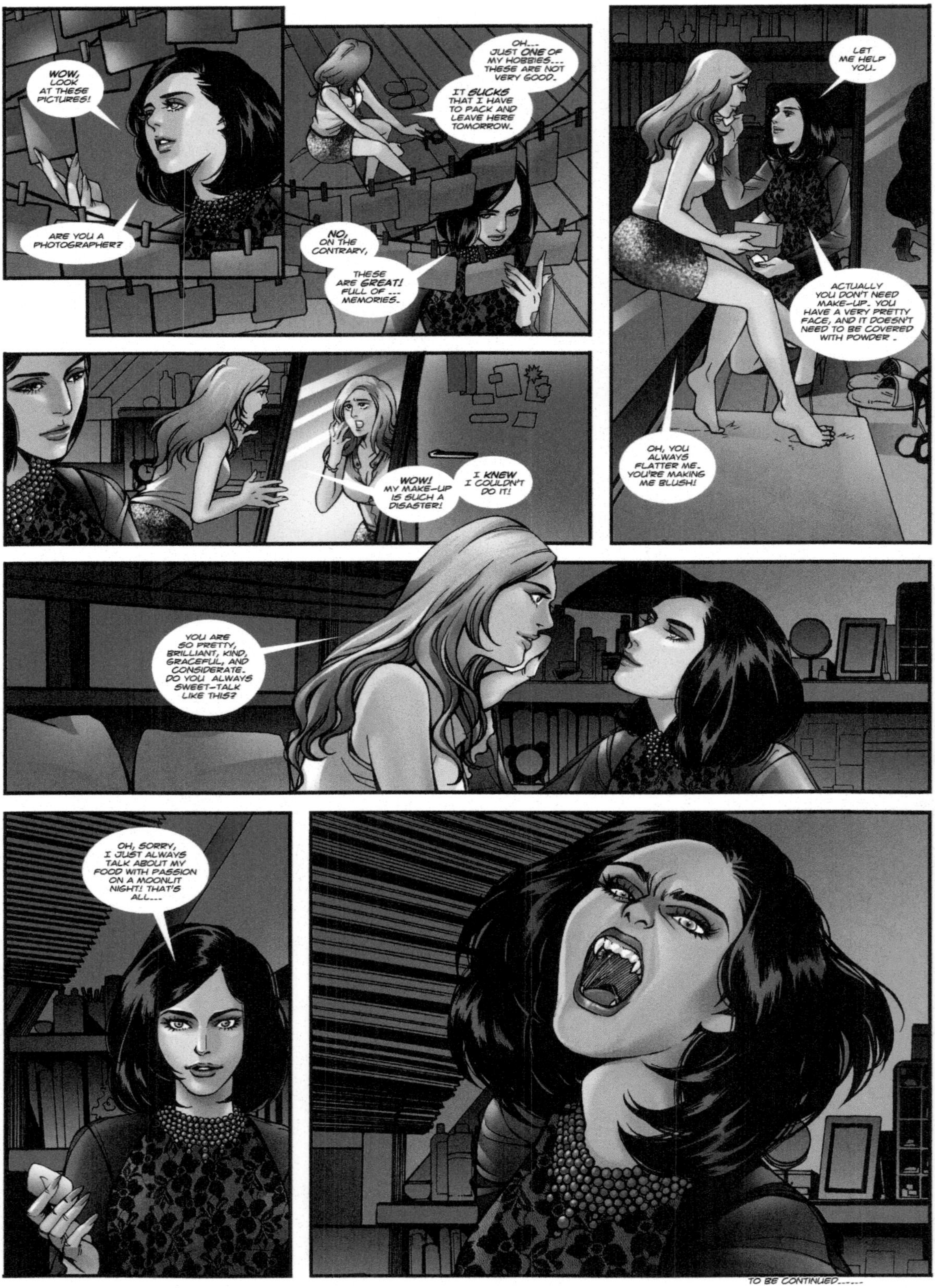
WOW, LOOK AT THESE PICTURES!
ARE YOU A PHOTOGRAPHER?
OH... JUST ONE OF MY HOBBIES... THESE ARE NOT VERY GOOD.
IT SUCKS THAT I HAVE TO PACK AND LEAVE HERE TOMORROW.
NO, ON THE CONTRARY,
THESE ARE GREAT! FULL OF ... MEMORIES.
LET ME HELP YOU.
ACTUALLY YOU DON'T NEED MAKE-UP. YOU HAVE A VERY PRETTY FACE, AND IT DOESN'T NEED TO BE COVERED WITH POWDER.
OH, YOU ALWAYS FLATTER ME. YOU'RE MAKING ME BLUSH!
WOW! MY MAKE-UP IS SUCH A DISASTER!
I KNEW I COULDN'T DO IT!
YOU ARE SO PRETTY, BRILLIANT, KIND, GRACEFUL, AND CONSIDERATE. DO YOU ALWAYS SWEET-TALK LIKE THIS?
OH, SORRY, I JUST ALWAYS TALK ABOUT MY FOOD WITH PASSION ON A MOONLIT NIGHT! THAT'S ALL...

TO BE CONTINUED......

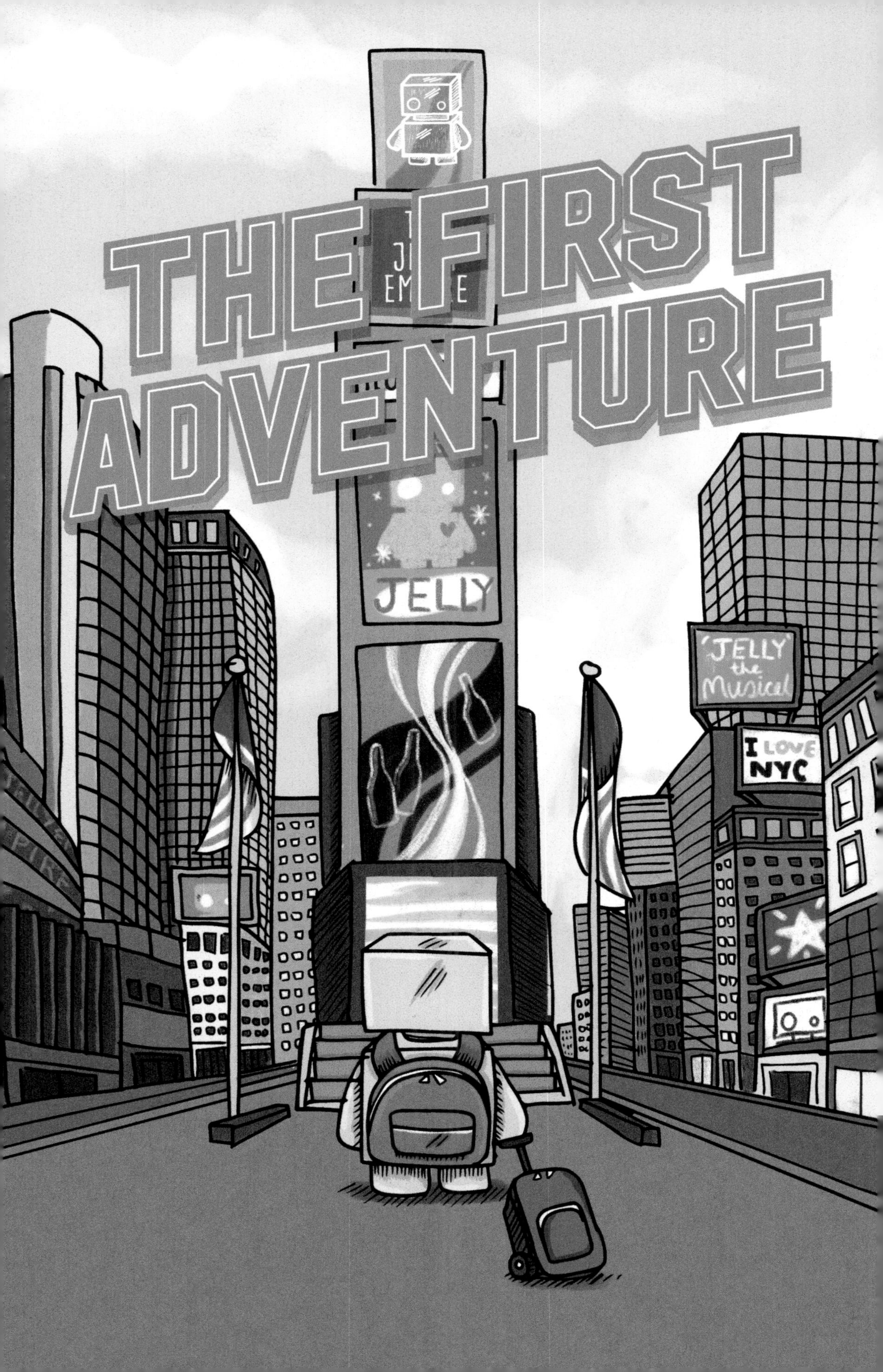
THE FIRST ADVENTURE
JELLY
'JELLY' the Musical
I LOVE NYC

Selina Briggs, Writer/Artist

England / USA

Selina Briggs, a UK native now living in Brooklyn, NY, is the creator and owner of The Jelly Empire. Inspired by science fiction, comics, robots, and pop culture, she has always dreamed of taking over the world with robots. Starting out as a 2D illustration, her little "Empire" has grown into much more, including her own line of collectible toys. She has recently moved into the world of comics, writing, and illustrating her own comic books, with a new issue currently in the works!

thejellyempire.com
@thejellyempire

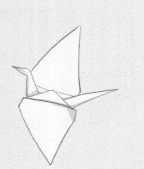

THE FIRST ADVENTURE

WRITTEN AND ILLUSTRATED
BY SELINA BRIGGS
OF
THE JELLY EMPIRE

TO MY MUM AND DAD,
WITHOUT YOUR LOVE, SUPPORT, AND
ENCOURAGEMENT TO SEIZE OPPORTUNITY,
THIS ADVENTURE WOULD NOT HAVE BEEN POSSIBLE.

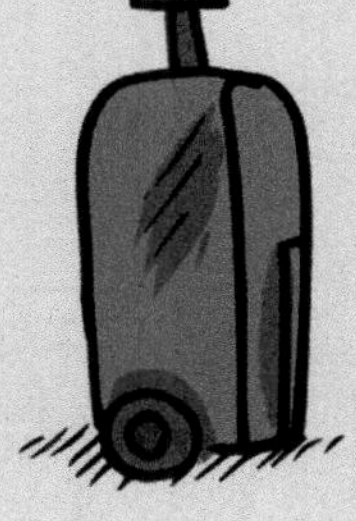

"THE JELLY EMPIRE"

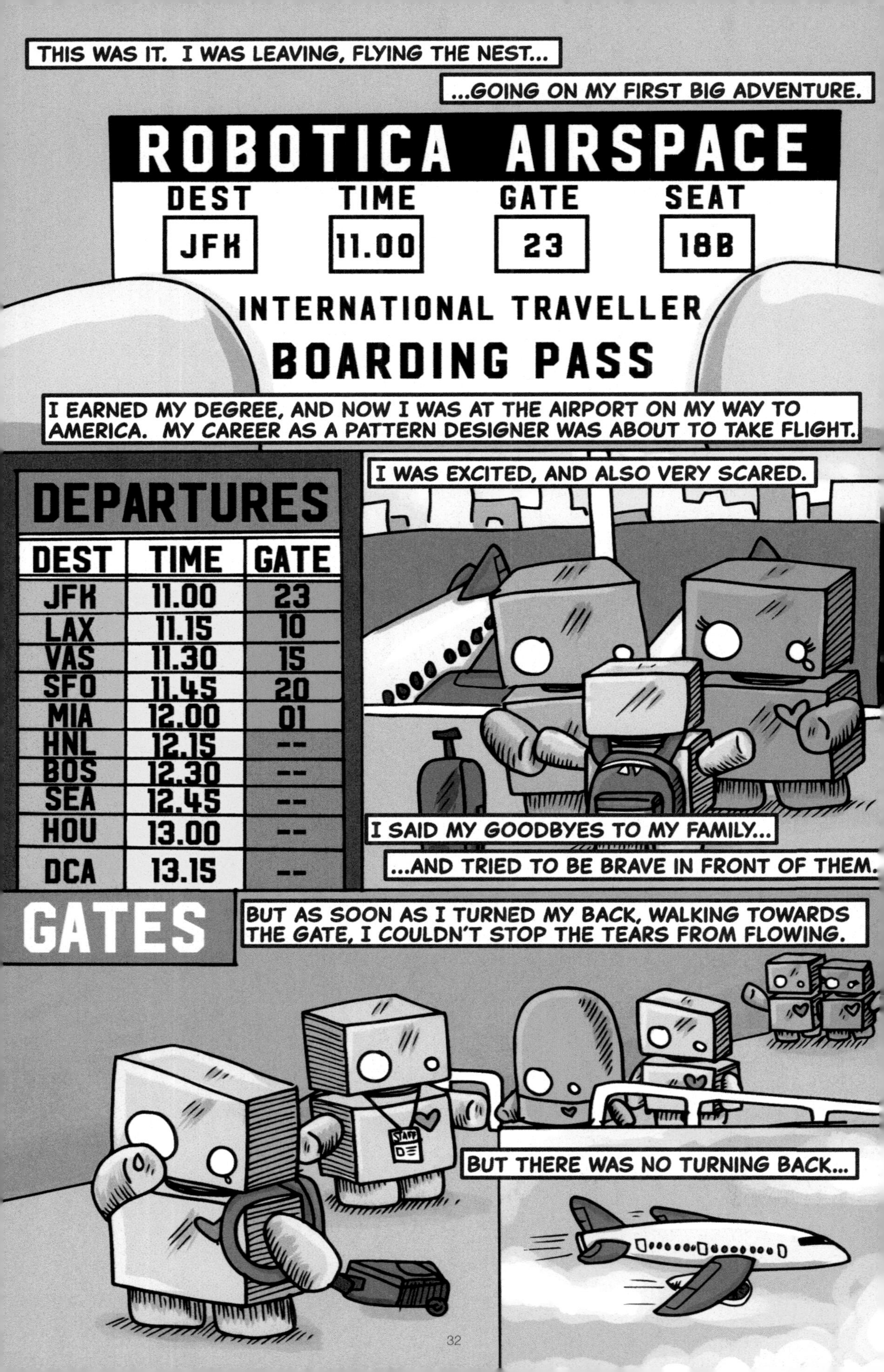
THIS WAS IT. I WAS LEAVING, FLYING THE NEST...
...GOING ON MY FIRST BIG ADVENTURE.
ROBOTICA AIRSPACE
DEST TIME GATE SEAT
JFK 11.00 23 18B
INTERNATIONAL TRAVELLER
BOARDING PASS
I EARNED MY DEGREE, AND NOW I WAS AT THE AIRPORT ON MY WAY TO AMERICA. MY CAREER AS A PATTERN DESIGNER WAS ABOUT TO TAKE FLIGHT.
DEPARTURES
DEST TIME GATE
JFK 11.00 23
LAX 11.15 10
VAS 11.30 15
SFO 11.45 20
MIA 12.00 01
HNL 12.15 --
BOS 12.30 --
SEA 12.45 --
HOU 13.00 --
DCA 13.15 --
I WAS EXCITED, AND ALSO VERY SCARED.
I SAID MY GOODBYES TO MY FAMILY...
...AND TRIED TO BE BRAVE IN FRONT OF THEM.
GATES
BUT AS SOON AS I TURNED MY BACK, WALKING TOWARDS THE GATE, I COULDN'T STOP THE TEARS FROM FLOWING.
STAFF
BUT THERE WAS NO TURNING BACK...

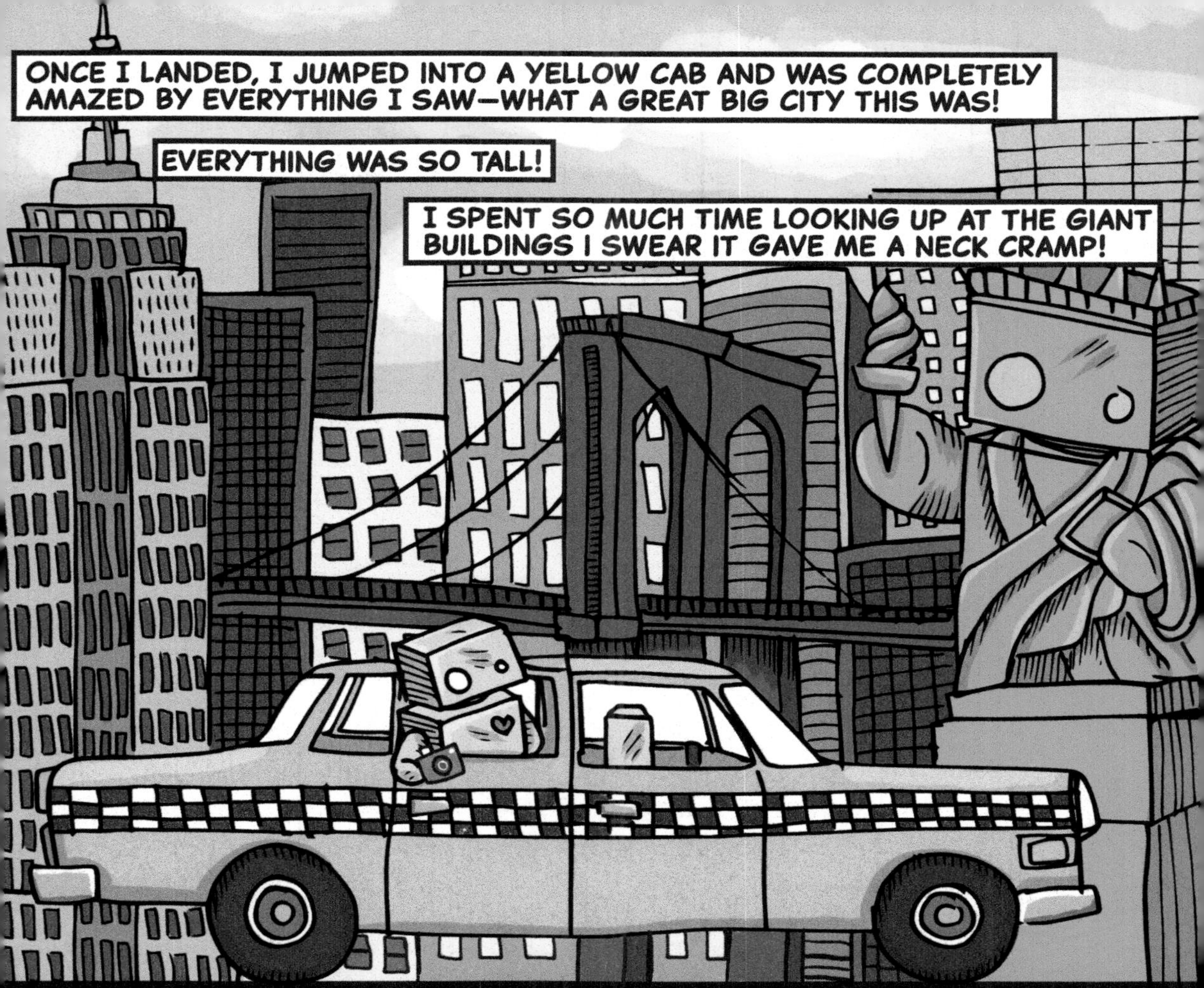
ONCE I LANDED, I JUMPED INTO A YELLOW CAB AND WAS COMPLETELY AMAZED BY EVERYTHING I SAW—WHAT A GREAT BIG CITY THIS WAS!
EVERYTHING WAS SO TALL!
I SPENT SO MUCH TIME LOOKING UP AT THE GIANT BUILDINGS I SWEAR IT GAVE ME A NECK CRAMP!

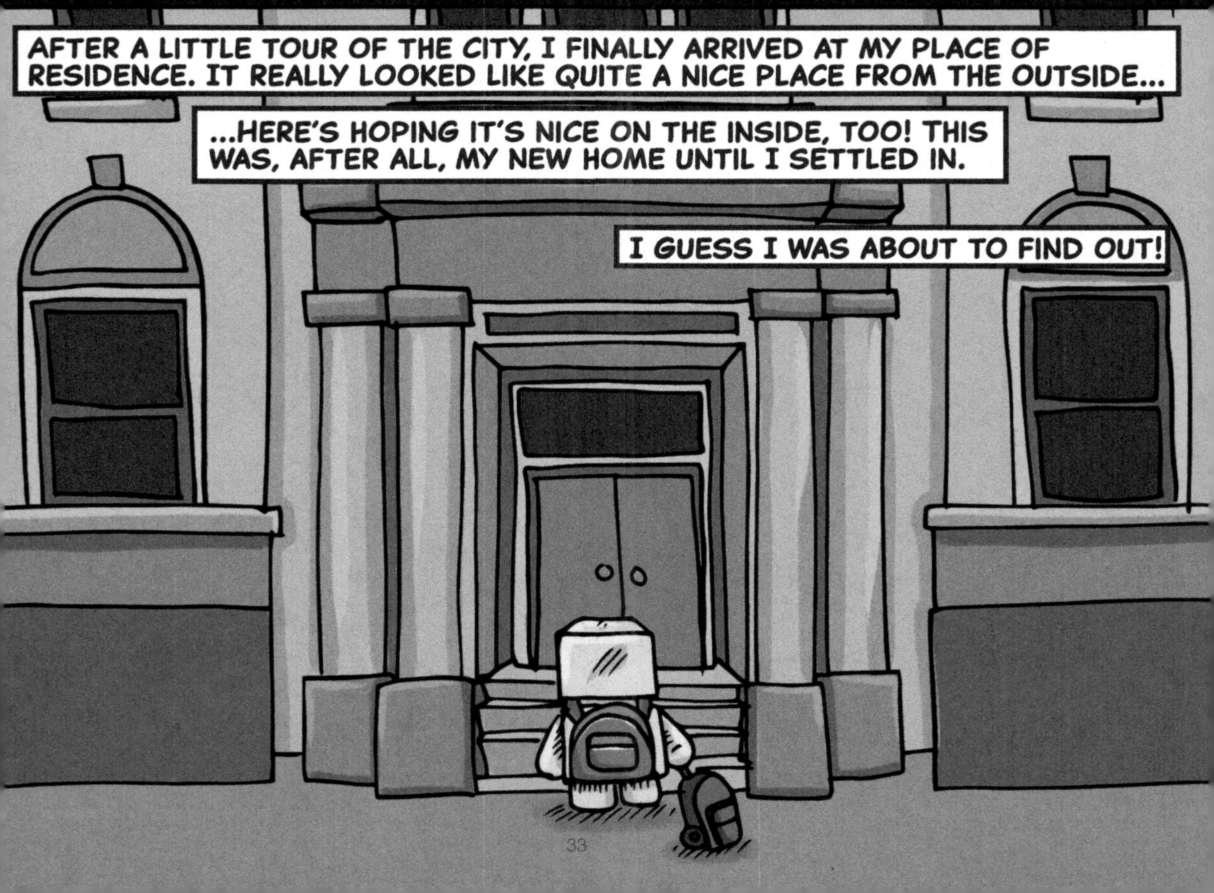
AFTER A LITTLE TOUR OF THE CITY, I FINALLY ARRIVED AT MY PLACE OF RESIDENCE. IT REALLY LOOKED LIKE QUITE A NICE PLACE FROM THE OUTSIDE...
...HERE'S HOPING IT'S NICE ON THE INSIDE, TOO! THIS WAS, AFTER ALL, MY NEW HOME UNTIL I SETTLED IN.
I GUESS I WAS ABOUT TO FIND OUT!

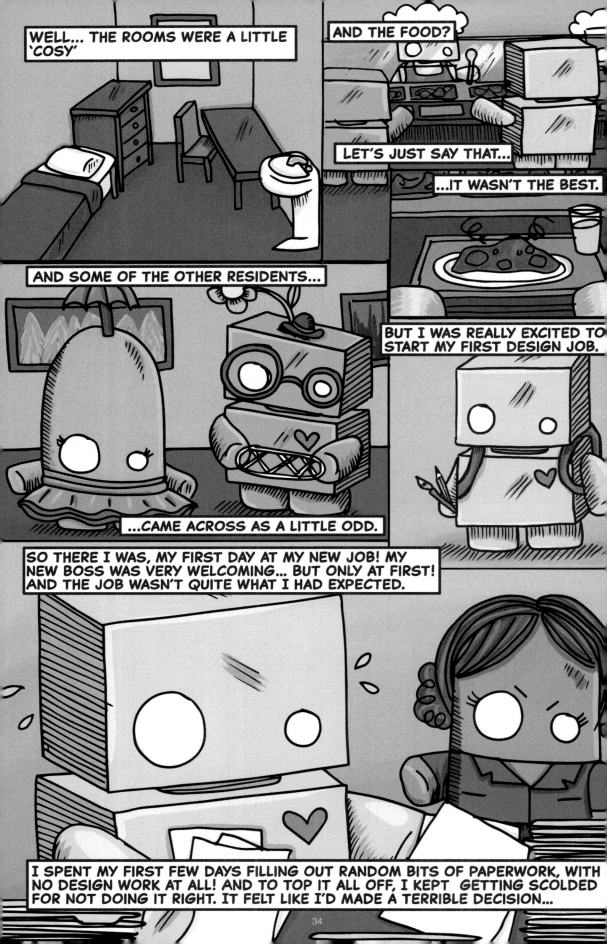

WELL... THE ROOMS WERE A LITTLE 'COSY'

AND THE FOOD?

LET'S JUST SAY THAT...

...IT WASN'T THE BEST.

AND SOME OF THE OTHER RESIDENTS...

BUT I WAS REALLY EXCITED TO START MY FIRST DESIGN JOB.

...CAME ACROSS AS A LITTLE ODD.

SO THERE I WAS, MY FIRST DAY AT MY NEW JOB! MY NEW BOSS WAS VERY WELCOMING... BUT ONLY AT FIRST! AND THE JOB WASN'T QUITE WHAT I HAD EXPECTED.

I SPENT MY FIRST FEW DAYS FILLING OUT RANDOM BITS OF PAPERWORK, WITH NO DESIGN WORK AT ALL! AND TO TOP IT ALL OFF, I KEPT GETTING SCOLDED FOR NOT DOING IT RIGHT. IT FELT LIKE I'D MADE A TERRIBLE DECISION...

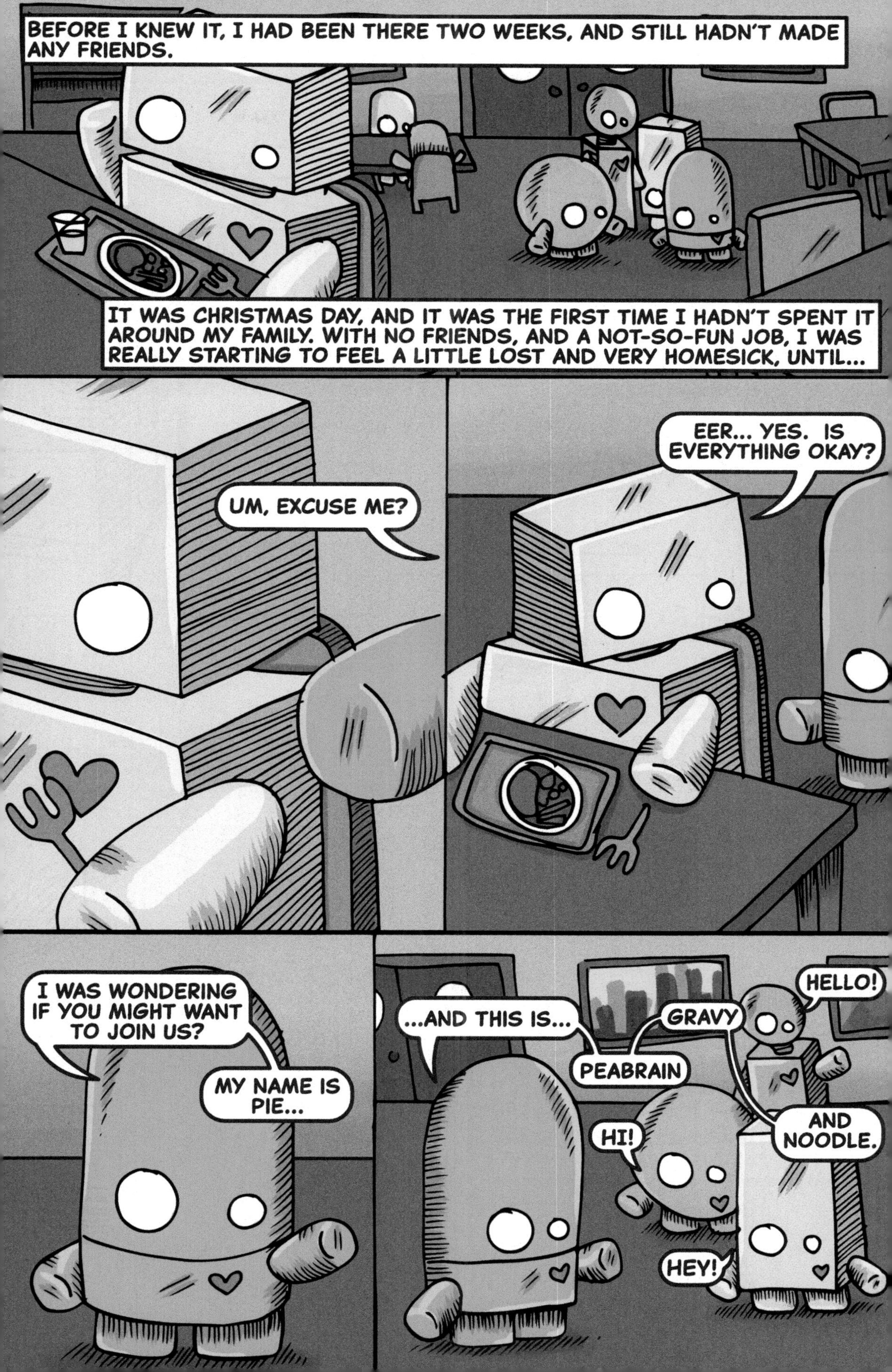
BEFORE I KNEW IT, I HAD BEEN THERE TWO WEEKS, AND STILL HADN'T MADE ANY FRIENDS.
IT WAS CHRISTMAS DAY, AND IT WAS THE FIRST TIME I HADN'T SPENT IT AROUND MY FAMILY. WITH NO FRIENDS, AND A NOT-SO-FUN JOB, I WAS REALLY STARTING TO FEEL A LITTLE LOST AND VERY HOMESICK, UNTIL...
UM, EXCUSE ME?
EER... YES. IS EVERYTHING OKAY?
I WAS WONDERING IF YOU MIGHT WANT TO JOIN US?
MY NAME IS PIE...
...AND THIS IS...
PEABRAIN
GRAVY
HELLO!
AND NOODLE.
HI!
HEY!

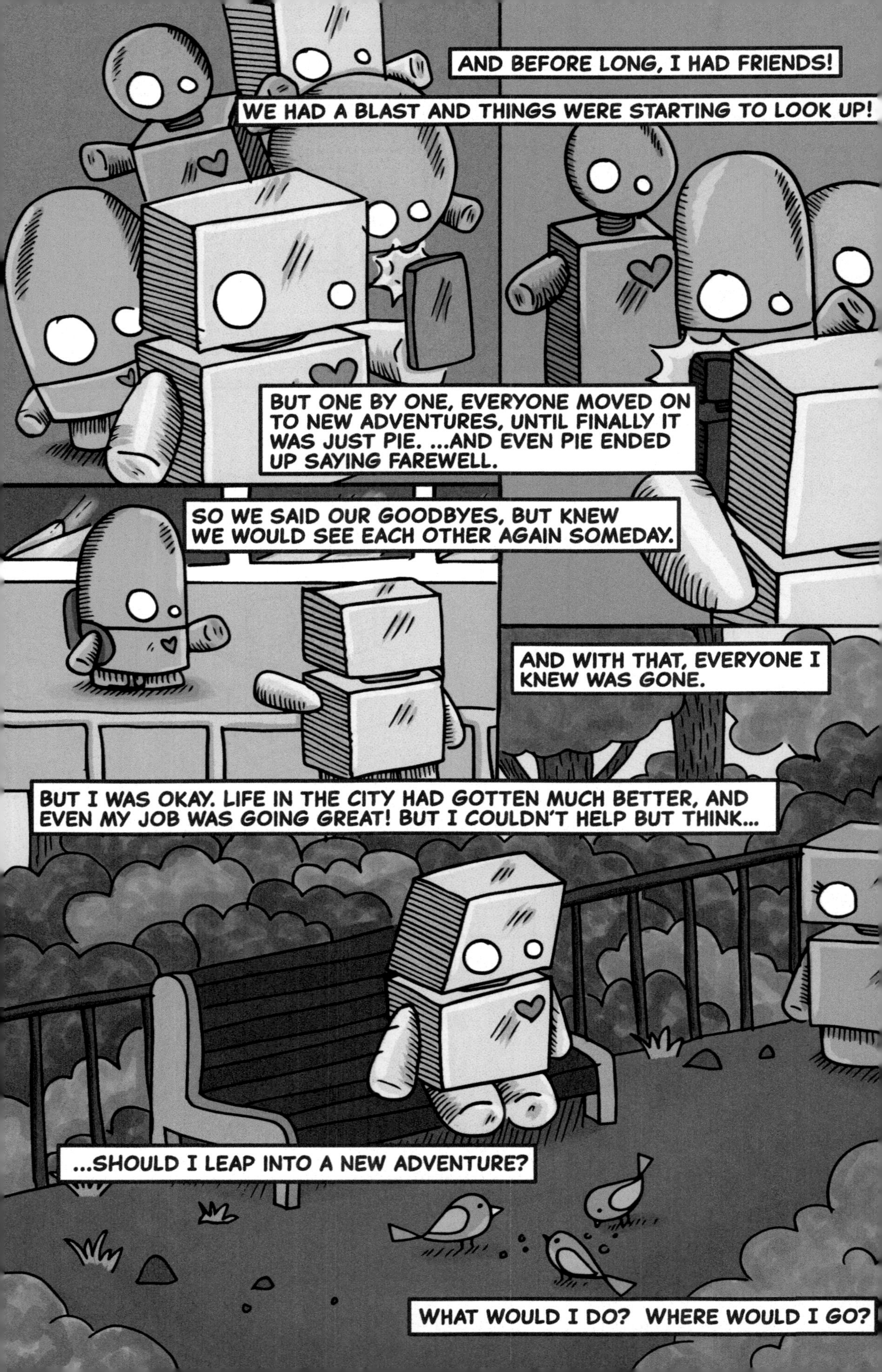
AND BEFORE LONG, I HAD FRIENDS!
WE HAD A BLAST AND THINGS WERE STARTING TO LOOK UP!
BUT ONE BY ONE, EVERYONE MOVED ON TO NEW ADVENTURES, UNTIL FINALLY IT WAS JUST PIE. ...AND EVEN PIE ENDED UP SAYING FAREWELL.
SO WE SAID OUR GOODBYES, BUT KNEW WE WOULD SEE EACH OTHER AGAIN SOMEDAY.
AND WITH THAT, EVERYONE I KNEW WAS GONE.
BUT I WAS OKAY. LIFE IN THE CITY HAD GOTTEN MUCH BETTER, AND EVEN MY JOB WAS GOING GREAT! BUT I COULDN'T HELP BUT THINK...
...SHOULD I LEAP INTO A NEW ADVENTURE?
WHAT WOULD I DO? WHERE WOULD I GO?

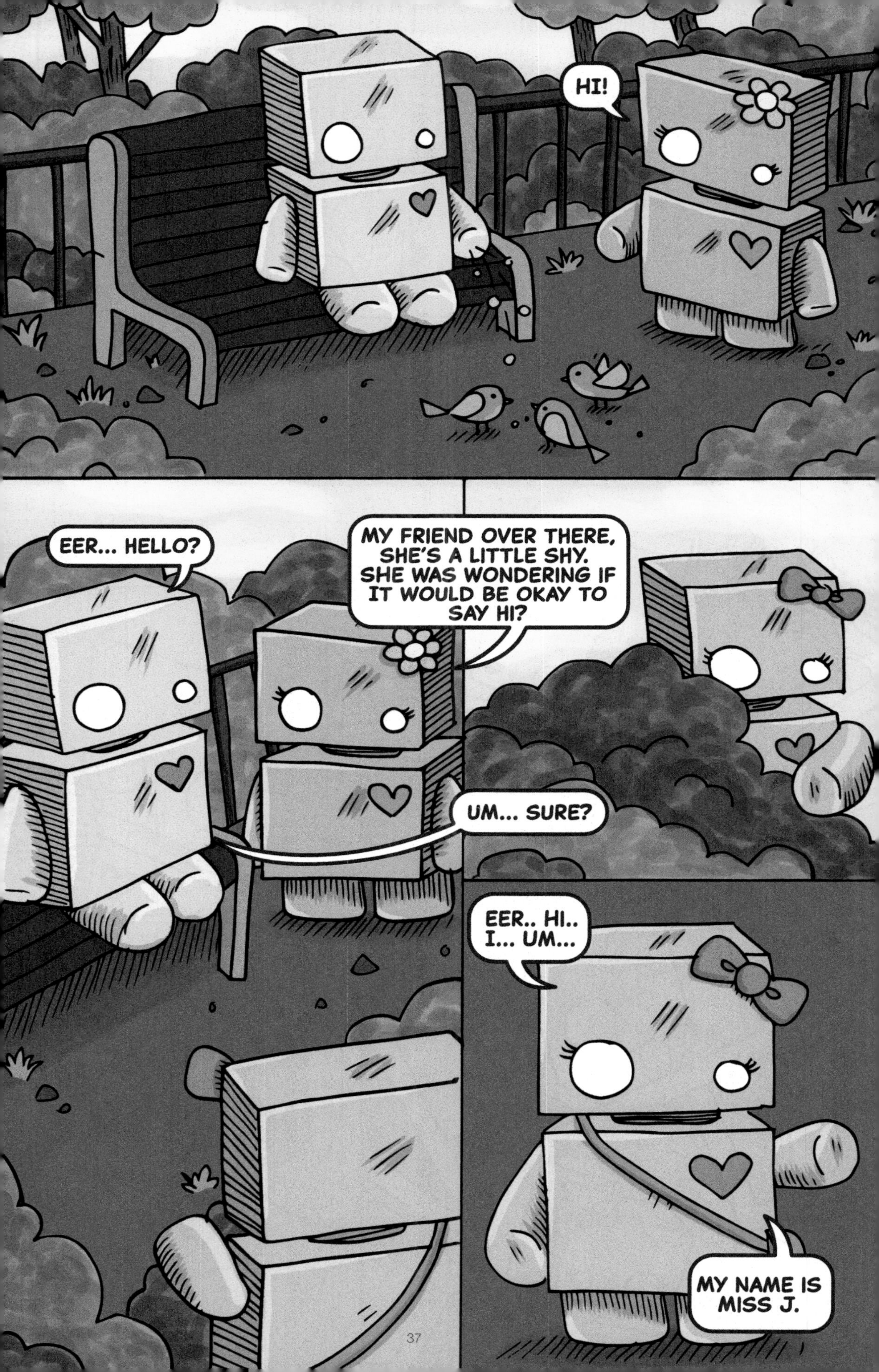
HI!
EER... HELLO?
MY FRIEND OVER THERE, SHE'S A LITTLE SHY. SHE WAS WONDERING IF IT WOULD BE OKAY TO SAY HI?
UM... SURE?
EER.. HI.. I... UM...
MY NAME IS MISS J.

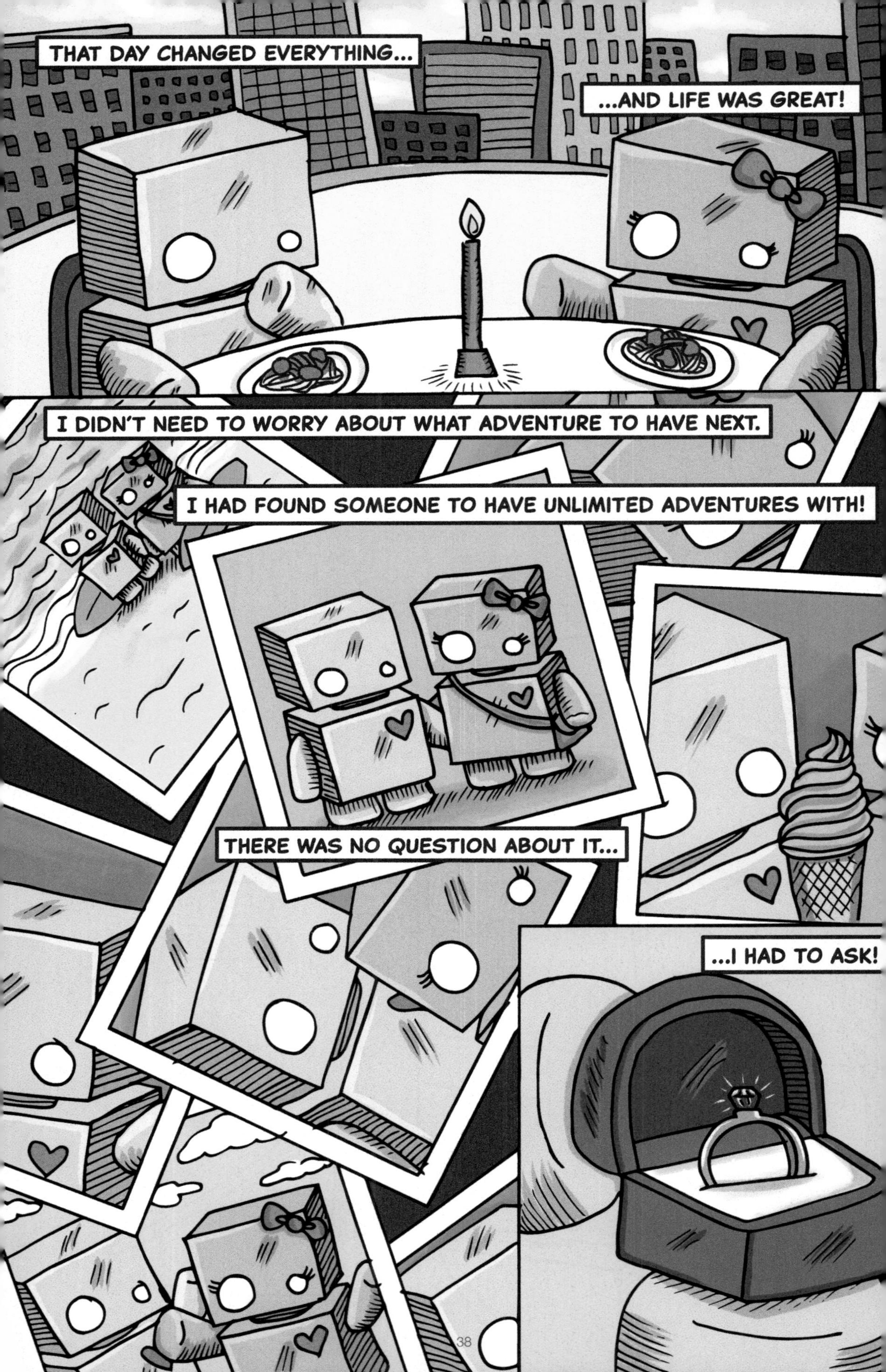
THAT DAY CHANGED EVERYTHING...
...AND LIFE WAS GREAT!
I DIDN'T NEED TO WORRY ABOUT WHAT ADVENTURE TO HAVE NEXT.
I HAD FOUND SOMEONE TO HAVE UNLIMITED ADVENTURES WITH!
THERE WAS NO QUESTION ABOUT IT...
...I HAD TO ASK!

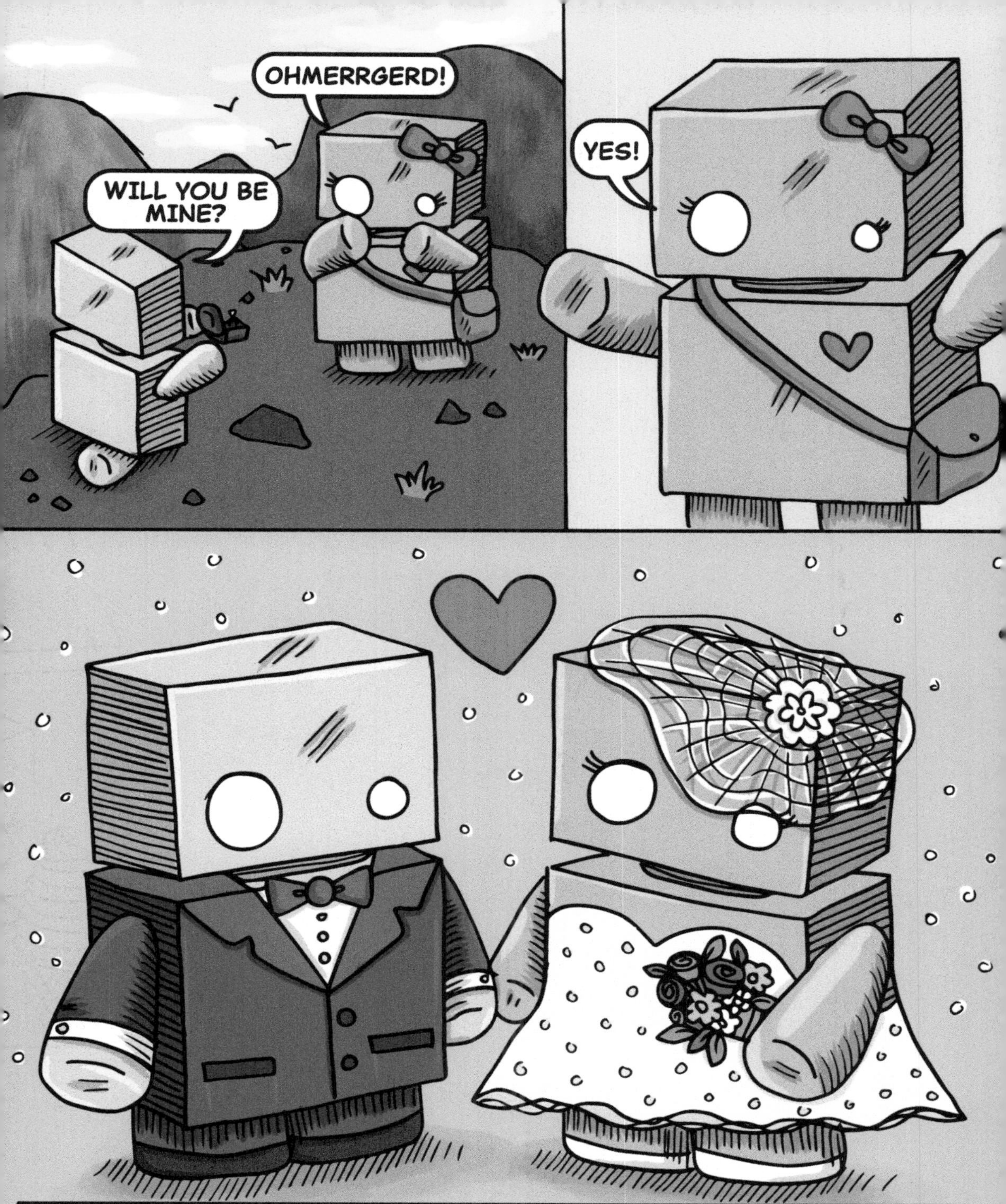
OHMERRGERD!
WILL YOU BE MINE?
YES!

LOOKING BACK, I AM GLAD I TOOK THE OPPORTUNITY TO GO ON MY FIRST REAL ADVENTURE. IT TOOK ME OUT OF MY COMFORT ZONE, HELPED ME TO GROW, CREATE GREAT NEW FRIENDSHIPS, AND NEVER, EVER GIVE UP. IT ALSO LED THE WAY TO MY NEXT ADVENTURE AND MANY MORE FUTURE ADVENTURES, BUT NOW I HAVE SOMEONE TO SHARE EVERYTHING WITH. IN GENERAL, YOU SHOULD ALWAYS TAKE THE OPPORTUNITIES TO GROW AND EXPAND YOUR WORLD. PUSHING YOURSELF TO DO THINGS YOU'RE NOT COMFORTABLE WITH CAN OFTEN LEAD TO GROWTH AND UNDERSTANDING THE WORLD BETTER.

AND NOW, OUR ADVENTURE CONTINUES...

Ramon Gil, Writer

The Philippines / United States

Ramon got his first professional strip published at 10 years old while growing up in the Philippines, where he often entertained his friends and teachers with hand-drawn comics in his notebooks. In 1982, he immigrated to Los Angeles, California, just in time for high school, and moved to New York City in 1993 after college to pursue his dream of becoming a comic book artist. After a few months of drawing NASCAR autobiographies for Vortex Comics, all the work dried up when the industry tanked in 1994. Ramon then got a job in advertising, and in 2006, he started his own graphic design company.

Eight years later, he realized how much he still wanted to create comic books, and began writing and self-publishing his own stories with artists like Trevor Von Eeden, Rudy Nebres, Roy Allan Martinez, Len Peralta, Cee Raymond, and Bill Walko among others. His comic work has been featured in *Indie Comics Magazine, Strange Tales, TV Times, Santa's Favorite Tales,* and *Asia World News,* and he recently did a comic on student life for the University of Southern California. His *Scifies* anthology *TPB* was recently published by Atlas Unleashed.

ramongil.com

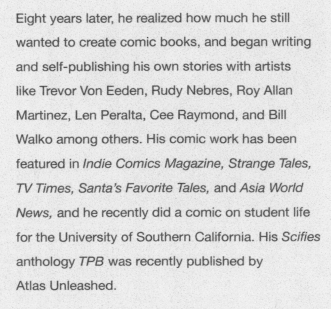

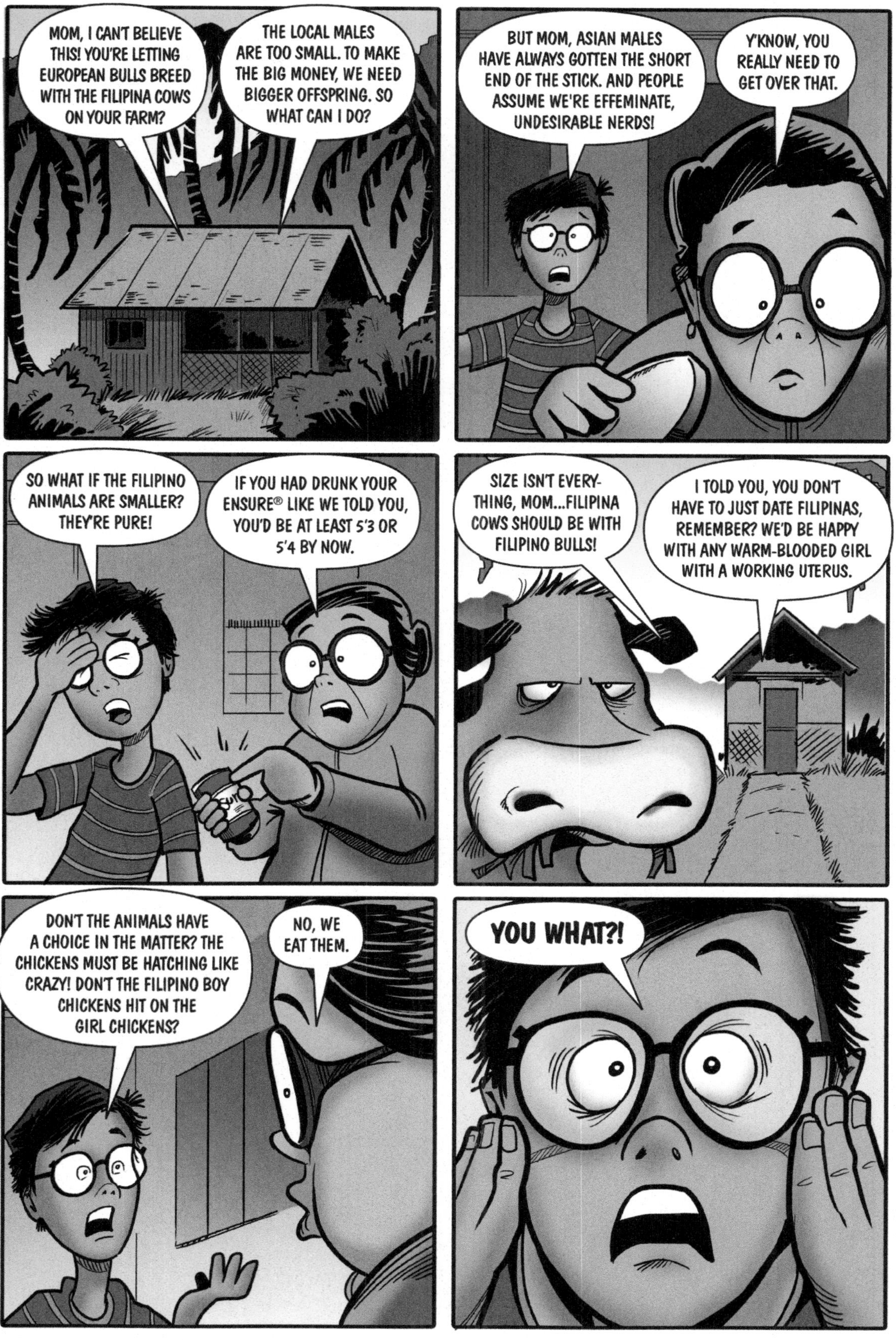
MOM, I CAN'T BELIEVE THIS! YOU'RE LETTING EUROPEAN BULLS BREED WITH THE FILIPINA COWS ON YOUR FARM?
THE LOCAL MALES ARE TOO SMALL. TO MAKE THE BIG MONEY, WE NEED BIGGER OFFSPRING. SO WHAT CAN I DO?
BUT MOM, ASIAN MALES HAVE ALWAYS GOTTEN THE SHORT END OF THE STICK. AND PEOPLE ASSUME WE'RE EFFEMINATE, UNDESIRABLE NERDS!
Y'KNOW, YOU REALLY NEED TO GET OVER THAT.
SO WHAT IF THE FILIPINO ANIMALS ARE SMALLER? THEY'RE PURE!
IF YOU HAD DRUNK YOUR ENSURE® LIKE WE TOLD YOU, YOU'D BE AT LEAST 5'3 OR 5'4 BY NOW.
SIZE ISN'T EVERY-THING, MOM...FILIPINA COWS SHOULD BE WITH FILIPINO BULLS!
I TOLD YOU, YOU DON'T HAVE TO JUST DATE FILIPINAS, REMEMBER? WE'D BE HAPPY WITH ANY WARM-BLOODED GIRL WITH A WORKING UTERUS.
DON'T THE ANIMALS HAVE A CHOICE IN THE MATTER? THE CHICKENS MUST BE HATCHING LIKE CRAZY! DON'T THE FILIPINO BOY CHICKENS HIT ON THE GIRL CHICKENS?
NO, WE EAT THEM.
YOU WHAT?!

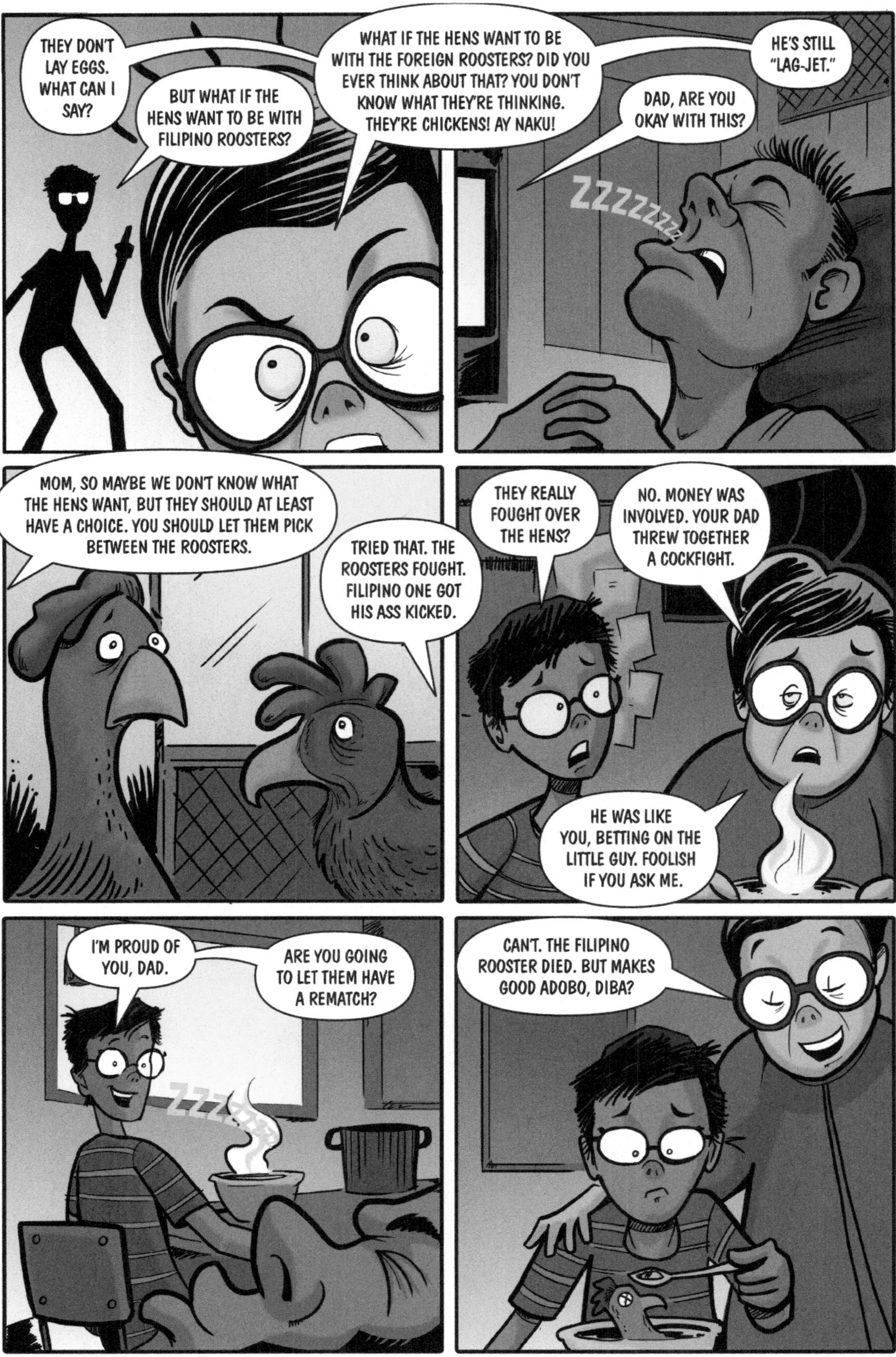
THEY DON'T LAY EGGS. WHAT CAN I SAY?
BUT WHAT IF THE HENS WANT TO BE WITH FILIPINO ROOSTERS?
WHAT IF THE HENS WANT TO BE WITH THE FOREIGN ROOSTERS? DID YOU EVER THINK ABOUT THAT? YOU DON'T KNOW WHAT THEY'RE THINKING. THEY'RE CHICKENS! AY NAKU!
HE'S STILL "LAG-JET."
DAD, ARE YOU OKAY WITH THIS?
ZZZZZZZZ
MOM, SO MAYBE WE DON'T KNOW WHAT THE HENS WANT, BUT THEY SHOULD AT LEAST HAVE A CHOICE. YOU SHOULD LET THEM PICK BETWEEN THE ROOSTERS.
TRIED THAT. THE ROOSTERS FOUGHT. FILIPINO ONE GOT HIS ASS KICKED.
THEY REALLY FOUGHT OVER THE HENS?
NO. MONEY WAS INVOLVED. YOUR DAD THREW TOGETHER A COCKFIGHT.
HE WAS LIKE YOU, BETTING ON THE LITTLE GUY. FOOLISH IF YOU ASK ME.
I'M PROUD OF YOU, DAD.
ARE YOU GOING TO LET THEM HAVE A REMATCH?
CAN'T. THE FILIPINO ROOSTER DIED. BUT MAKES GOOD ADOBO, DIBA?

Police Nab Asian Baby Smugglers

By Ramon Gil for *Asians in America Magazine*

(April 1, 2002 - New York, NY) The Marsh family had been trying to adopt a baby for five years. But they had been turned down by every agency in this country. "What's wrong with us?" asked James, during a conjugal visit at the Riker's Island Correctional Facility where he is serving 10 years for felony assault. His wife Melissa, clearly distraught, sat beside him.

This was common knowledge on cell block 24601 when he was approached by a Chitanoo Balawing Osmond, a man of mixed race and mysterious origins. Balawing told them that he knew someone who knew someone who knew someone who could get them a healthy baby for about $10,000. Half what it cost to adopt a baby through legal channels. Melissa was desperate enough to consider it, claiming "I'm never ovulating during these conjugal visits, which is really frustrating." But James reasoned that if he was sent back to jail for buying a baby on the black market, then he wouldn't be able to experience the joy of watching her grow up and earn her GED. And so they went to the authorities in hopes of getting his sentence shortened and perhaps a letter of recommendation for future adoption interviews.

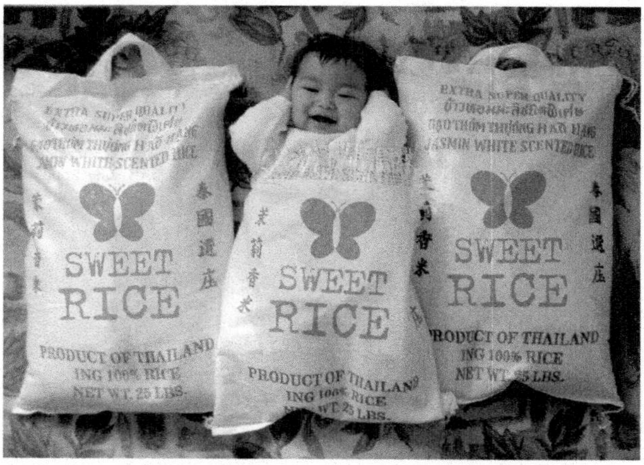
SWEET RICE
SWEET RICE
SWEET RICE
PRODUCT OF THAILAND
Baby Jasmine, newly rescued from the smugglers.

So on April 1st, a sting operation was carefully coordinated by a joint task force between New York Police, The Department of Social Services, and Homeland Security, who just wanted to make sure the incoming babies weren't terrorists. A deal was struck between the Marshes and the alleged baby dealers and arrangements were made to meet and exchange $9,999.98 for a new daughter. Police detectives insisted on bargaining the price down to throw off any suspicions on the part of the smugglers.

Melissa showed up at a small fish market in the Lower East Side with the cash and was led to the back of the store where she was handed what looked like a sack of imported Jasmine rice. Inside was a seven-month old baby, three fresh diapers and a cookbook by Ming Tsai. As soon as she left the store, she spoke the signal into a hidden wireless mike: "She made a poopie!" Instantly, the police moved in and arrested everyone on the premises. One woman was later released when it was learned that she was simply a customer who was there to buy eel.

"We rescued eight Asian babies ranging from two months to a year old. We also recovered 200 lbs of salmon, 100 lbs. of tuna and 500 lbs of albacore. The street price for the fish and the babies was estimated at about $200,000. "There was some eel and squid too, but they were old and wouldn't have sold well," mentioned one of the arresting officers.

Through the course of the investigation, police learned that with the recent popularity of adopting babies from Asia, a group of soy sauce smugglers decided to try to get in on the action. So they started posing as married couples and adopting babies from all over Asia. This was made doubly hard as the smugglers were all men and one of them always had to dress in drag. Sister Alice "Boom-boom" Basilio, of the Our Lady of Perpetual Motion Orphanage in Zamboanga

City, Philippines remembers the couple who adopted 17 children. "I thought it was so strange, the mother was so ugly." But dismissed her suspicions for the sake of the orphans. "She was so ugly that I didn't think they should be producing their own children...she was just so ugly."

Once adopted the babies were loaded onto a cargo ship bound for America. Buyers for the children would be found en route. "Let's get something clear right off the bat...the babies were not shipped in the rice sacks. They were only put in there when they reached customs," said a police spokesperson. "Though they were made to sleep in them while in their cribs so that they'd get used to the feel and texture." Welfare officials called in a child specialist to give a thorough medical examination of the eight rescued babies. Dr. Edith Chang, podiatrist,

smugglers had originally tried to use eBay, but realized that they couldn't accept credit cards or Paypal as the per-transaction fees were too high. They spread the word among their soy sauce distributors that babies were available, who then looked out for eligible couples. Once a couple showed interest, they would be given a password to the website where they could open up an account and browse through pictures of available infants. If they saw a baby they liked they simply had to click "Add to shopping cart."

The website also sold other staples like soy sauce, dried fish, and rice at a huge discount. Prices for the infants ranged anywhere from $10,000 to $25,000. When the smugglers were asked how the price for individual babies were determined, he simply answered, "By the kilo." He later added, "The skinny babies always went first."

"She was so ugly that I didn't think they should be producing their own children...she was just so ugly."

declared them in perfect health. "Though one eight-month-old boy had flat feet," she added. "They were actually very well cared for. Rice sacks provide really good insulation. They would make excellent blankets," Chang said.

Records seized by Asian authorities indicated a total of 45 babies had been adopted by the smugglers over the past two years, but could only find adoption records for 39 of them. When questioned about the six missing children, the smugglers admitted to taking some of the children for their own. "They were so cute we just fell in love with them!" They would have kept more of them, but that would have been bad for business, they said through an interpreter. This was confirmed by authorities who found the remainder of the children well cared for at the smugglers' individual homes in Thailand, Singapore, and the Nevernever-land Ranch in California.

The babies were sold on the internet through a password protected website. The

For what could have been such a heart-wrenching story, the ending has turned out quite pleasant for everyone involved. Seven of the babies have already found homes in the United States, and James and Melissa are LEGALLY adopting the baby she picked up during the sting operation. They have named the child "Jasmine," which would have been even more appropriate had he been a girl.

James has received early parole for his part in the case. The smugglers are facing child trafficking charges here in the US, though authorities in Asia are not prosecuting as they claimed that all of the adoption papers seemed to be in order.

However, one of the smugglers is facing indecency charges in Malaysia for dressing up as a woman in public. Police in Kuala Lumpur stated "It wasn't so much that she was dressed up as a woman...it was just that she was so ugly."◆

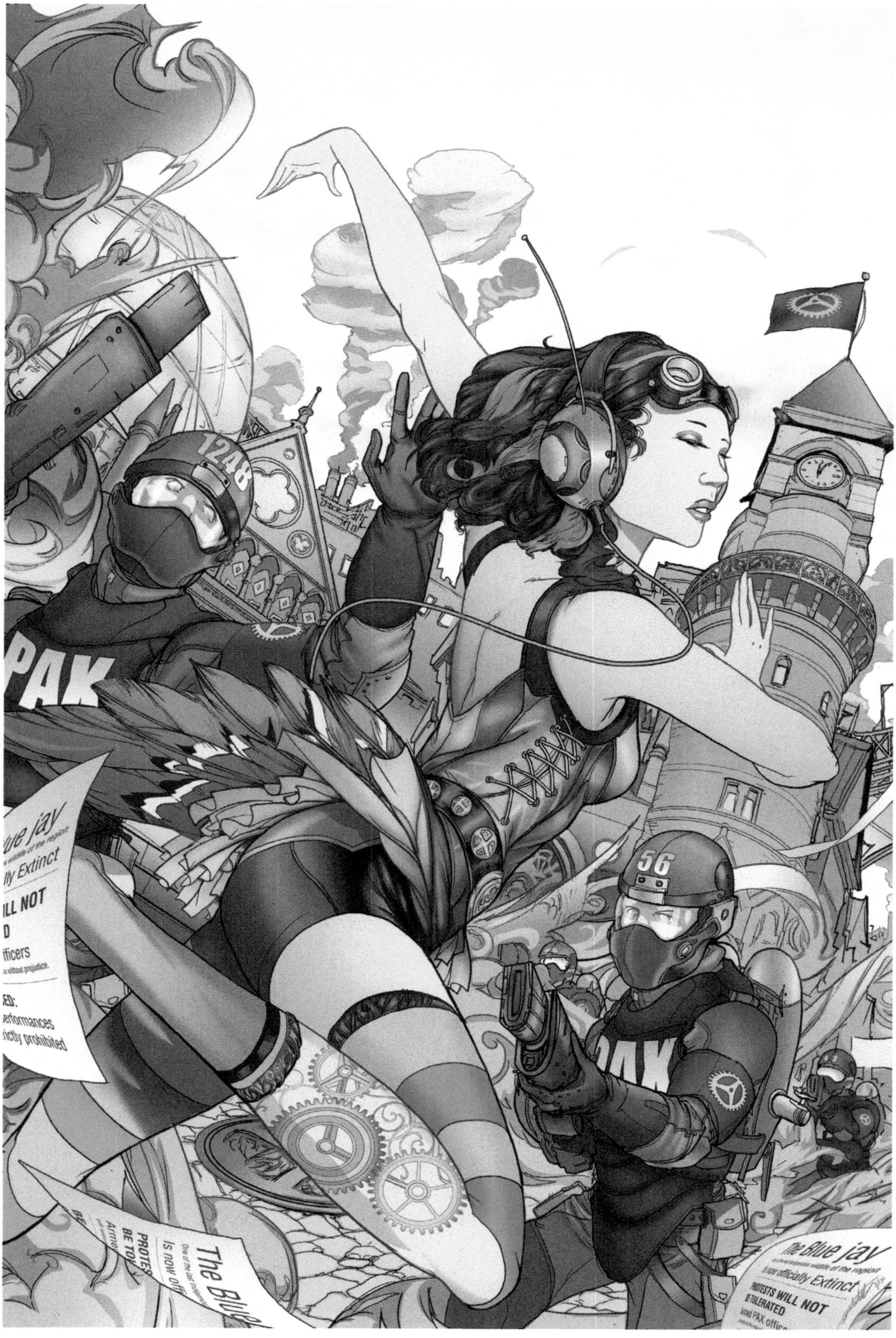
1248
PAK
56
PAK
The Blue jay
is now officially Extinct
PROTESTS WILL NOT
BE TOLERATED

Jerome Walford
Jamaica / United States

Last Dance for the Extinct Blue Jay
forwardcomix.com

Len Cicio, Artist

United States

My background in textile design helps me see patterns, textures, forms, and movement in the landscapes and architectural subjects I draw. Living more than 20 years right next to Inwood Park, the last natural forest in Manhattan, I found a rich, primal, and supernatural quality in its landscapes, which I've explored with quiet joy.

However, I'm increasingly drawn to the structures of the NYC subway system, with its powerful blend of dramatic gothic and sexy qualities. Both the manmade subways and landscapes of nature hold intricately woven patterns, filled with myriad details. I want to encourage people to rediscover their surroundings and really see the subway platforms, visually elevated to a higher level, and their walk through the park as entering into a live piece of artwork. When the sunlight hits the cold, steel structures of the subway, it brings out blues, purples, and reds that light up the surface. My goal is to make an analytical study with an attempt to show a deeper, more supernatural vision behind our natural world that we see every day. The Creator stamped the color of love into the life, movement, and power of His creations, including the subways and landscapes of New York City.

lencicio.com

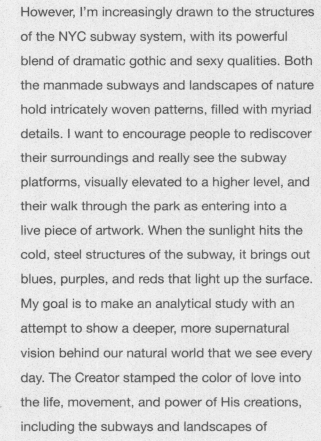

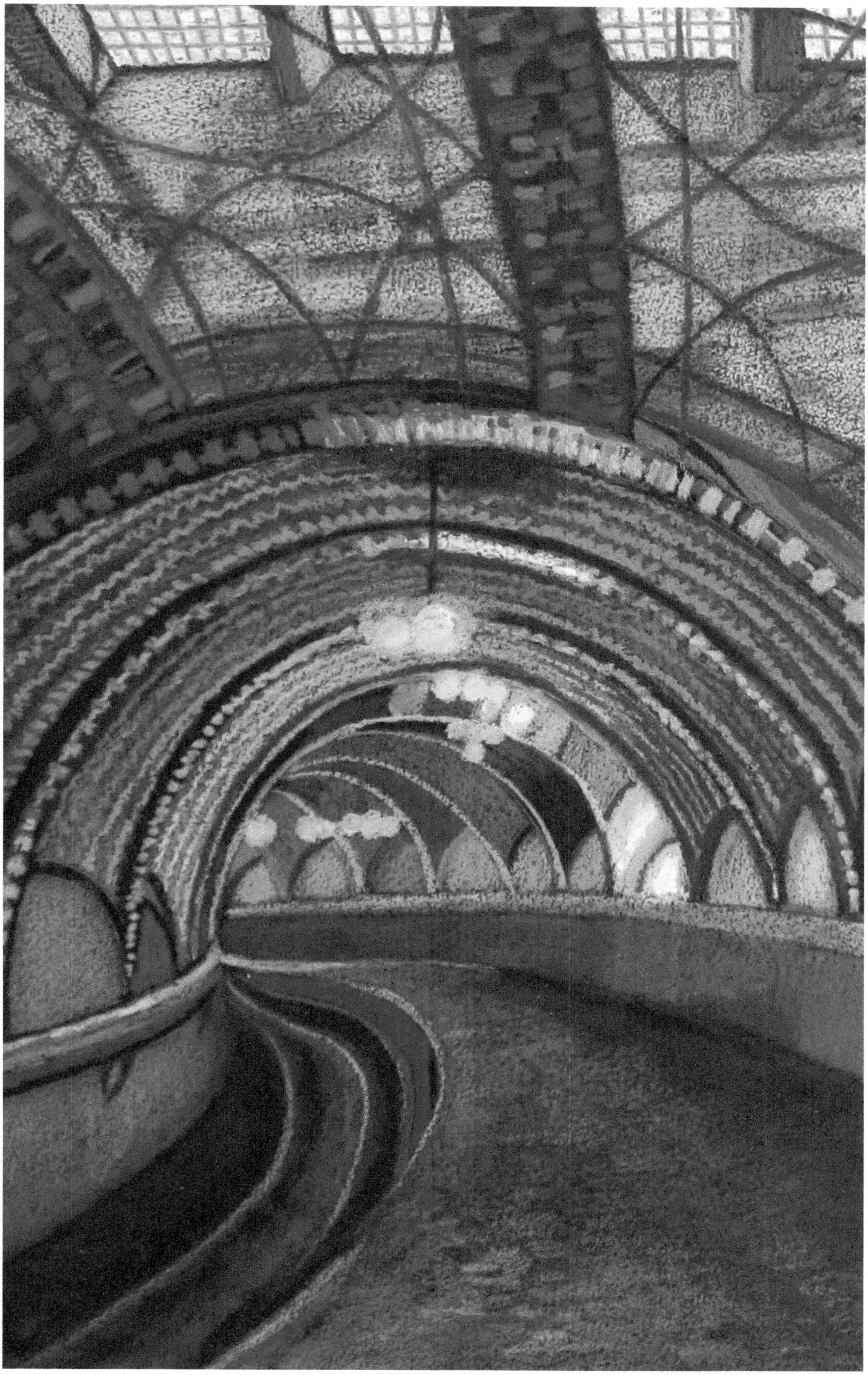

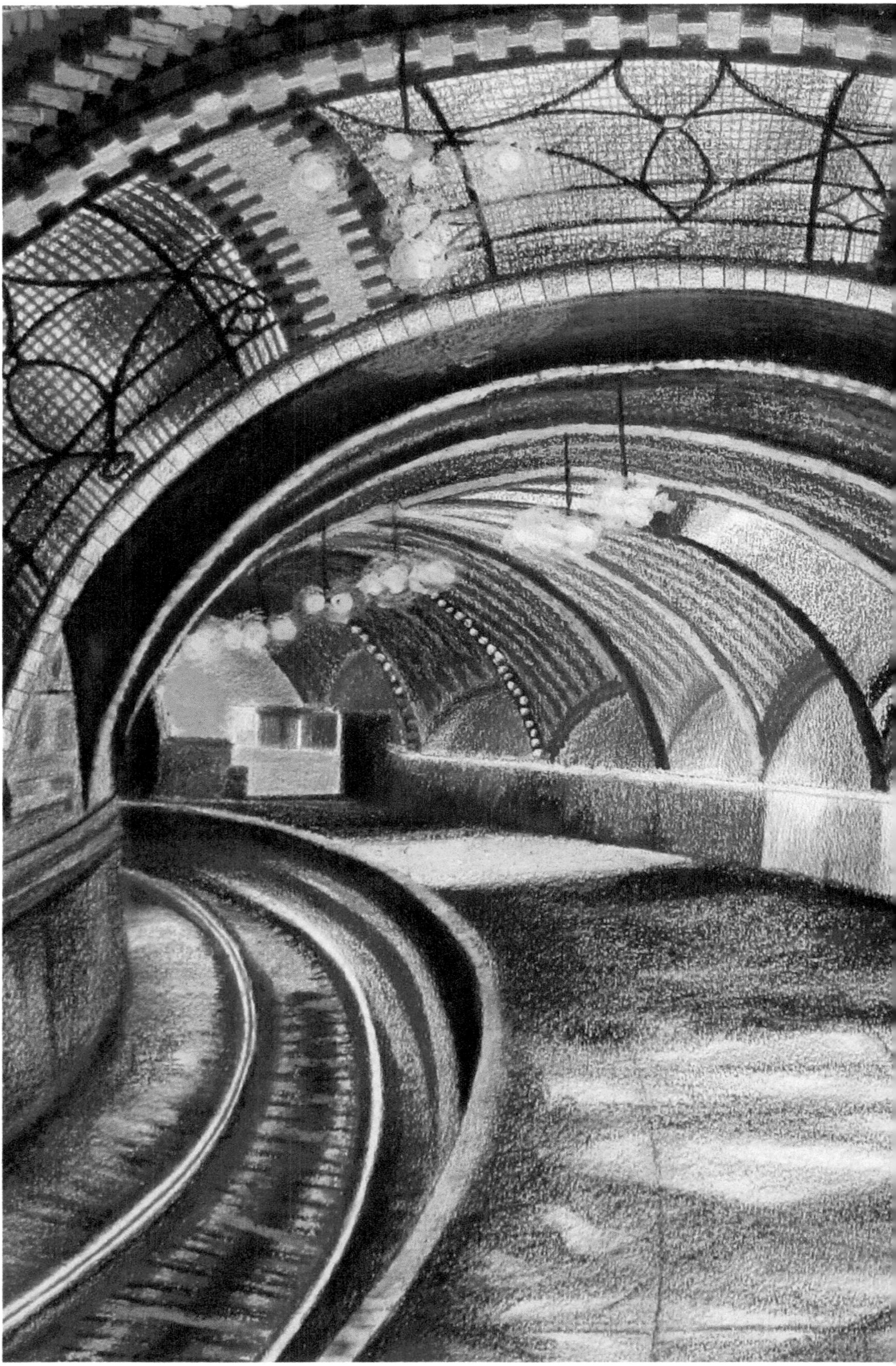

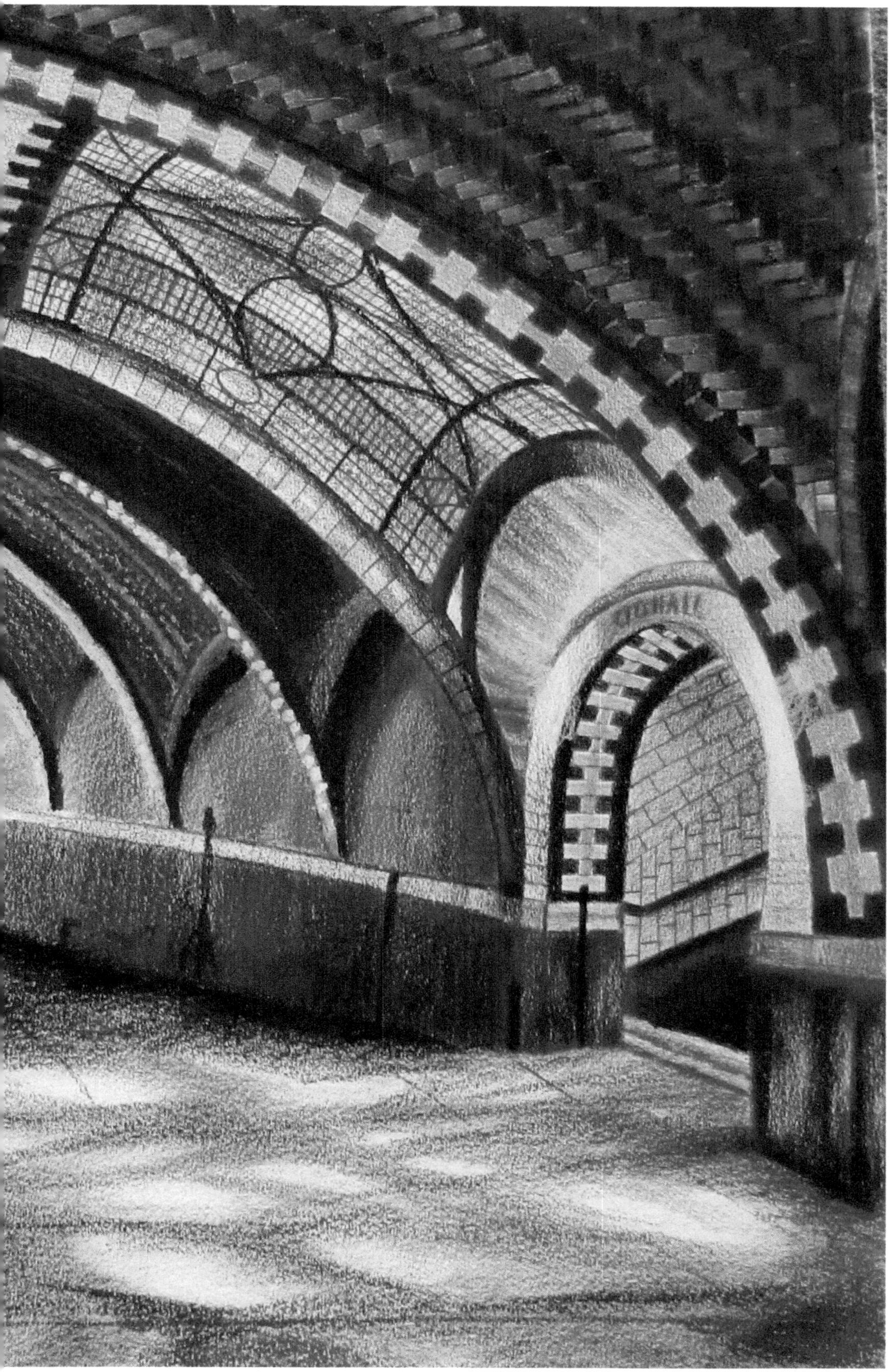

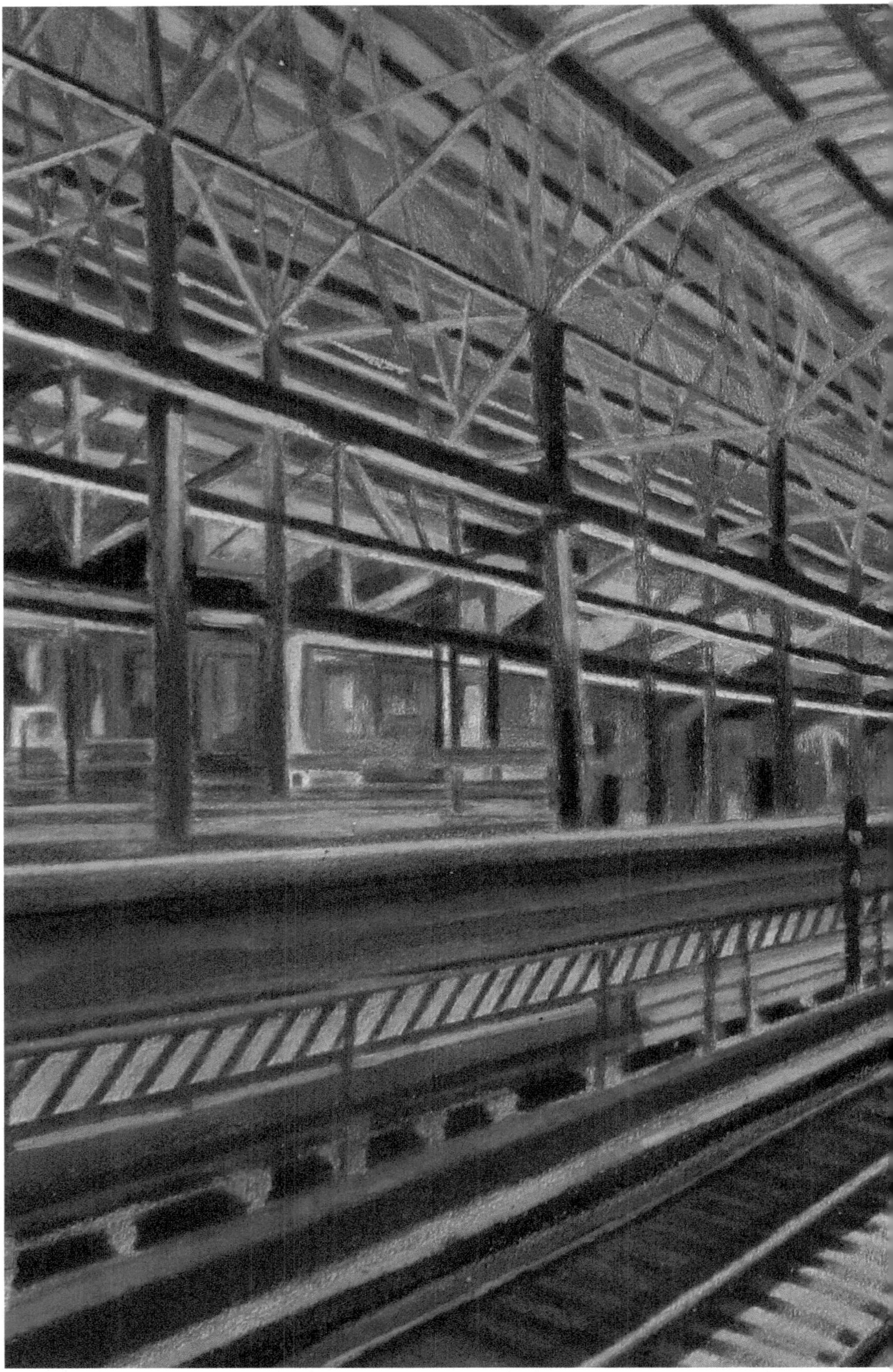

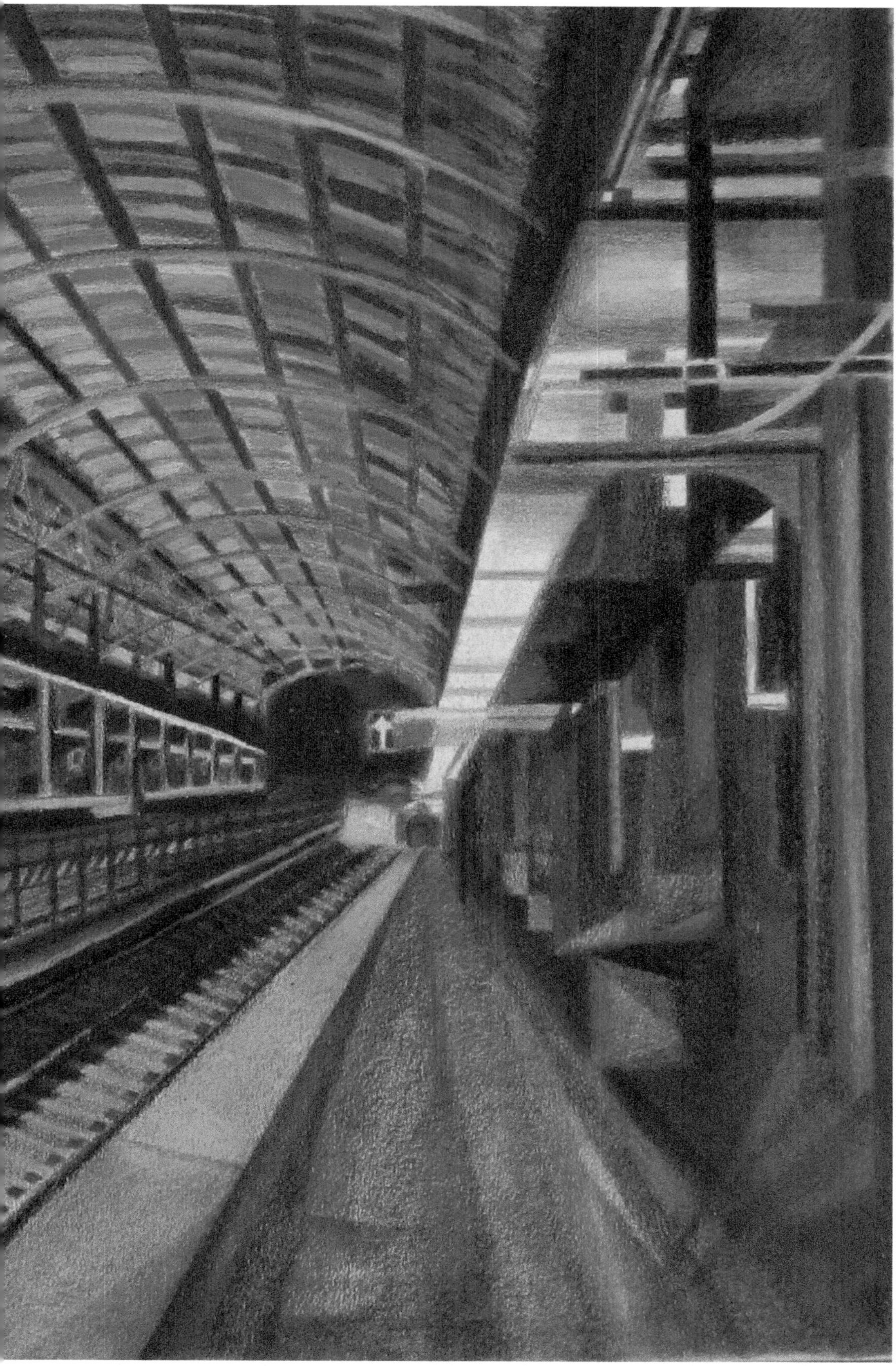

Julia Cawley, Photographer

Germany / United States / Germany

Hello, my name is Julia Cawley. I was born and raised in Germany. I studied and earned a degree in photography in Dortmund, Germany. I had a strong interest in architectural photography and got to work on some amazing projects, including one with my father, to document a potential landmark restoration project. I got to see a different side of my dad and developed an appreciation for how passionate he is about his work.

Soon, love pulled me back to New York City, where I first met my husband. We have lived in New York for a few years, raising our daughter Clementine and our crazy Pit Bull mix, Lola.

In New York I got to expand my horizons as a photographer, shooting food and newborns. Although I love the Big Apple, it's not for the faint of heart. For the next step in my journey, my husband and I are relocating our family to Germany, making a fresh start in Hamburg. I can't wait to see what this new adventure brings.

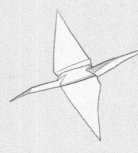

juliacawley.com

Weg Isser

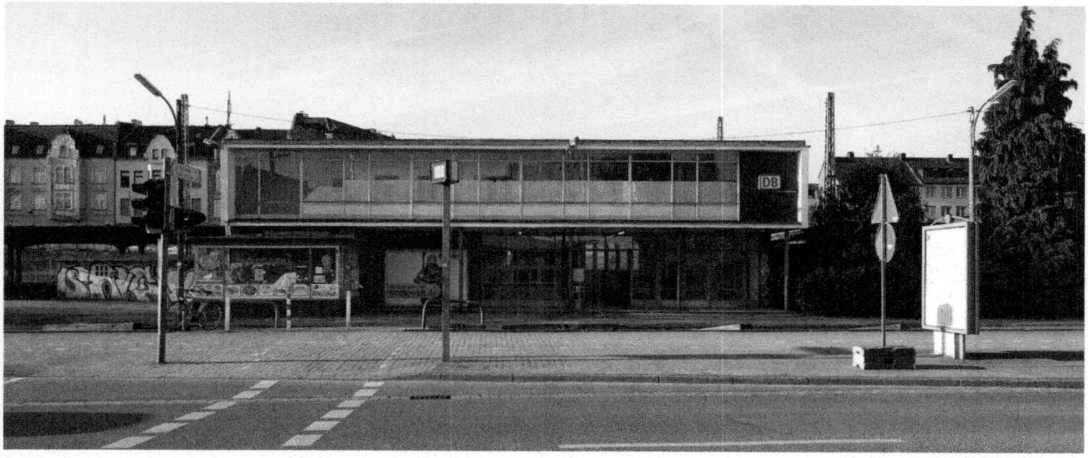
DB

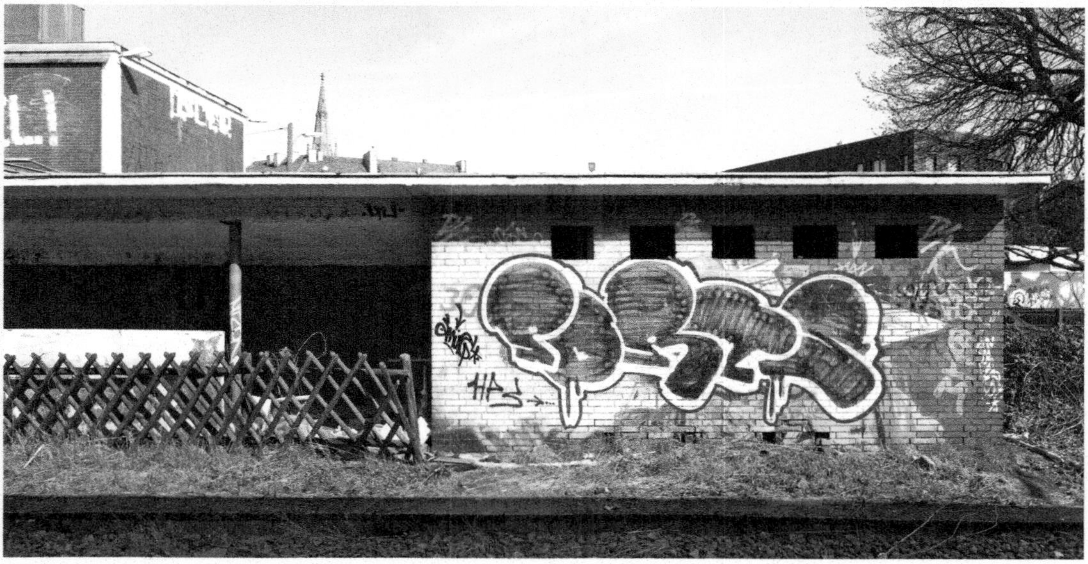

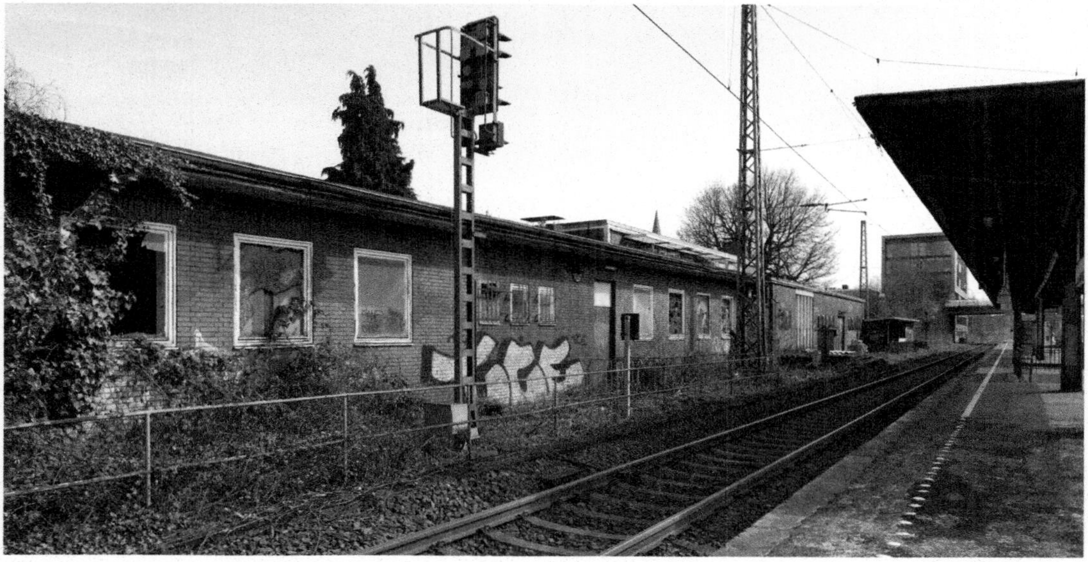

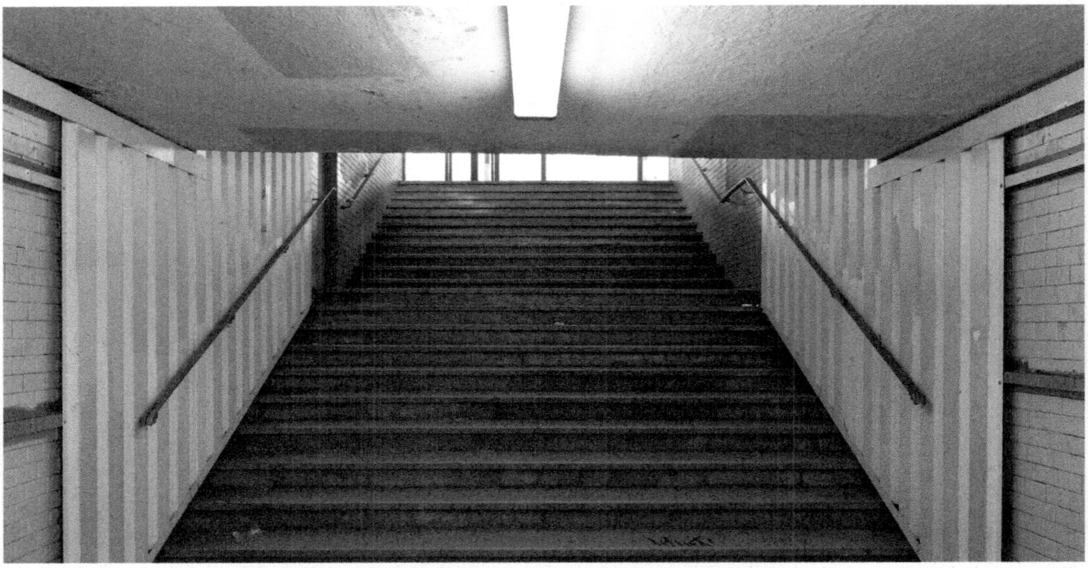

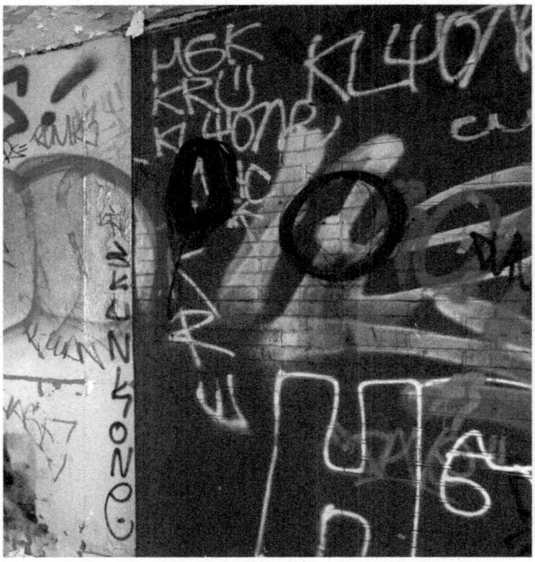

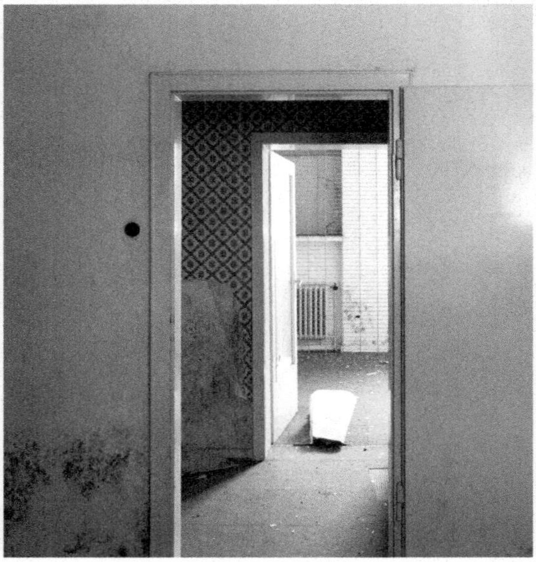

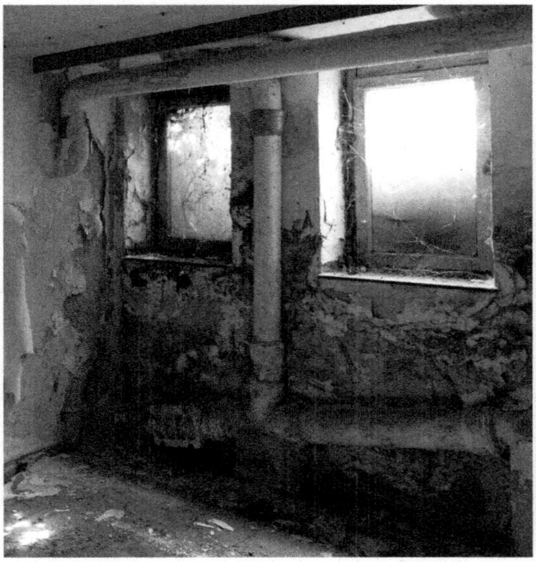

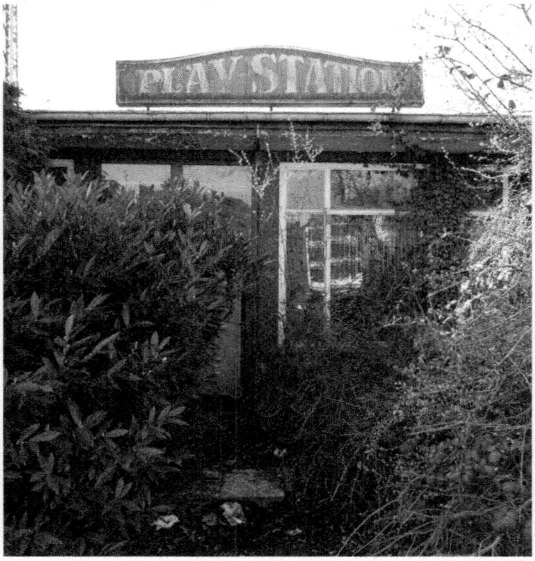
PLAY STATION

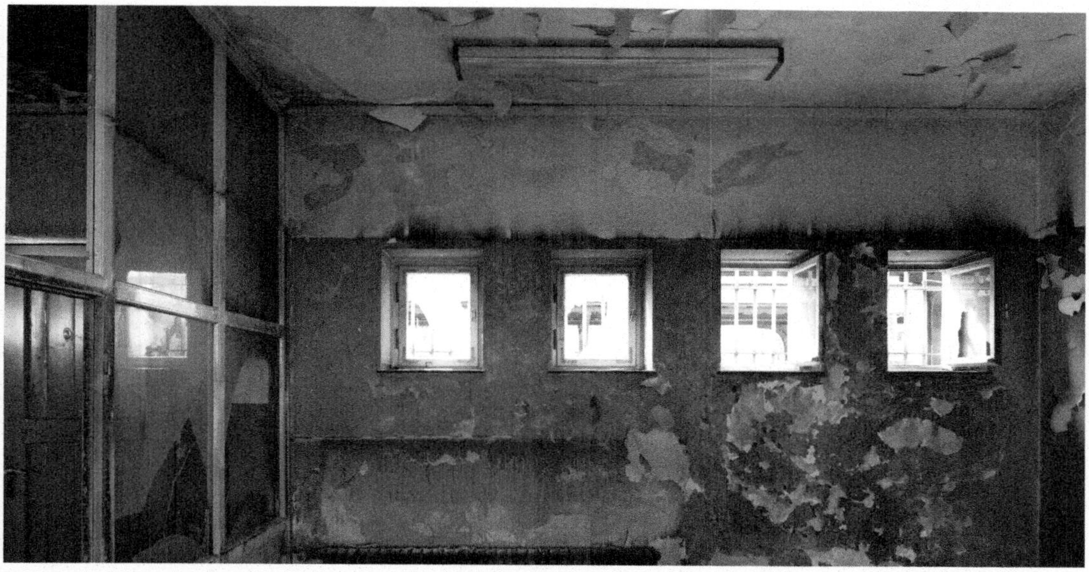

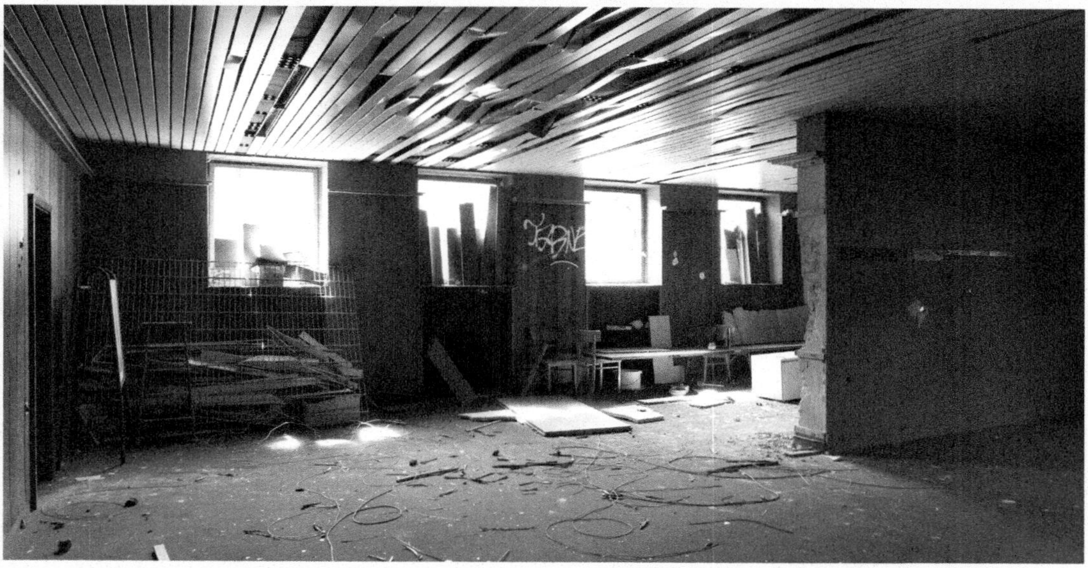

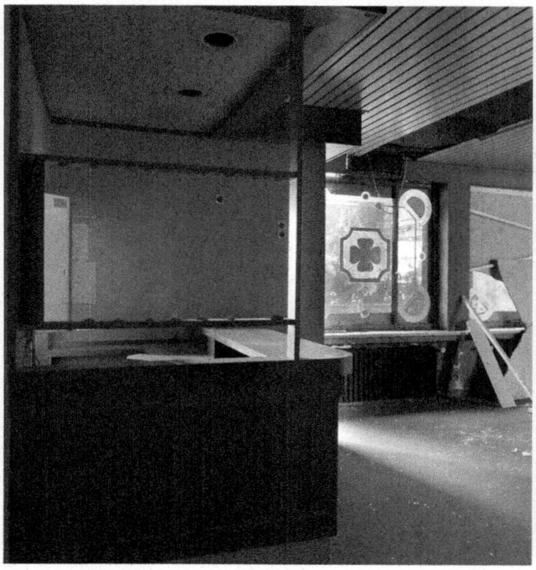

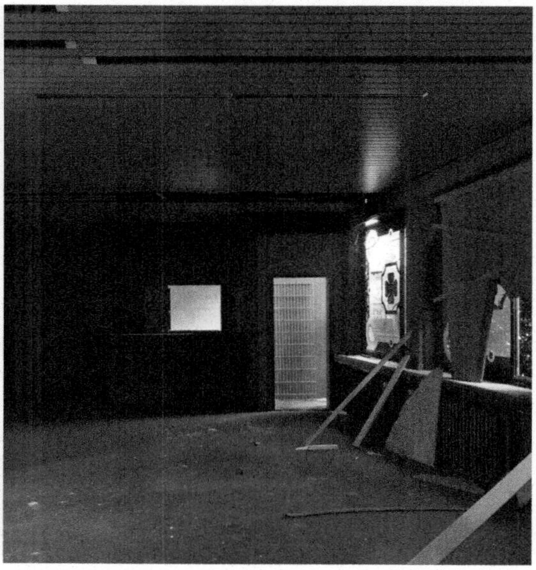

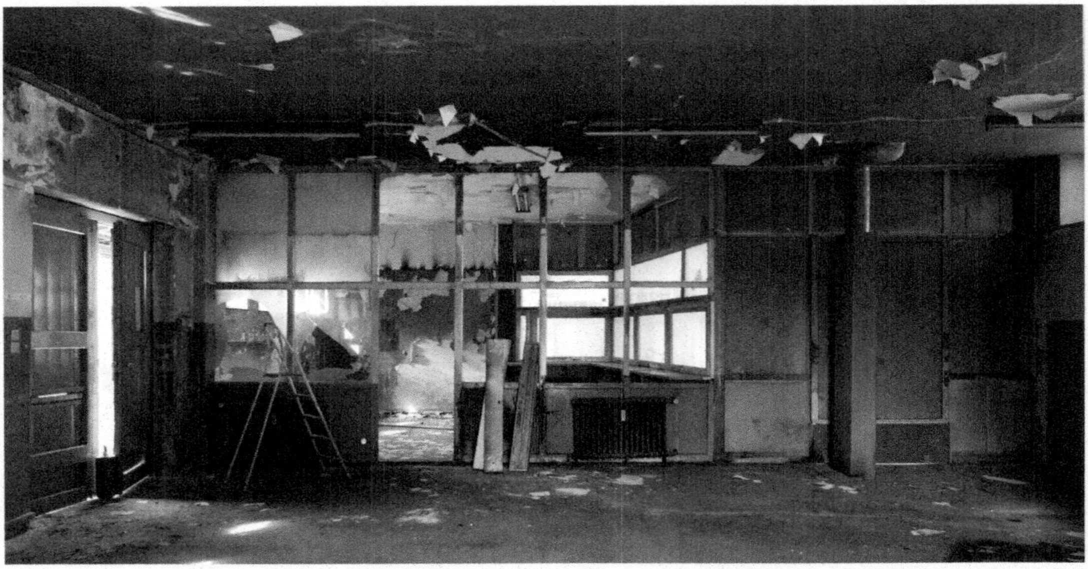

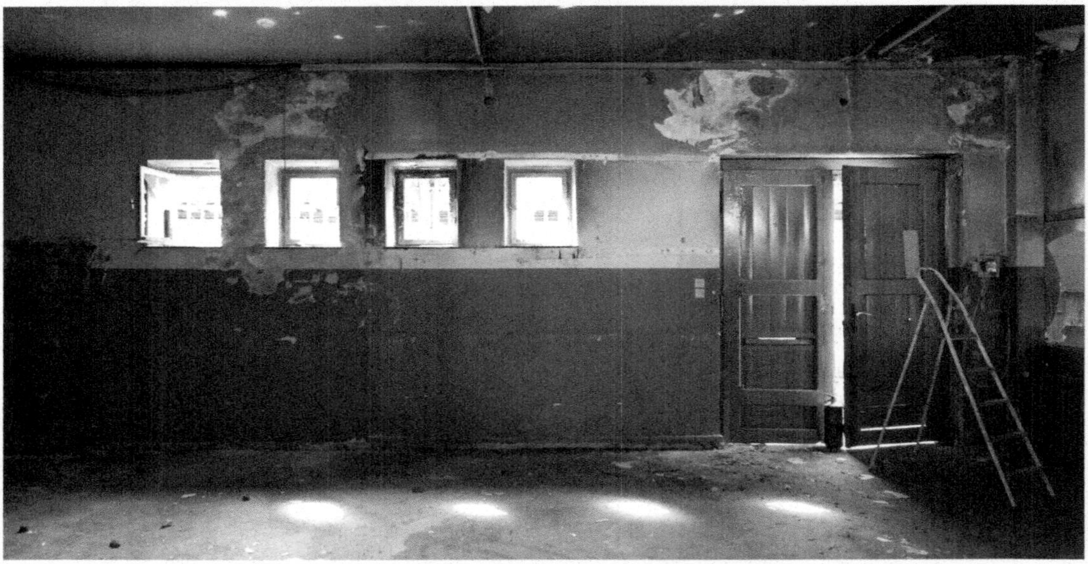

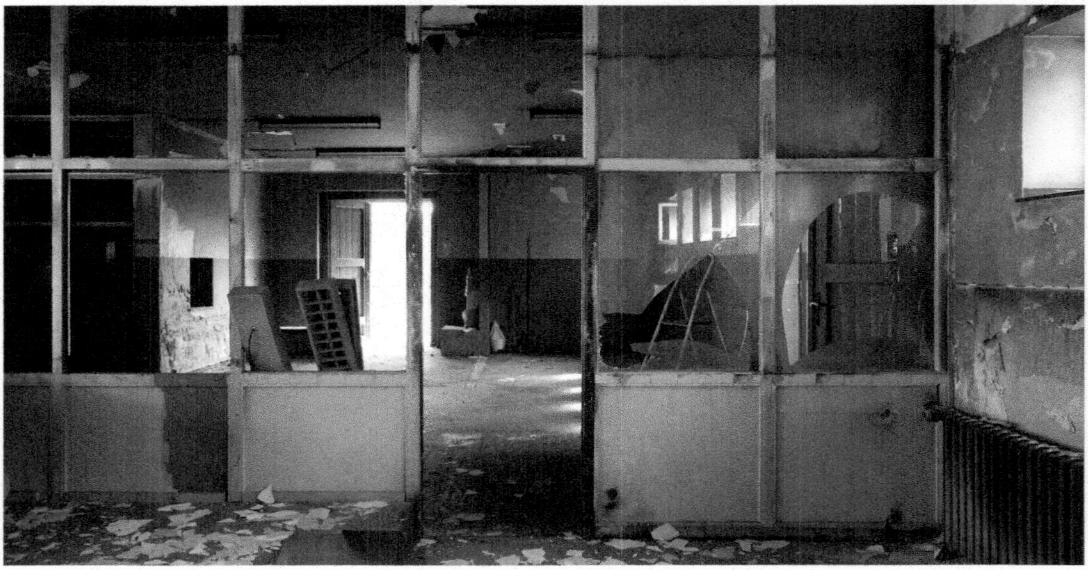

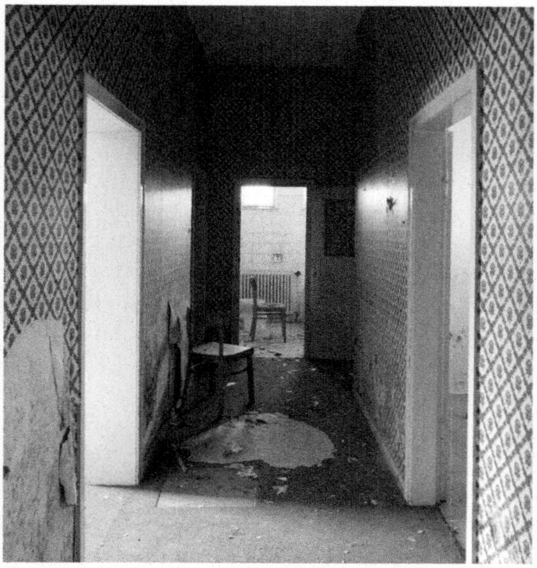

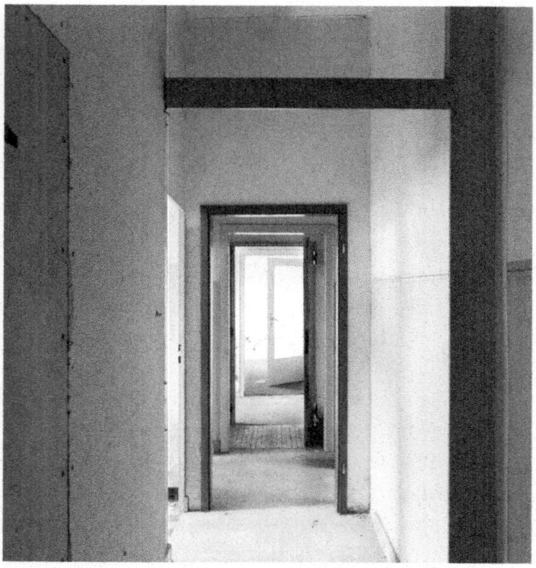

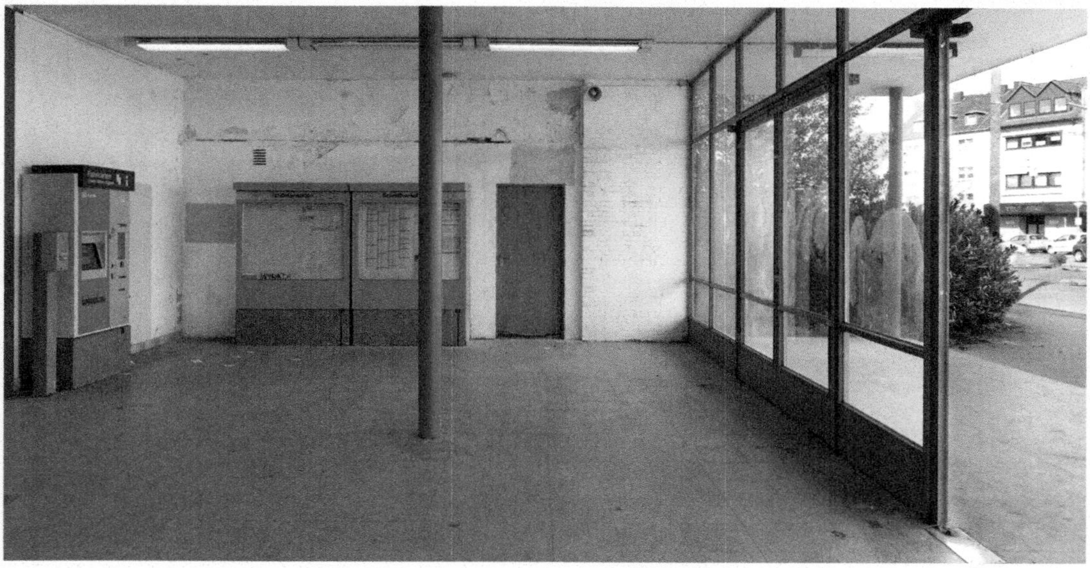

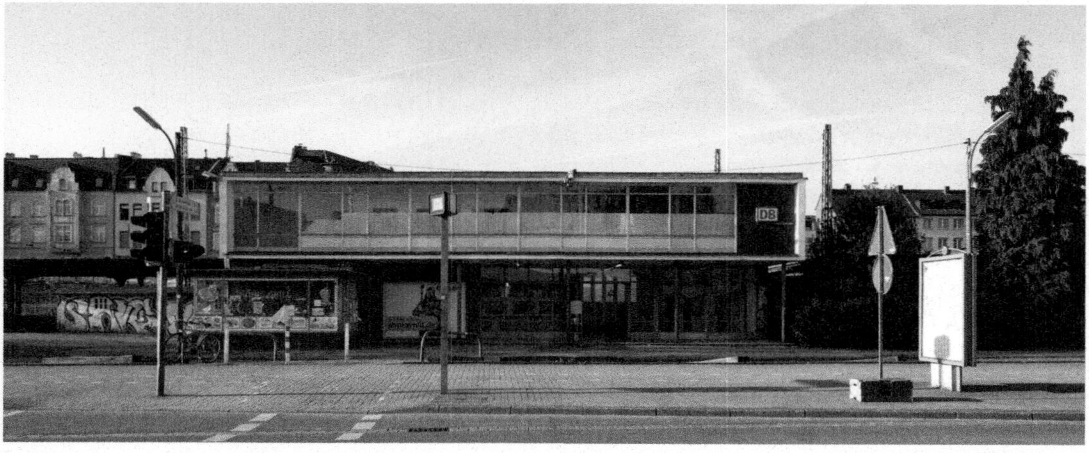
DB

Former train station in Hörde, Germany

Weg Isser (It's Gone)

Based on a true story

There was something grand here once. If you listened quietly,
you could still hear the echoes of laughter, loud clacks of high
heels, and the roar of locomotive engines. The train station in
the small town of Hörde, Germany was built in the 1950s. "Built
to last," they said.

Sure, train stations are for getting out and about, and fast.
Yet, they also offer chance meetings, and exposure to something
new and unexpected. That is, after all, how we grow and learn.
Whether a connection was planned or serendipitous; whether
someone new comes to town or we explore beyond the city limits
and return more cultured, traveled, and refined; mass transit is
a means for grand transformation.

That era had a certain style and charm which we don't see much
of these days. Even in a decaying state, there is something
beautiful and hard to replicate. But things don't have to fall
apart.

Mr. Holtkötter was employed by the Historic Monuments Protection
Authority to preserve places just like this train station, a
landmark unto itself, despite the lack of funding to restore it
to its former glory. He and his colleagues fought long and hard,
exercising every legal option to safeguard the classic station
in Hörde.

Institutional and administrative barriers weren't enough; even
the majority of residents seemed to want something more modern,
with shopping opportunities. A mall seemed more reasonable and
profitable. But there is - there was - historic value there that
can't be replaced.

"*Weg isser,*" Mr. Holtkötter murmured with a sigh.

He hunched in front of his computer in the quiet of his office as
he looked through the photos from his daughter, Julia. Being a
trained photographer, he brought her alongside to document the
former station during its final days.

He smiled broadly as he recalled them working together that
summer - a special treat, indeed. With hopes of saving the next
one, Mr. Holtkötter took a deep breath and reached for his
project folders.

Written by Jerome Walford   Images by Julia Cawley

ON THE GRIND
BY GEORGE GANT
SO I'M ON MY EX'S FACEBOOK, AND I SEE THAT HE'S ALREADY TALKING TO ANOTHER WOMAN!
SHE AIN'T ALL THAT!
HER FEET ARE TOO BIG!
IT DOESN'T MATTER ANYWAY– I DON'T NEED HIM! I DON'T NEED NO MAN!
I'M GONNA DO ME!
...AS SOON AS I BLOCK HIM FROM MY FACEBOOK AND MY TWITTER AND MY LINKEDIN PROFILES!
I'M SORRY ABOUT THAT...THE FIRST CUP FROM A FRESH BATCH IS USUALLY BITTER.
WHO YOU CALLIN' BITTER?
HI! WHAT CAN I GET YOU?
A LARGE PUMPKIN SPICE LATTE!
UM...WE DON'T HAVE PUMPKIN SPICE YET. IT COMES NEXT WEEK.
WHAT?!?
MAYBE I CAN GET YOU SOMET–
SHH!
I DON'T THINK SETTING YOUR WATCH FORWARD IS GOING TO HELP.
YOU DON'T KNOW THAT!
HI, WHAT CAN I GET YOU?
I WANT A COFFEE... BLACK.
GOTCHA WHAT SI–
HERE. I HAVE MY OWN MUG.
POP!
THERE'S MORE WHERE THAT CAME FROM, IF YOU'D LIKE TO SEE.
I'M GOOD.
D'SHAWN, I NEED YOU THE CLEAN THE MEN'S ROOM.
WHY ME? I ALREADY DID THE BAR, THE DISHES, AND THE FLOOR!
BECAUSE I HAVE ALL THIS "SUPERVISOR STUFF" TO FINISH!
WHAT SUPERVISOR STUFF? I'M READIN' YOUR HANDBOOK RIGHT NOW!
SHIFT SUPERVISOR JOB DUTIES: EVERYTHING A BARISTA DOES, BUT WITH ACCOUNTABILITY, STORE KEYS, AND THAT'S IT.
DANG.
...AND THIS WAS TYPED IN COMIC SANS, SO YOU KNOW IT'S LEGIT!

George Gant, Cartoonist

United States

George Gant is the creator of the all-ages video-game-themed comic *The Reset Button*, and the slice-of-life retail satire *On the Grind*. He has work featured in books published by Dark Horse Comics and Hound Comics, and has illustrated children's books, and two *On the Grind* book collections. George is also planning his first *The Reset Button* book. He currently lives in Chicago with his wife and young son.

geogantart.com

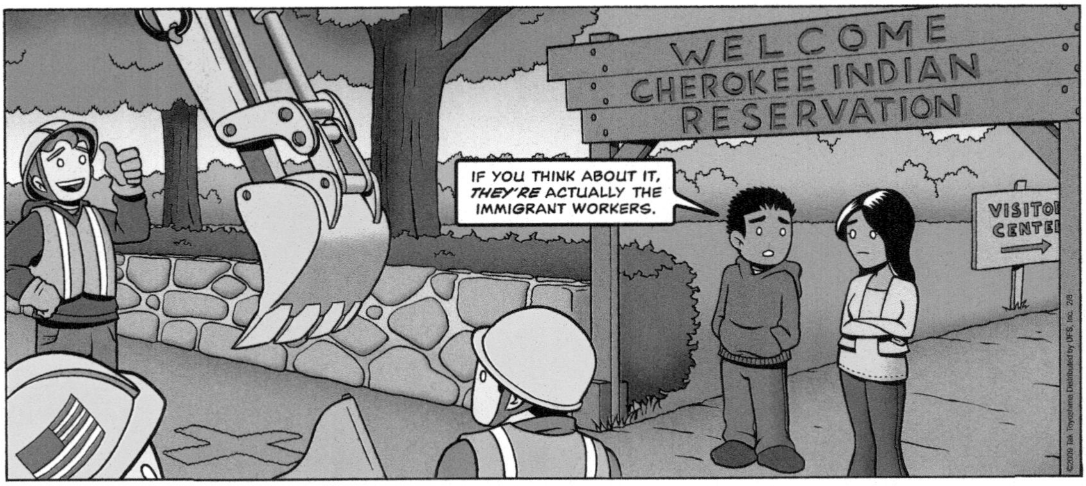
WELCOME
CHEROKEE INDIAN
RESERVATION
IF YOU THINK ABOUT IT, *THEY'RE* ACTUALLY THE IMMIGRANT WORKERS.
VISITO
CENTE

SECRET ASIAN MAN By Tak

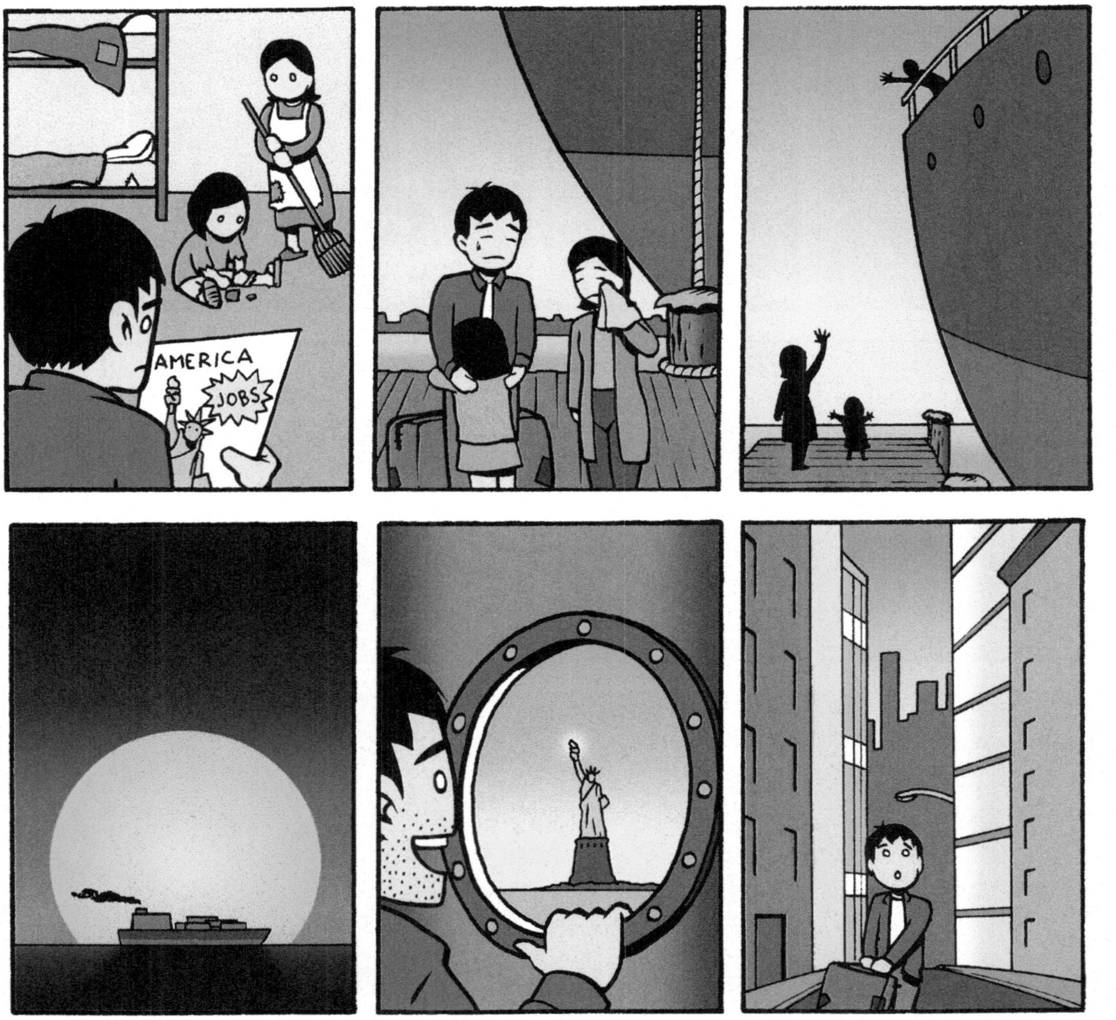
AMERICA
JOBS

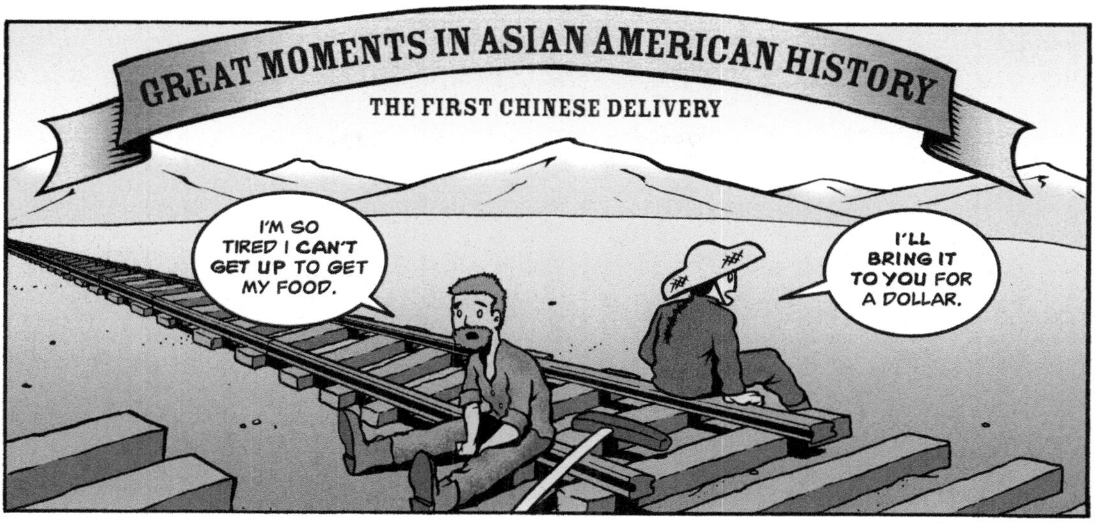
GREAT MOMENTS IN ASIAN AMERICAN HISTORY
THE FIRST CHINESE DELIVERY
I'M SO TIRED I CAN'T GET UP TO GET MY FOOD.
I'LL BRING IT TO YOU FOR A DOLLAR.

tak@secreatasianman.com • www.secretasianman.com •

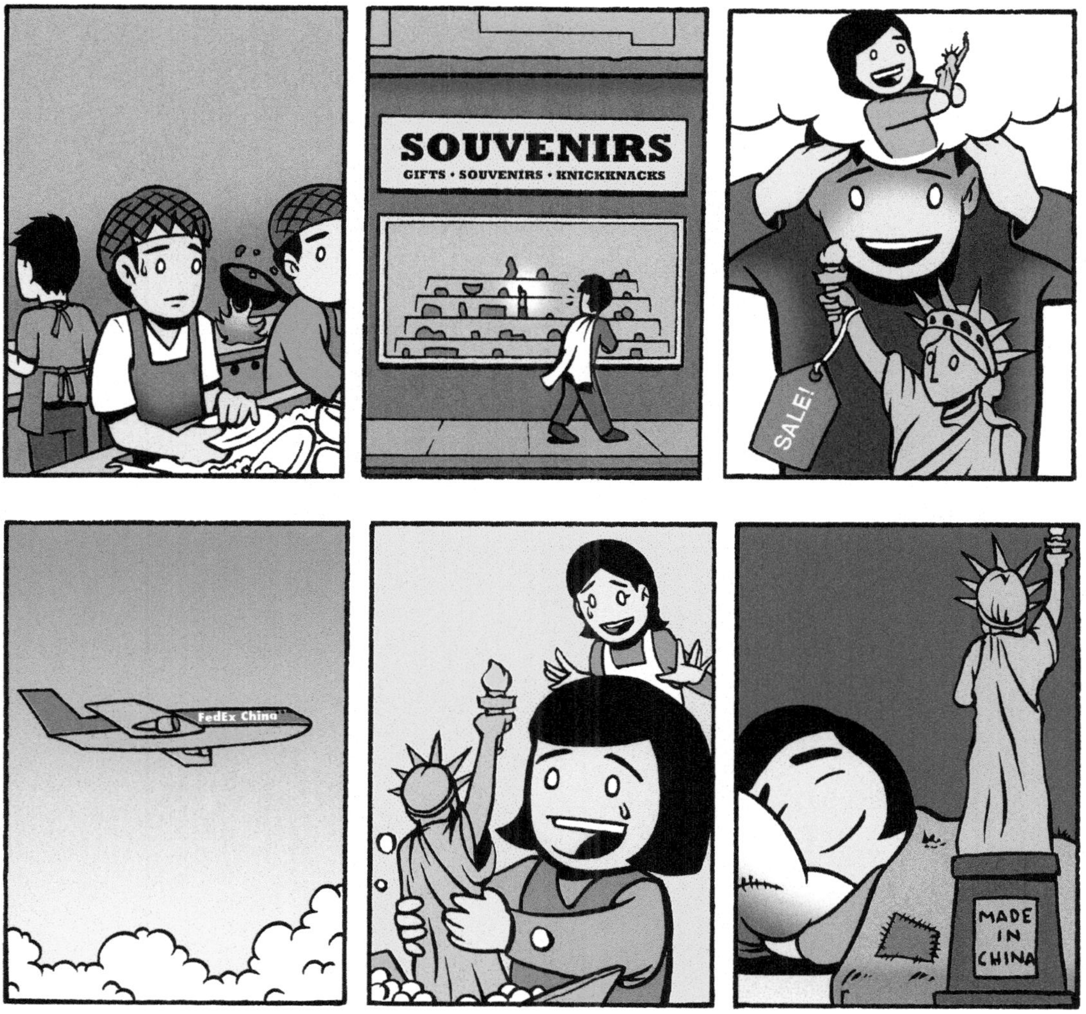
SOUVENIRS
GIFTS • SOUVENIRS • KNICKKNACKS
SALE!
FedEx China
MADE IN CHINA

Marta Tanrikulu, Writer

United States

Marta Tanrikulu is a writer and editor from the United States who has close ties to relatives in Italy and Turkey. Her stories have appeared in various anthologies, often with elements of loss, exploration, or humor.
vizyonentertainment.com

Lucho Inzunza, Artist

Chile

Lucho Inzunza is a comic book artist, character designer, and concept artist from Chile. His work includes *Halloween Man* and *Raupatu*.
facebook.com/luchoinzunzacomicartist

Kóte Carvajal, Colorist

Chile

Kóte Carvajal is a colorist and writer from Chile. Since Chile has a limited comics industry, he has also worked on several projects with creators from the US, New Zealand, and the UK. His colors are featured in stories such as *The Warden* and *One Must Break*.
kotecarvajal.com

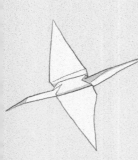

E.T. Dollman, Letterer

Italy

E.T. Dollman is an Italian writer, letterer, and designer who works with creators in several countries. He has lettered comics for Image Comics, Arcana, and Big Dog Ink.
facebook.com/ETDollman

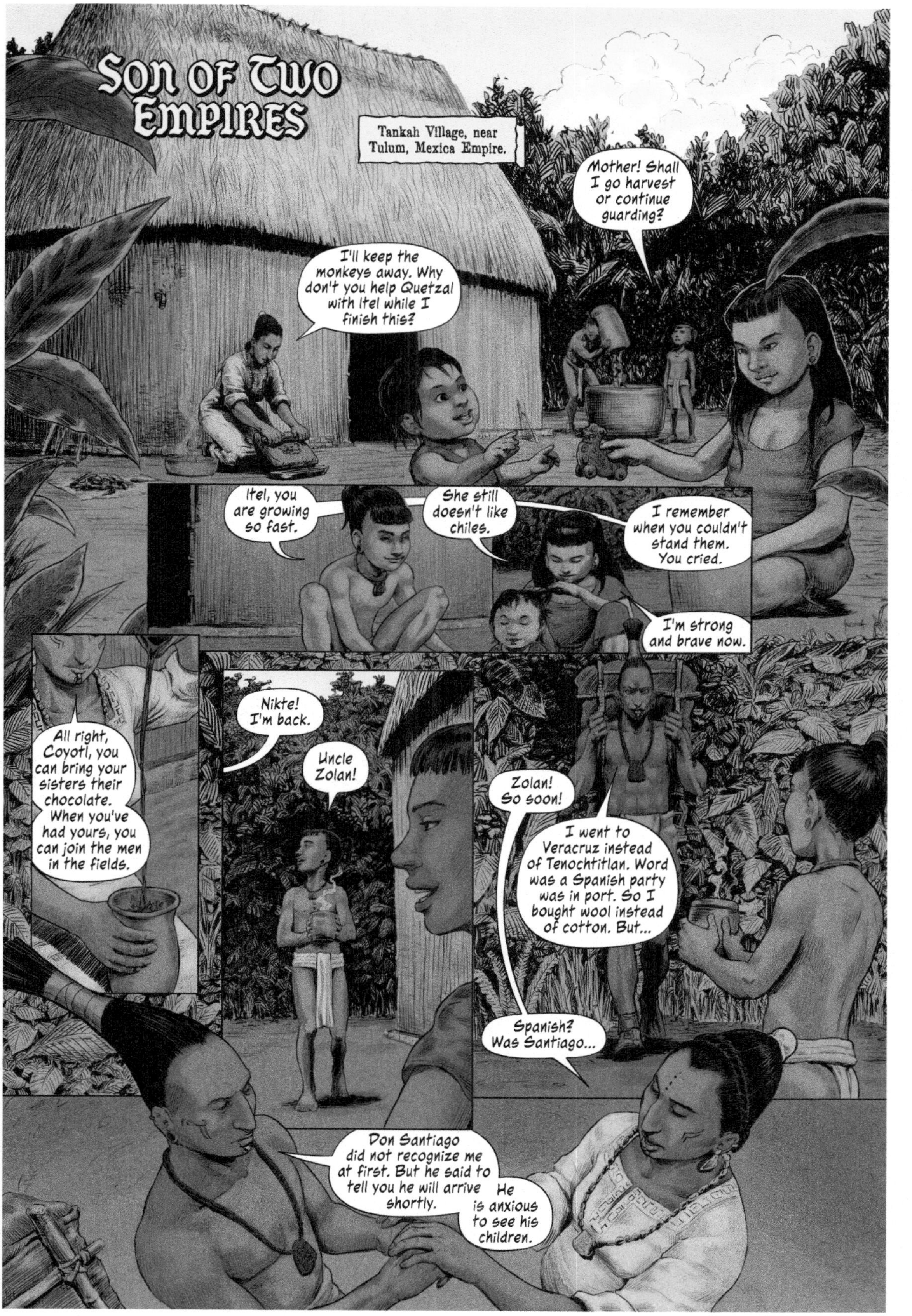

Son of Two Empires
Tankah Village, near Tulum, Mexica Empire.
Mother! Shall I go harvest or continue guarding?
I'll keep the monkeys away. Why don't you help Quetzal with Itel while I finish this?
Itel, you are growing so fast.
She still doesn't like chiles.
I remember when you couldn't stand them. You cried.
I'm strong and brave now.
All right, Coyotl, you can bring your sisters their chocolate. When you've had yours, you can join the men in the fields.
Nikte! I'm back.
Uncle Zolan!
Zolan! So soon!
I went to Veracruz instead of Tenochtitlan. Word was a Spanish party was in port. So I bought wool instead of cotton. But...
Spanish? Was Santiago...
Don Santiago did not recognize me at first. But he said to tell you he will arrive shortly.
He is anxious to see his children.

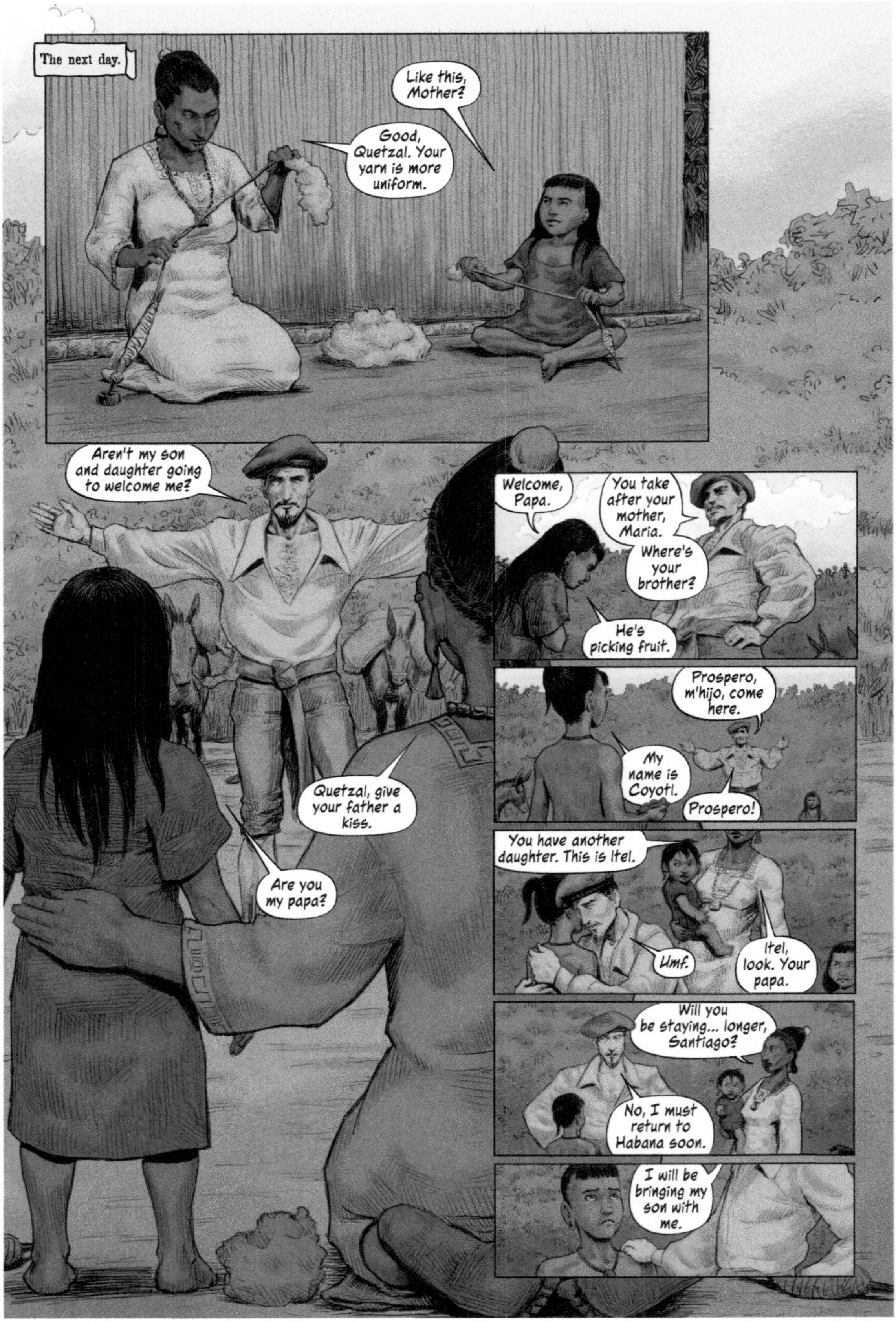

The next day.
Like this, Mother?
Good, Quetzal. Your yarn is more uniform.
Aren't my son and daughter going to welcome me?
Quetzal, give your father a kiss.
Are you my papa?
Welcome, Papa.
You take after your mother, Maria.
Where's your brother?
He's picking fruit.
Prospero, m'hijo, come here.
My name is Coyotl.
Prospero!
You have another daughter. This is Itel.
Umf.
Itel, look. Your papa.
Will you be staying... longer, Santiago?
No, I must return to Habana soon.
I will be bringing my son with me.

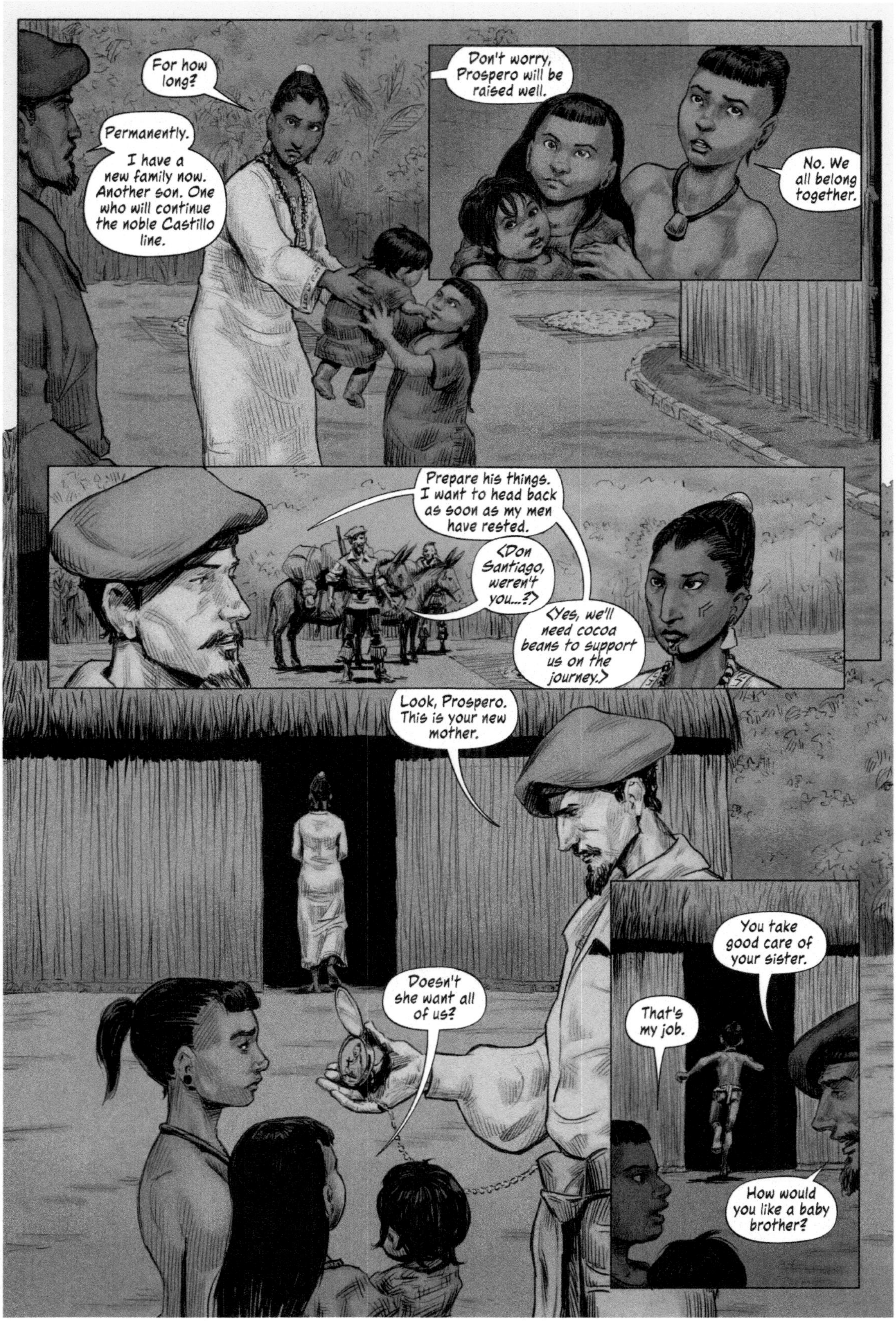
For how long?
Permanently.
I have a new family now. Another son. One who will continue the noble Castillo line.
Don't worry, Prospero will be raised well.
No. We all belong together.
Prepare his things. I want to head back as soon as my men have rested.
<Don Santiago, weren't you...?>
<Yes, we'll need cocoa beans to support us on the journey.>
Look, Prospero. This is your new mother.
Doesn't she want all of us?
You take good care of your sister.
That's my job.
How would you like a baby brother?

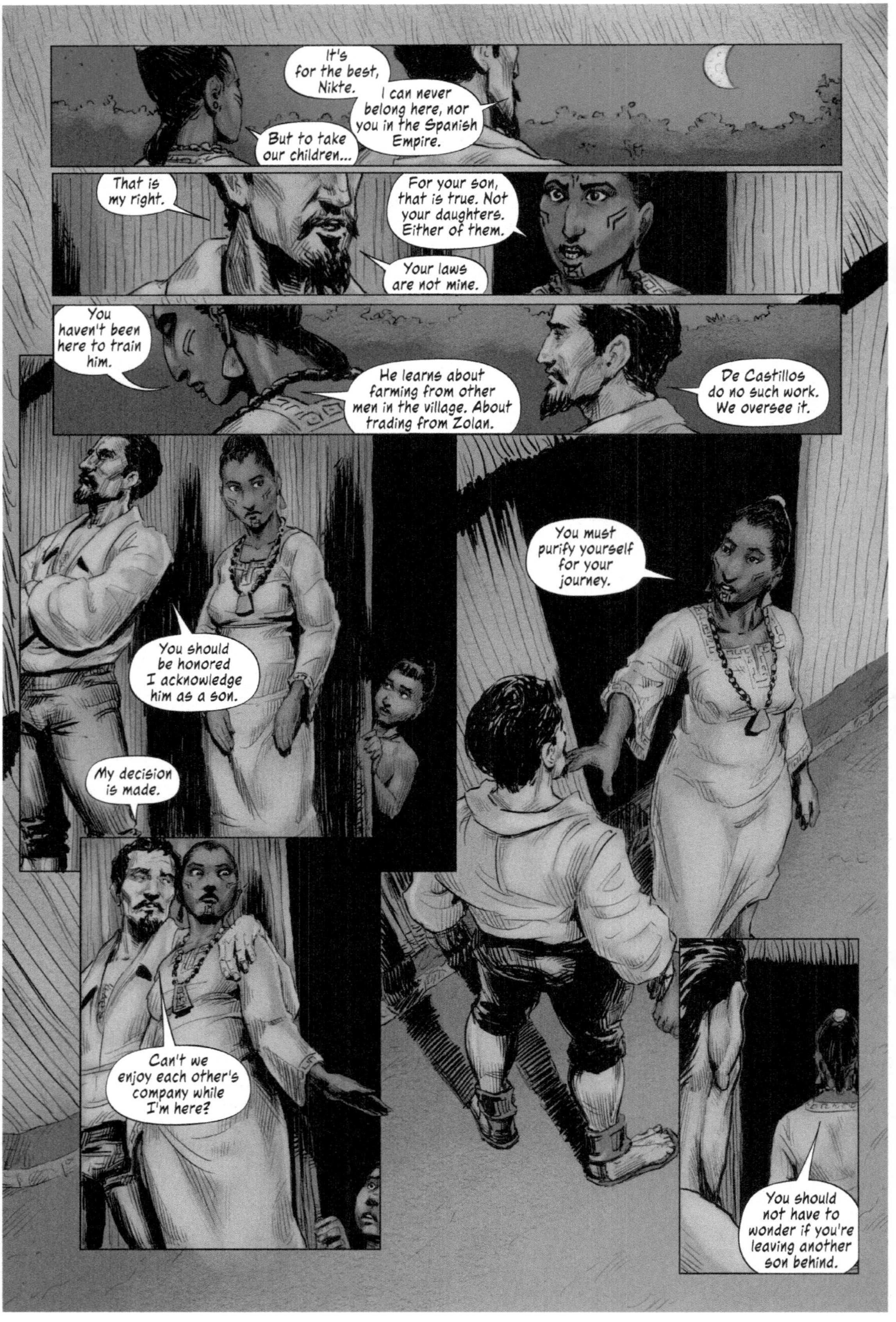
It's for the best, Nikte.
I can never belong here, nor you in the Spanish Empire.
But to take our children...
That is my right.
For your son, that is true. Not your daughters. Either of them.
Your laws are not mine.
You haven't been here to train him.
He learns about farming from other men in the village. About trading from Zolan.
De Castillos do no such work. We oversee it.
You should be honored I acknowledge him as a son.
My decision is made.
You must purify yourself for your journey.
Can't we enjoy each other's company while I'm here?
You should not have to wonder if you're leaving another son behind.

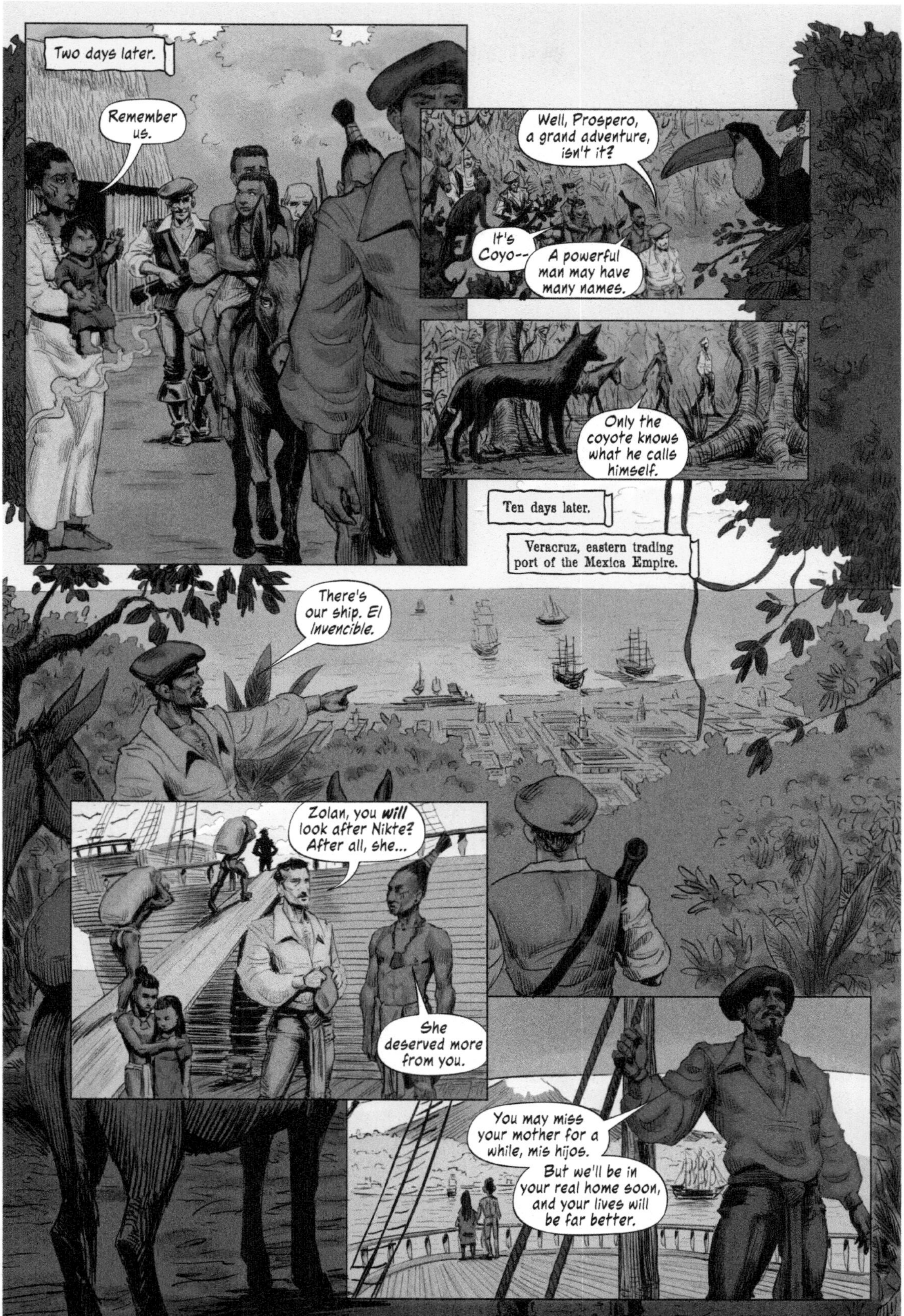

Two days later.
Remember us.
Well, Prospero, a grand adventure, isn't it?
It's Coyo--
A powerful man may have many names.
Only the coyote knows what he calls himself.
Ten days later.
Veracruz, eastern trading port of the Mexica Empire.
There's our ship. El Invencible.
Zolan, you **will** look after Nikte? After all, she...
She deserved more from you.
You may miss your mother for a while, mis hijos.
But we'll be in your real home soon, and your lives will be far better.

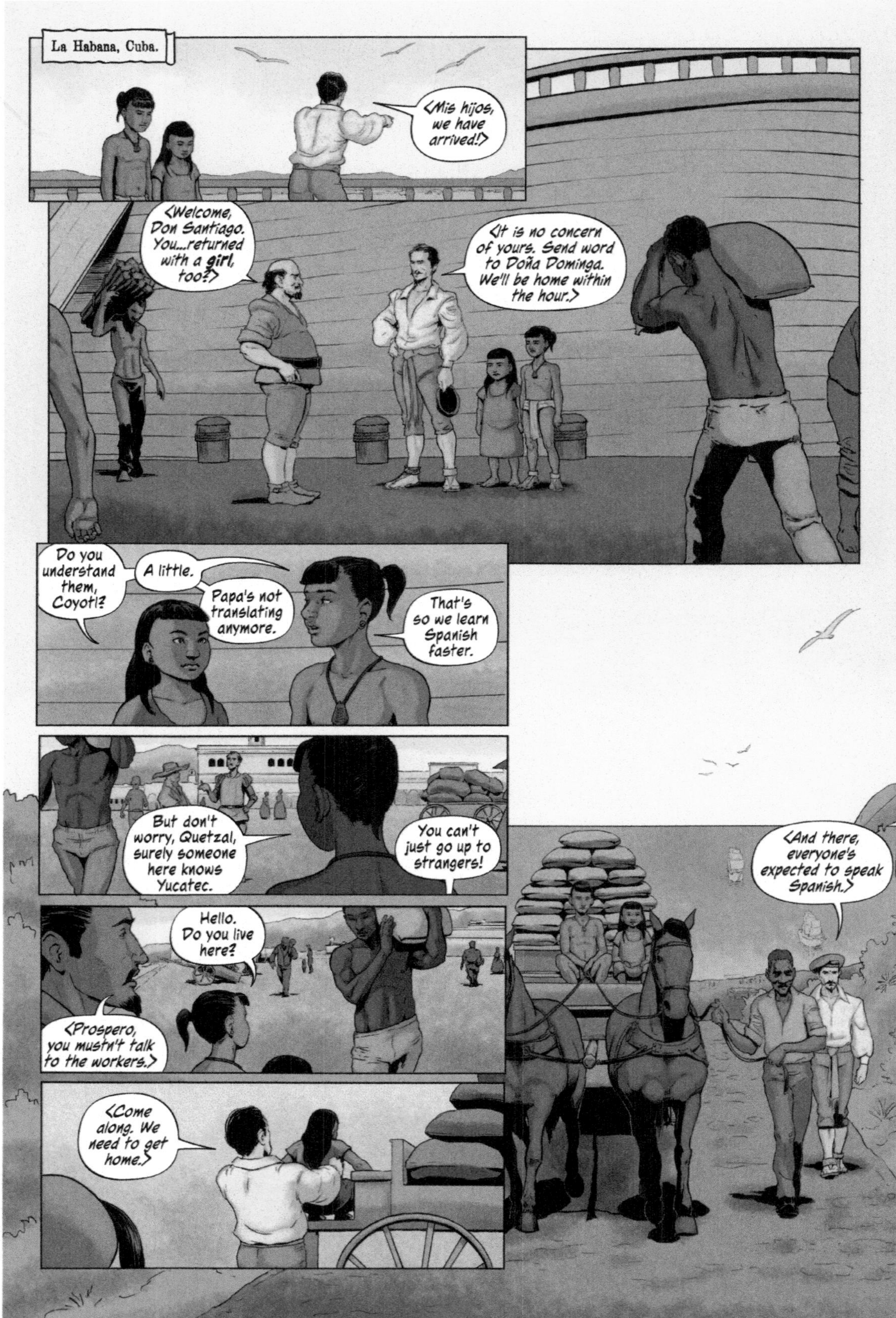
La Habana, Cuba.
<Mis hijos, we have arrived!>
<Welcome, Don Santiago. You...returned with a girl, too?>
<It is no concern of yours. Send word to Doña Dominga. We'll be home within the hour.>
Do you understand them, Coyotl?
A little.
Papa's not translating anymore.
That's so we learn Spanish faster.
But don't worry, Quetzal, surely someone here knows Yucatec.
You can't just go up to strangers!
<And there, everyone's expected to speak Spanish.>
Hello. Do you live here?
<Prospero, you mustn't talk to the workers.>
<Come along. We need to get home.>

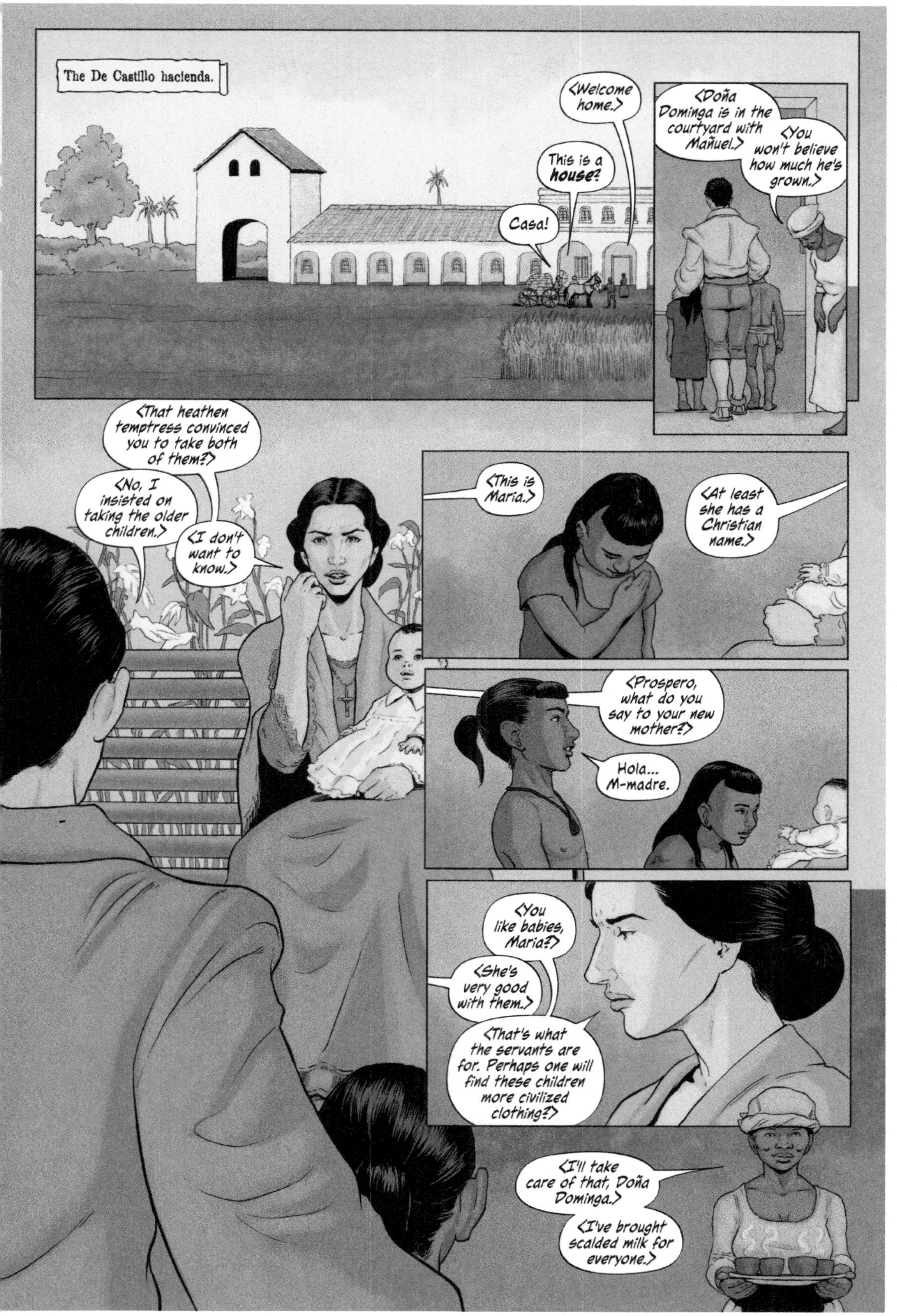

The De Castillo hacienda.
<Welcome home.>
This is a house?
Casa!
<Doña Dominga is in the courtyard with Mañuel.>
<You won't believe how much he's grown.>
<That heathen temptress convinced you to take both of them?>
<No, I insisted on taking the older children.>
<I don't want to know.>
<This is Maria.>
<At least she has a Christian name.>
<Prospero, what do you say to your new mother?>
Hola... M-madre.
<You like babies, Maria?>
<She's very good with them.>
<That's what the servants are for. Perhaps one will find these children more civilized clothing?>
<I'll take care of that, Doña Dominga.>
<I've brought scalded milk for everyone.>

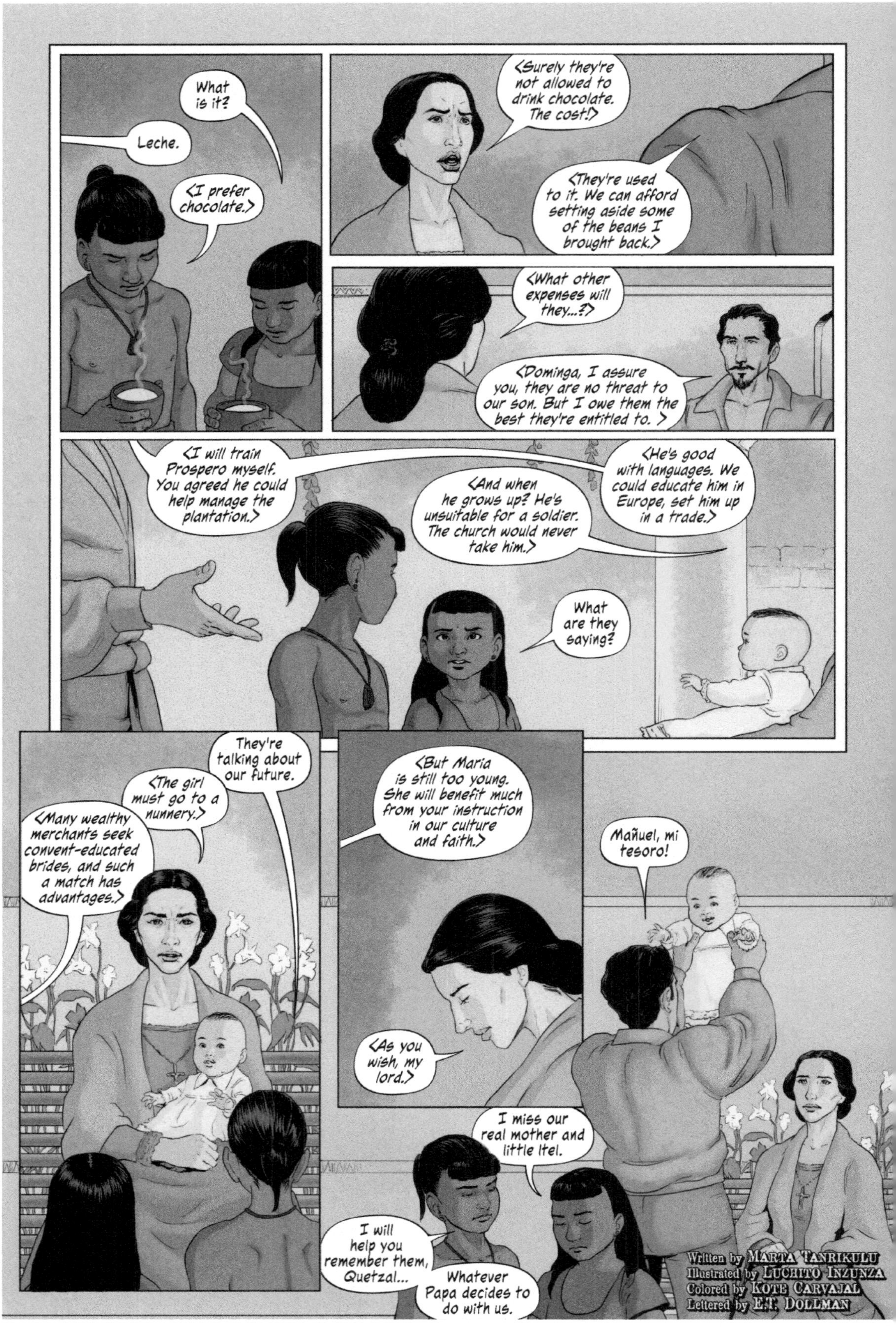
What is it?
Leche.
<I prefer chocolate.>
<Surely they're not allowed to drink chocolate. The cost!>
<They're used to it. We can afford setting aside some of the beans I brought back.>
<What other expenses will they...?>
<Dominga, I assure you, they are no threat to our son. But I owe them the best they're entitled to.>
<I will train Prospero myself. You agreed he could help manage the plantation.>
<He's good with languages. We could educate him in Europe, set him up in a trade.>
<And when he grows up? He's unsuitable for a soldier. The church would never take him.>
What are they saying?
<Many wealthy merchants seek convent-educated brides, and such a match has advantages.>
<The girl must go to a nunnery.>
They're talking about our future.
<But Maria is still too young. She will benefit much from your instruction in our culture and faith.>
<As you wish, my lord.>
Mañuel, mi tesoro!
I miss our real mother and little Itel.
I will help you remember them, Quetzal...
Whatever Papa decides to do with us.
Written by Marta Tanrikulu
Illustrated by Luchito Inzunza
Colored by Kote Carvajal
Lettered by E.T. Dollman

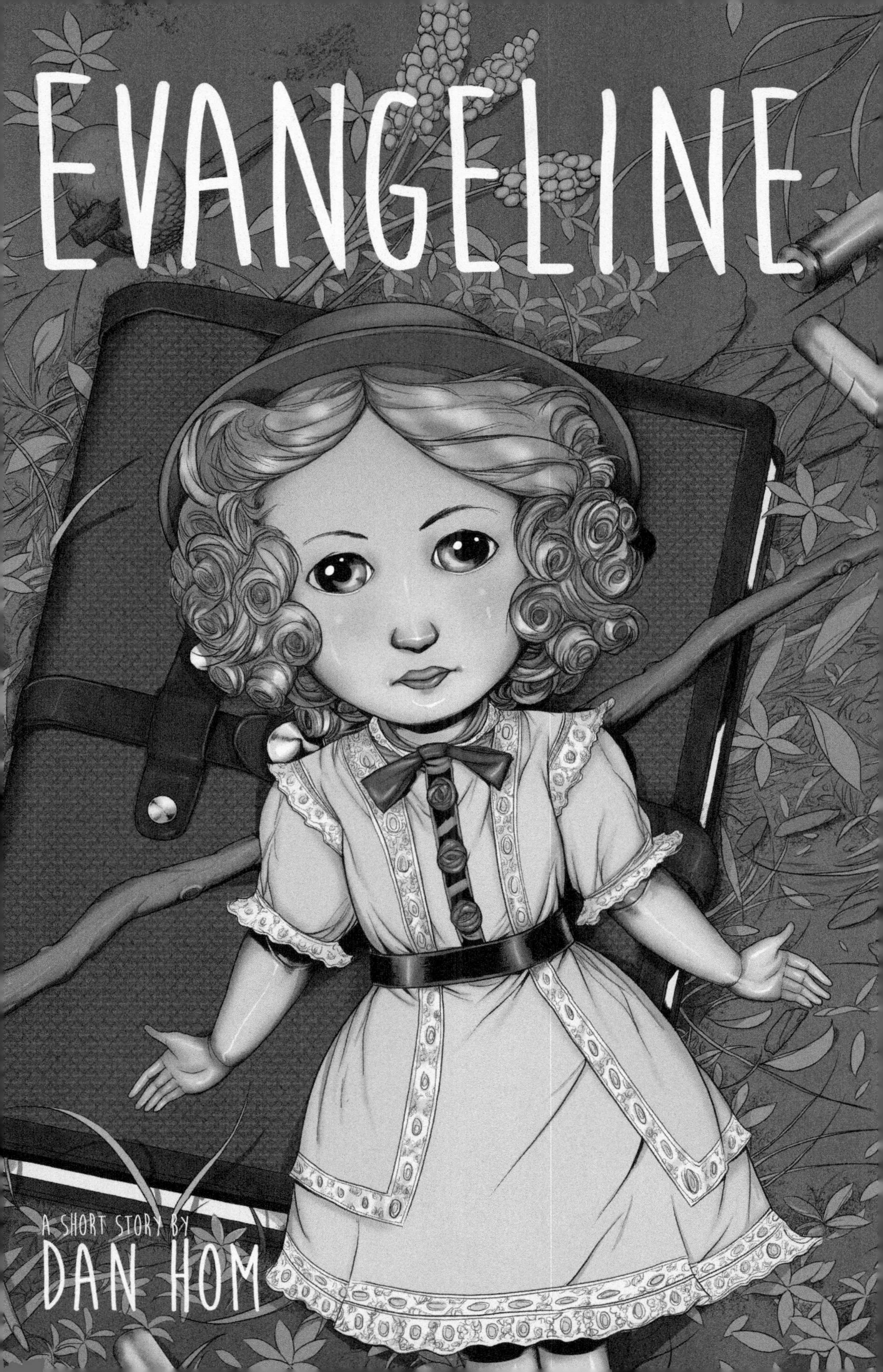
EVANGELINE
A SHORT STORY BY
DAN HOM

Dan Hom, Writer
United States

So, surprise. My name is Dan.

I work in tech, am an amateur photographer and wannabe chef, musician, and on occasion, and only on occasion, I write.

I think the world is pretty fascinating and exploring it is a ton of fun. I love running through mega-cities, small towns, and remote trails. But more than anything, I like to meet the people on this planet, find out what their stories are and what makes them tick. And then I like to write about it. But usually I'm lazy so I just ending up writing about me. Either way, writing is good practice for writing.

Thanks for humoring me.
</smile>

danhom.com

12 July

I miss home. I want to go back but I am scared that home is too far away to ever go back.

Father and I have been gone for so many days now. I remember he woke me up in the night. It was quite cold, and I thought maybe it was a big bad dream. Father said he loved me but we must go and I only had time to bring a very small bag with me. He said to not carry many things because we will come back home soon. But we have been wandering through the northern mountains and I forgot how many days it has been since we left.

Today a strange boy found us. I think he is my age but he looks strange so I do not know for sure. Father asked for help, and the boy took us to a camp where the boy lives with other strange people. I have never seen people like them before.

Their camp is far away from home and I have never been here. It's scary and hard to find and there are lots of tall trees. I wonder if they are hiding.

The people here aren't like me. They look different and I don't understand the words they say. Father says he understands some of their language. It sounds like aliens. And their hair is so bright, almost like gold. I wonder if it is valuable and like the gold coins at home.

I want to see Mother. But Father says we won't see Mother again. He looked like he might cry. And then he said he loves me and he really wants me to know that so he said it three or four or ten times.

This is the first day at the camp with the strange people. Father said we won't be here for very long. I looked very close at his eyes when he said this. I really hope he is not lying.

13 July

The strange people here say my name wrong. My name is
Evangeline. It sounds so pretty when I say it out loud.
It sounds strong and ambitious but also kind and sweet.
When the strange people say Evangeline it sounds like
Yewanjoelay. Like eww when you see something gross. My
name is not gross. It is the name of a beautiful girl with
hair like dark chocolate, lips like roses and eyes like the
cute little birds in our garden. It is the name of a queen
and I rule over the world.

Father says to not think that I am a queen. He says I am
more like a cowboy. I go get the bad guys and bring good
news to people. He says that's what my name means, bring
good news to people. I am sure you can bring good news
to people and still be a queen.

I learned one word today from the strange people.
Rosho. It is how they say hello. Father said it does
not quite mean hello but it is like the same thing. I
don't understand. If you use it to say hello why doesn't
it mean hello? Father said it's complicated. Why is it
complicated? That is Father's reason for many questions.
Maybe he does not know the answers. Or maybe he does
not want to tell me because it is something only older
people understand. I still wish he would try.

15 July

The boy came to visit Father and me today. He's the one who found us when we were lost. He is very nice and brought us some food. It was something that tastes like chicken and it tasted very good. I said rosho to him and he smiled. He tried to say hello but it sounds like halu.

He wrote his name and it looks like L'anzoh. The ' thing is funny and I don't know why it is there. I don't know anyone who has a ' in their name. You only use it to put two words together and make the word less long. Like don't.

L'anzoh is very hard to say so I call him Lance now because it's easier. Lance also sounds like a hunky name which is perfect for a queen like me. Maybe Lance doesn't like it though. I don't like it when he calls me Yewanjoelay. He says my name over and over but it still sounds wrong and then he looks confused.

I miss my friends Gwendolyn and Alvina. And Alistaire too. They all knew how to say my name the right way. I did not have to teach them about me because they already knew.

18 July

Rosho! Everytime I see Lance he says rosho like he is very happy and very excited. That is why I used the ! sign. Today, he came over to play and he brought some long sticks. He gave one to me and I think you play a game with them. The stick is something you use to hit things with but also to stop someone else from hitting you. I think a queen should have other people carry the sticks for her and do the hitting, but it is still fun and I like it.

Father tells me I shouldn't play sticks. He brought some dolls for me to play with. I would rather play with the sticks. If we had to leave home so quickly I don't know why he packed so many dolls for me.

Father also said I shouldn't play with the boys and girls here. He said they are dangerous and I should be careful. He says if Lance is a good boy then he should give me flowers. I like flowers but I have not seen any in a long time. Maybe this place has no flowers. That would be very sad, a place that has no flowers.

Father told me again that we won't be here for very long. He has been leaving the camp very often and comes back at nighttime when I am asleep. I am a little scared so I asked if he is going to leave me here and he said no and don't worry because he will always come back. He said he promised. And that I am a very good girl. He never used to say that to me.

A non. That is how you say goodbye to the strange people.

23 July

Lance comes to say hi everyday and he practices lots of words. He can say come, okay and yes. He still says hello like halu.

When he says halu he smiles. He has a very hunky smile. I will make sure he is my soldier when I am the queen. I think Lance is like a friend and so I am not mad when he does not say my name properly. I am happy because he keeps trying to say it better.

There is one of the strange people who can say my name. She is an old lady with grey hair and she has a voice that sounds like she is singing. When she calls me Evangeline it sounds like a song and it makes me smile. Mother used to sing songs to me.

A non.

24 July

A long time ago I asked Father what he does when he leaves home during the day. He said he must perform his duty and that he is a soldier. Maybe he is one of the people who will carry a stick for me when I am the queen. I think that is what a soldier does.

Today, Father told me a confusing story. He said this place with the strange people is hidden and that the people here ran away because they were bad. He has been looking for this place for a long time. It does not make sense. Lance came to help us because we did not have food and we were lost. That seems like a nice thing to do. All the people here seem like nice people, but they are weird. And I do not think weird means that they are bad.

I asked Father where Mother is, and he did not answer for a long time. I was scared so I did not move. And then he said not to ask him that question ever again.

25 July

I am so sorry! I did something bad and Lance is in trouble.

Lance came to visit and showed me a bow and arrow. I think he received it as a gift. He let me try it and I don't know what happened and I hit one of the old men at the camp. It was not on purpose! There was a lot of yelling and crying and yelling again. I was so scared. They hit Lance, they hit him very hard and they took him away. And when he said goodbye he said cez' afi a non.

When Father came he yelled at me and hit me. I am so scared. He said it is my fault and that when you do something wrong, you deserve to be punished for it so do not do things that are wrong and that is the rule of the land. I did not know it was wrong! It was a mistake.

I want Mother. I yelled back at Father and said I want to see Mother and then Father screamed and said that Mother is dead. He started to cry and said he is being punished and that is why she is dead. He said that is why we are here.

I want to go home. If I say please enough times, can I go home? Maybe Father is wrong and Mother will be there when we go back. But if mother is gone forever, will it still be home? I love Father too but I am so scared when he yells. I am scared that he does not love me and maybe he will hit me again.

And now Lance is also in trouble and I will not see him. I do not know what to do. It is so complicated.

Much later, I asked Father what cez' afi a non means. He said it is like goodbye but much more sad and you do not say it very often because you do not know if you will ever see the person again.

Cez' afi a non, Mother.

26 July

I cried today. I tried not to but I could not help it. Father told me not to cry and that he does not like to see me cry. Why? Why am I not allowed to cry? I am sad. I made Lance get in trouble and he was my friend. I am sad because Father hit me. And now I have no friends again because we are not at home and cannot see my old friends. It is very lonely.

I do not think Father wants me to go outside anymore but I do anyway because I like it. At home I always stay in the garden. Here I can go outside and say rosho to people. Some people smile but some people whisper about me and I think it is mean. But most people smile at me. I like that I can wander in the forest on my own. The nice lady with the grey hair tried to show me how to use the bow and arrow the right way. It is very difficult but I like that she is teaching me. It is like how Mother used to teach me to pick flowers from the garden.

Father told me that he loves me again. His eyes were very scared when he said it though, and I can tell when he is scared. He said again to not do things that are wrong so that you are not punished. He says he does not want to lose me and he does everything for me. I do not know if I believe him. He did give me these dolls because he loves me but I do not really enjoy dolls. I hope he does not do bad things because he loves me. I do not want him to do bad things for me because that would be lying. I do not think that is love.

28 July

I miss home. I wonder if maybe home was a dream. Perhaps I have always lived here in this strange place in the mountains.

1 August

Rosho! There was a surprise today. Lance came back. I mean L'anzoh. He tried to tell me what happened but I didn't understand and Father had to explain to me. He said they hit him to teach him a lesson but that the elder people also said Lance is strong and fights for what is right. Lance pointed to himself and said tak'ski. I think tak'ski means cool but it is probably complicated and doesn't quite mean that.

He said he likes the name Lance. I told him I still don't like Yewanjolay. He is better about saying Evangeline. He said it over and over and over again but it still sounds wrong.

I told Father that Lance is very tak'ski and Father became angry and said you cannot say that word that way. But Lance seemed to understand what I mean. And then Father said he doesn't ever want to see me with Lance again.

I asked him how come. I thought he would say it is complicated but he said it is because he does not want to lose me. Why would he lose me? I do not understand Father. He is becoming very strange to me.

A non.

5 August

I want to understand Father so I decided to follow
Father when he left the strange people's camp. I made
sure that Father did not see that I was close behind him.

He carried the bag with my dolls in it. When he got to
the top of one hill, he took out a doll and put it on
the ground. I don't know why he is leaving my dolls
everywhere. Then he went to another hill and put another
doll there too. They are my dolls but I don't really like
them so it's okay. But why is he doing it?

6 August

I am so scared. I know Lance is scared too.

I thought Father was strange yesterday so I told Lance
to come with me today and we followed Father again. We
followed all the hills that have the dolls on them. And then
we saw Father light a small fire on a nearby mountain. You
can see the smoke from very far away.

And then also very far away we saw some people walking
towards the smoke. The people look like me and they have a
lot of large sticks with them. I think they are guns. Guns
are very loud and scary. I'm scared. I'm scared that Father
is bringing the people here to the strange people's camp.

Lance is scared. He has a very sad look in his eyes. He
pointed to the people coming, and then he pointed to his
heart and then he fell over and said something like da'vos. I
think that means the people who look like me want to hurt
Lance.

Did Father bring the people here on purpose? Is this what
he meant when he said he is being punished and that is why
Mother is gone and we are at the strange people's camp?

Have I done something wrong too?

7 August

I am with Lance right now. It is nighttime and Father is asleep. We ran back to the camp and Lance brought me to all the rest of his people. Everyone has packed everything and they look like they will run away. Lance pointed into the mountains and said come.

I am scared. I don't know what will happen to Father. But I want to do the right thing. The strange people are not so bad. I want him to know it isn't okay to bring bad people here.

If I go with the people, will I never go home? Will I never see the gardens and flowers? What about my friends? But I do not know if I can stay here with Father. I do not know if he truly is my father. I do not want a father who does bad things to people.

I do not often know when something is wrong. But how do I know when something is right?

I will leave this journal here. I will leave it for Father. I hope that he will find it and read it, so that he will understand why I am leaving with these people.

Goodbye Father. Cez' afi a non.

Love,
Evangeline

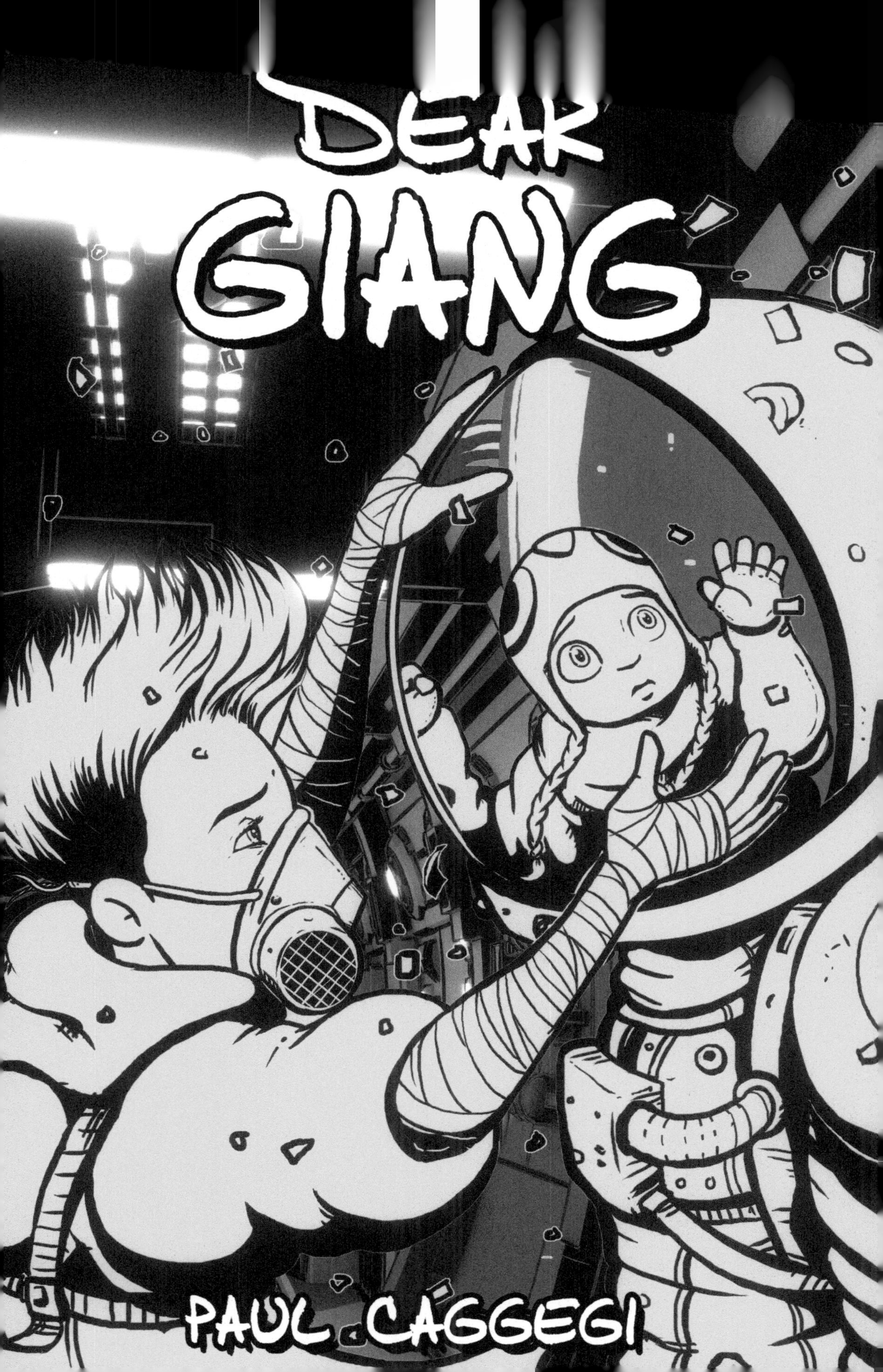
DEAR
GIANG
PAUL CAGGEGI

Paul Caggegi, Writer / Artist

Australia

Paul Caggegi is the first generation Australian son of Italian immigrants. He is married to a Vietnamese refugee whose family fled from Communists in 1981.

Paul lectures on design at JMC Academy in Sydney. He is also an illustrator and motion graphics designer. He has worked on storyboards, motion graphics promotional content, and TV commercials for prominent studios such as Nickelodeon, Saachi & Saachi, and Leo Burnett. His comic work includes the ongoing sci-fi title, *Pandeia*, as well as several contributions of short comics and illustrations for a range of anthologies. He frequently appears at local comic and gaming conventions.

You can see his work over at his official website or follow him on social media: Tumblr, Instagram and DeviantArt by searching for pcaggegi.

paulcaggegi.com

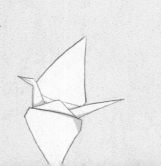

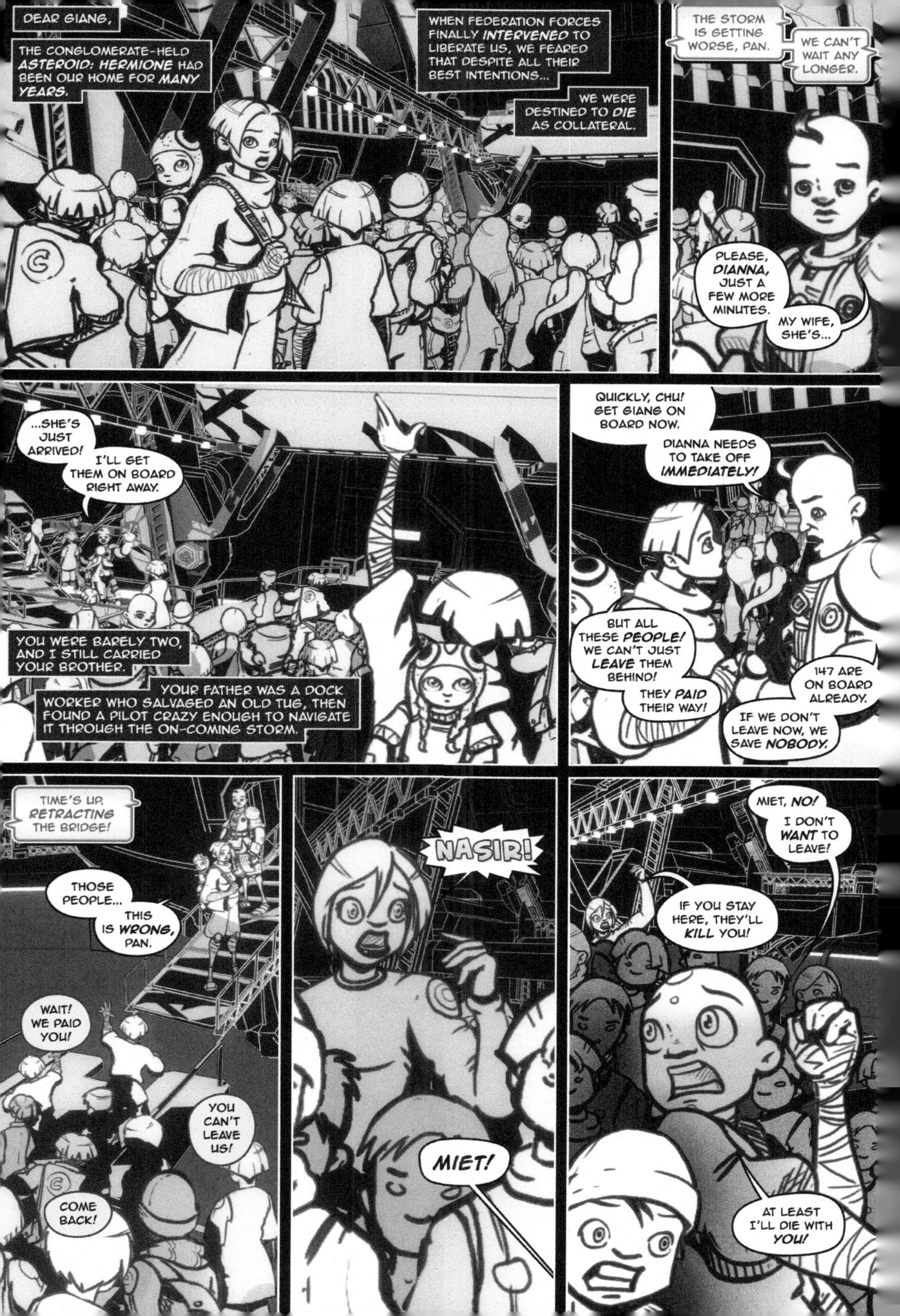
DEAR GIANG,
THE CONGLOMERATE-HELD ASTEROID: HERMIONE HAD BEEN OUR HOME FOR MANY YEARS.
WHEN FEDERATION FORCES FINALLY INTERVENED TO LIBERATE US, WE FEARED THAT DESPITE ALL THEIR BEST INTENTIONS...
WE WERE DESTINED TO DIE AS COLLATERAL.
THE STORM IS GETTING WORSE, PAN.
WE CAN'T WAIT ANY LONGER.
PLEASE, DIANNA, JUST A FEW MORE MINUTES.
MY WIFE, SHE'S...
...SHE'S JUST ARRIVED!
I'LL GET THEM ON BOARD RIGHT AWAY.
YOU WERE BARELY TWO, AND I STILL CARRIED YOUR BROTHER.
YOUR FATHER WAS A DOCK WORKER WHO SALVAGED AN OLD TUG, THEN FOUND A PILOT CRAZY ENOUGH TO NAVIGATE IT THROUGH THE ON-COMING STORM.
QUICKLY, CHU! GET GIANG ON BOARD NOW.
DIANNA NEEDS TO TAKE OFF IMMEDIATELY!
BUT ALL THESE PEOPLE! WE CAN'T JUST LEAVE THEM BEHIND!
THEY PAID THEIR WAY!
147 ARE ON BOARD ALREADY.
IF WE DON'T LEAVE NOW, WE SAVE NOBODY.
TIME'S UP, RETRACTING THE BRIDGE!
THOSE PEOPLE...
THIS IS WRONG, PAN.
WAIT! WE PAID YOU!
YOU CAN'T LEAVE US!
COME BACK!
NASIR!
MIET!
MIET, NO!
I DON'T WANT TO LEAVE!
IF YOU STAY HERE, THEY'LL KILL YOU!
AT LEAST I'LL DIE WITH YOU!

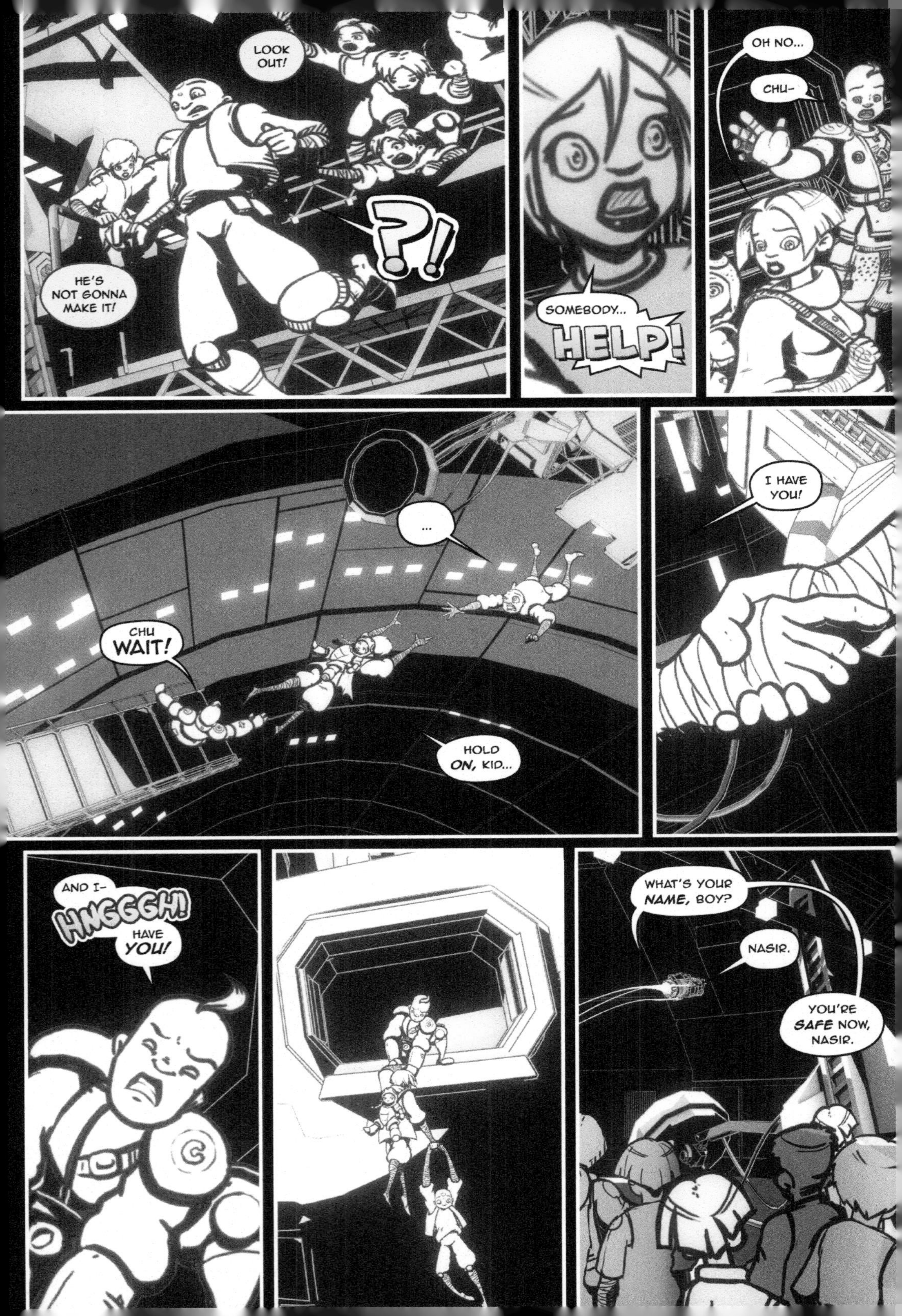

LOOK OUT!
HE'S NOT GONNA MAKE IT!
?!
SOMEBODY...
HELP!
OH NO...
CHU-
...
CHU WAIT!
HOLD ON, KID...
I HAVE YOU!
AND I-
HNGGGH!
HAVE YOU!
WHAT'S YOUR NAME, BOY?
NASIR.
YOU'RE SAFE NOW, NASIR.

WHAT WERE YOU *THINKING*, CHU?!

YOU COULD HAVE *DIED!* OR WORSE,

TAKEN OUR *FAMILY* WITH YOU!

I KNEW YOU'D *ALWAYS* BE THERE FOR US.

A DAY MIGHT COME WHEN I *WON'T* BE.

THAT SEEMS MORE LIKELY NOW.

WHAT HAPPENS THEN?

LADIES AND GENTLEMEN...

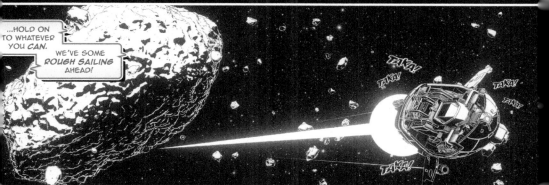

...HOLD ON TO WHATEVER YOU *CAN*.

WE'VE SOME *ROUGH SAILING* AHEAD!

TAKA!
TAKA!
TAKA!
TAKA!
TAKA!
TAKA!

IT TOOK SEVERAL HOURS TO CLEAR THE DUST STORM.

TAKA!
TAKA!

TAKA!
TAKA!

TAKA!
TAKA!
TAKA!

WE OFTEN THOUGHT THAT WE WOULDN'T MAKE IT THROUGH...

BUT OUR PILOT DID NOT LET US DOWN.

HEY PAN? IS EVERYONE DOING OK DOWN THERE?

THEY'RE A LITTLE SHAKEN. BUT THEY'LL LIVE.

MY SENSORS ARE SHOWING ME WE TOOK QUITE A *BEATING*.

ARE YOU UP FOR A WALK OUTSIDE?

PAN? WHAT'S GOING ON?

I HAVE TO *CHECK* SOME OF THE SHIELDING.

I'M SURE IT'S FINE, BUT JUST TO BE SAFE,

YOU AND *GIANG* SHOULD STAY AS CLOSE TO THE FRONT AS *POSSIBLE*.

WHAT ABOUT THE OTHERS?

WE DON'T WANT TO *PANIC* EVERYONE

YOU'RE PANICKING *ME*.

IT'S JUST A... *SIGH*

IF YOU'RE *THAT* WORRIED, TAKE *THIS*. SO YOU CAN HEAR ME.

PLEASE, CHU? FOR *GIANG*?

FOR MISTER *BUMP* HERE?

OK, PAN. BE SAFE.

"HOW BAD IS IT, PAN?"

THE LEAD SHIELDING IS *DAMAGED* IN SECTIONS 18 THROUGH TO... 23.

HOW *FAR* DO WE HAVE TO TRAVEL?

"THE ROCK WE'RE AIMING FOR IS A FORTNIGHT'S BURN AWAY...

...BUT WE SHOULD HIT *FEDERATION SPACE* INSIDE A DAY OR SO."

"COULD WE CLOSE OFF *THOSE* SECTIONS? GET EVERYONE UP FRONT?"

WE'RE ALREADY OVERCROWDED, DIANNA.

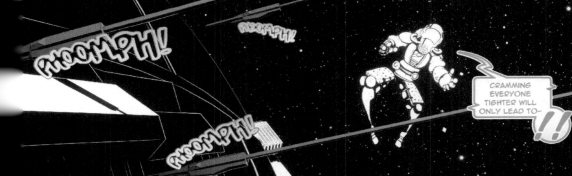

FROOMPH!

FROOMPH!

FROOMPH!

CRAMMING EVERYONE TIGHTER WILL ONLY LEAD TO—

!!

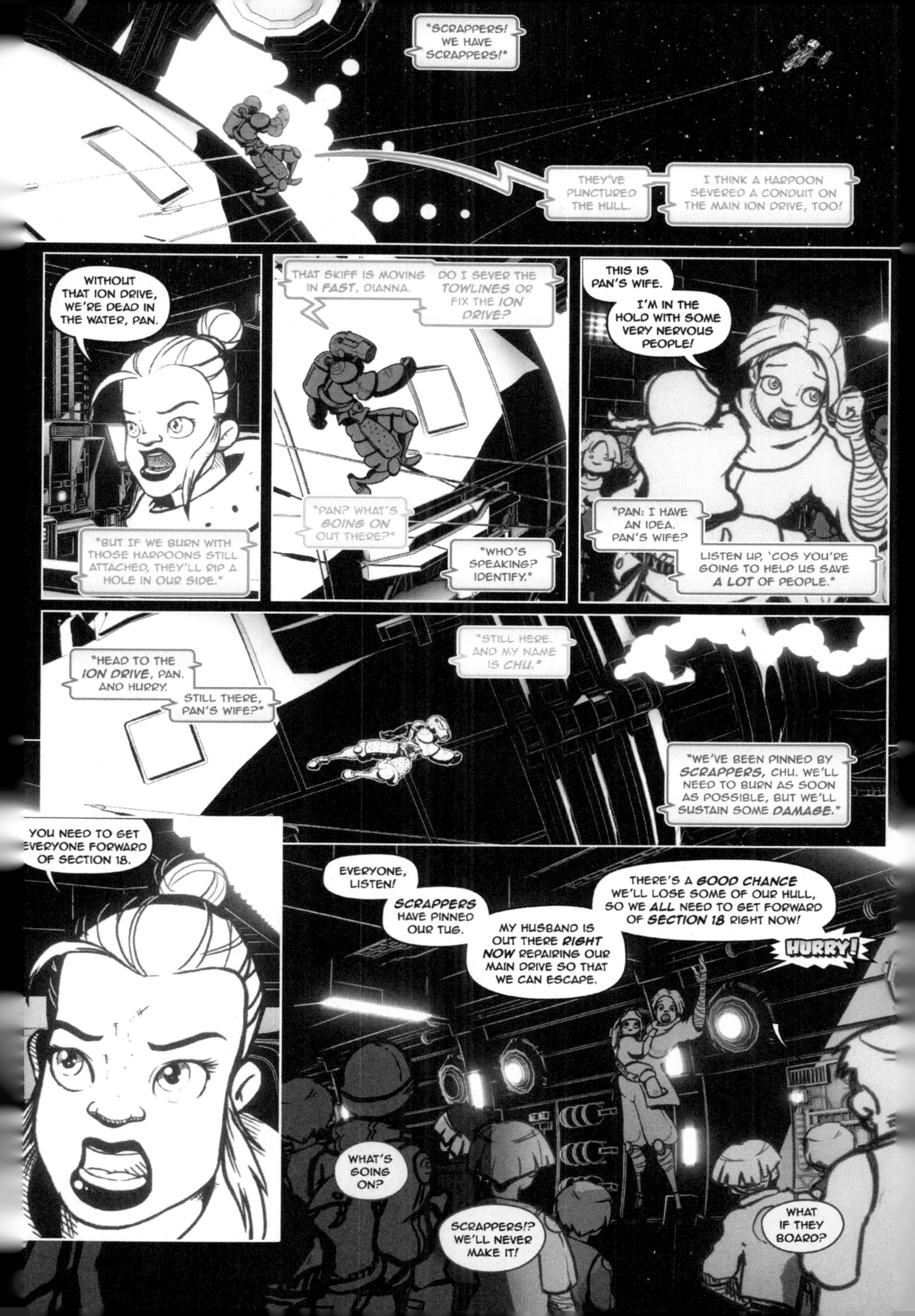
"SCRAPPERS! WE HAVE SCRAPPERS!"
THEY'VE PUNCTURED THE HULL.
I THINK A HARPOON SEVERED A CONDUIT ON THE MAIN ION DRIVE, TOO!
WITHOUT THAT ION DRIVE, WE'RE DEAD IN THE WATER, PAN.
"BUT IF WE BURN WITH THOSE HARPOONS STILL ATTACHED, THEY'LL RIP A HOLE IN OUR SIDE."
THAT SKIFF IS MOVING IN FAST, DIANNA.
DO I SEVER THE TOWLINES OR FIX THE ION DRIVE?
"PAN? WHAT'S GOING ON OUT THERE?"
"WHO'S SPEAKING? IDENTIFY."
THIS IS PAN'S WIFE.
I'M IN THE HOLD WITH SOME VERY NERVOUS PEOPLE!
"PAN: I HAVE AN IDEA. PAN'S WIFE?
LISTEN UP, 'COS YOU'RE GOING TO HELP US SAVE A LOT OF PEOPLE."
"HEAD TO THE ION DRIVE, PAN. AND HURRY.
STILL THERE, PAN'S WIFE?"
"STILL HERE. AND MY NAME IS CHU."
"WE'VE BEEN PINNED BY SCRAPPERS, CHU. WE'LL NEED TO BURN AS SOON AS POSSIBLE, BUT WE'LL SUSTAIN SOME DAMAGE."
YOU NEED TO GET EVERYONE FORWARD OF SECTION 18.
EVERYONE, LISTEN!
SCRAPPERS HAVE PINNED OUR TUG.
MY HUSBAND IS OUT THERE RIGHT NOW REPAIRING OUR MAIN DRIVE SO THAT WE CAN ESCAPE.
THERE'S A GOOD CHANCE WE'LL LOSE SOME OF OUR HULL, SO WE ALL NEED TO GET FORWARD OF SECTION 18 RIGHT NOW!
HURRY!
WHAT'S GOING ON?
SCRAPPERS!? WE'LL NEVER MAKE IT!
WHAT IF THEY BOARD?

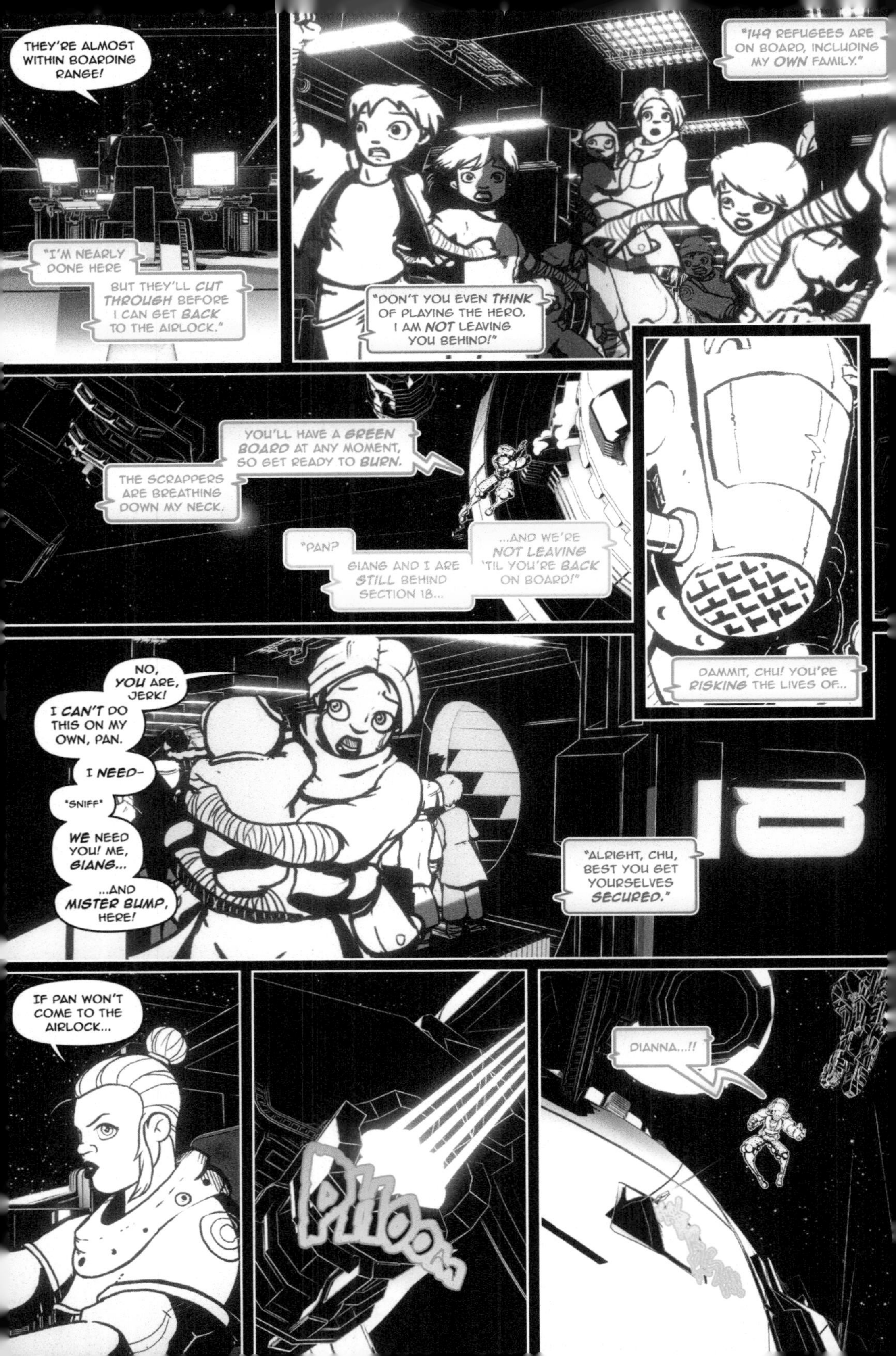
THEY'RE ALMOST WITHIN BOARDING RANGE!
"I'M NEARLY DONE HERE
BUT THEY'LL CUT THROUGH BEFORE I CAN GET BACK TO THE AIRLOCK."
"149 REFUGEES ARE ON BOARD, INCLUDING MY OWN FAMILY."
"DON'T YOU EVEN THINK OF PLAYING THE HERO. I AM NOT LEAVING YOU BEHIND!"
THE SCRAPPERS ARE BREATHING DOWN MY NECK.
YOU'LL HAVE A GREEN BOARD AT ANY MOMENT, SO GET READY TO BURN.
"PAN?
GIANG AND I ARE STILL BEHIND SECTION 18...
...AND WE'RE NOT LEAVING 'TIL YOU'RE BACK ON BOARD!"
DAMMIT, CHU! YOU'RE RISKING THE LIVES OF...
NO, YOU ARE, JERK!
I CAN'T DO THIS ON MY OWN, PAN.
I NEED-
SNIFF
WE NEED YOU! ME, GIANG...
...AND MISTER BUMP, HERE!
18
"ALRIGHT, CHU, BEST YOU GET YOURSELVES SECURED."
IF PAN WON'T COME TO THE AIRLOCK...
DIANNA...!!

MOMENTS LATER

I WON'T BE LONG, GIANG.

I HAVE TO GO LET DADDY IN, 'KAY?

I'M NEARLY... INSIDE!

I SEE YOU!

JUST A LITTLE BIT FURTHER!

COME ON, PAN! YOU CAN MAKE IT!

I CAN...

ALMOST...

MET!

SNAP!

PAN!

CHU...

NO!

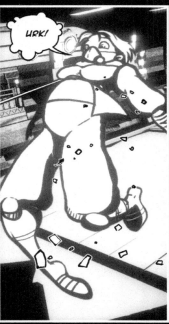

URK!

NASIR!

DOOR 18 IS SHUT.

BURN IT, DIANNA!

YOU ALL BETTER BE HOLDING ONTO SOMETHING!

THE SCRAPPER'S HARPOONS TORE A HOLE IN OUR SIDE...

...BUT WE LOST NOBODY TO SPACE.

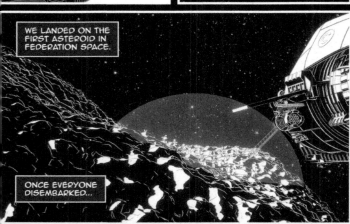

WE LANDED ON THE FIRST ASTEROID IN FEDERATION SPACE.

ONCE EVERYONE DISEMBARKED...

...WE DESTROYED THE TUG.

NOBODY KNEW IF HELP WOULD EVER COME.

SOME PRAYED TO THEIR GODS

SOME SAT SILENTLY IN HOPE.

IF WE EVER GET RESCUED, GIANG...

...I HOPE YOU AND YOUR BROTHER WILL SEE THAT WE HAD TO LEAVE...

...SO THAT YOU MIGHT HAVE A TOMORROW.

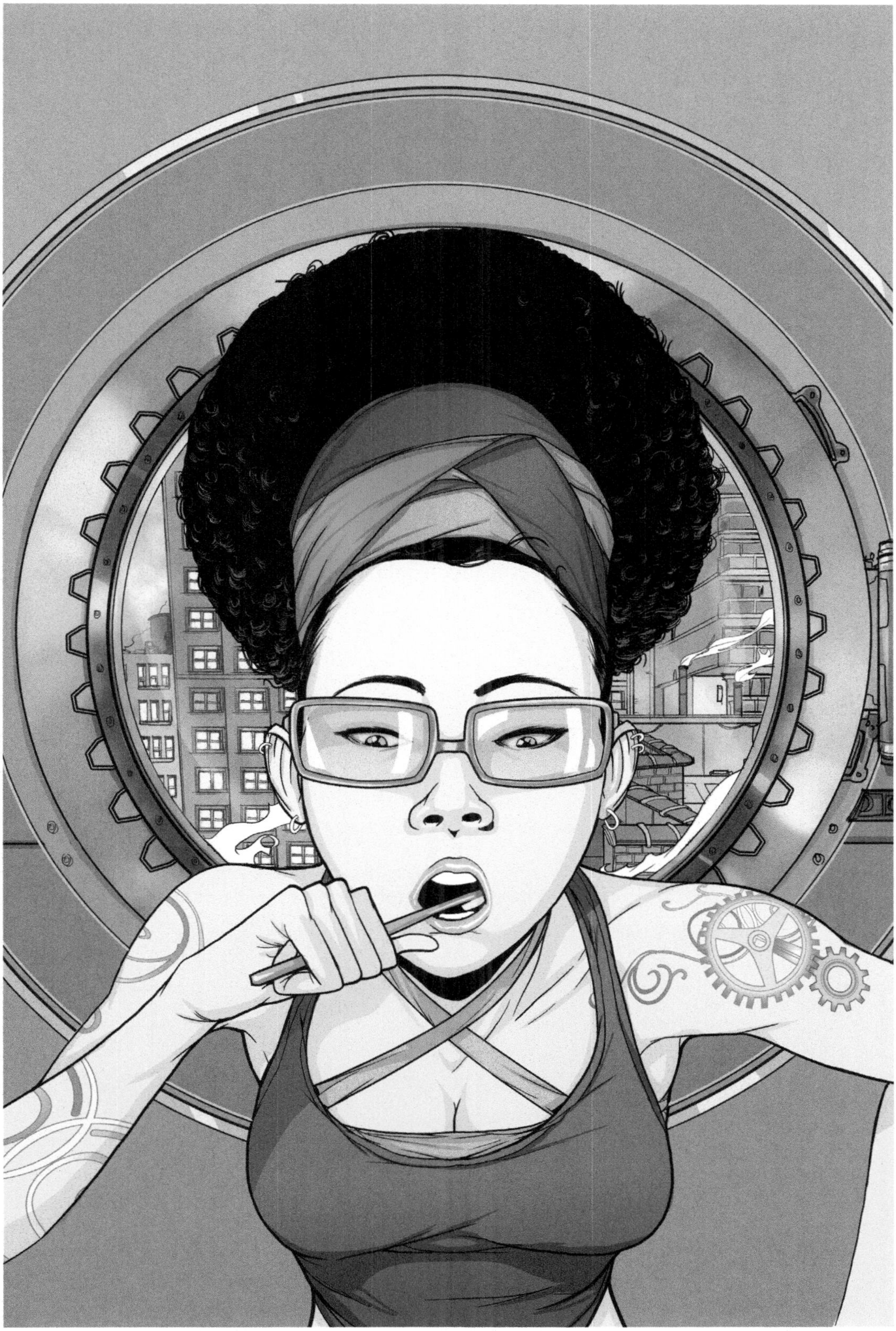

Jerome Walford
Jamaica / United States

Afrosia
forwardcomix.com

Marta Tanrikulu, Writer

United States

Marta Tanrikulu is a writer and editor from the United States who has close ties to relatives in Italy and Turkey. Her stories have appeared in various anthologies, often with elements of loss, exploration, or humor.

vizyonentertainment.com

Leila del Duca, Artist

United States

Leila del Duca is a comic book artist from the United States who's drawing *SHUTTER* and writing *AFAR*, both from Image Comics.

Twitter: @leiladelduca

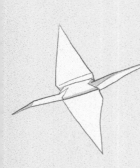

E.T. Dollman, Letterer

Italy

E.T. Dollman is an Italian writer, letterer, and designer who works with creators in several countries. He has lettered comics for Image Comics, Arcana, and Big Dog Ink.

facebook.com/ETDollman

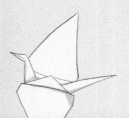

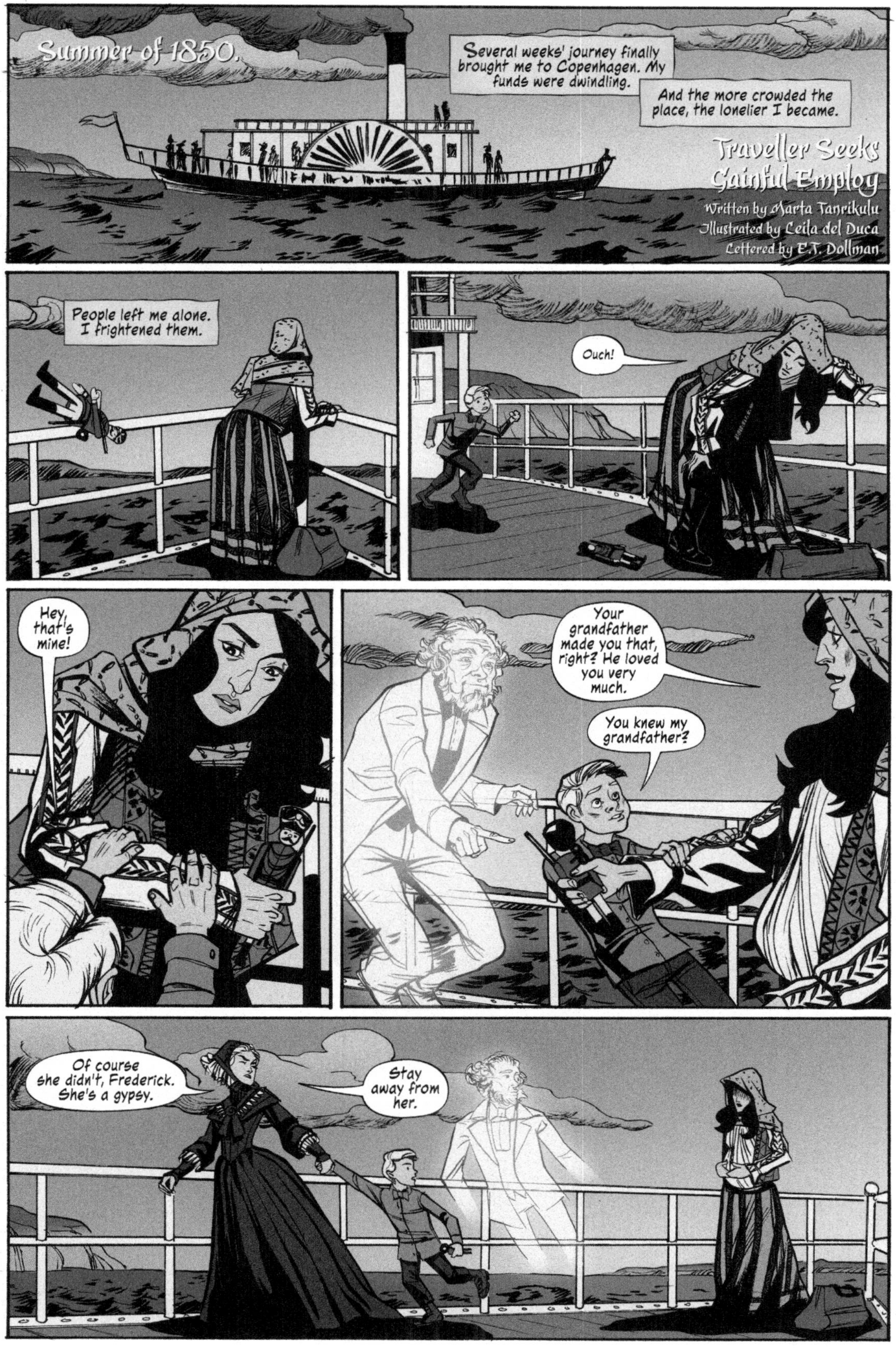

Summer of 1850.
Several weeks' journey finally brought me to Copenhagen. My funds were dwindling.
And the more crowded the place, the lonelier I became.
Traveller Seeks Gainful Employ
Written by Marta Tanrikulu
Illustrated by Leila del Duca
Lettered by E.T. Dollman
People left me alone. I frightened them.
Ouch!
Hey, that's mine!
Your grandfather made you that, right? He loved you very much.
You knew my grandfather?
Of course she didn't, Frederick. She's a gypsy.
Stay away from her.

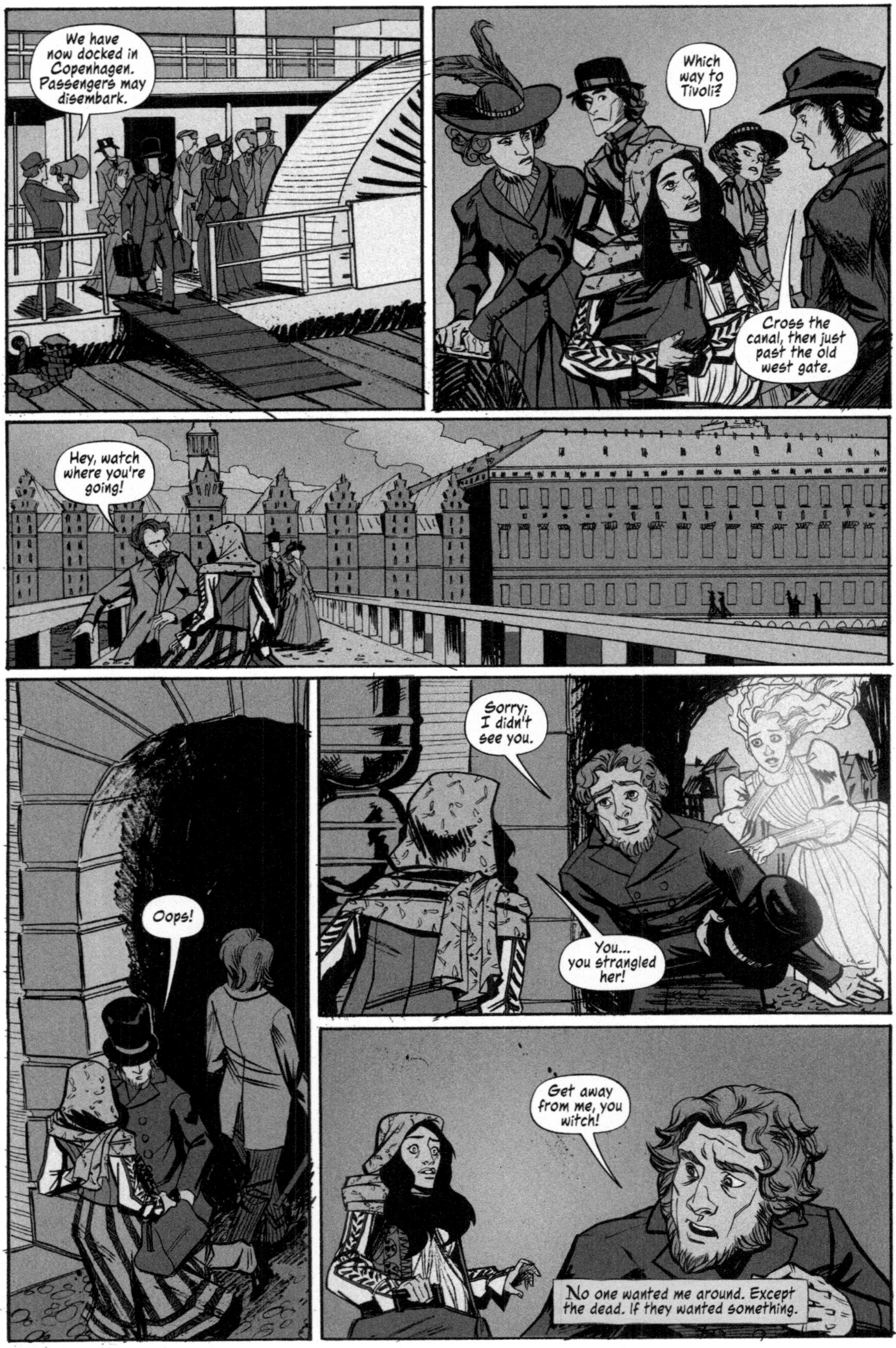
We have now docked in Copenhagen. Passengers may disembark.
Which way to Tivoli?
Cross the canal, then just past the old west gate.
Hey, watch where you're going!
Oops!
Sorry; I didn't see you.
You... you strangled her!
Get away from me, you witch!
No one wanted me around. Except the dead. If they wanted something.

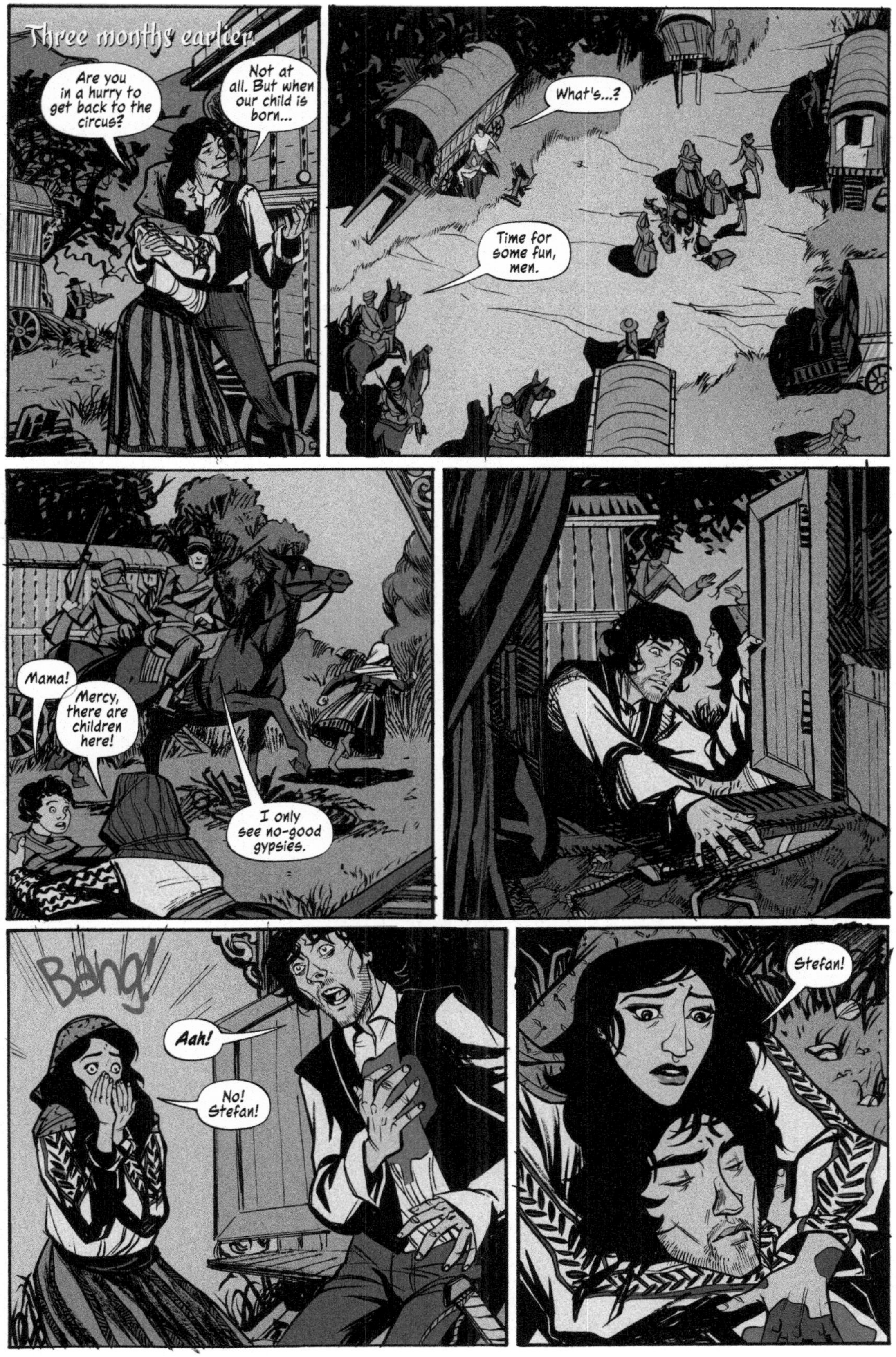
Three months earlier.
Are you in a hurry to get back to the circus?
Not at all. But when our child is born...
What's...?
Time for some fun, men.
Mama!
Mercy, there are children here!
I only see no-good gypsies.
Bang!
Aah!
No! Stefan!
Stefan!

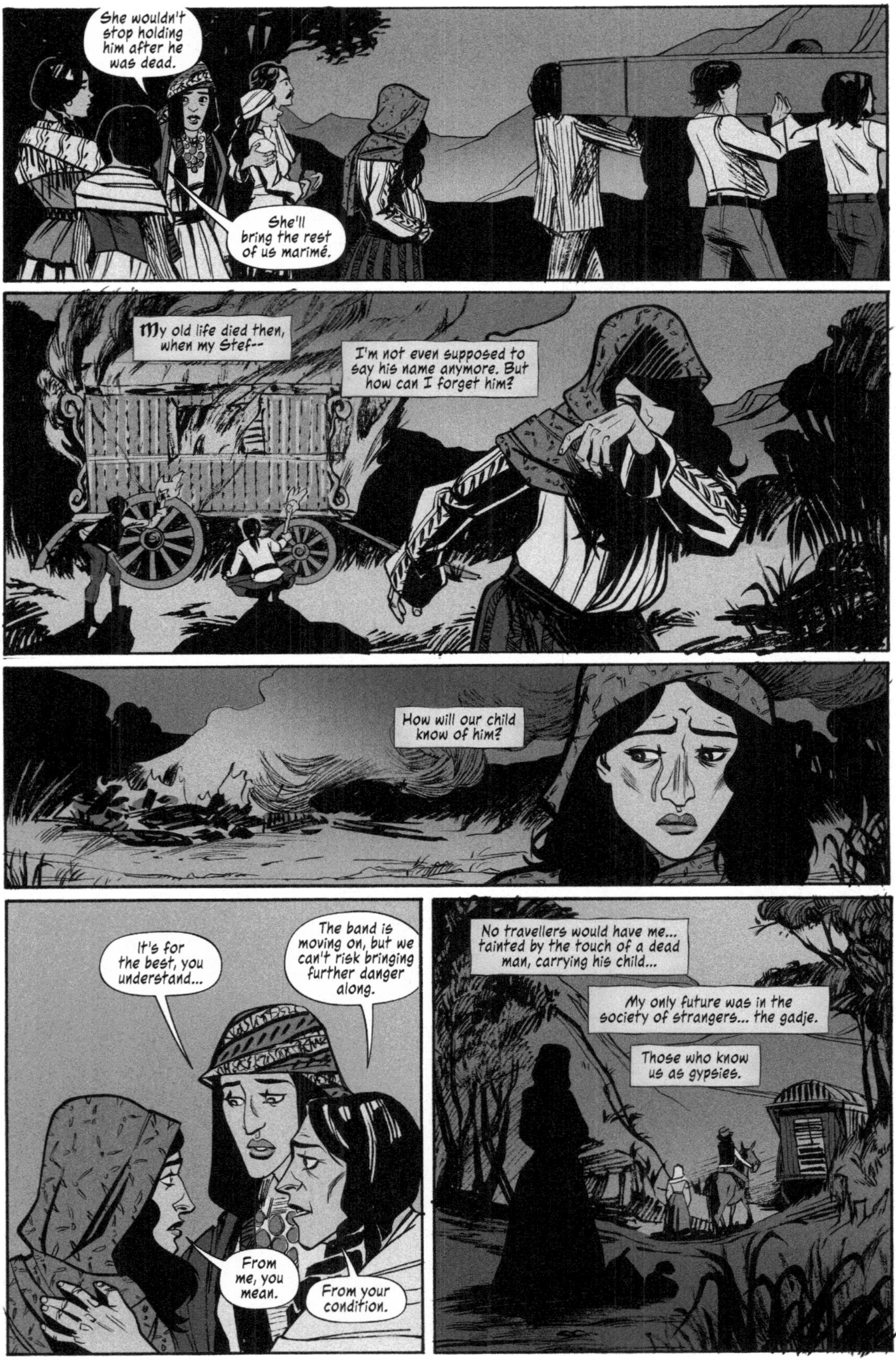
She wouldn't stop holding him after he was dead.
She'll bring the rest of us marimé.
My old life died then, when my Stef--
I'm not even supposed to say his name anymore. But how can I forget him?
How will our child know of him?
It's for the best, you understand...
The band is moving on, but we can't risk bringing further danger along.
From me, you mean.
From your condition.
No travellers would have me... tainted by the touch of a dead man, carrying his child...
My only future was in the society of strangers... the gadje.
Those who know us as gypsies.

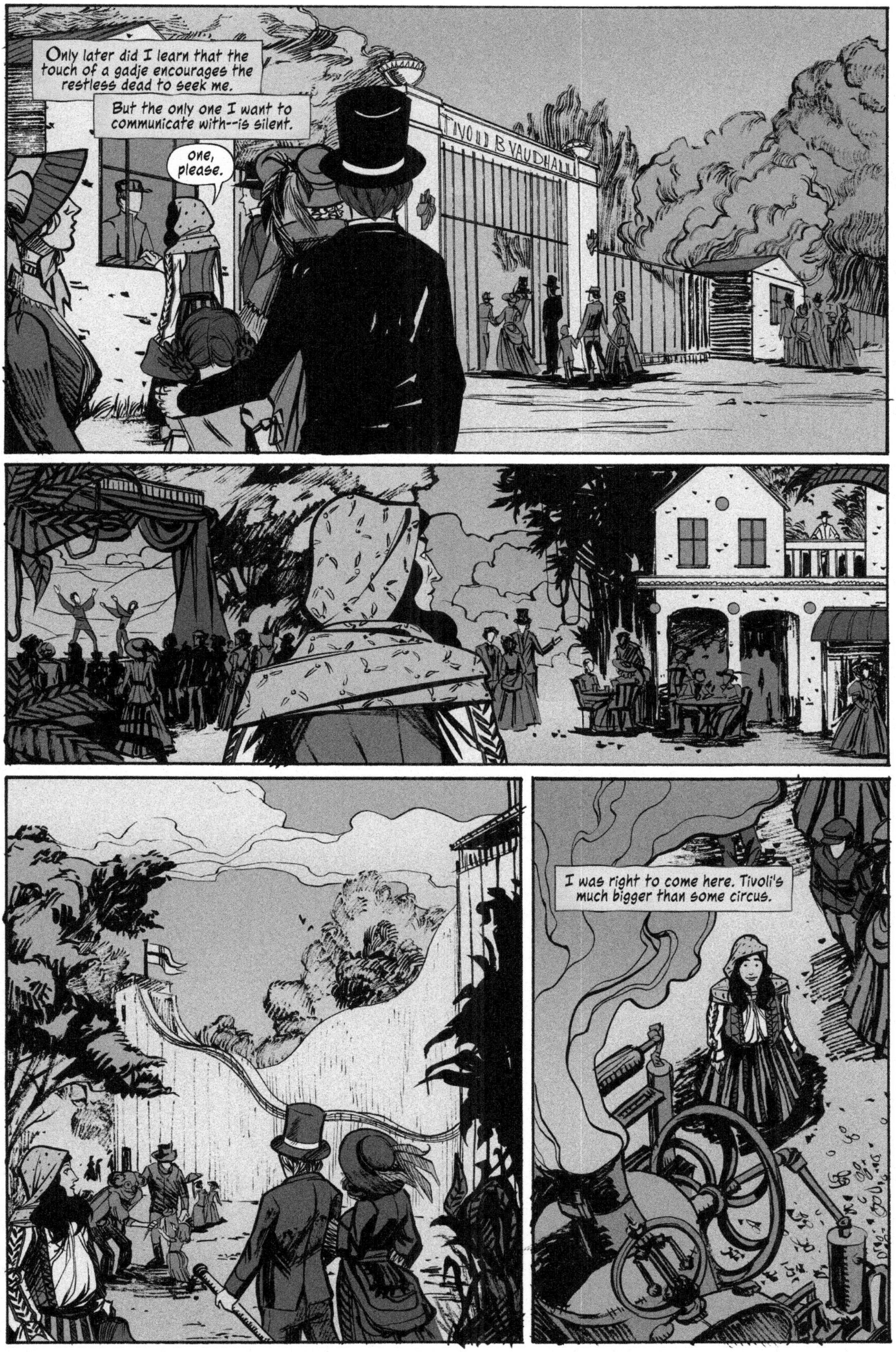
Only later did I learn that the touch of a gadje encourages the restless dead to seek me.
But the only one I want to communicate with--is silent.
one, please.
TIVOLI B VAUDHALL
I was right to come here. Tivoli's much bigger than some circus.

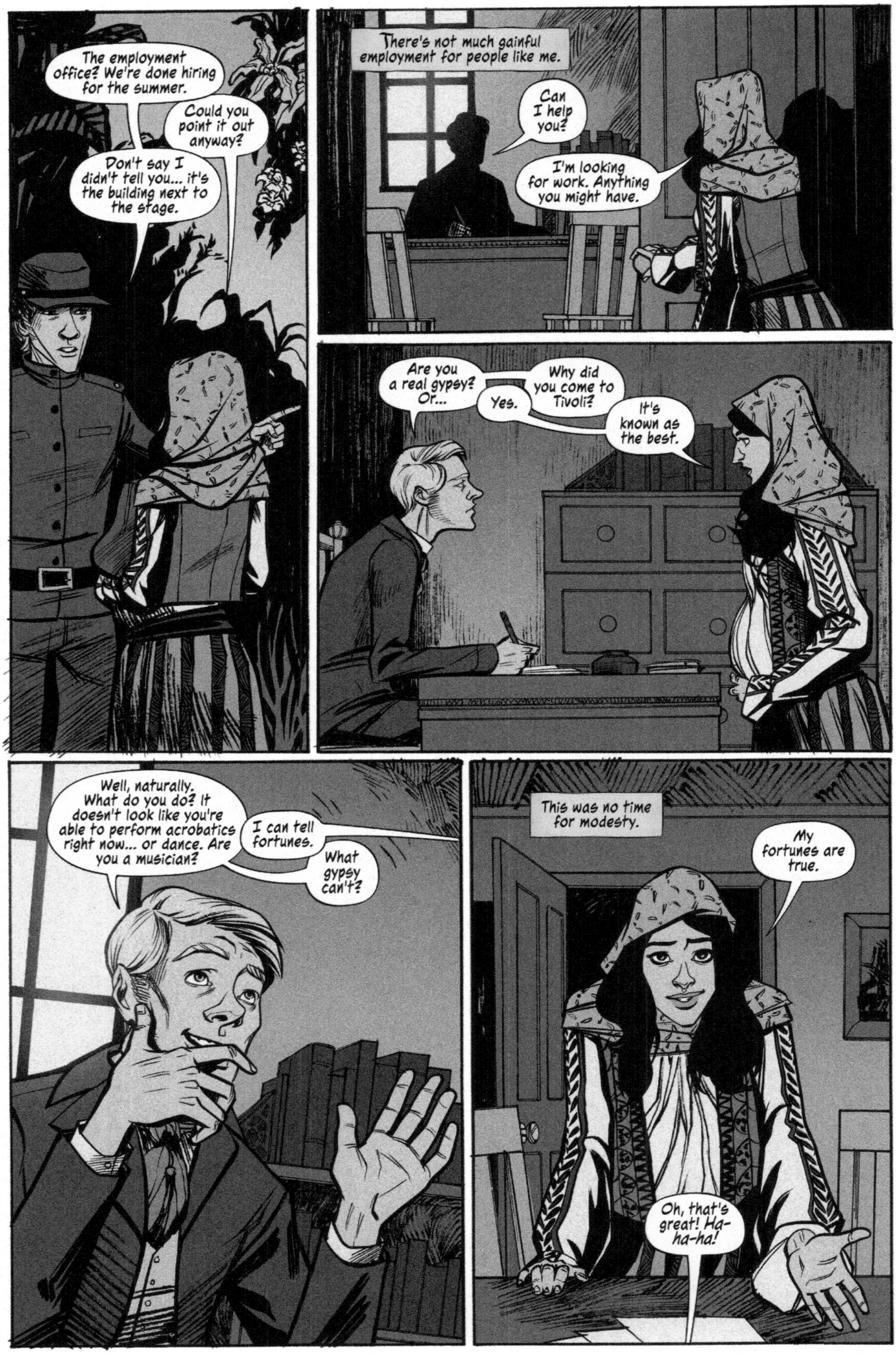

The employment office? We're done hiring for the summer.
Could you point it out anyway?
Don't say I didn't tell you... it's the building next to the stage.
There's not much gainful employment for people like me.
Can I help you?
I'm looking for work. Anything you might have.
Are you a real gypsy? Or...
Yes.
Why did you come to Tivoli?
It's known as the best.
Well, naturally. What do you do? It doesn't look like you're able to perform acrobatics right now... or dance. Are you a musician?
I can tell fortunes.
What gypsy can't?
This was no time for modesty.
My fortunes are true.
Oh, that's great! Ha-ha-ha!

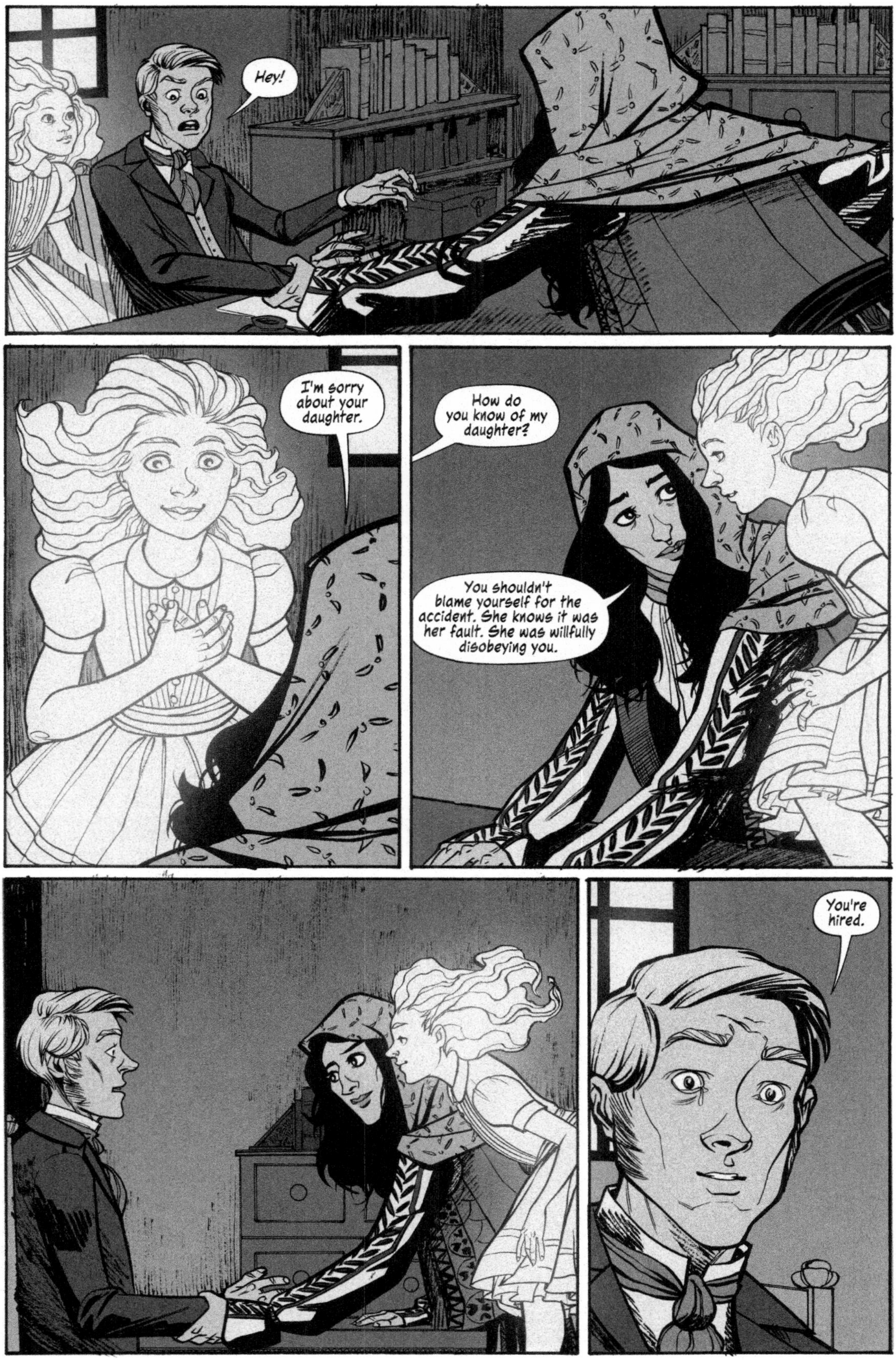
Hey!
I'm sorry about your daughter.
How do you know of my daughter?
You shouldn't blame yourself for the accident. She knows it was her fault. She was willfully disobeying you.
You're hired.

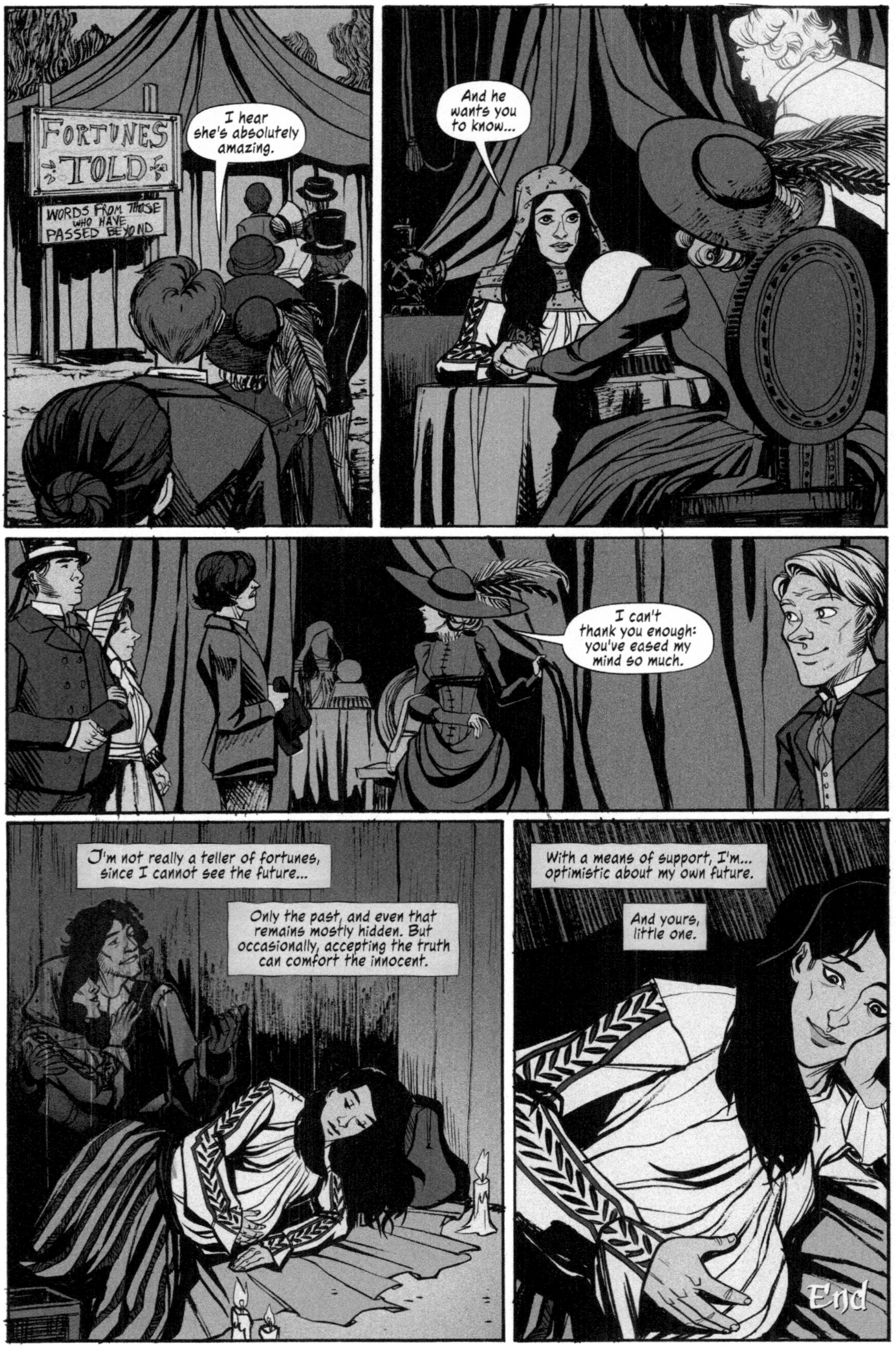
FORTUNES TOLD
WORDS FROM THOSE WHO HAVE PASSED BEYOND
I hear she's absolutely amazing.
And he wants you to know...
I can't thank you enough: you've eased my mind so much.
I'm not really a teller of fortunes, since I cannot see the future...
Only the past, and even that remains mostly hidden. But occasionally, accepting the truth can comfort the innocent.
With a means of support, I'm... optimistic about my own future.
And yours, little one.
End

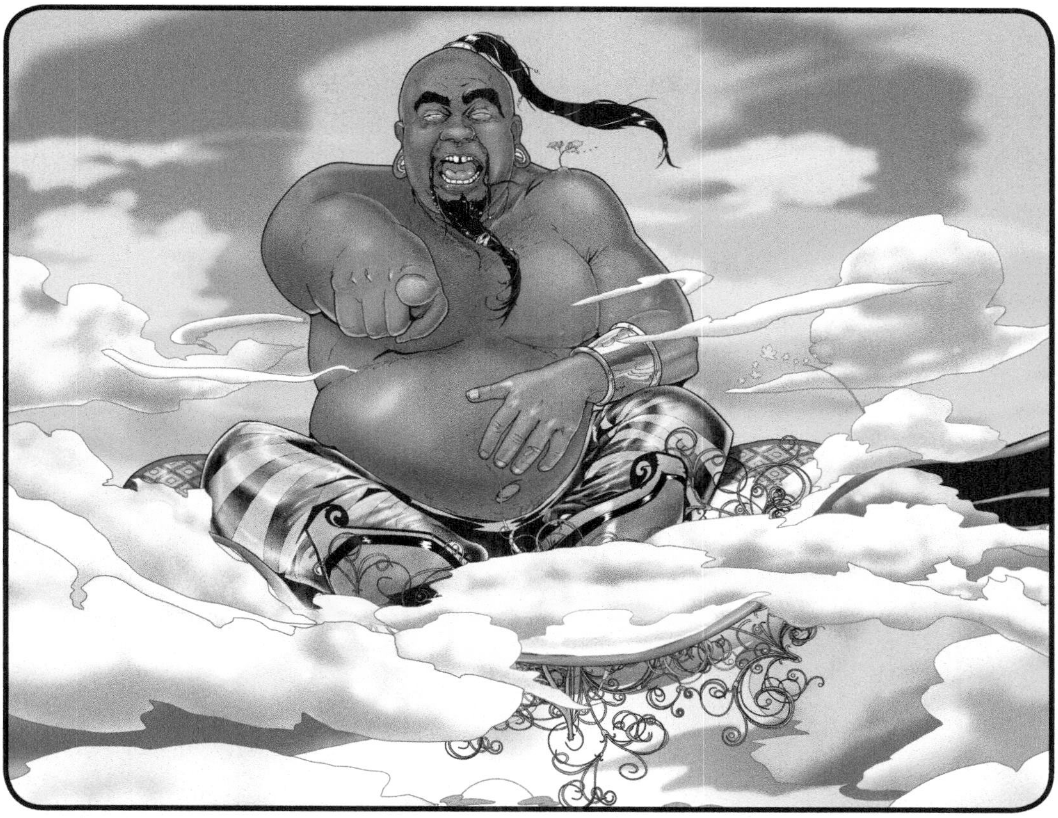

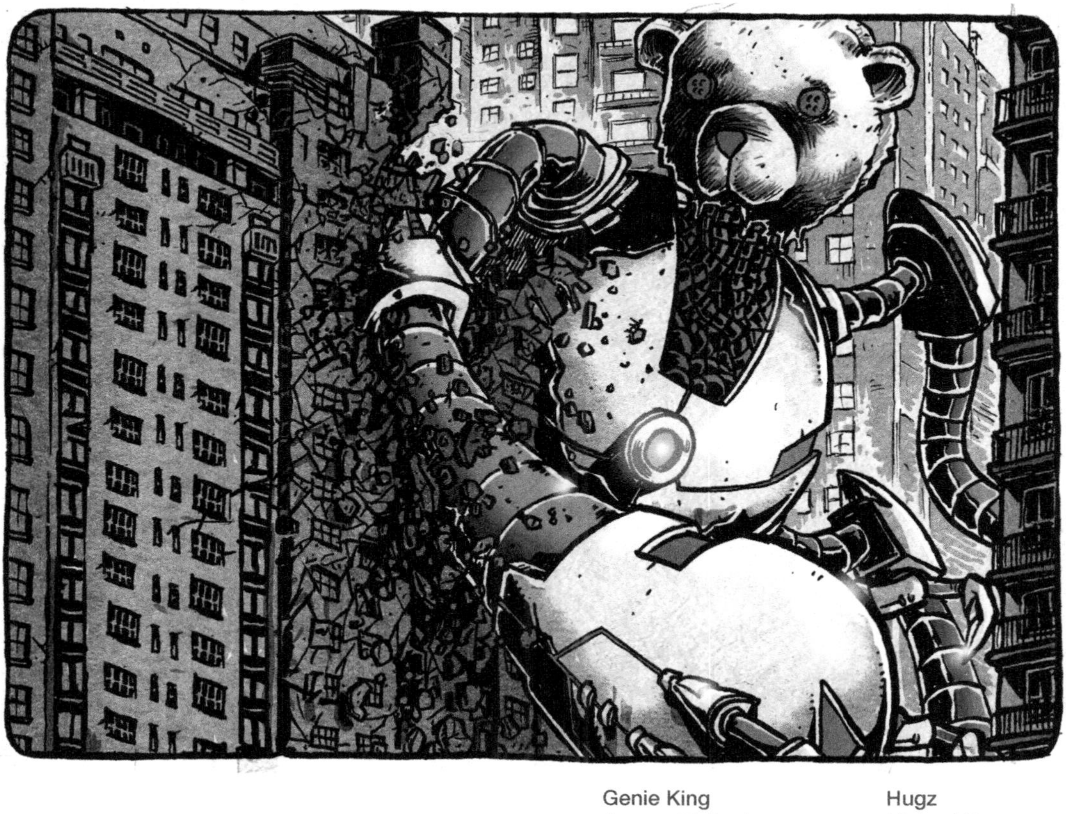

Genie King
Jerome Walford
forwardcomix.com

Hugz
Michael Bracco

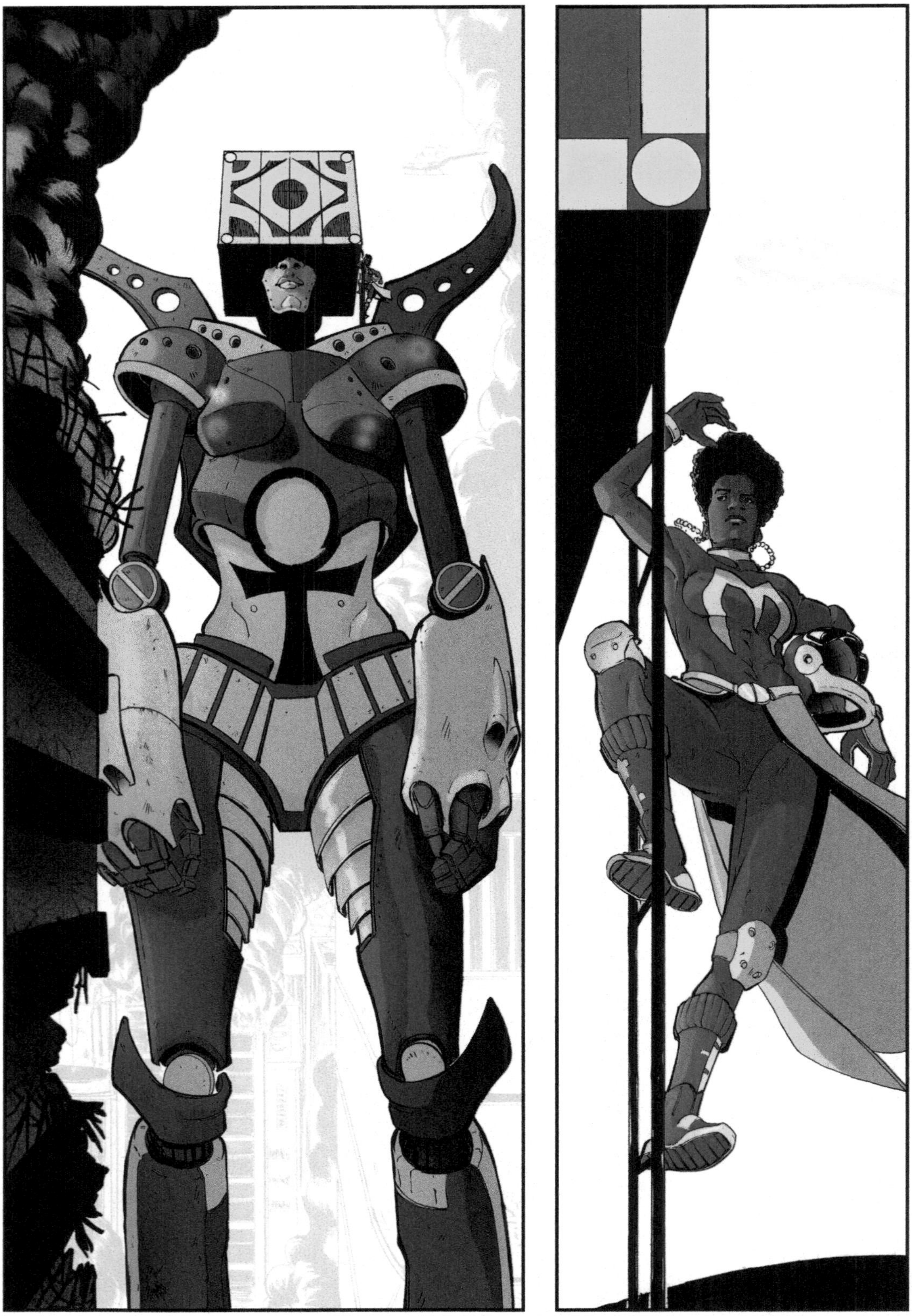

N Steven Harris
United States

Courtesy of Maia Crown Williams and Mecca Con
nstevenharris.deviantart.com

YAMZ/BRUTHA YAMZ
Concept/creation by Joseph R Wheeler III
Pencils by N Steven Harris
Digital inks and color by Chris Miller
ONYXCON Fifth Anniversary

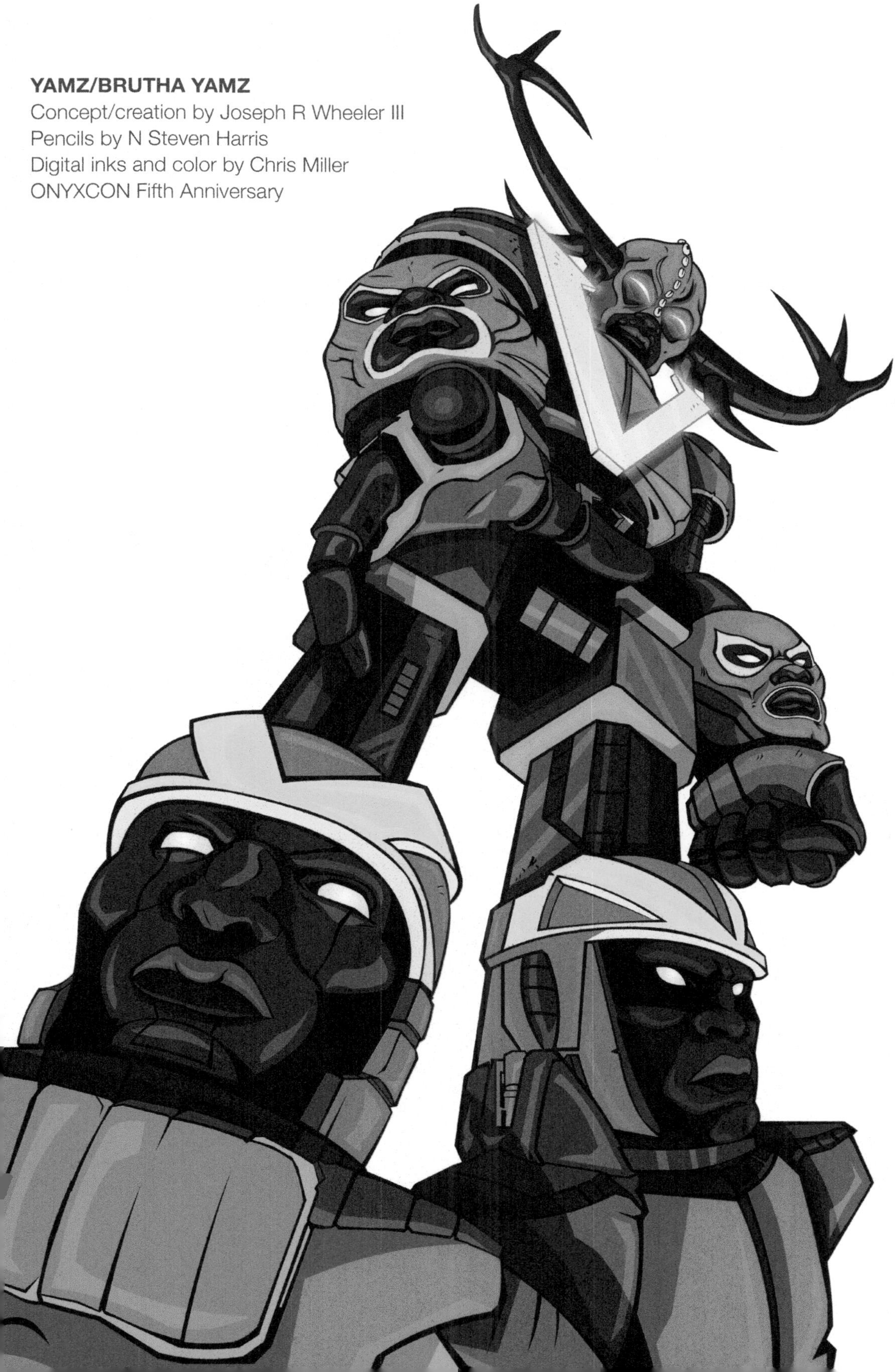

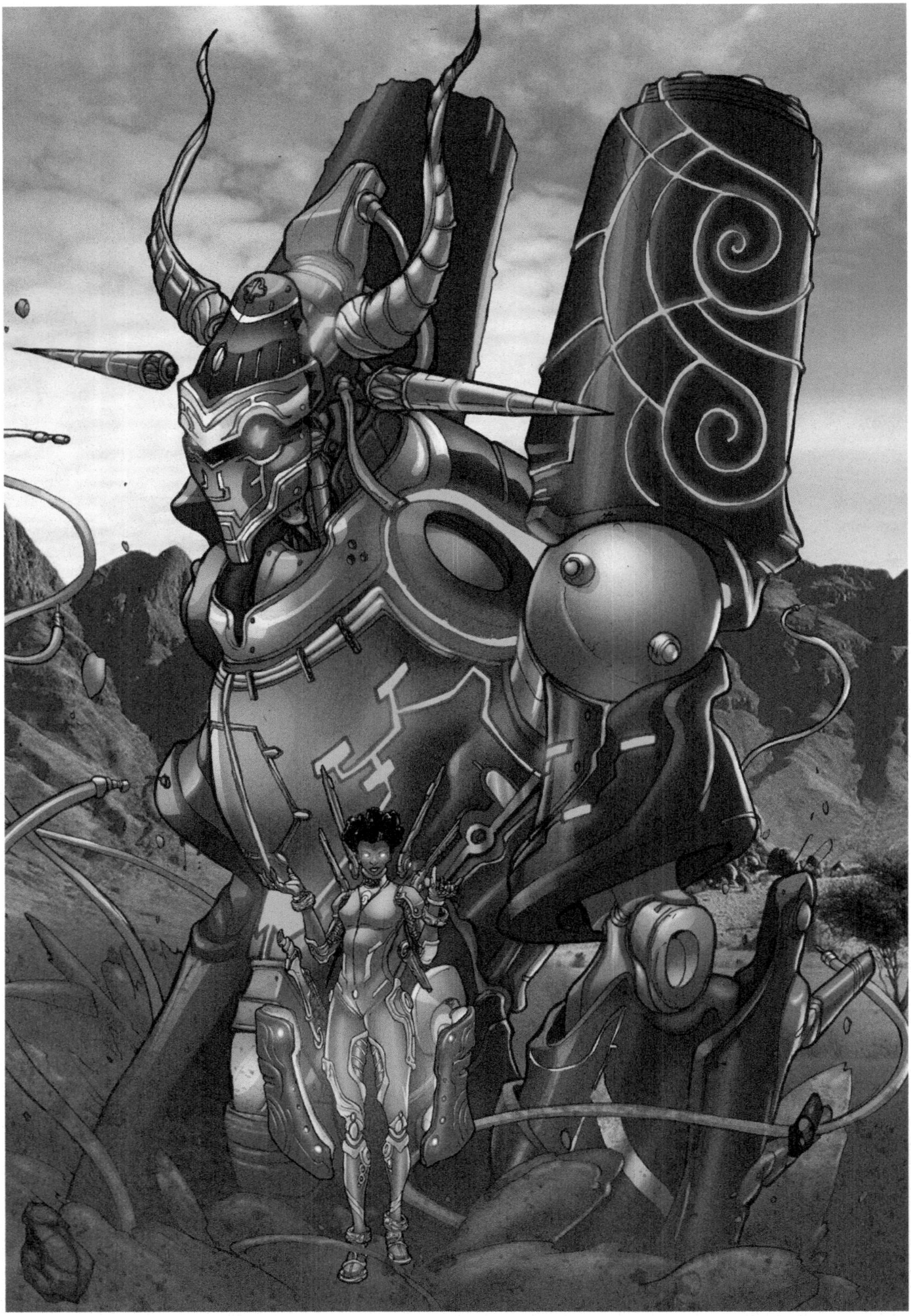

Shawn Alleyne
Barbados / United States

Afro Mech
pyroglyphics1.deviantart.com

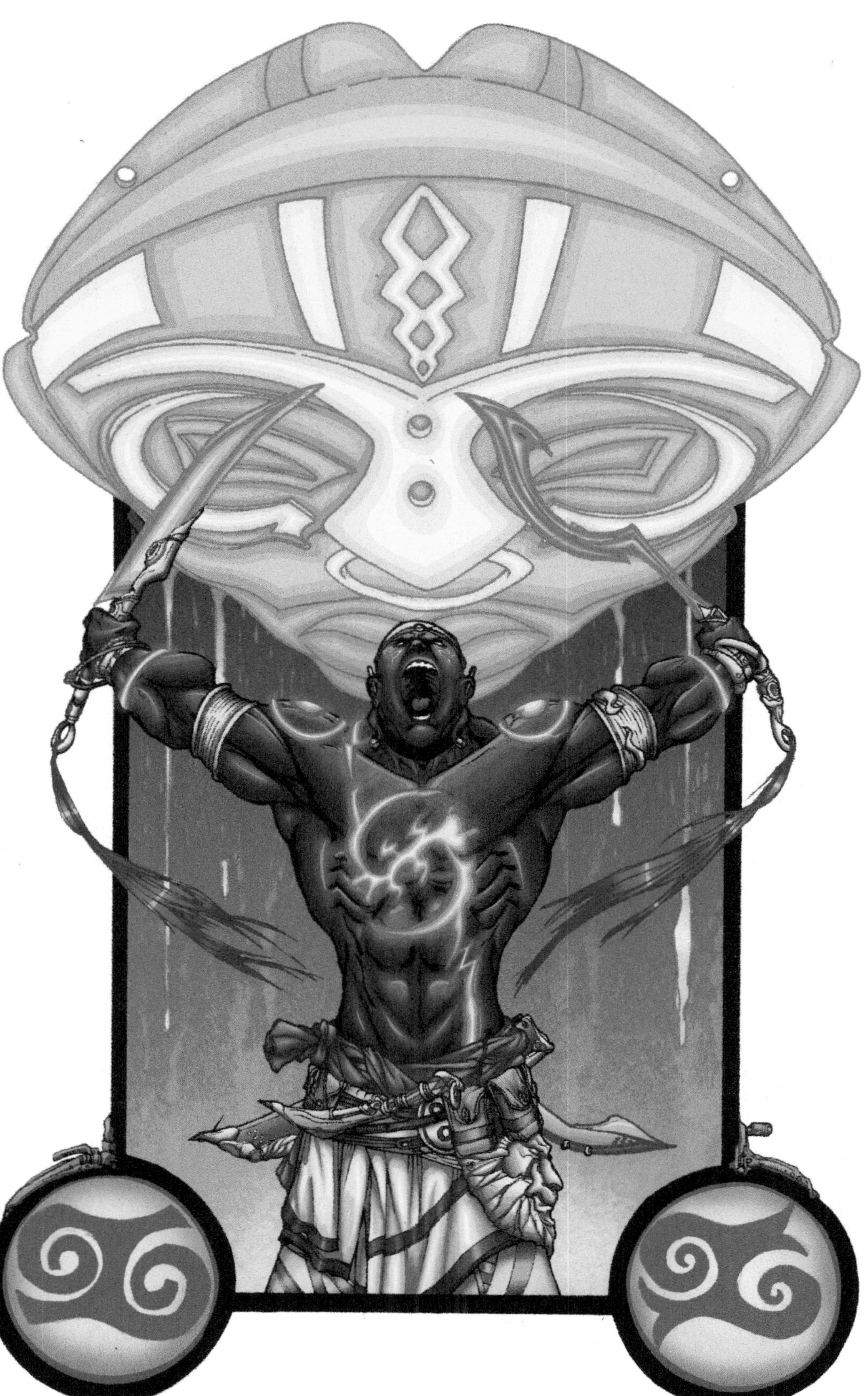

Shawn Alleyne
Barbados / United States

Sep-Krado
pyroglyphics1.deviantart.com

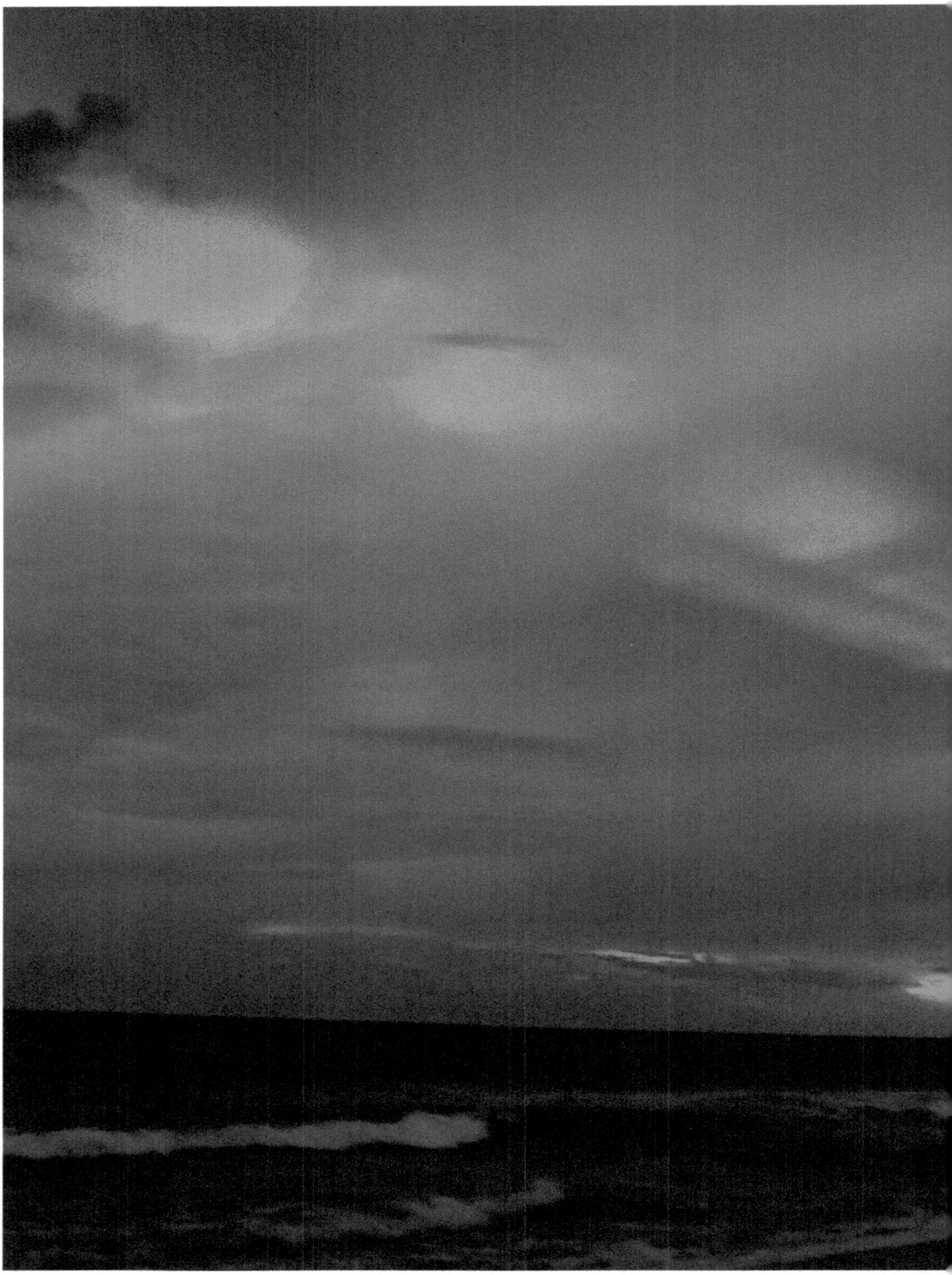

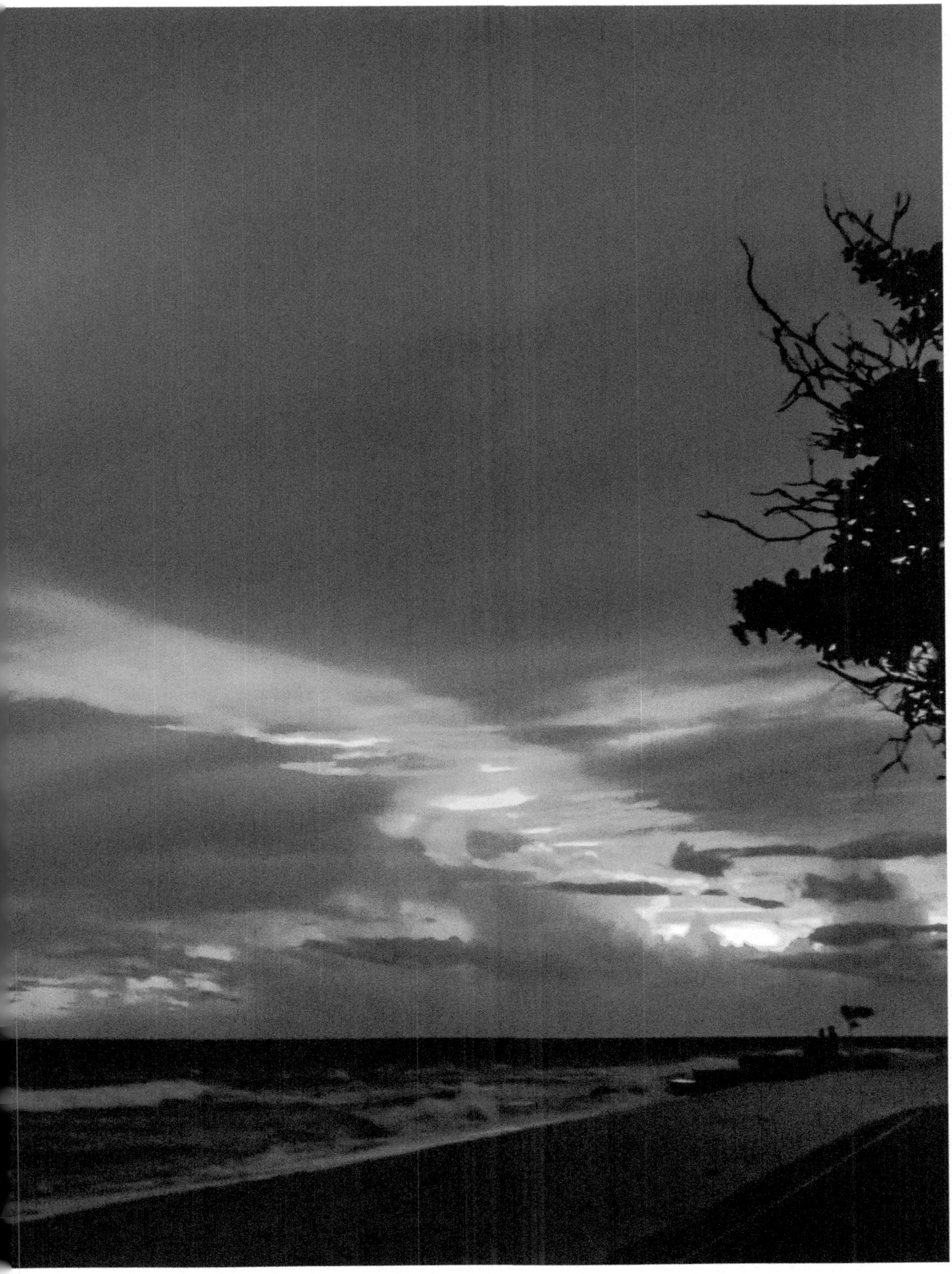

Jason Scott Jones
United States

MajorLaserSunset
Barbados
jsjcreative.net

Leonardo Gonzalez, Artist
United States

Leonardo Gonzalez is an artist, and
Illustration is his career of choice. Originally
from Ridgewood, Queens, Leo now resides
in New Britain, Connecticut, where he lives
with his girlfriend and tons of animals. He's
a graduate from the University of Hartford
with a degree in Illustration, and also
earned an Associate's degree in Fine Arts
at Tunxis Community College.

While in college, Leonardo pursued
a career in the comics field, and after
attending many New York Comic-Con
conventions he was hired as a cover
and interior illustrator by UK Comics
Publisher T-Publications. He is currently
Illustrating *Theatrics,* a new graphic novel
written by Neil Gibson, to be published by
T-Publications in 2017. Aside from comics,
Leo also creates whimsical illustrations
that focus on nature, creatures, monsters,
and ghouls.

leonardoillustration.com

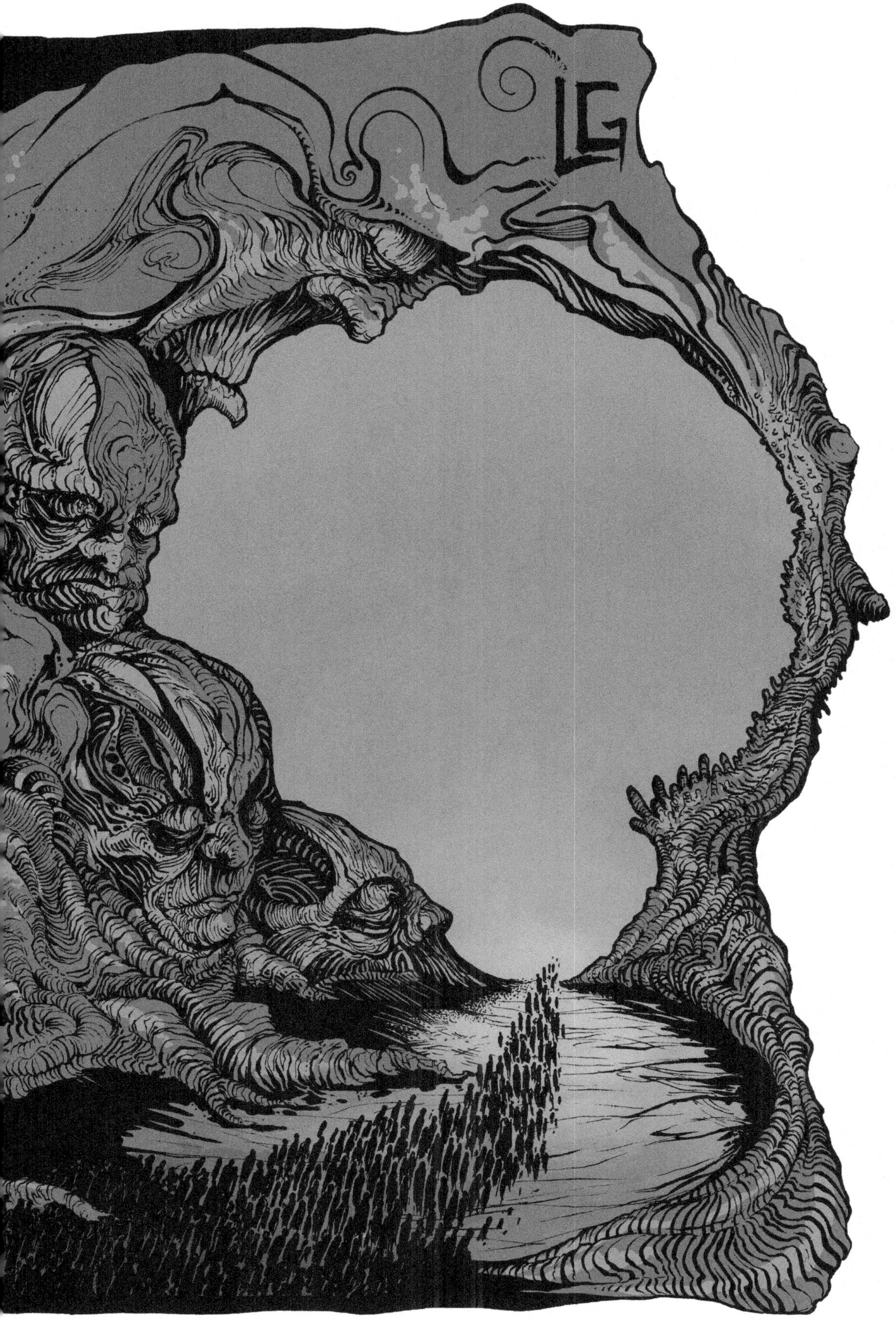

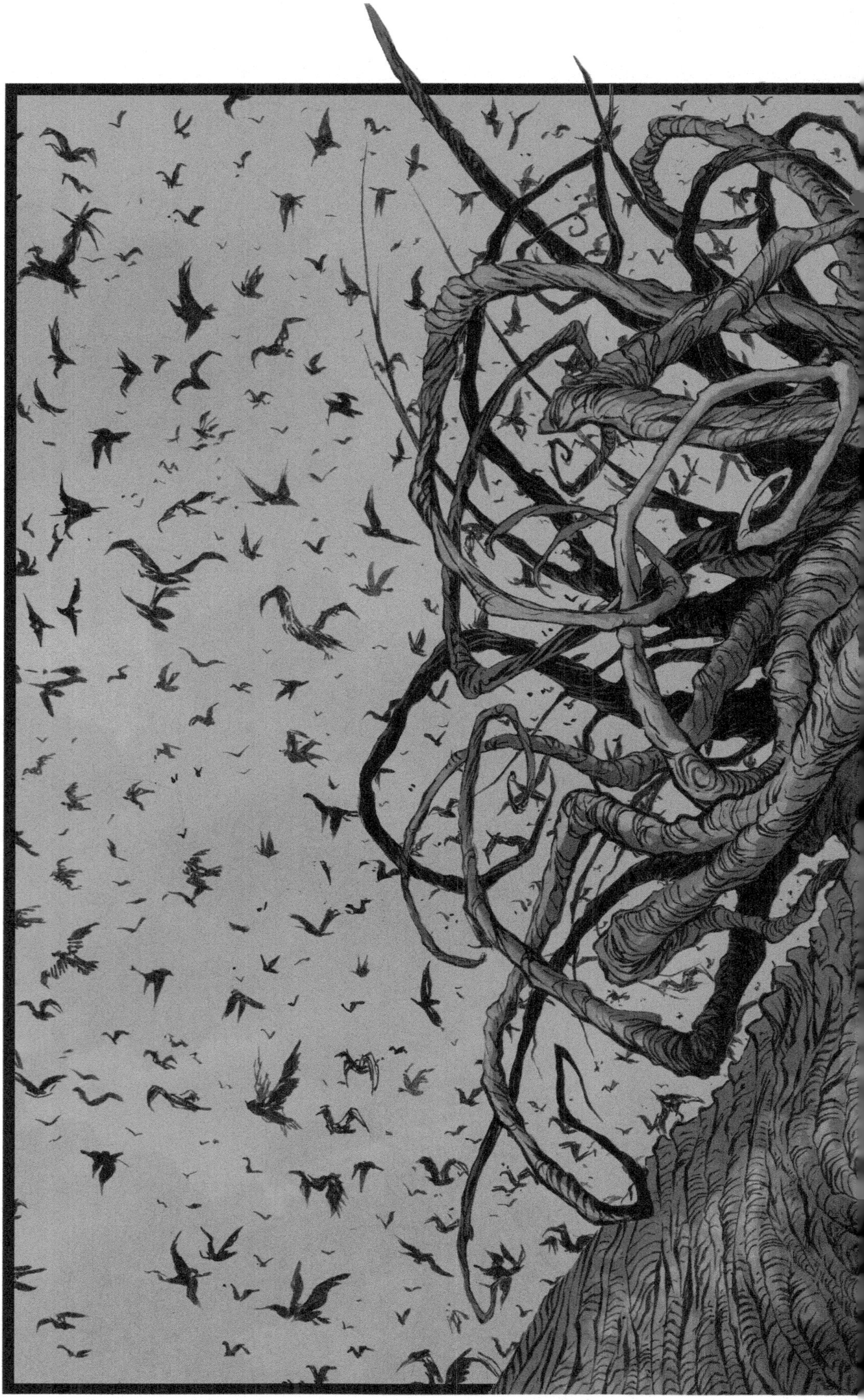

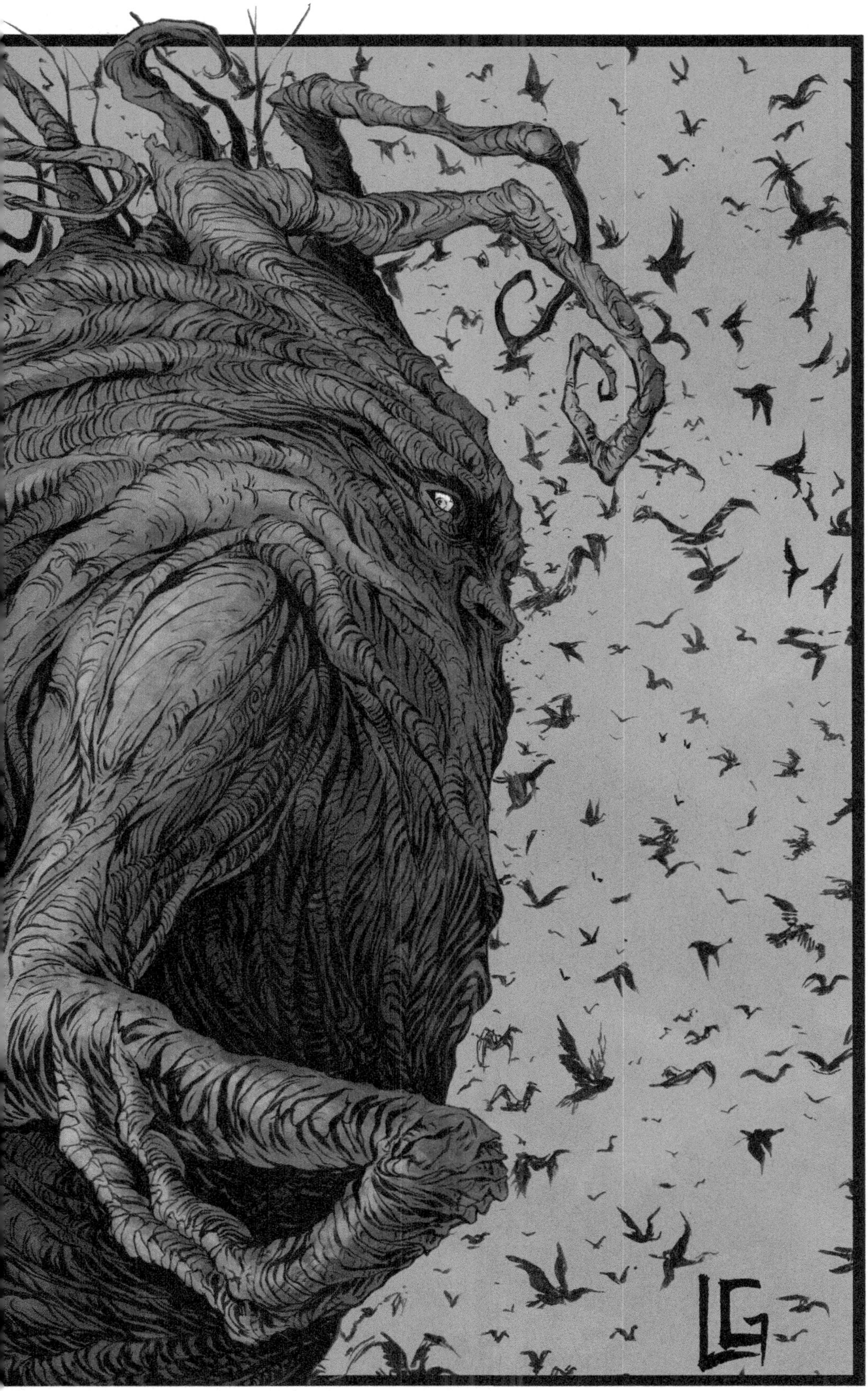

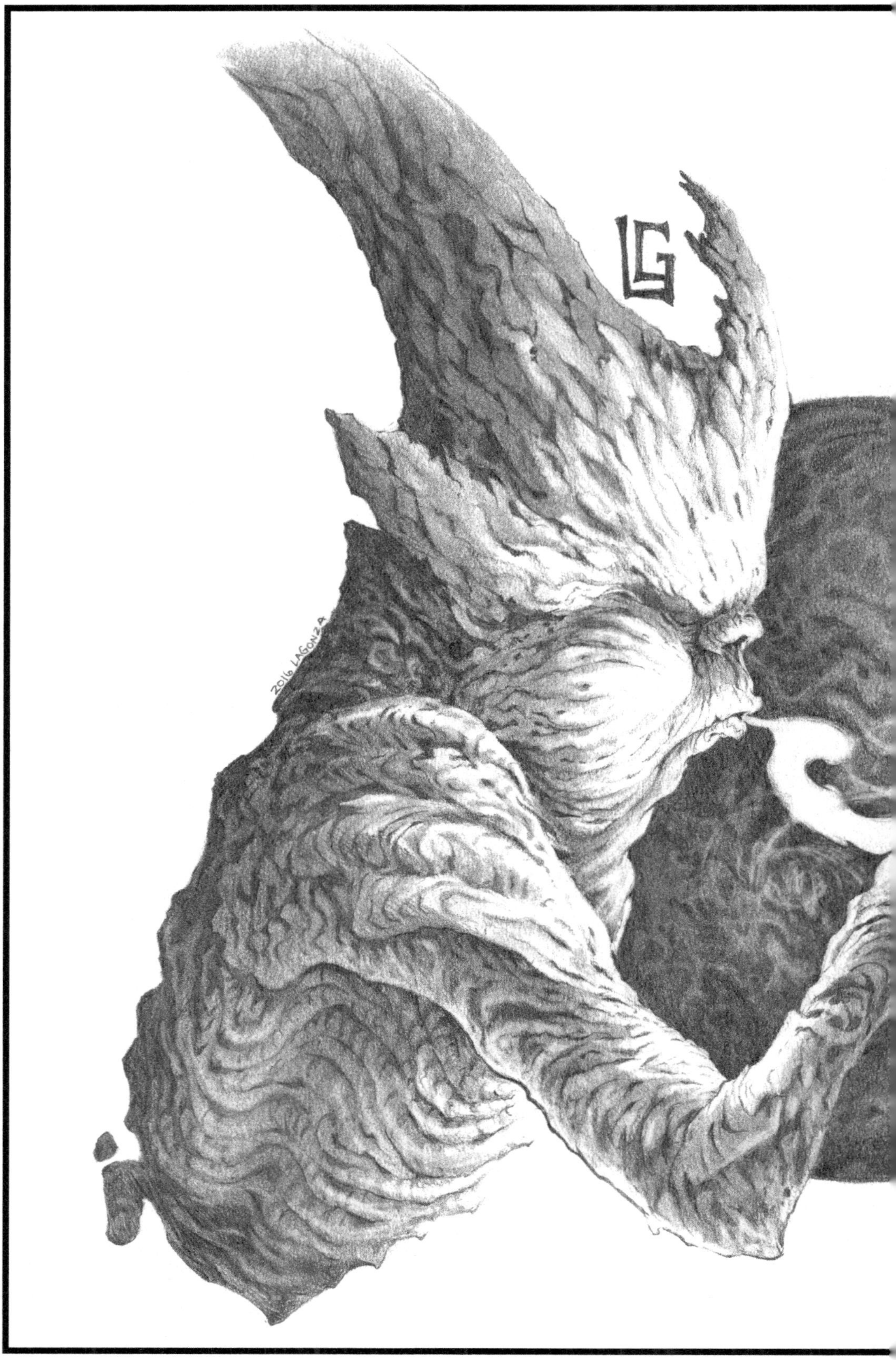
2016 LAGONZA

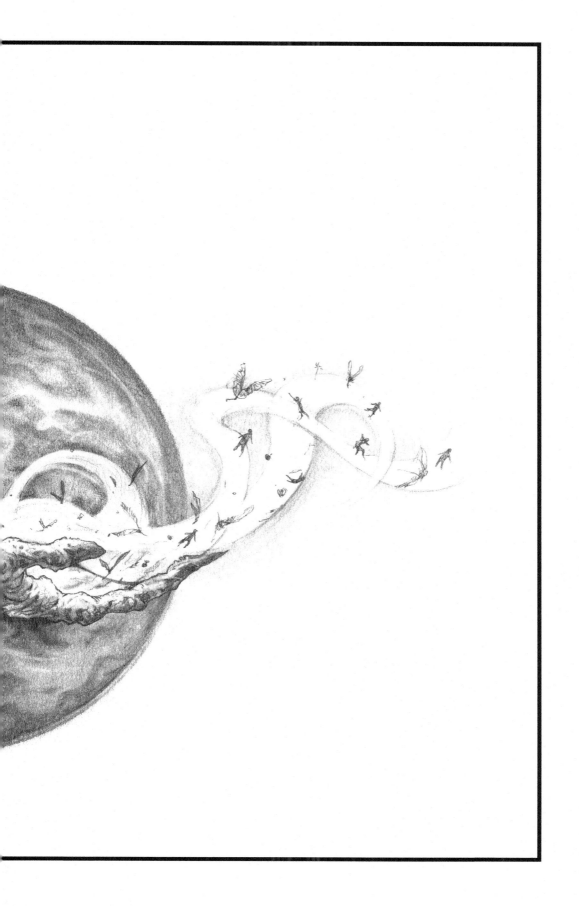

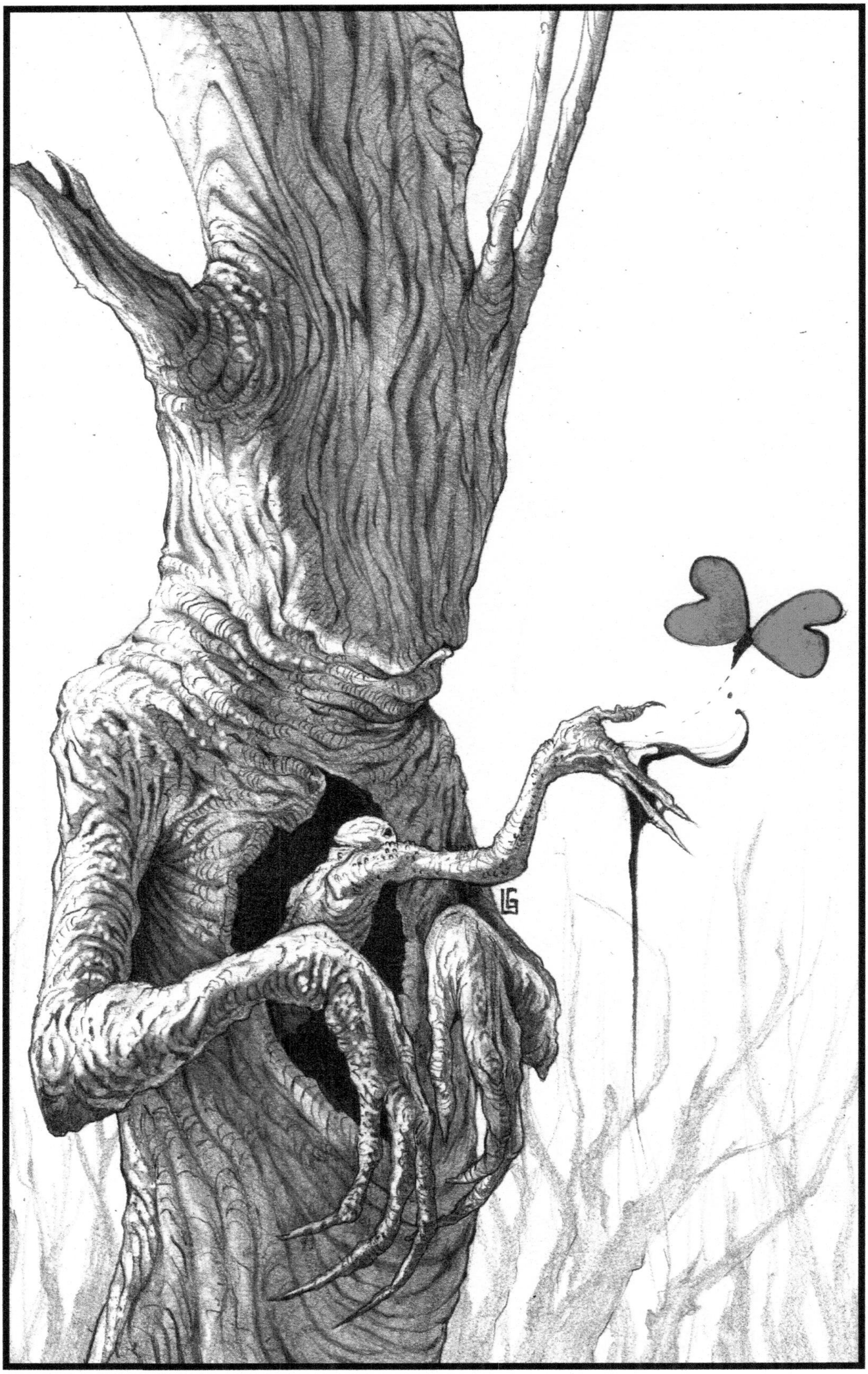

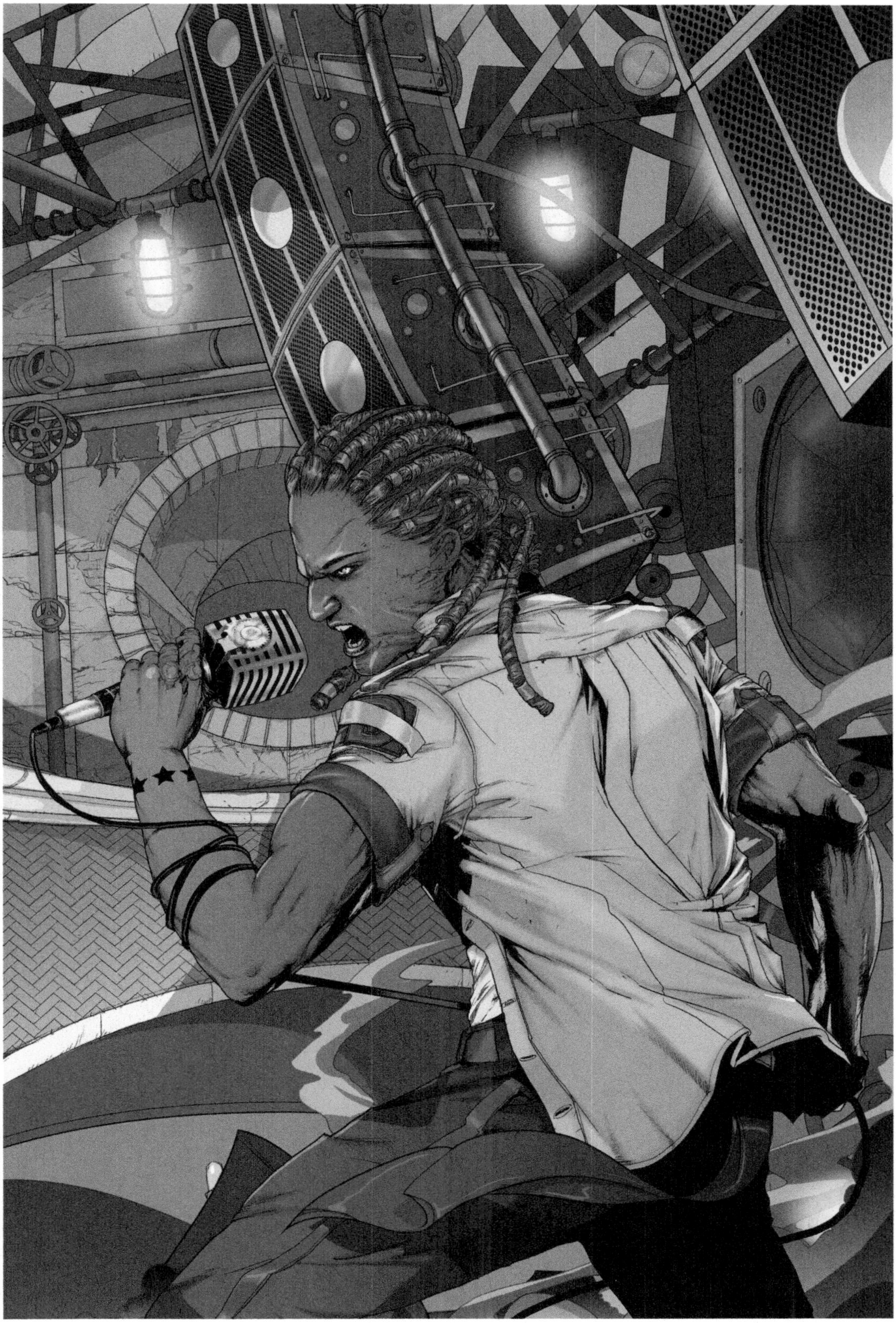

Jerome Walford
Jamaica / United States

Grass Mon Underground Rock Performance
Curse of the Griffin

Jacques Nyemb, Writer

Cameroon / United States

Jacques Nyemb was born in Cameroon, Africa and moved with his family to the United States when he was 11. Having an African father and an American mother allowed him to see the world through various perspectives.

The thing that kept the culture shock at bay was his love for comics. That was the one constant regardless of where he lived. Comics were somehow always accessible.

Fast forward many years later and his appreciation for comics is still present. He founded an independent publishing company whose goal is to create quality comics that everyone can enjoy.

This experience has allowed him to work with the likes of Skuds Mckinley, Justin Wood, and Michael Neno, all of which helped him create *Tribal Quest*.

When he's not making comics, he enjoys watching his young girls grow. He also loves binge-watching cerebral documentaries on Netflix.

notsosupercomics.com

FOR THOUSANDS OF YEARS OUR VILLAGE HAS SENT TWO PEOPLE TO THE EDGE OF THE WORLD.

TRIBAL QUEST

THE GOAL WAS ALWAYS THE SAME: TO REPORT THEIR FINDINGS TO THE ELDERS.

FOR THE FIRST HUNDRED YEARS, THIS WAS THE EDGE OF OUR WORLD.

ART: SKUDS MCKINLEY
COLORS: JUSTIN WOOD
LETTERS: MICHAEL NENO

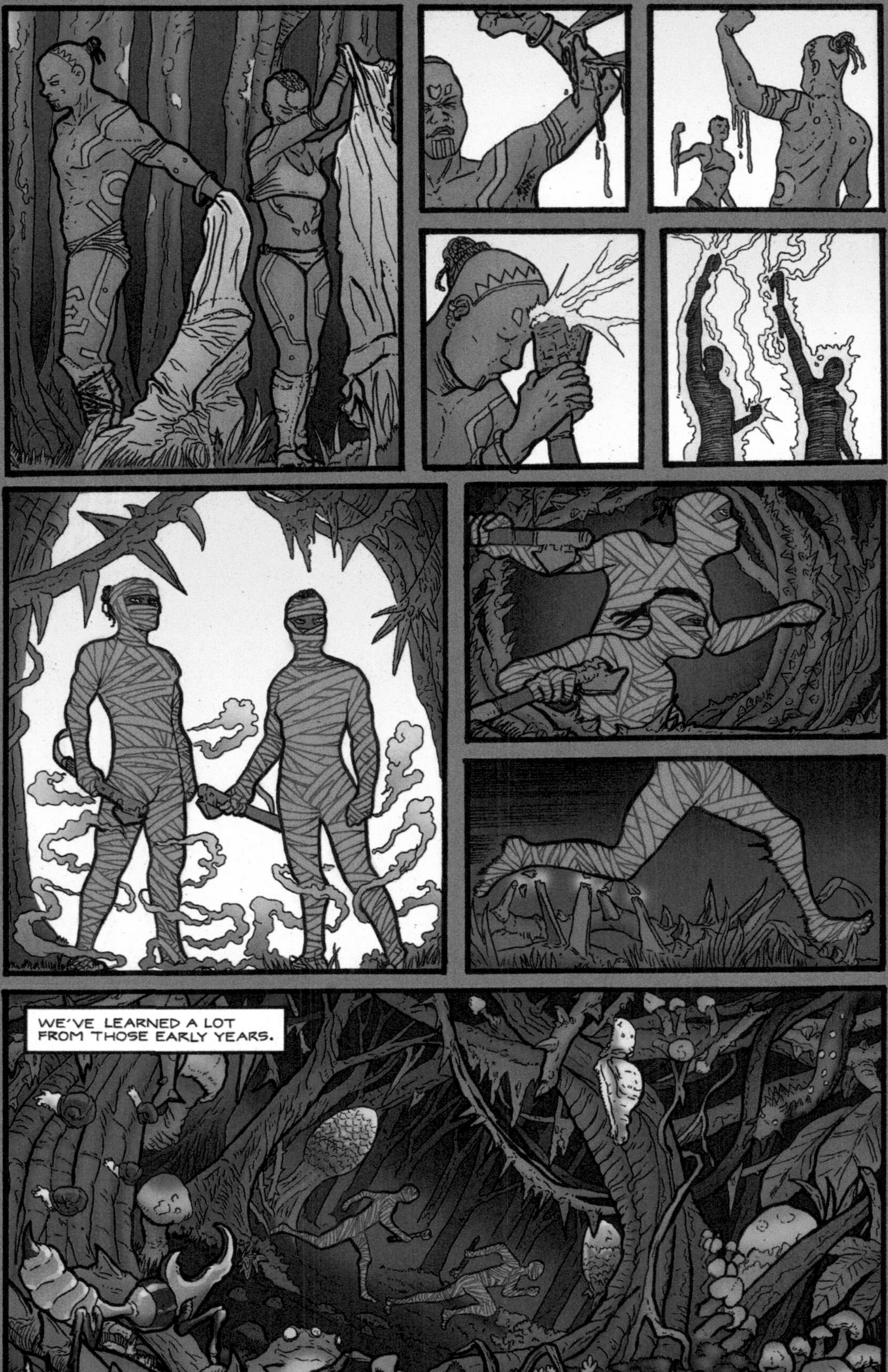
WE'VE LEARNED A LOT
FROM THOSE EARLY YEARS.

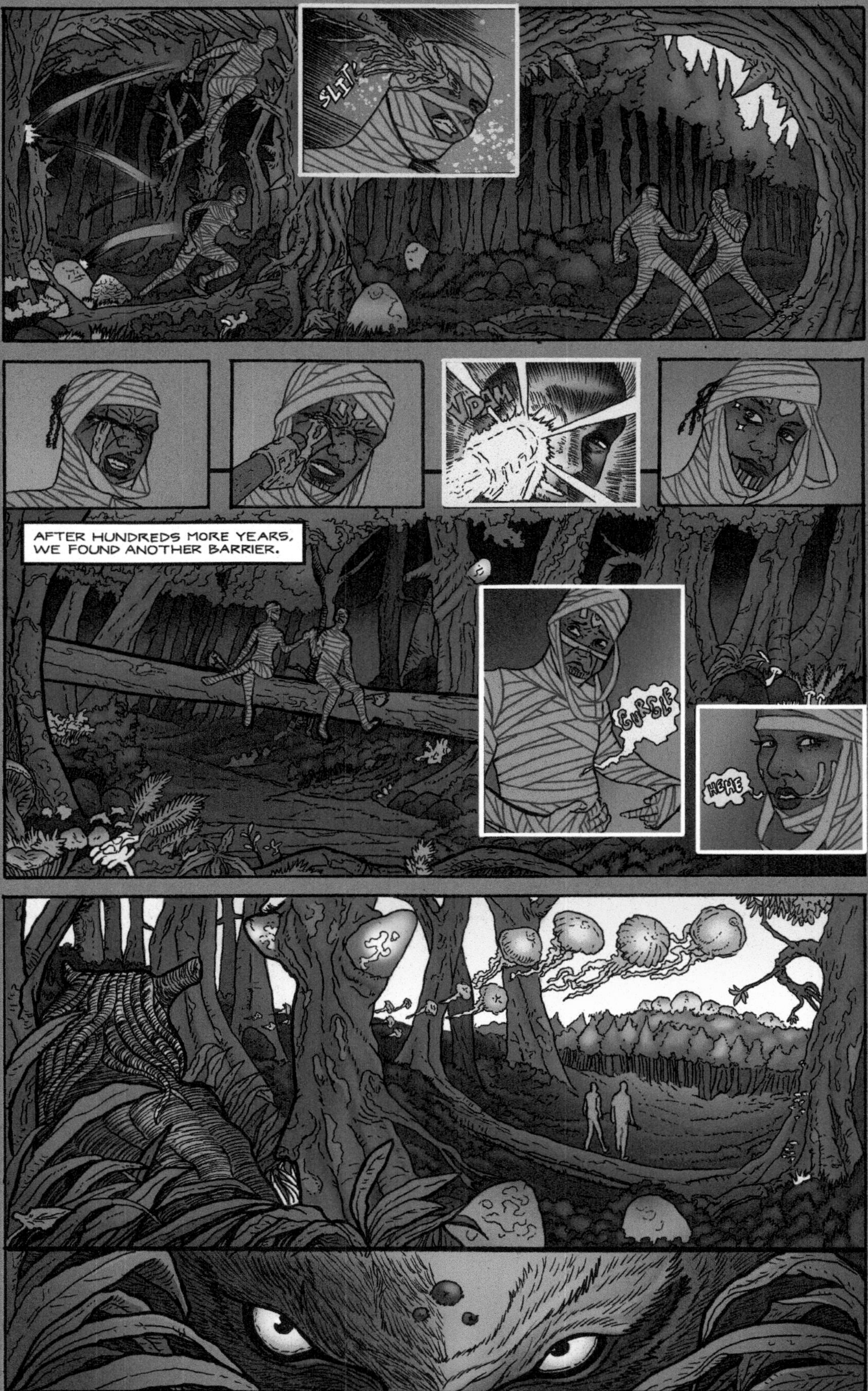
SLIT
VDAM
AFTER HUNDREDS MORE YEARS, WE FOUND ANOTHER BARRIER.
GURGLE
HEHE

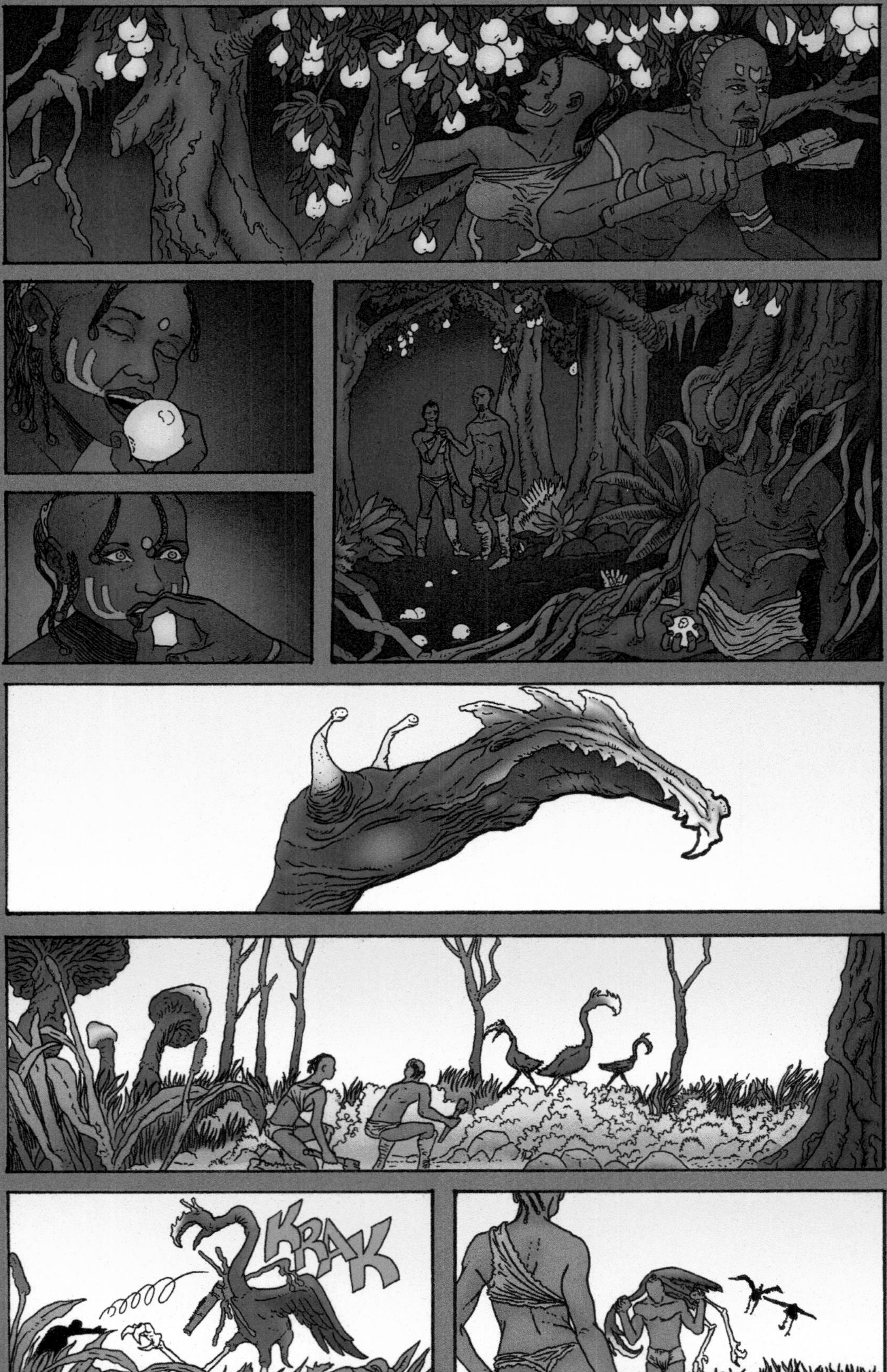
KRAK

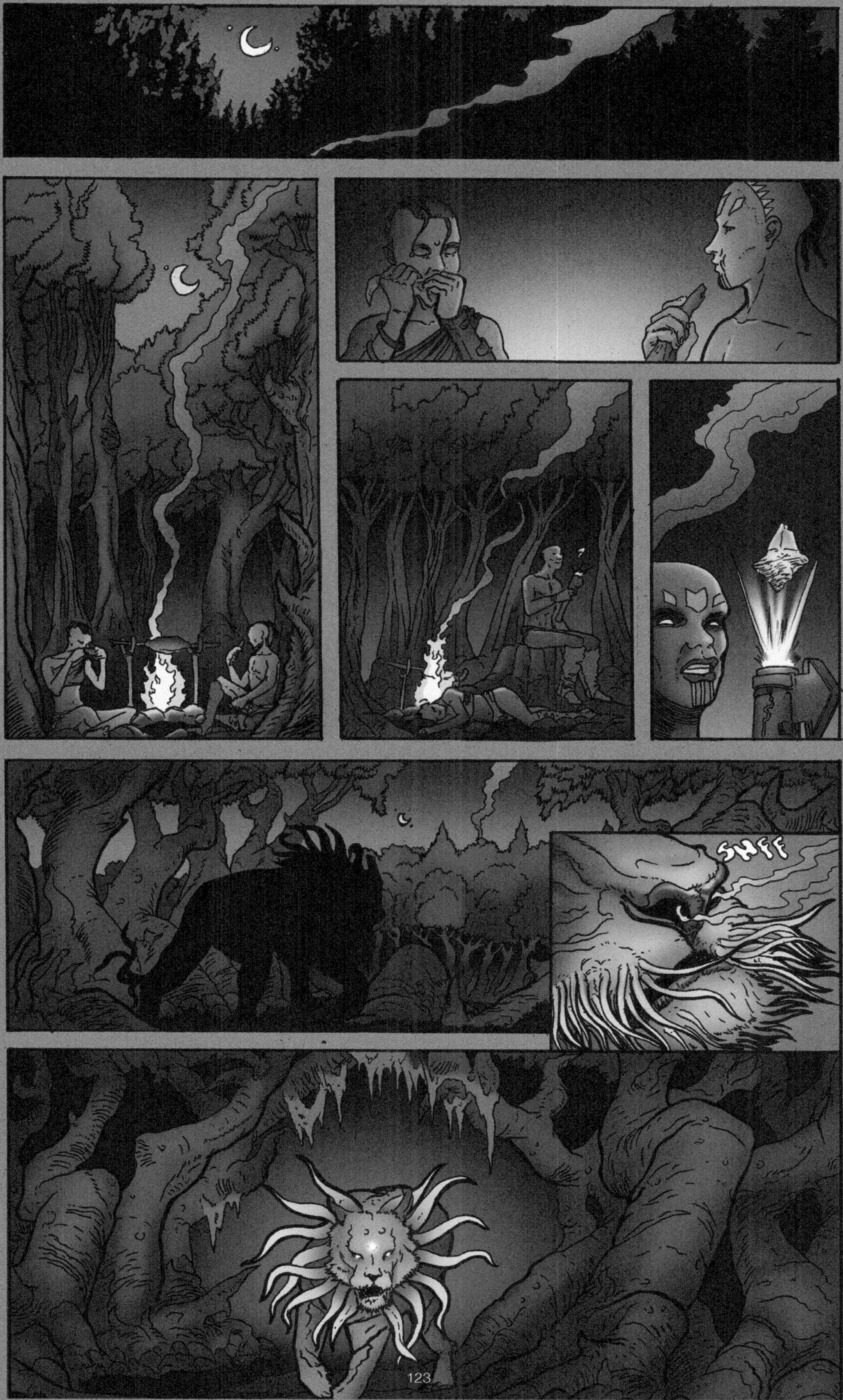
SNFF

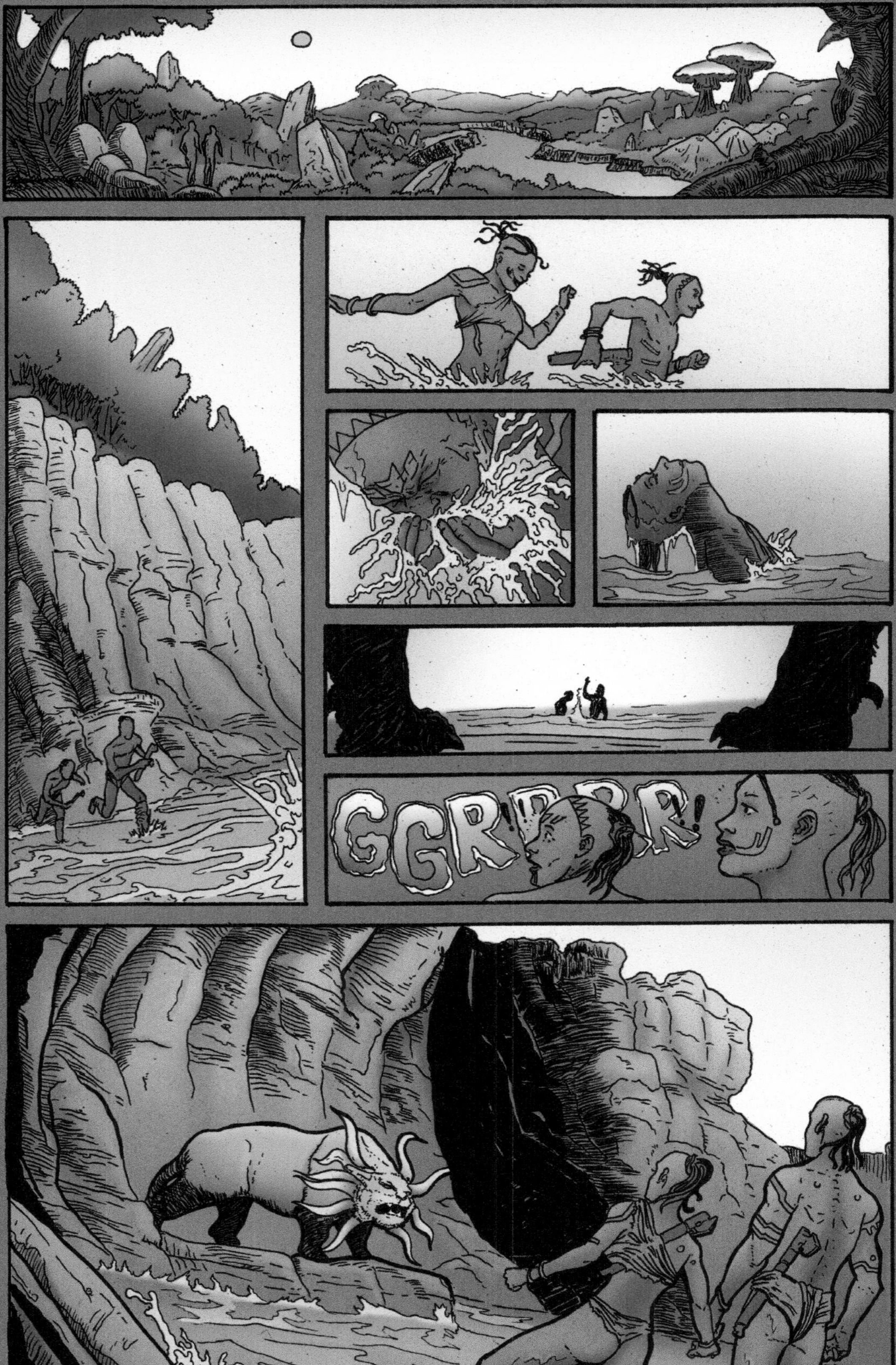
GGRRRR!!

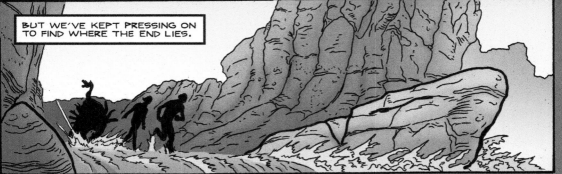

WE'VE LOST A LOT OF PEOPLE IN THIS CORNER OF THE WORLD.

BUT WE'VE KEPT PRESSING ON TO FIND WHERE THE END LIES.

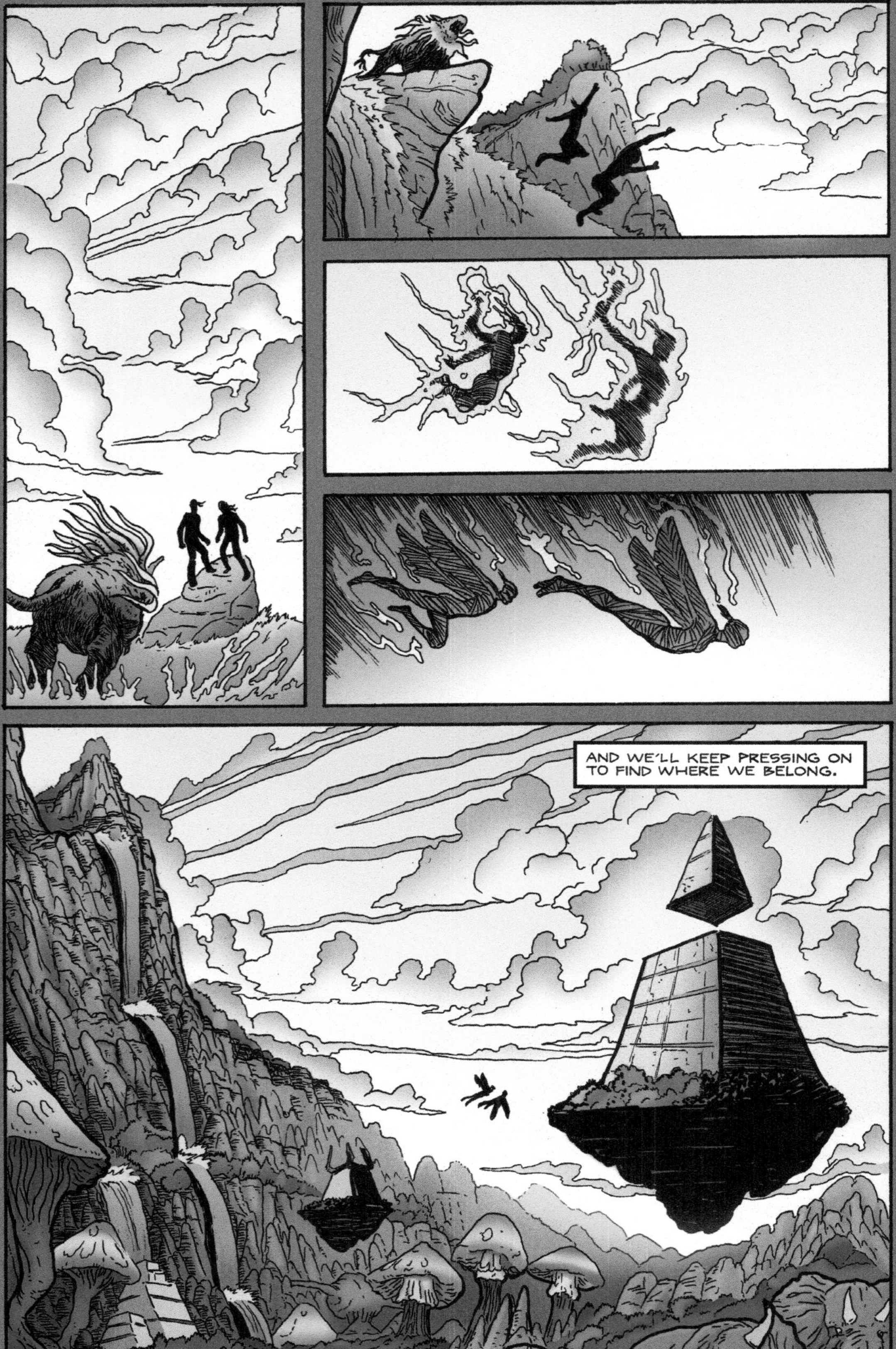
AND WE'LL KEEP PRESSING ON
TO FIND WHERE WE BELONG.

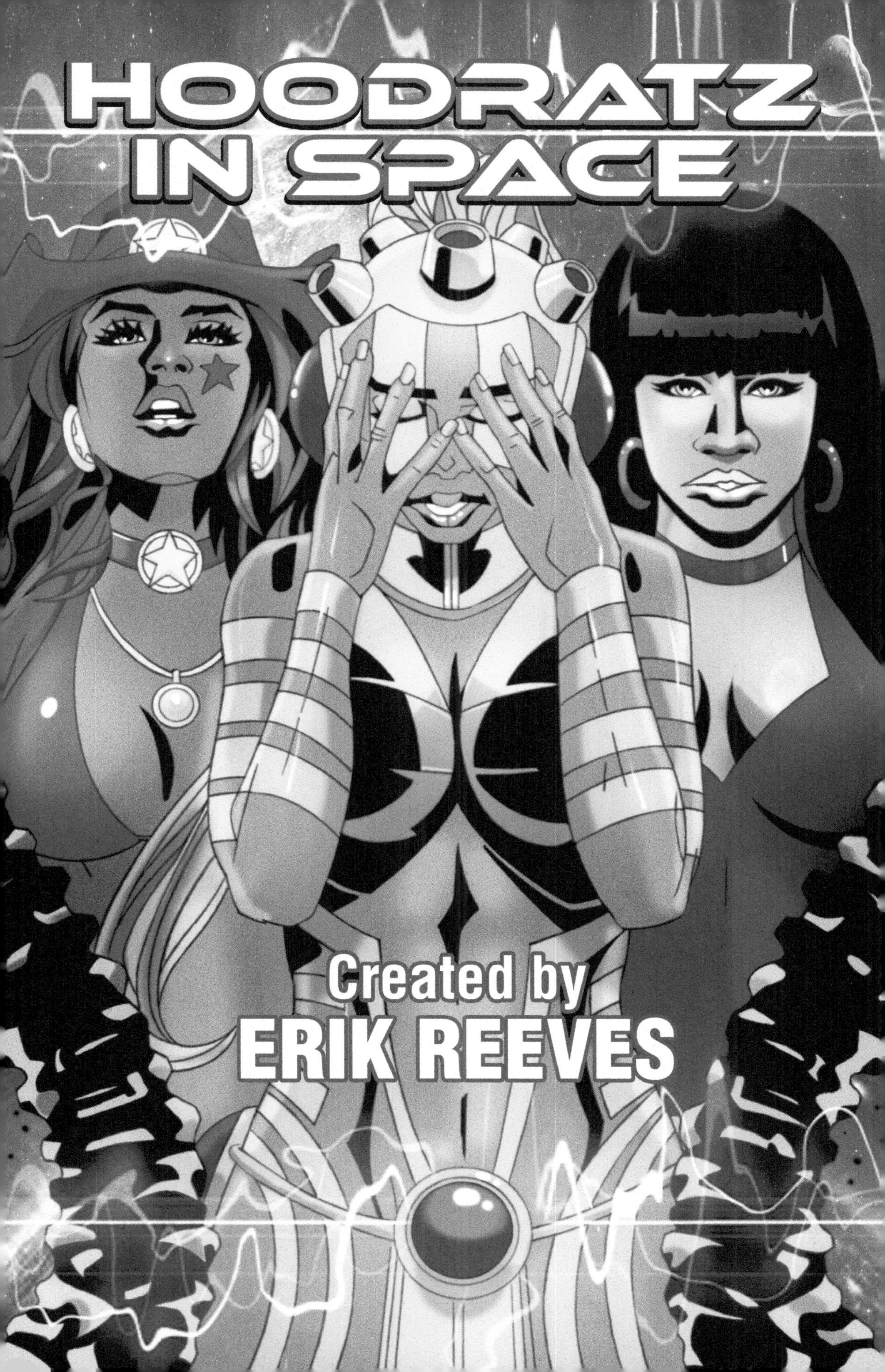
HOODRATZ
IN SPACE
Created by
ERIK REEVES

Erik Reeves, Writer / Artist

United States

Artist: Hoodratz In Space, Peacekeeper, Throwd comic series; Concept Artist: Transformers: War for Cybertron video Game; Sketchcard Artist: Marvel Now, Iron Man 3, Guardians of the Galaxy, Marvel Premiere

Erik Reeves worked as a concept artist in video games for a few years for companies including THQ, Activision, and Blizzard. He has worked as a penciler, inker, and writer on several independent comics for companies such as Image Comics, Antarctic Press, and Viper comics. He is currently working as a sketchcard artist for Marvel and Upperdeck Entertainment while self publishing his Kickstarter funded *Hoodratz In Space* comic series and more...

Erik grew up, like so many, a victim of a broken marriage, without a mother to help guide him in a world of so many different paths.

Cut off from many family members spread out in different states, it's a real honest contrast to being an immigrant living within the United States.

Disconnected from a stable family life, Erik found himself creating worlds that reflect his outlook on survival in today's modern society.

Like his fan page on Facebook and follow him on Twitter and Instagram @Erikreevesart

erockalipse.deviantart.com

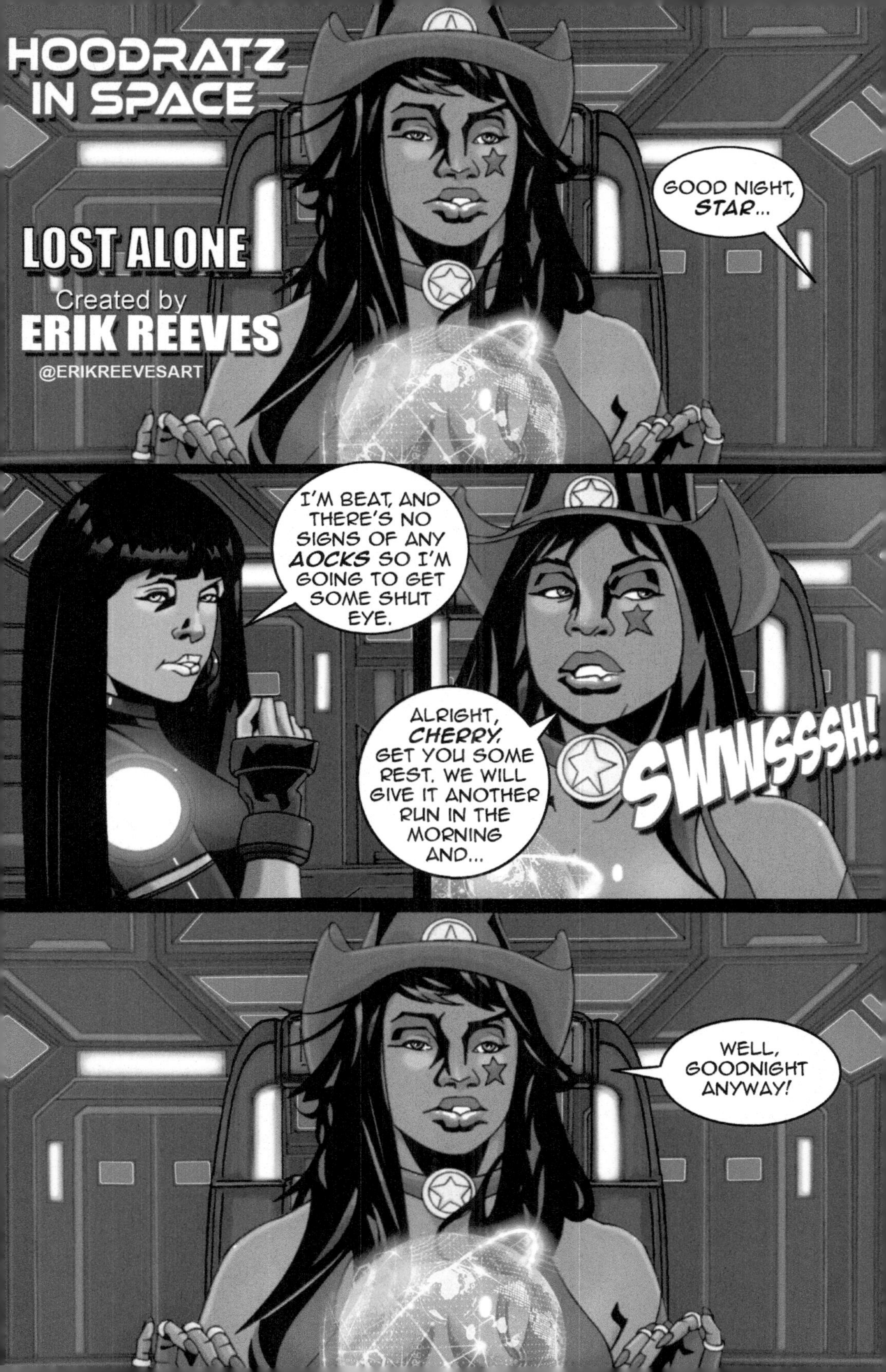
HOODRATZ IN SPACE
LOST ALONE
Created by
ERIK REEVES
@ERIKREEVESART
GOOD NIGHT, STAR...
I'M BEAT, AND THERE'S NO SIGNS OF ANY AOCKS SO I'M GOING TO GET SOME SHUT EYE.
ALRIGHT, CHERRY, GET YOU SOME REST. WE WILL GIVE IT ANOTHER RUN IN THE MORNING AND...
SWWSSSH!
WELL, GOODNIGHT ANYWAY!

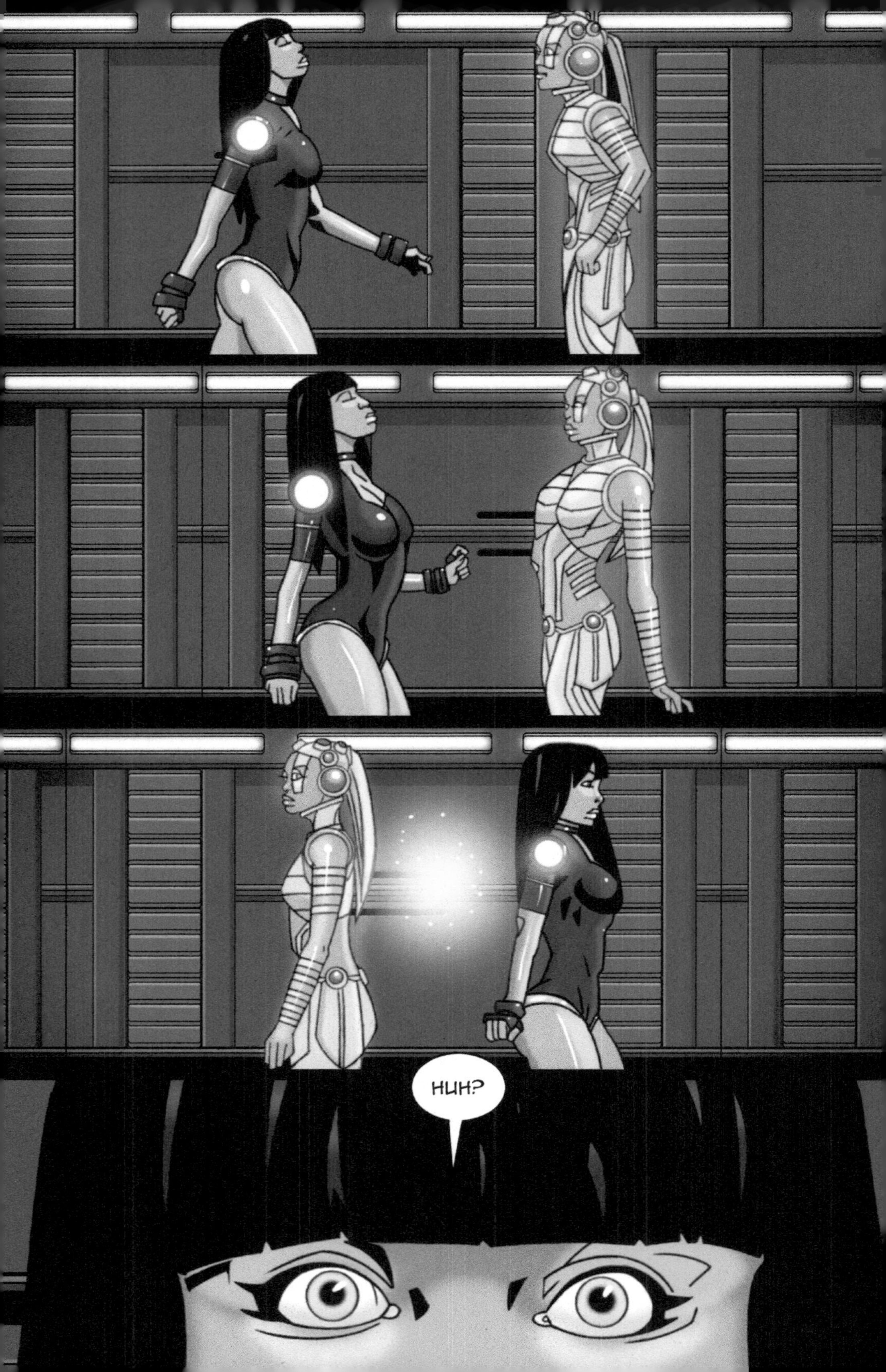
HUH?

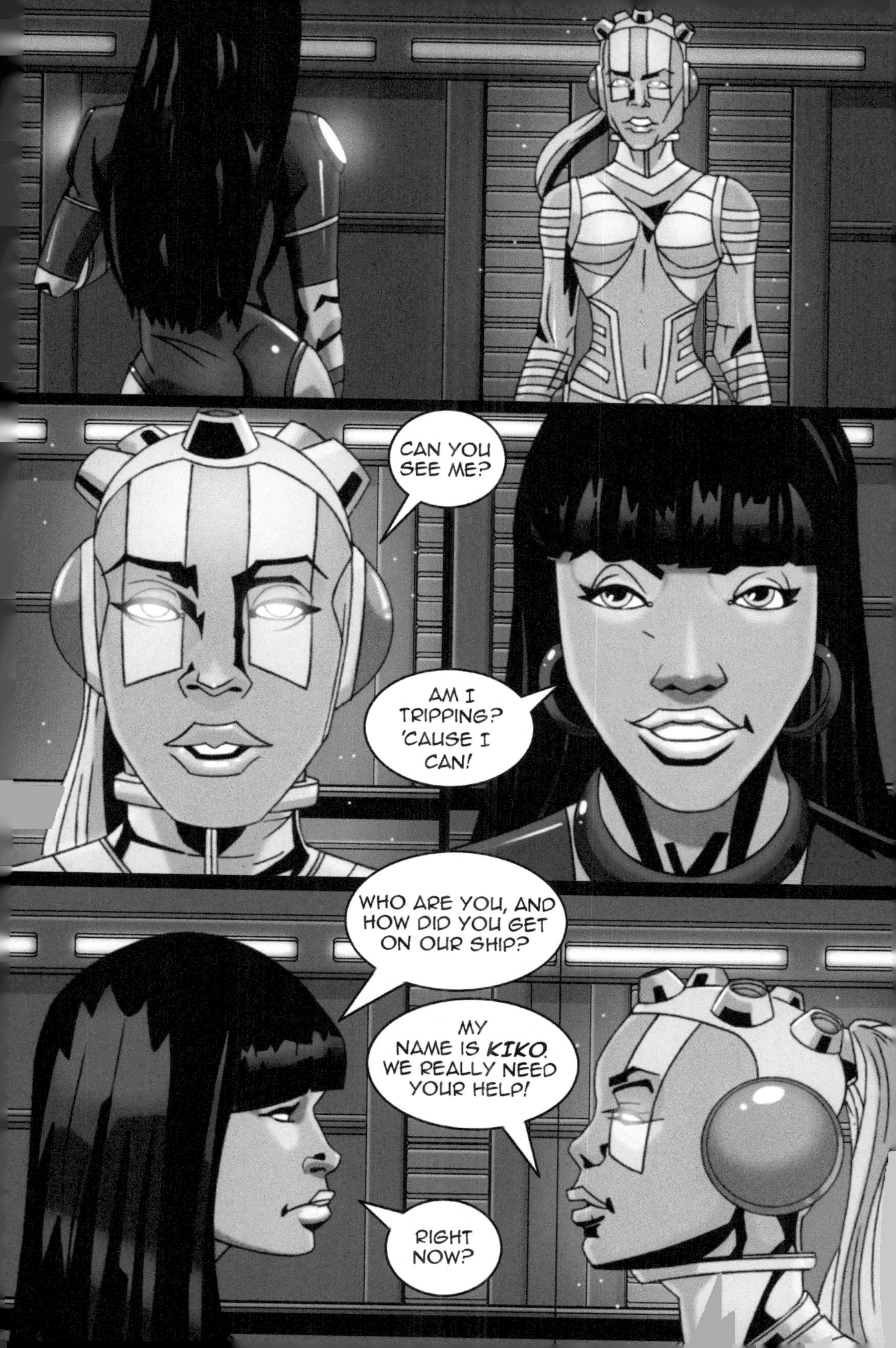
CAN YOU SEE ME?
AM I TRIPPING? 'CAUSE I CAN!
WHO ARE YOU, AND HOW DID YOU GET ON OUR SHIP?
MY NAME IS ***KIKO***. WE REALLY NEED YOUR HELP!
RIGHT NOW?

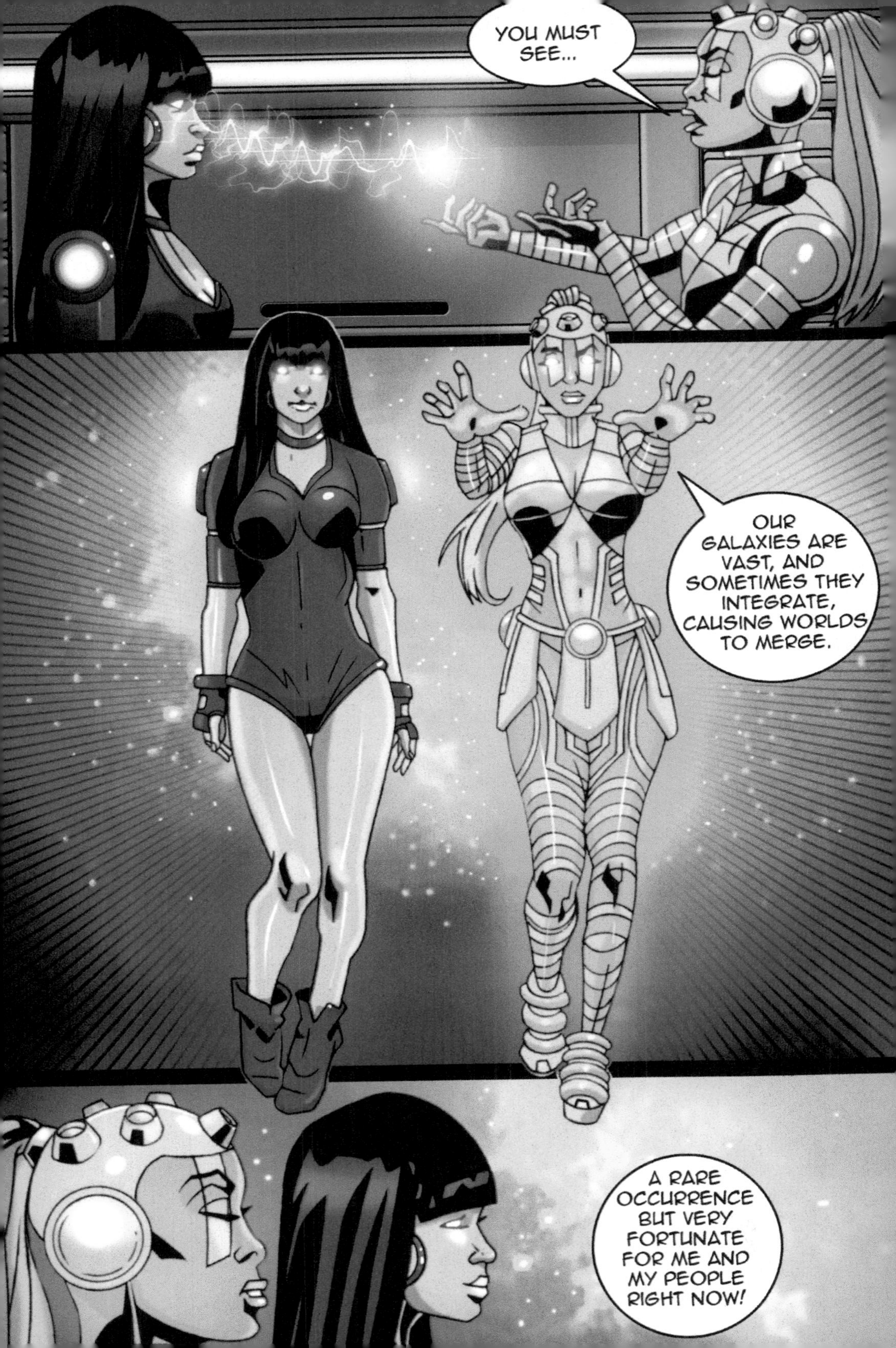
YOU MUST SEE...
OUR GALAXIES ARE VAST, AND SOMETIMES THEY INTEGRATE, CAUSING WORLDS TO MERGE.
A RARE OCCURRENCE BUT VERY FORTUNATE FOR ME AND MY PEOPLE RIGHT NOW!

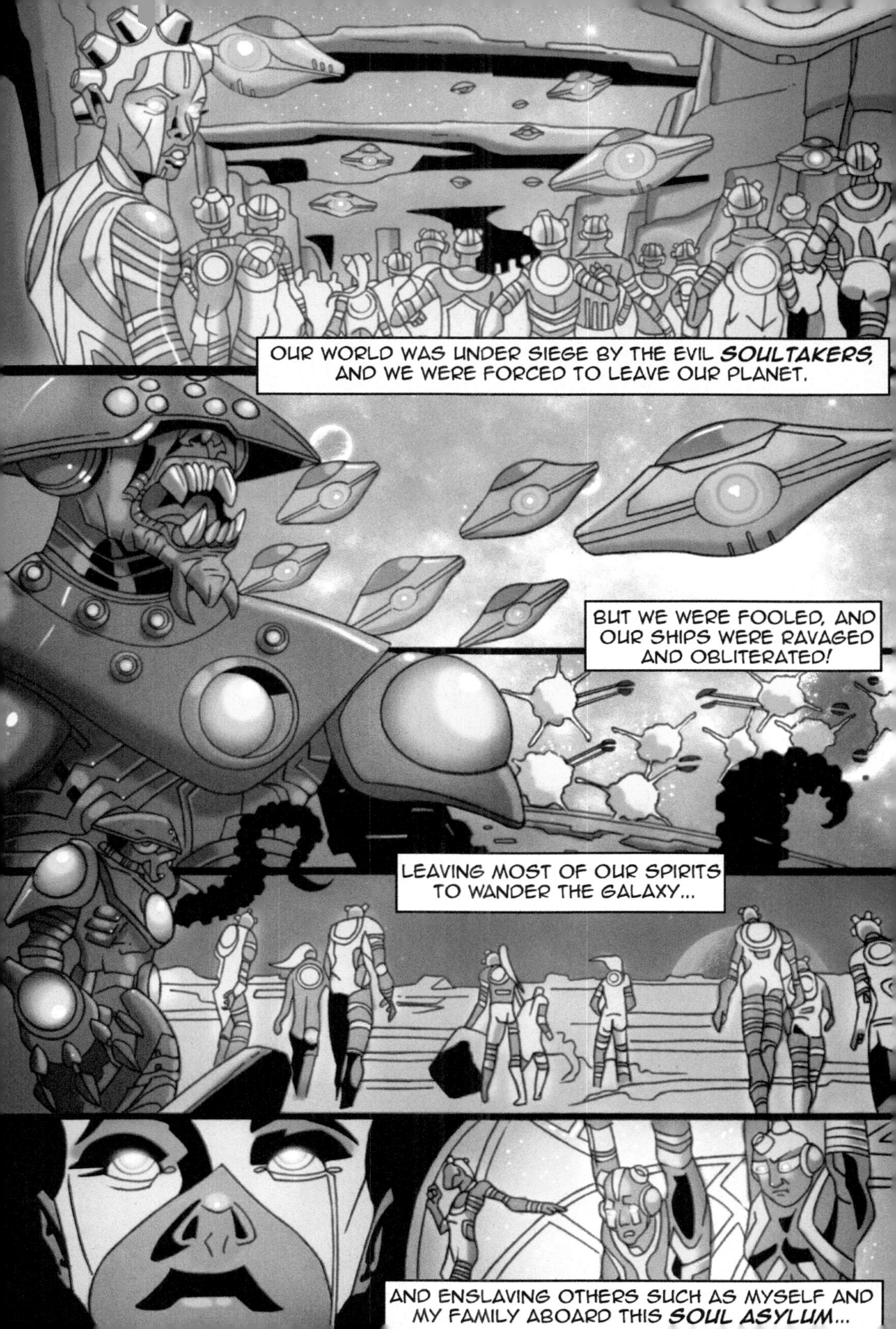
OUR WORLD WAS UNDER SIEGE BY THE EVIL *SOULTAKERS*, AND WE WERE FORCED TO LEAVE OUR PLANET.
BUT WE WERE FOOLED, AND OUR SHIPS WERE RAVAGED AND OBLITERATED!
LEAVING MOST OF OUR SPIRITS TO WANDER THE GALAXY...
AND ENSLAVING OTHERS SUCH AS MYSELF AND MY FAMILY ABOARD THIS *SOUL ASYLUM*...

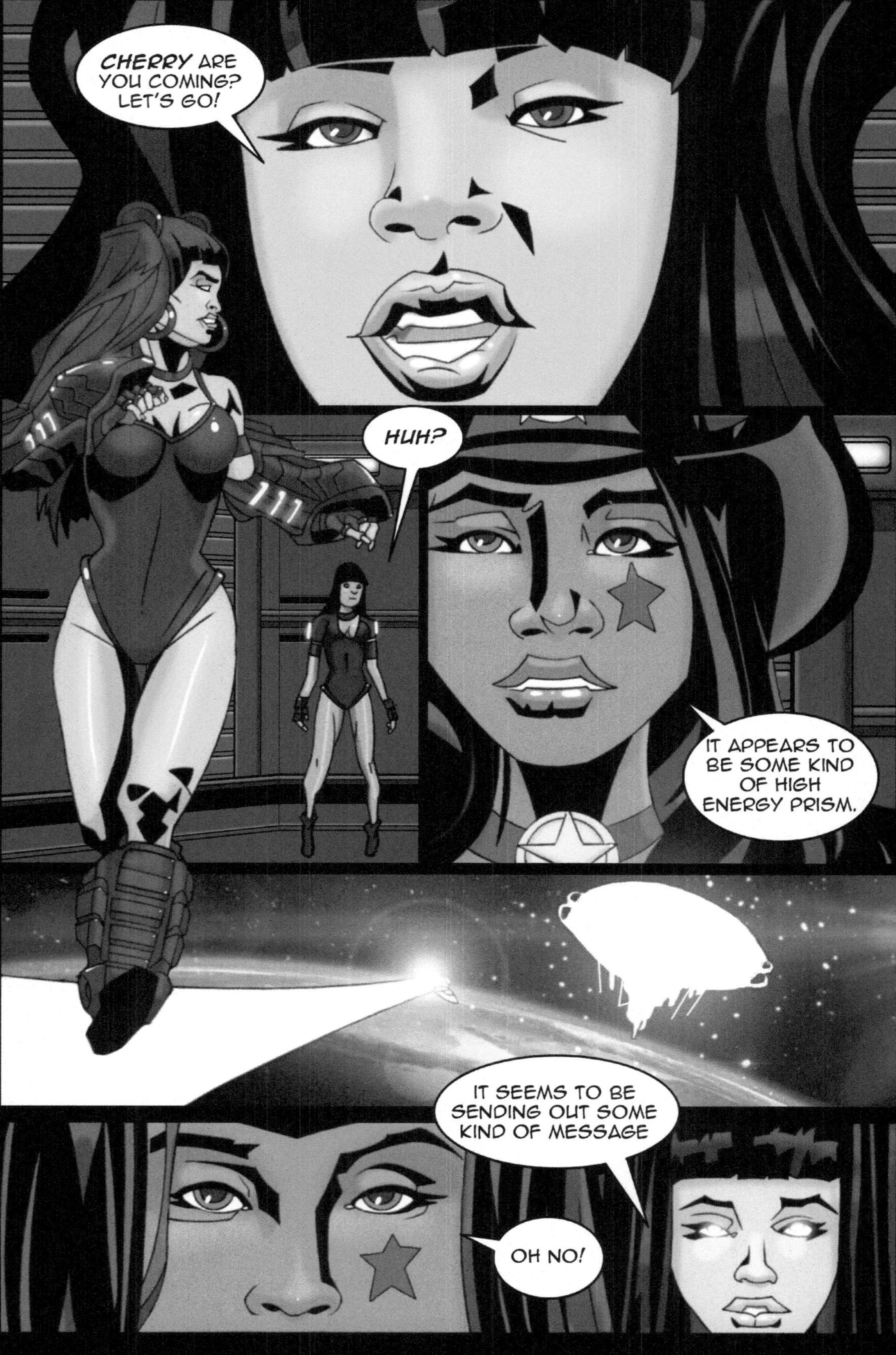
CHERRY ARE YOU COMING? LET'S GO!
HUH?
IT APPEARS TO BE SOME KIND OF HIGH ENERGY PRISM.
IT SEEMS TO BE SENDING OUT SOME KIND OF MESSAGE
OH NO!

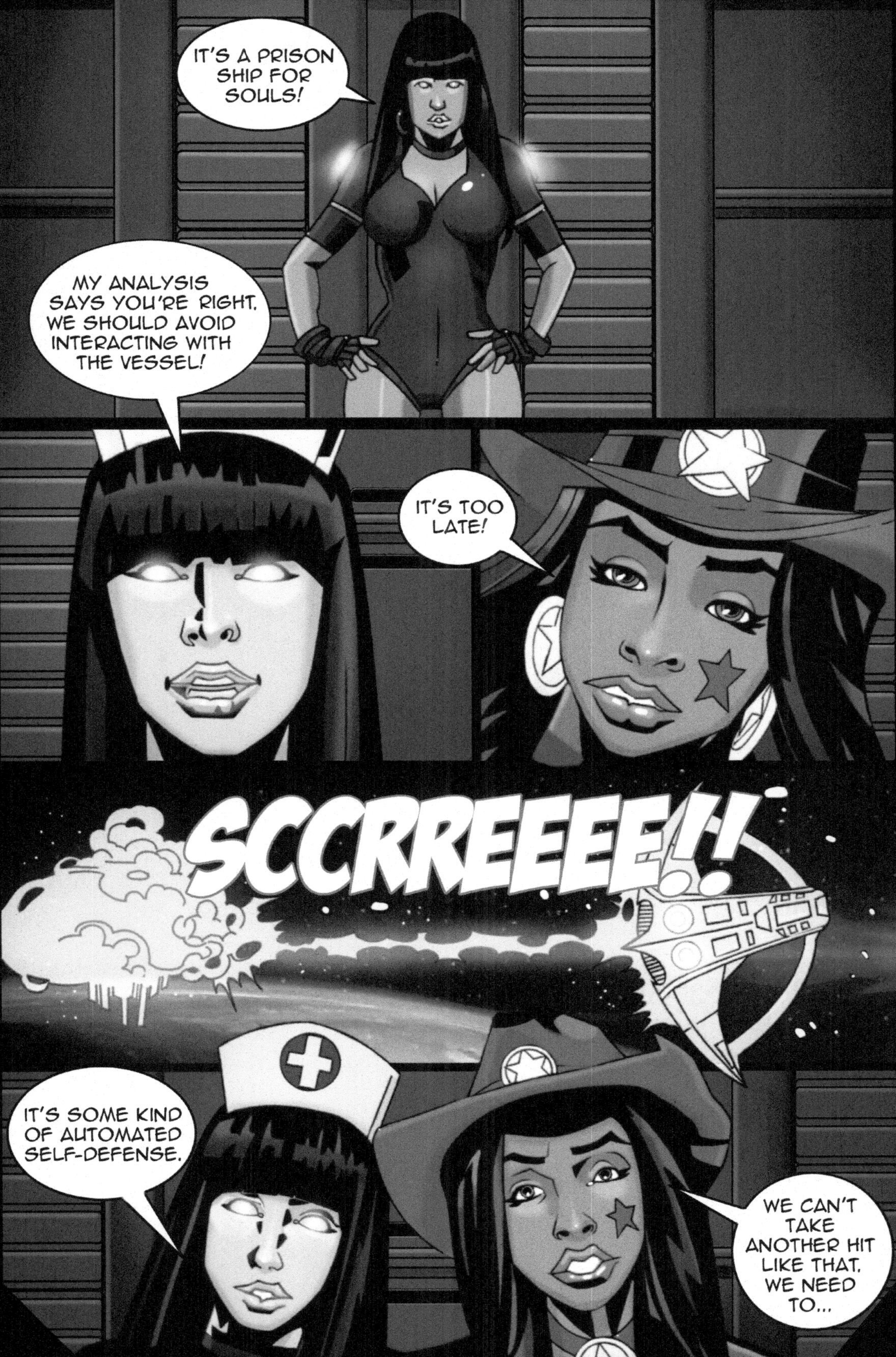
IT'S A PRISON SHIP FOR SOULS!
MY ANALYSIS SAYS YOU'RE RIGHT. WE SHOULD AVOID INTERACTING WITH THE VESSEL!
IT'S TOO LATE!
SCCRREEEEE!!
IT'S SOME KIND OF AUTOMATED SELF-DEFENSE.
WE CAN'T TAKE ANOTHER HIT LIKE THAT. WE NEED TO...

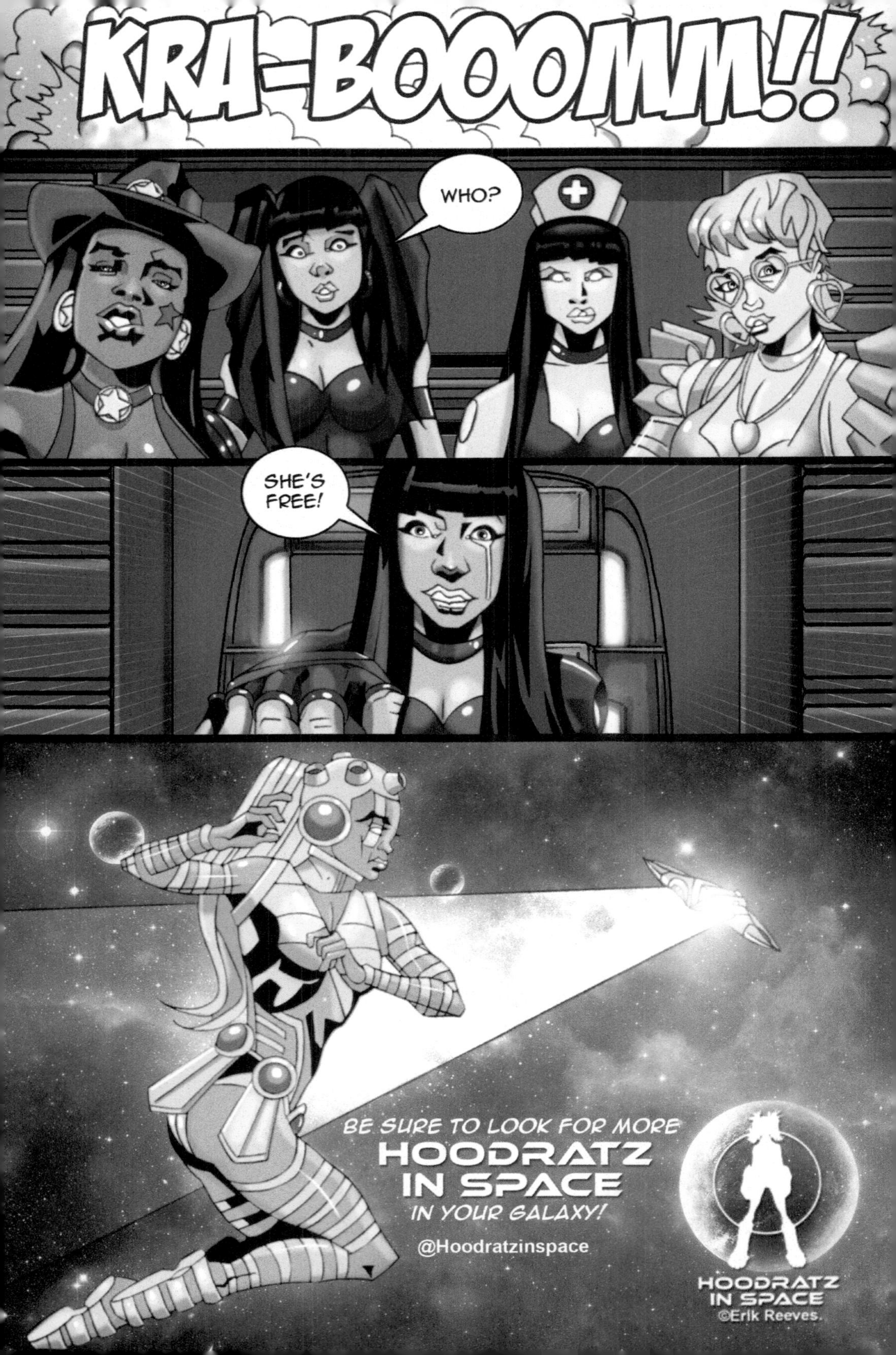
KRA-BOOOMM!!
WHO?
SHE'S FREE!
BE SURE TO LOOK FOR MORE
HOODRATZ IN SPACE
IN YOUR GALAXY!
@Hoodratzinspace
HOODRATZ IN SPACE
©Erik Reeves.

The Festival of Wishes

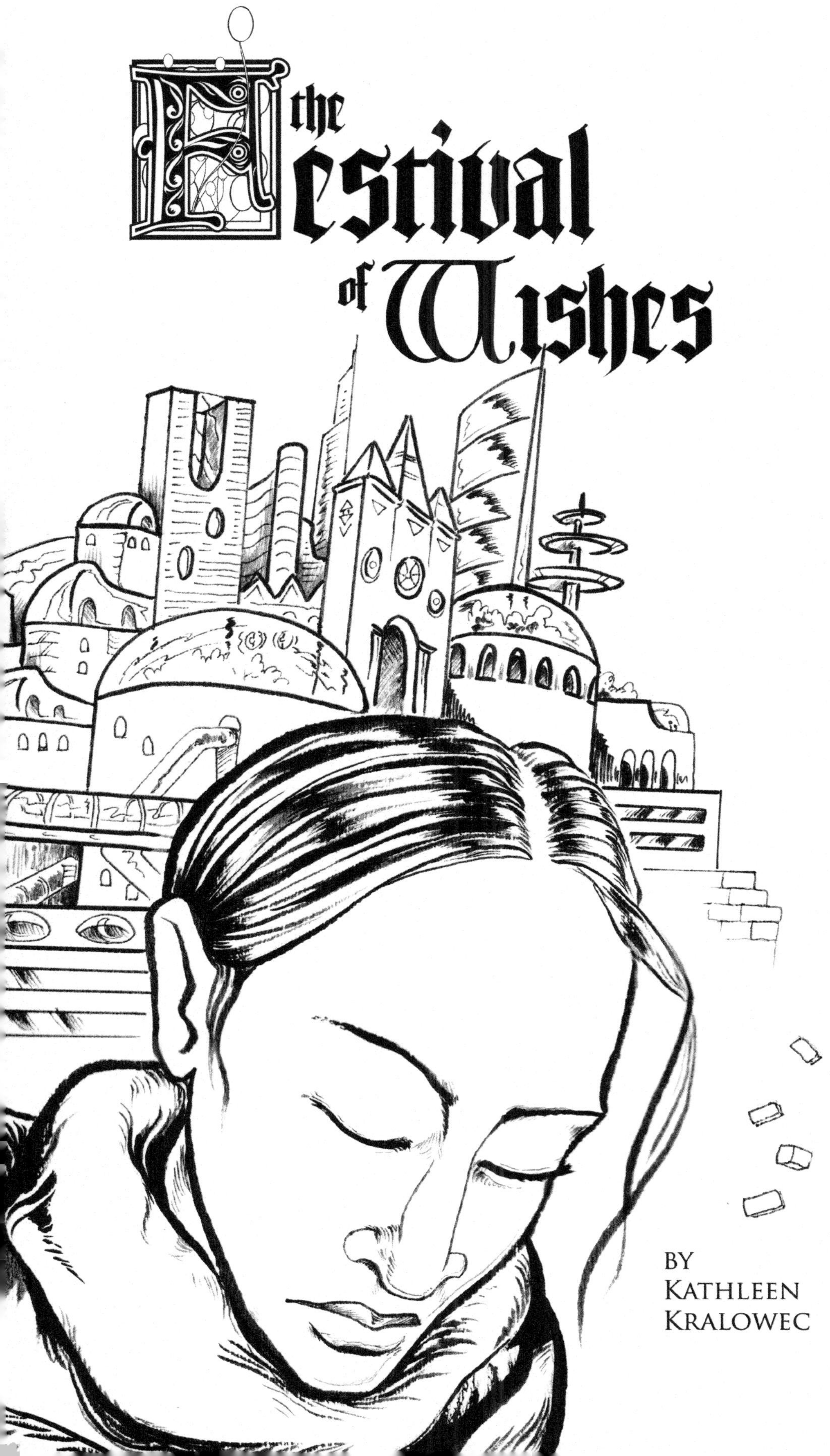

BY
KATHLEEN
KRALOWEC

Kathleen Kralowec, Writer / Artist

United States / Czech Republic / United States

Kathleen M Kralowec is from Central California and majored in Art at Scripps College. After graduating, she lived for three years in the Czech Republic, where she wrote for the *Prague Post* newspaper and began studying digital media. She returned to the US in 2008 to continue with digital media in a master's program at UC Santa Cruz. It seemed for a while she'd be going into animation, however, her first several jobs were in the game industry.

Throughout these many transitions, she continued working on an idea for a graphic novel, and after several years in Silicon Valley, she decided to focus on bringing that idea to life. She now lives in New York.

cargocollective.com/kkralowec

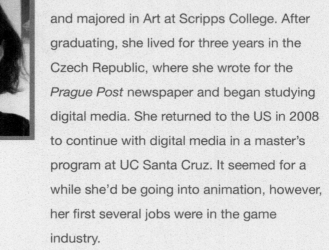

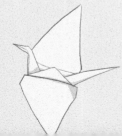

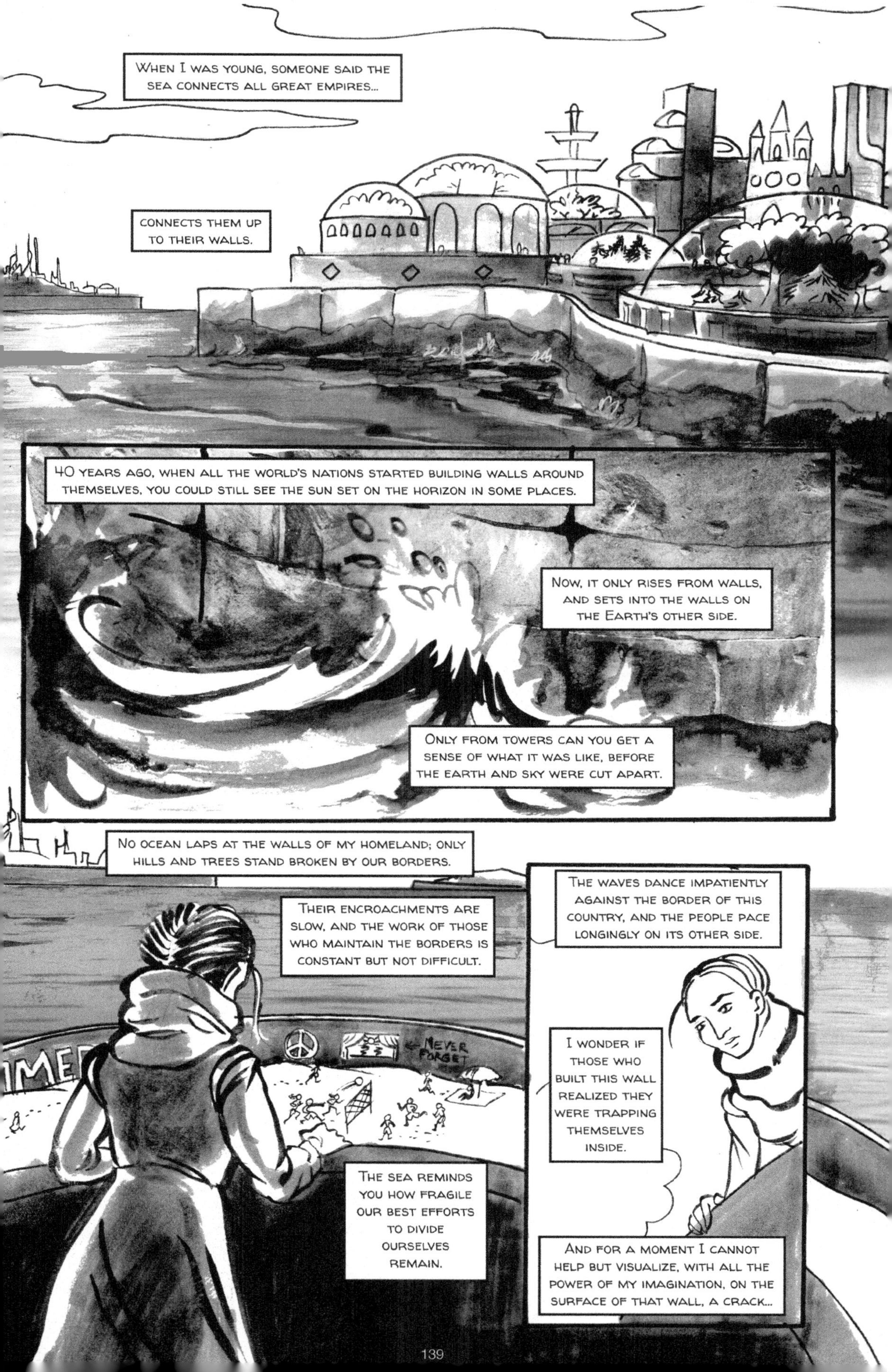

WHEN I WAS YOUNG, SOMEONE SAID THE SEA CONNECTS ALL GREAT EMPIRES...
CONNECTS THEM UP TO THEIR WALLS.
40 YEARS AGO, WHEN ALL THE WORLD'S NATIONS STARTED BUILDING WALLS AROUND THEMSELVES, YOU COULD STILL SEE THE SUN SET ON THE HORIZON IN SOME PLACES.
NOW, IT ONLY RISES FROM WALLS, AND SETS INTO THE WALLS ON THE EARTH'S OTHER SIDE.
ONLY FROM TOWERS CAN YOU GET A SENSE OF WHAT IT WAS LIKE, BEFORE THE EARTH AND SKY WERE CUT APART.
NO OCEAN LAPS AT THE WALLS OF MY HOMELAND; ONLY HILLS AND TREES STAND BROKEN BY OUR BORDERS.
THEIR ENCROACHMENTS ARE SLOW, AND THE WORK OF THOSE WHO MAINTAIN THE BORDERS IS CONSTANT BUT NOT DIFFICULT.
NEVER FORGET
THE SEA REMINDS YOU HOW FRAGILE OUR BEST EFFORTS TO DIVIDE OURSELVES REMAIN.
THE WAVES DANCE IMPATIENTLY AGAINST THE BORDER OF THIS COUNTRY, AND THE PEOPLE PACE LONGINGLY ON ITS OTHER SIDE.
I WONDER IF THOSE WHO BUILT THIS WALL REALIZED THEY WERE TRAPPING THEMSELVES INSIDE.
AND FOR A MOMENT I CANNOT HELP BUT VISUALIZE, WITH ALL THE POWER OF MY IMAGINATION, ON THE SURFACE OF THAT WALL, A CRACK...

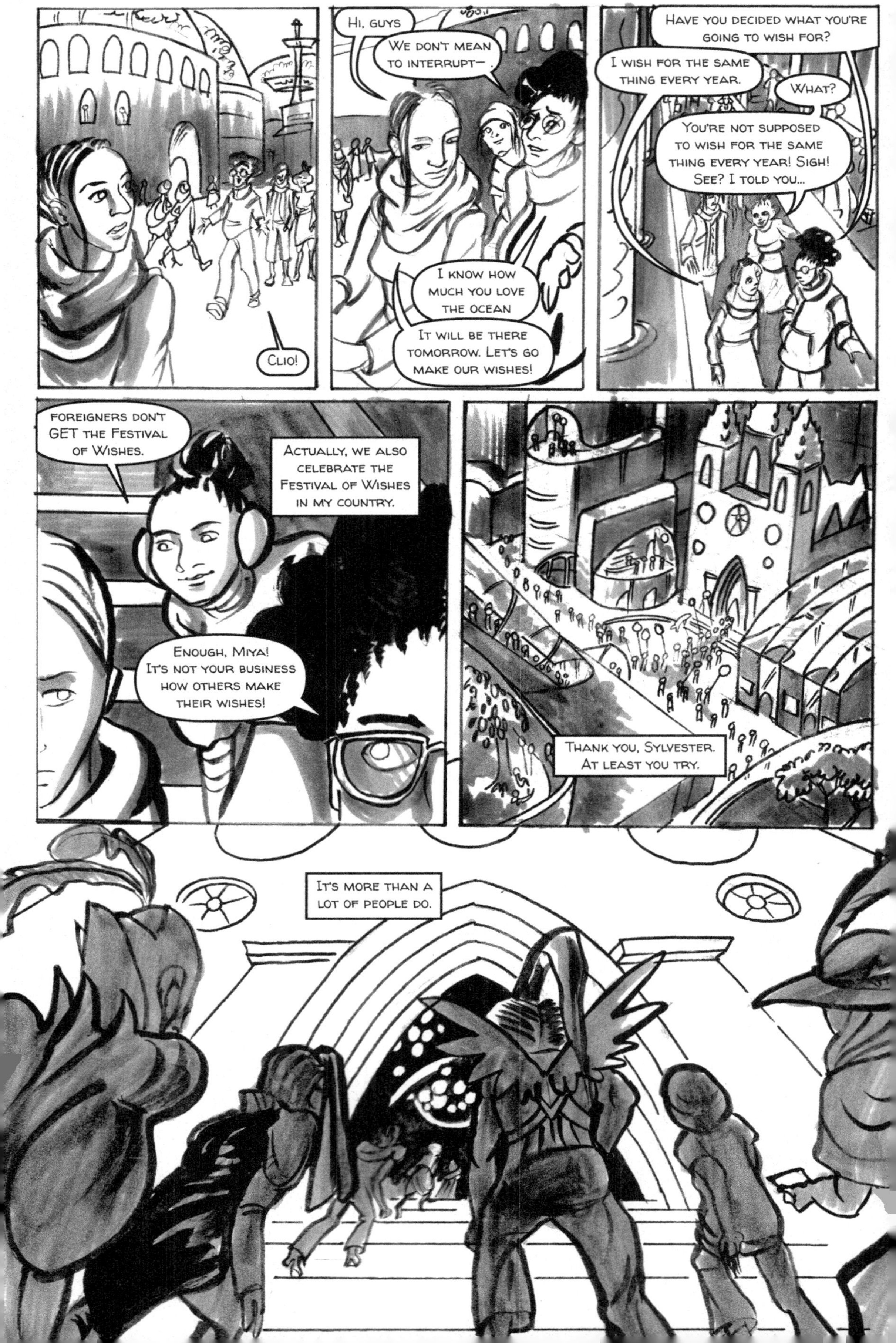
Clio!
Hi, guys
We don't mean to interrupt—.
I know how much you love the ocean
It will be there tomorrow. Let's go make our wishes!
Have you decided what you're going to wish for?
I wish for the same thing every year.
What?
You're not supposed to wish for the same thing every year! Sigh! See? I told you...
Foreigners don't GET the Festival of Wishes.
Actually, we also celebrate the Festival of Wishes in my country.
Enough, Miya! It's not your business how others make their wishes!
Thank you, Sylvester. At least you try.
It's more than a lot of people do.

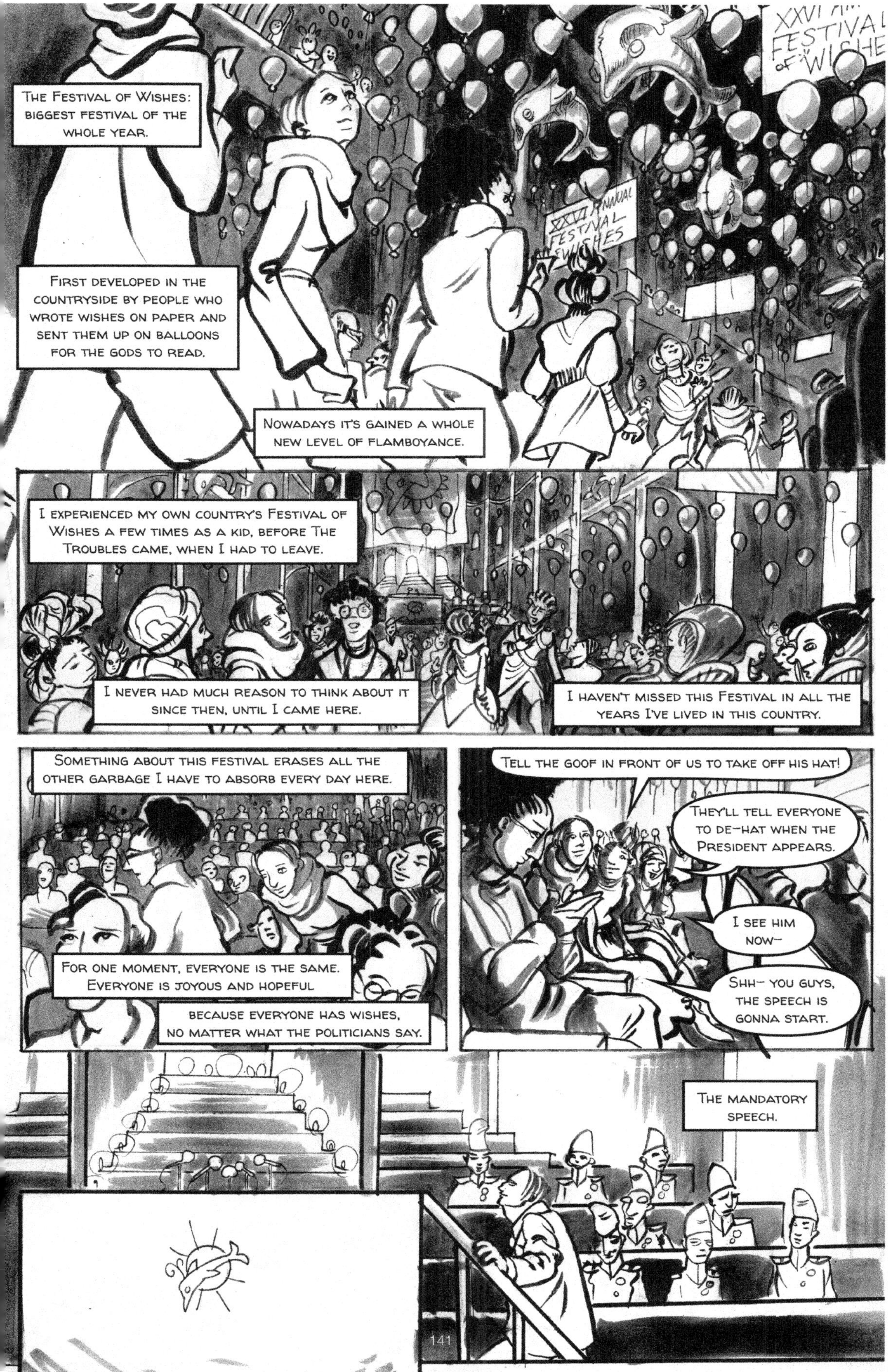
The Festival of Wishes: biggest festival of the whole year.
First developed in the countryside by people who wrote wishes on paper and sent them up on balloons for the gods to read.
Nowadays it's gained a whole new level of flamboyance.
I experienced my own country's Festival of Wishes a few times as a kid, before The Troubles came, when I had to leave.
I never had much reason to think about it since then, until I came here.
I haven't missed this Festival in all the years I've lived in this country.
Something about this festival erases all the other garbage I have to absorb every day here.
For one moment, everyone is the same. Everyone is joyous and hopeful
because everyone has wishes, no matter what the politicians say.
Tell the goof in front of us to take off his hat!
They'll tell everyone to de-hat when the President appears.
I see him now–
Shh– you guys, the speech is gonna start.
The mandatory speech.

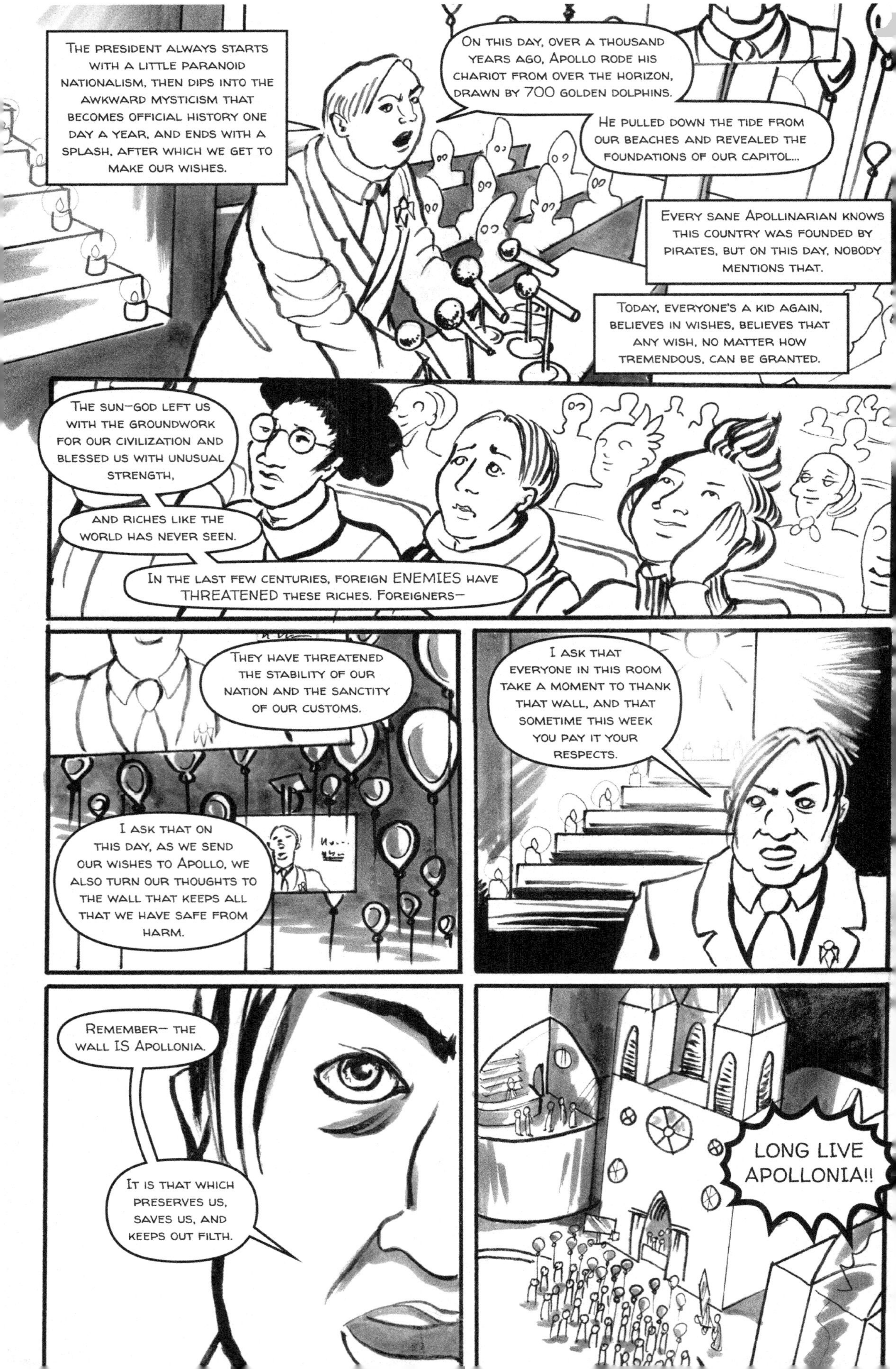
The president always starts with a little paranoid nationalism, then dips into the awkward mysticism that becomes official history one day a year, and ends with a splash, after which we get to make our wishes.
On this day, over a thousand years ago, Apollo rode his chariot from over the horizon, drawn by 700 golden dolphins.
He pulled down the tide from our beaches and revealed the foundations of our capitol...
Every sane Apollinarian knows this country was founded by pirates, but on this day, nobody mentions that.
Today, everyone's a kid again, believes in wishes, believes that any wish, no matter how tremendous, can be granted.
The sun-god left us with the groundwork for our civilization and blessed us with unusual strength,
and riches like the world has never seen.
In the last few centuries, foreign ENEMIES have THREATENED these riches. Foreigners—
They have threatened the stability of our nation and the sanctity of our customs.
I ask that on this day, as we send our wishes to Apollo, we also turn our thoughts to the wall that keeps all that we have safe from harm.
I ask that everyone in this room take a moment to thank that wall, and that sometime this week you pay it your respects.
Remember— the wall IS Apollonia.
It is that which preserves us, saves us, and keeps out filth.
LONG LIVE APOLLONIA!!

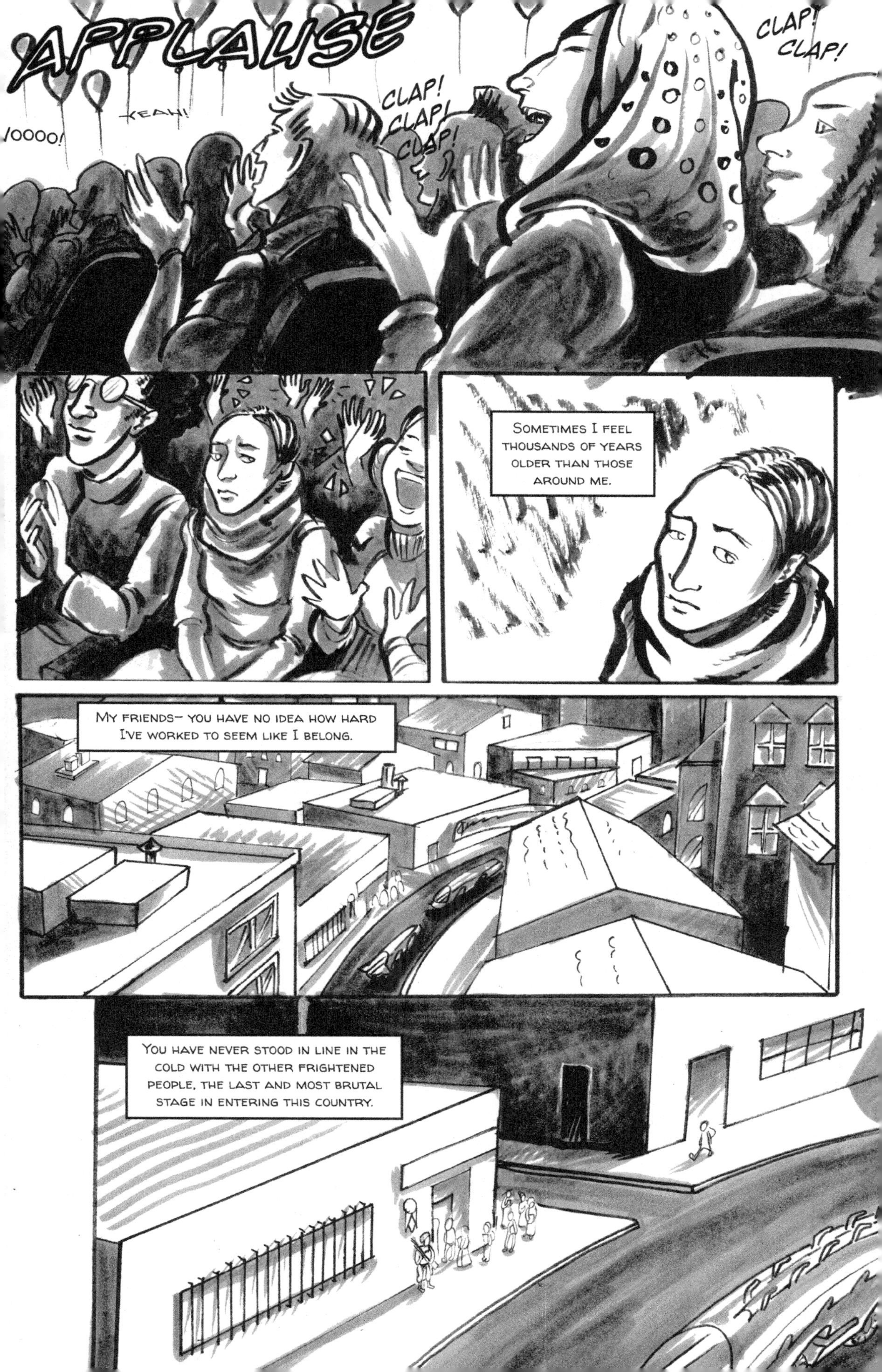
APPLAUSE
WOOOO!
YEAH!
CLAP! CLAP! CLAP!
CLAP! CLAP!
Sometimes I feel thousands of years older than those around me.
My friends– you have no idea how hard I've worked to seem like I belong.
You have never stood in line in the cold with the other frightened people, the last and most brutal stage in entering this country.

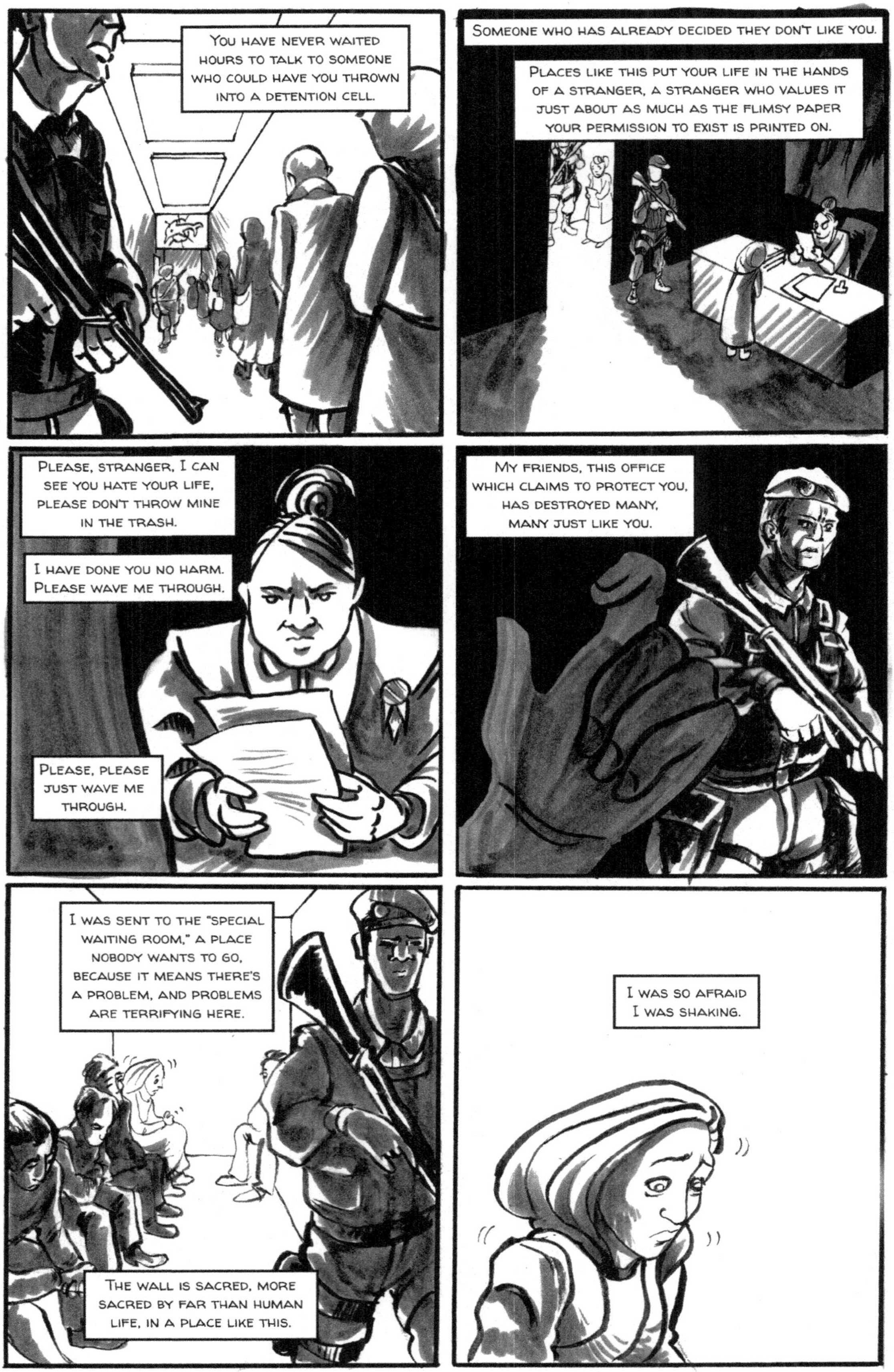
You have never waited hours to talk to someone who could have you thrown into a detention cell.
Someone who has already decided they don't like you.
Places like this put your life in the hands of a stranger, a stranger who values it just about as much as the flimsy paper your permission to exist is printed on.
Please, stranger, I can see you hate your life, please don't throw mine in the trash.
I have done you no harm. Please wave me through.
Please, please just wave me through.
My friends, this office which claims to protect you, has destroyed many, many just like you.
I was sent to the "special waiting room," a place nobody wants to go, because it means there's a problem, and problems are terrifying here.
The wall is sacred, more sacred by far than human life, in a place like this.
I was so afraid I was shaking.

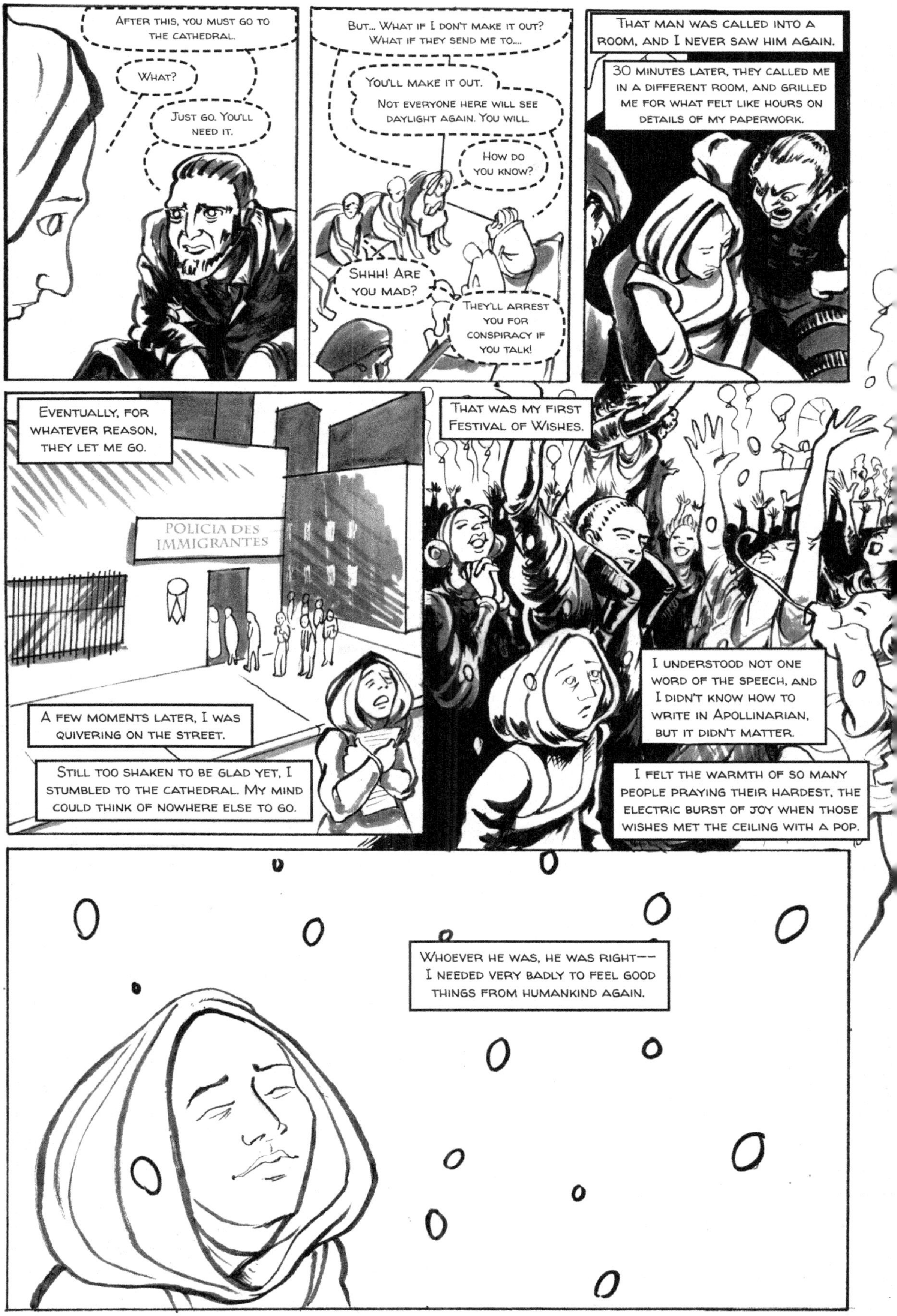
After this, you must go to the cathedral.
What?
Just go. You'll need it.
But... What if I don't make it out? What if they send me to....
You'll make it out.
Not everyone here will see daylight again. You will.
How do you know?
Shhh! Are you mad?
They'll arrest you for conspiracy if you talk!
That man was called into a room, and I never saw him again.
30 minutes later, they called me in a different room, and grilled me for what felt like hours on details of my paperwork.
Eventually, for whatever reason, they let me go.
POLICIA DES IMMIGRANTES
A few moments later, I was quivering on the street.
Still too shaken to be glad yet, I stumbled to the cathedral. My mind could think of nowhere else to go.
That was my first Festival of Wishes.
I understood not one word of the speech, and I didn't know how to write in Apollinarian, but it didn't matter.
I felt the warmth of so many people praying their hardest, the electric burst of joy when those wishes met the ceiling with a pop.
Whoever he was, he was right-- I needed very badly to feel good things from humankind again.

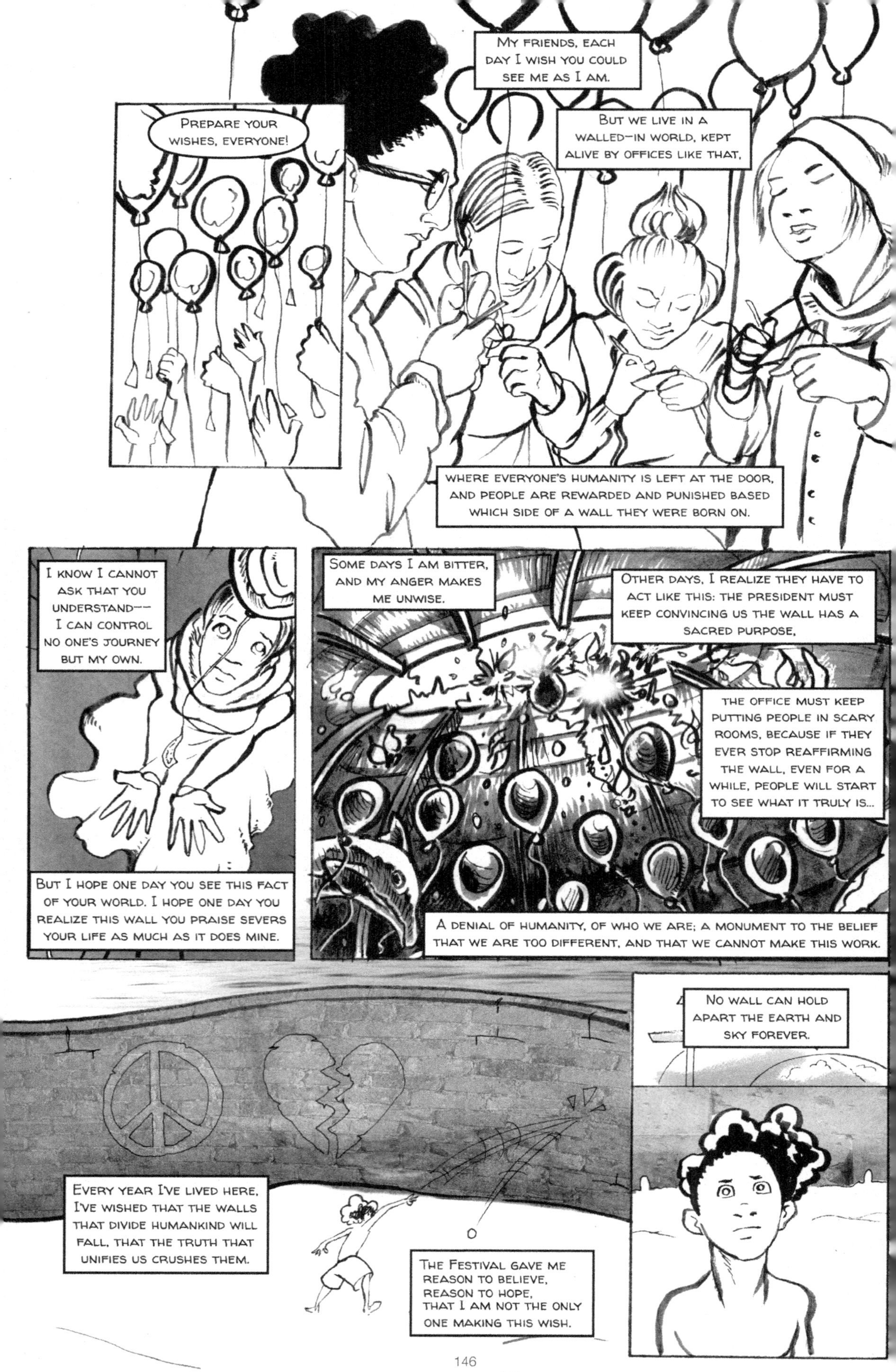
Prepare your wishes, everyone!
My friends, each day I wish you could see me as I am.
But we live in a walled—in world, kept alive by offices like that,
where everyone's humanity is left at the door, and people are rewarded and punished based which side of a wall they were born on.
I know I cannot ask that you understand-- I can control no one's journey but my own.
But I hope one day you see this fact of your world. I hope one day you realize this wall you praise severs your life as much as it does mine.
Some days I am bitter, and my anger makes me unwise.
Other days, I realize they have to act like this: the president must keep convincing us the wall has a sacred purpose,
the office must keep putting people in scary rooms, because if they ever stop reaffirming the wall, even for a while, people will start to see what it truly is...
A denial of humanity, of who we are; a monument to the belief that we are too different, and that we cannot make this work.
Every year I've lived here, I've wished that the walls that divide humankind will fall, that the truth that unifies us crushes them.
The Festival gave me reason to believe, reason to hope, that I am not the only one making this wish.
No wall can hold apart the earth and sky forever.

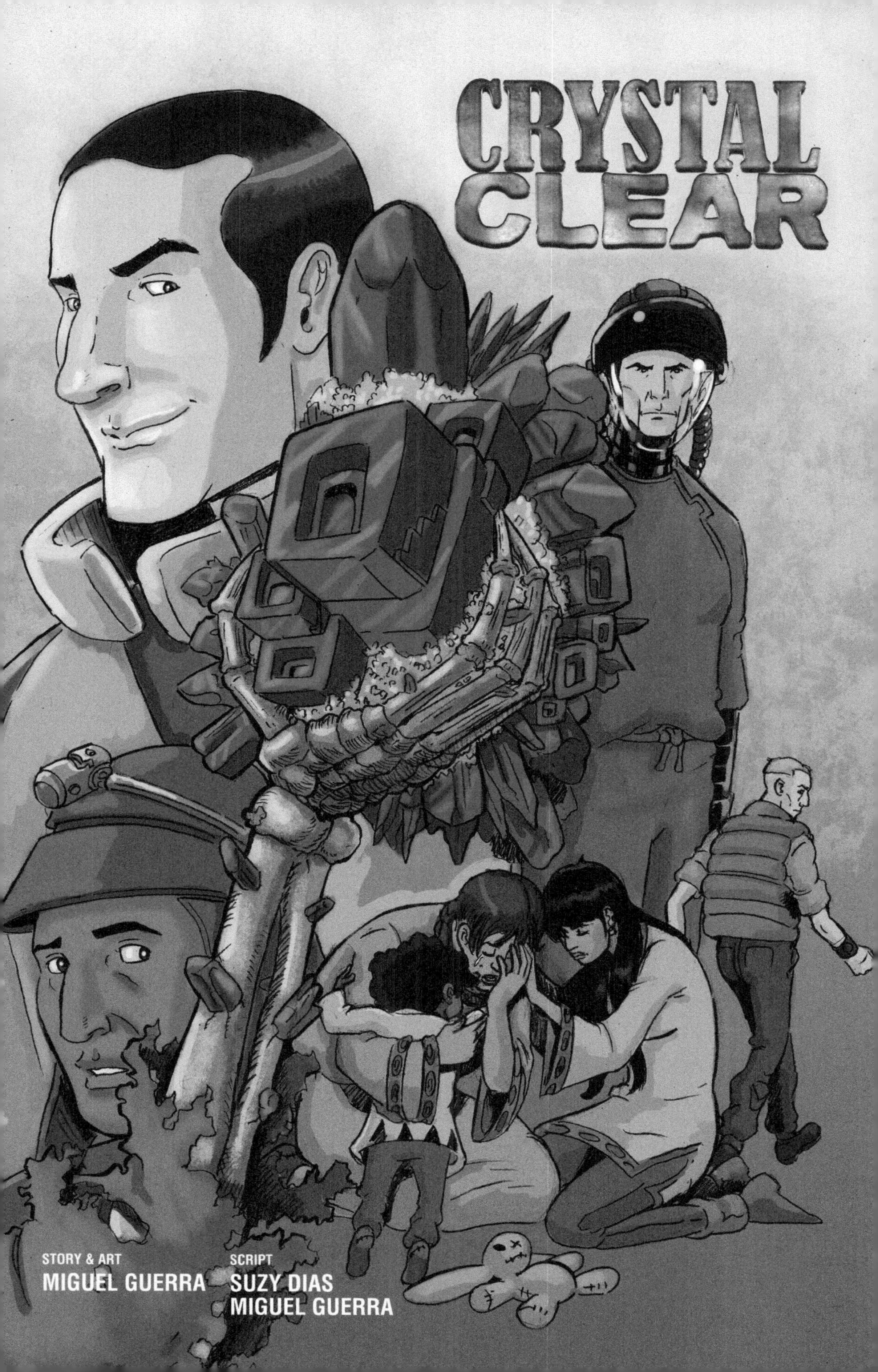
CRYSTAL CLEAR
STORY & ART
MIGUEL GUERRA
SCRIPT
SUZY DIAS
MIGUEL GUERRA

Miguel Guerra, Writer / Artist

United States / Spain / Europe

My name is Miguel Guerra. I'm co-founder of 7 Robots, Inc., where I publish various titles: *Super Corporate Heroes, Samurai Elf* and *Wolf Boy and His Magical warriors*, and our absolutely free annual indie anthology - *Earth Dream*. I've published in *Heavy Metal* and Antarctic Press, and have collaborated with some great indie presses like Forward Comix. I'm also a freelance illustrator for businesses and individuals looking for something unique, as well as Forbes and The NY National Book Foundation.

I'm an American comic creator living in Europe, and I also grew up in Canada. Moving around has exposed me to both European and American styles and approaches to comics. Since Europe is a big consumer of manga and animé, Japanese artists and stories have been a big influence on my work. Each has a very unique approach to the medium, and my own goal has been to fuse the three.

Samurai Elf
Super Corporate Heroes
Earth Dream
Wolf Boy and his Magical Warriors
Crash Boom Pop!

7robots.com

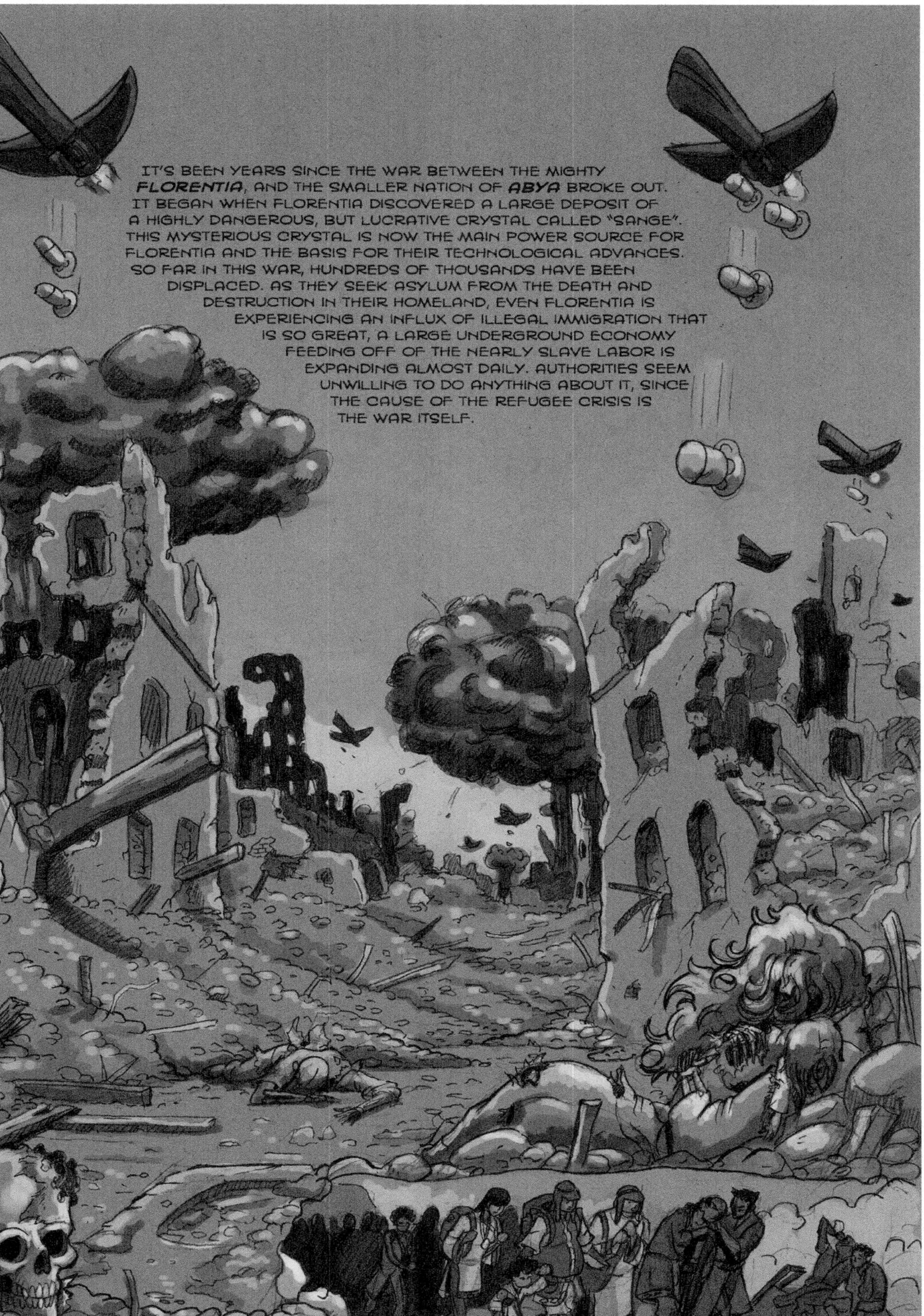
IT'S BEEN YEARS SINCE THE WAR BETWEEN THE MIGHTY FLORENTIA, AND THE SMALLER NATION OF ABYA BROKE OUT. IT BEGAN WHEN FLORENTIA DISCOVERED A LARGE DEPOSIT OF A HIGHLY DANGEROUS, BUT LUCRATIVE CRYSTAL CALLED "SANGE". THIS MYSTERIOUS CRYSTAL IS NOW THE MAIN POWER SOURCE FOR FLORENTIA AND THE BASIS FOR THEIR TECHNOLOGICAL ADVANCES. SO FAR IN THIS WAR, HUNDREDS OF THOUSANDS HAVE BEEN DISPLACED. AS THEY SEEK ASYLUM FROM THE DEATH AND DESTRUCTION IN THEIR HOMELAND, EVEN FLORENTIA IS EXPERIENCING AN INFLUX OF ILLEGAL IMMIGRATION THAT IS SO GREAT, A LARGE UNDERGROUND ECONOMY FEEDING OFF OF THE NEARLY SLAVE LABOR IS EXPANDING ALMOST DAILY. AUTHORITIES SEEM UNWILLING TO DO ANYTHING ABOUT IT, SINCE THE CAUSE OF THE REFUGEE CRISIS IS THE WAR ITSELF.

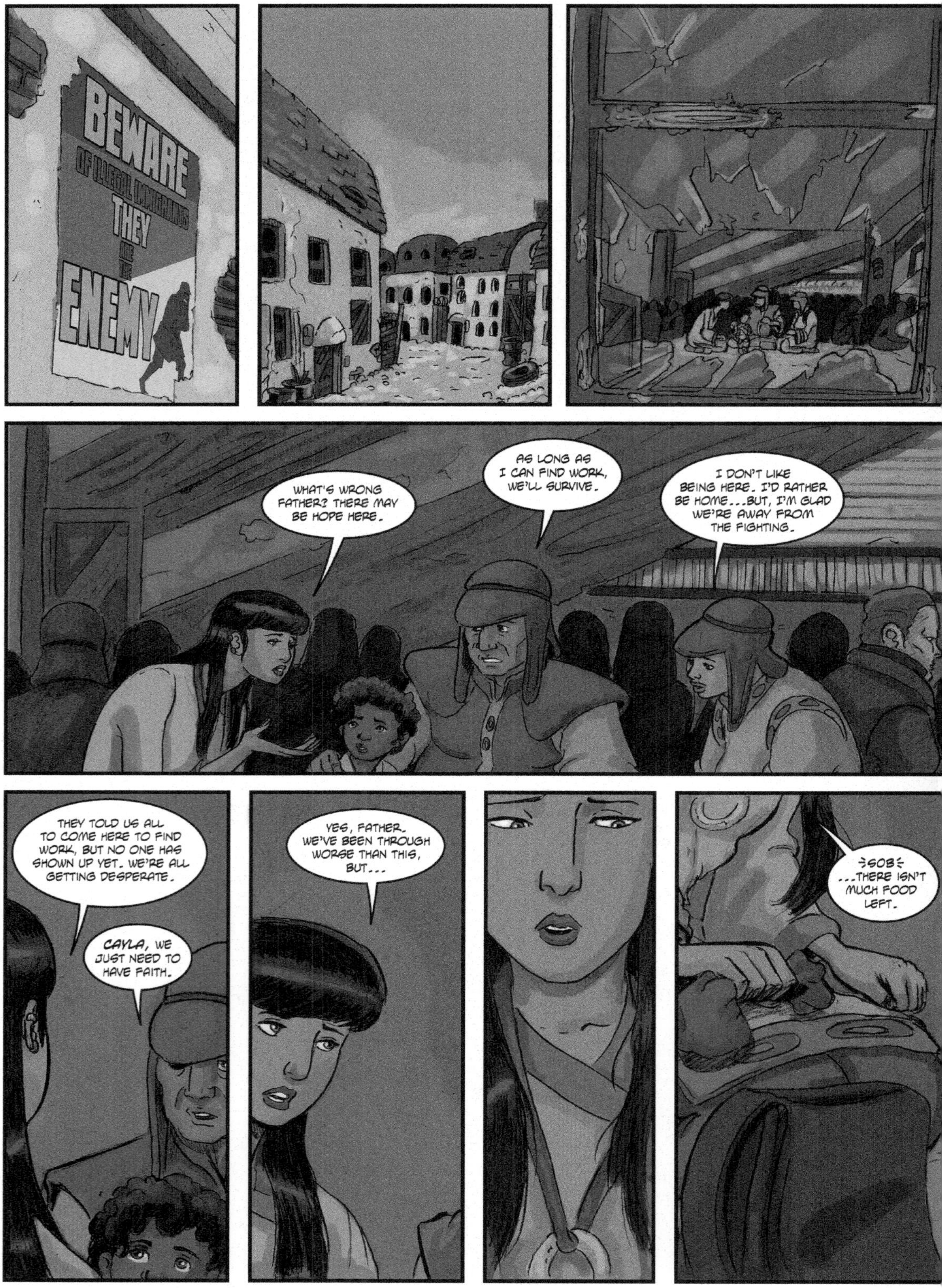
BEWARE
OF ILLEGAL IMMIGRANTS
THEY
ARE THE
ENEMY
WHAT'S WRONG FATHER? THERE MAY BE HOPE HERE.
AS LONG AS I CAN FIND WORK, WE'LL SURVIVE.
I DON'T LIKE BEING HERE. I'D RATHER BE HOME...BUT, I'M GLAD WE'RE AWAY FROM THE FIGHTING.
THEY TOLD US ALL TO COME HERE TO FIND WORK, BUT NO ONE HAS SHOWN UP YET. WE'RE ALL GETTING DESPERATE.
CAYLA, WE JUST NEED TO HAVE FAITH.
YES, FATHER. WE'VE BEEN THROUGH WORSE THAN THIS, BUT...
SOB ...THERE ISN'T MUCH FOOD LEFT.

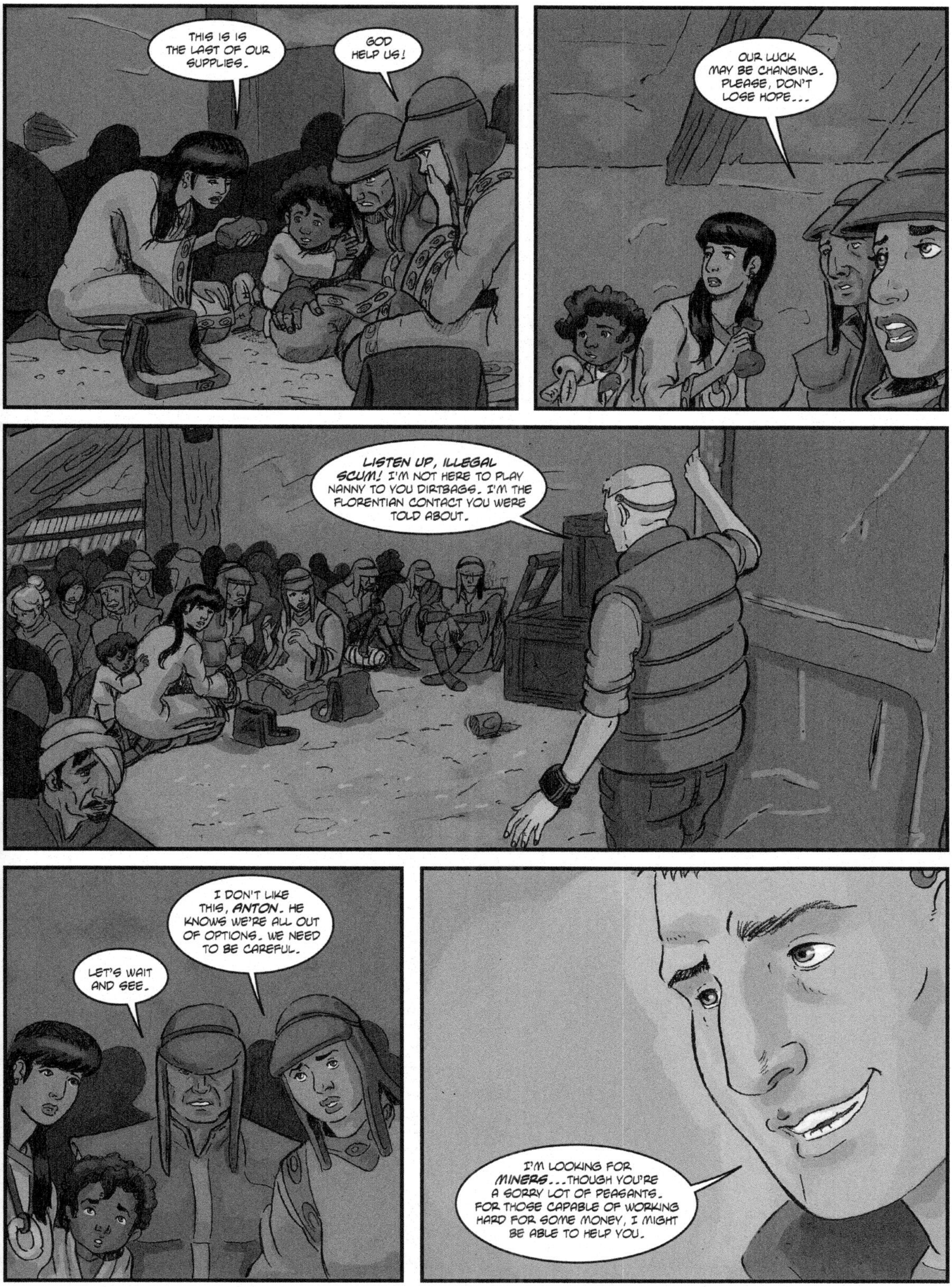
THIS IS IS THE LAST OF OUR SUPPLIES.
GOD HELP US!
OUR LUCK MAY BE CHANGING. PLEASE, DON'T LOSE HOPE...
LISTEN UP, ILLEGAL SCUM! I'M NOT HERE TO PLAY NANNY TO YOU DIRTBAGS. I'M THE FLORENTIAN CONTACT YOU WERE TOLD ABOUT.
I DON'T LIKE THIS, ANTON. HE KNOWS WE'RE ALL OUT OF OPTIONS. WE NEED TO BE CAREFUL.
LET'S WAIT AND SEE.
I'M LOOKING FOR MINERS...THOUGH YOU'RE A SORRY LOT OF PEASANTS. FOR THOSE CAPABLE OF WORKING HARD FOR SOME MONEY, I MIGHT BE ABLE TO HELP YOU.

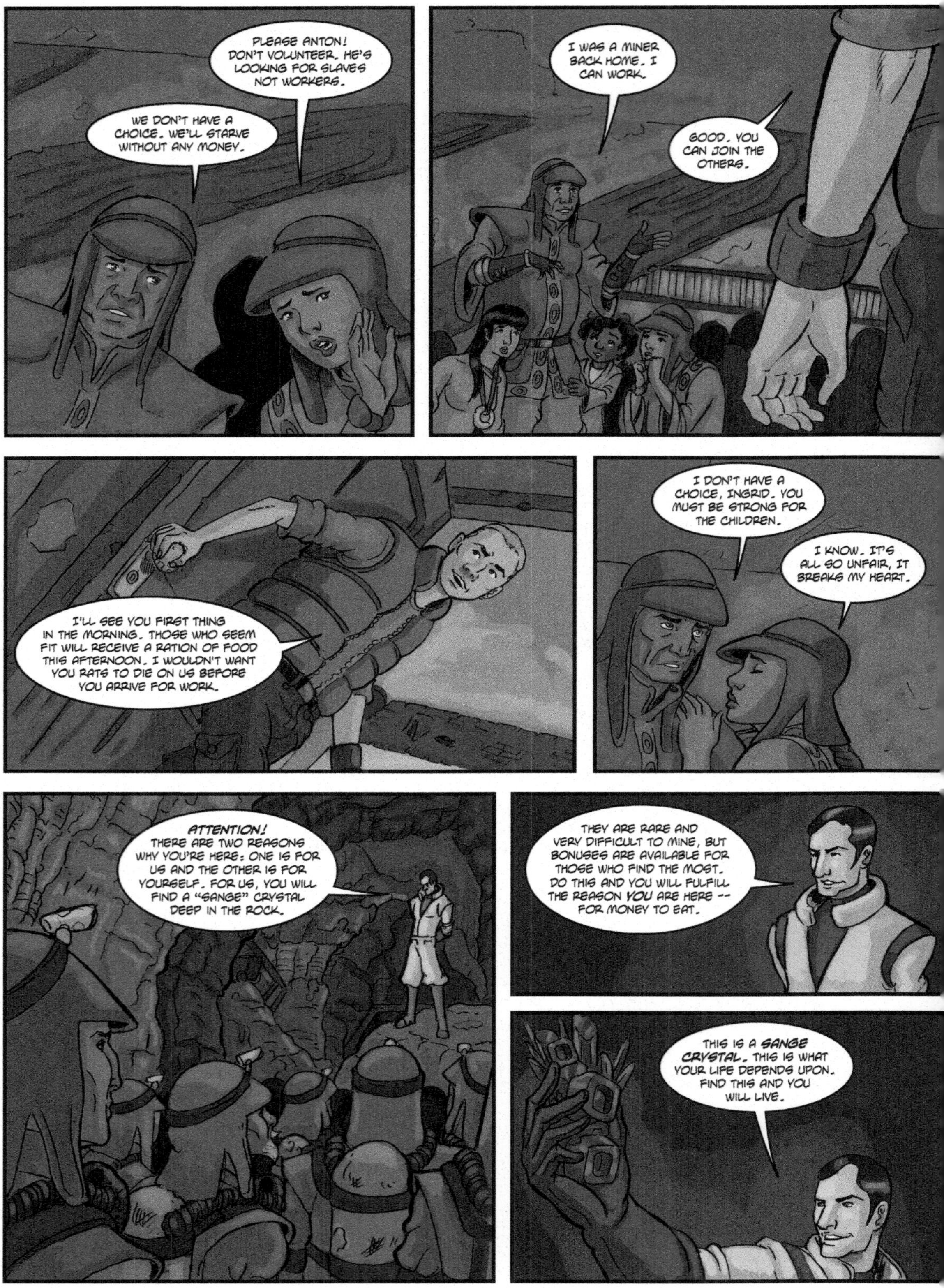
PLEASE ANTON! DON'T VOLUNTEER. HE'S LOOKING FOR SLAVES NOT WORKERS.
WE DON'T HAVE A CHOICE. WE'LL STARVE WITHOUT ANY MONEY.
I WAS A MINER BACK HOME. I CAN WORK.
GOOD. YOU CAN JOIN THE OTHERS.
I'LL SEE YOU FIRST THING IN THE MORNING. THOSE WHO SEEM FIT WILL RECEIVE A RATION OF FOOD THIS AFTERNOON. I WOULDN'T WANT YOU RATS TO DIE ON US BEFORE YOU ARRIVE FOR WORK.
I DON'T HAVE A CHOICE, INGRID. YOU MUST BE STRONG FOR THE CHILDREN.
I KNOW. IT'S ALL SO UNFAIR, IT BREAKS MY HEART.
ATTENTION! THERE ARE TWO REASONS WHY YOU'RE HERE: ONE IS FOR US AND THE OTHER IS FOR YOURSELF. FOR US, YOU WILL FIND A "SANGE" CRYSTAL DEEP IN THE ROCK.
THEY ARE RARE AND VERY DIFFICULT TO MINE, BUT BONUSES ARE AVAILABLE FOR THOSE WHO FIND THE MOST. DO THIS AND YOU WILL FULFILL THE REASON YOU ARE HERE -- FOR MONEY TO EAT.
THIS IS A SANGE CRYSTAL. THIS IS WHAT YOUR LIFE DEPENDS UPON. FIND THIS AND YOU WILL LIVE.

I MUST FIND THAT CRYSTAL.

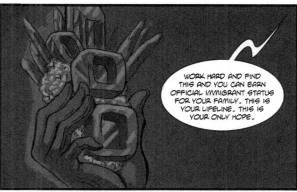

WORK HARD AND FIND THIS AND YOU CAN EARN OFFICIAL IMMIGRANT STATUS FOR YOUR FAMILY. THIS IS YOUR LIFELINE. THIS IS YOUR ONLY HOPE.

ANTON WORKED NIGHT AND DAY, CLINGING TO THE HOPE THE SANGE CRYSTAL WOULD BRING HIS FAMILY A NEW LIFE. MONTHS PASSED BUT THE CRYSTALS WERE ELUSIVE, BUT THE MINERS WORKED ON, STRUGGLING ON MEAGER RATIONS.

ALL OF THE MINERS EVENTUALLY SUCCUMBED TO THE POISONOUS FUMES THAT LURKED DEEP IN THE MINES AND COLLAPSED FROM EXHAUSTION.

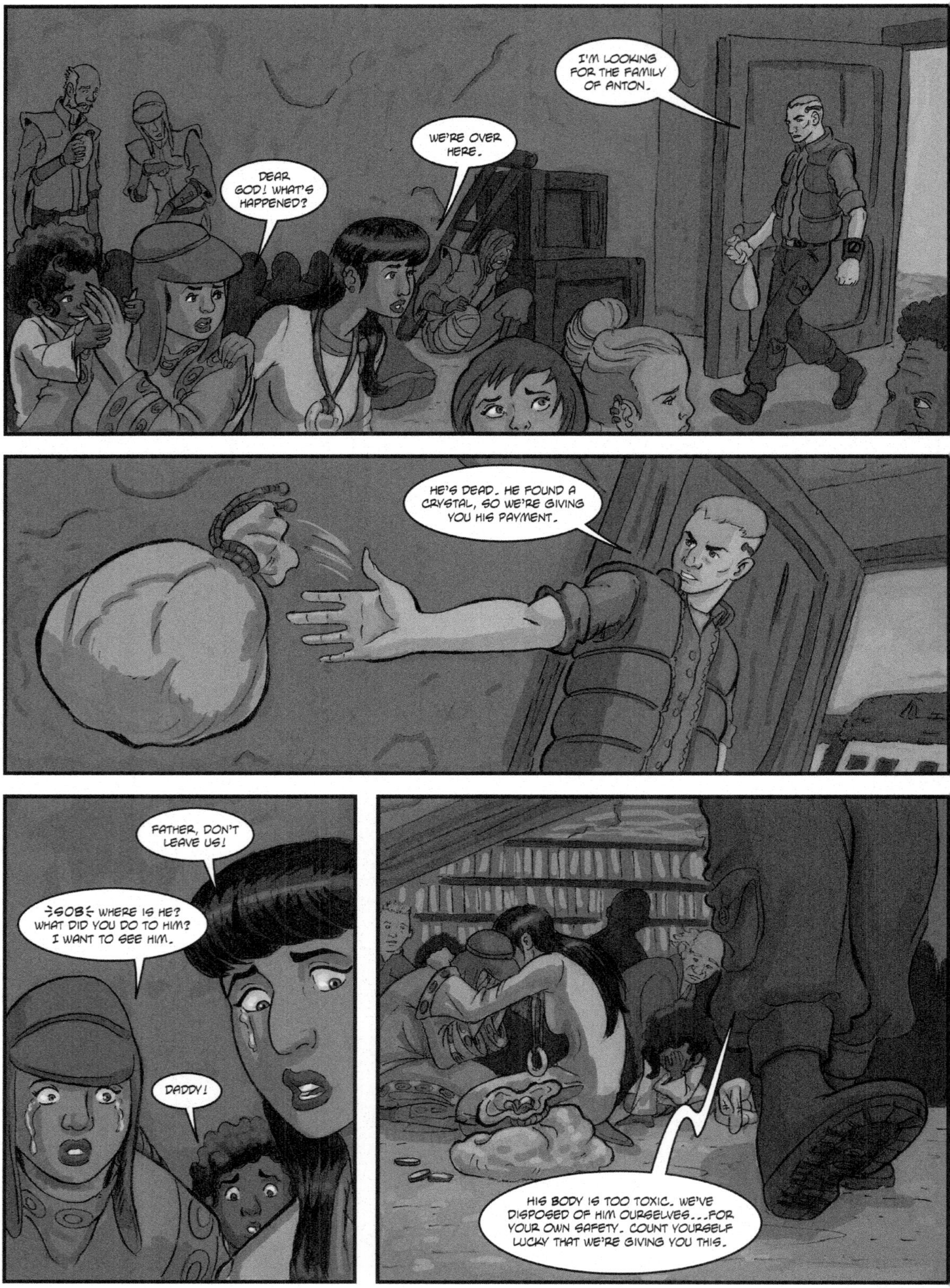
I'M LOOKING FOR THE FAMILY OF ANTON.
WE'RE OVER HERE.
DEAR GOD! WHAT'S HAPPENED?
HE'S DEAD. HE FOUND A CRYSTAL, SO WE'RE GIVING YOU HIS PAYMENT.
FATHER, DON'T LEAVE US!
≶SOB≷ WHERE IS HE? WHAT DID YOU DO TO HIM? I WANT TO SEE HIM.
DADDY!
HIS BODY IS TOO TOXIC. WE'VE DISPOSED OF HIM OURSELVES...FOR YOUR OWN SAFETY. COUNT YOURSELF LUCKY THAT WE'RE GIVING YOU THIS.

THE SUBJECT IS NOW READY FOR EXTRACTION.
HE IS OF ABYAN ORIGIN, CLOSE TO 40. THE GESTATION PERIOD IS IN ITS LAST STAGE.
BEGINNING THE INCISION.
THE CRYSTAL HAS GROWN TO FULL SIZE AND IS COMPLETELY INTACT. EXTRAORDINARY.
BE CAREFUL! I DON'T WANT ONE SINGLE CRACK... IT'S BEAUTIFUL.

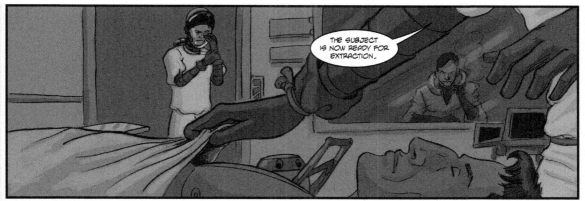

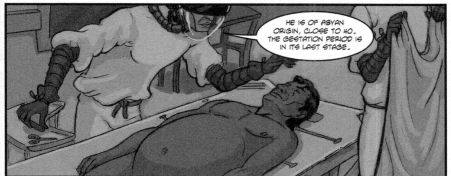

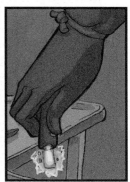

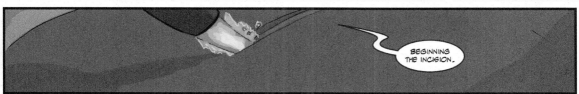

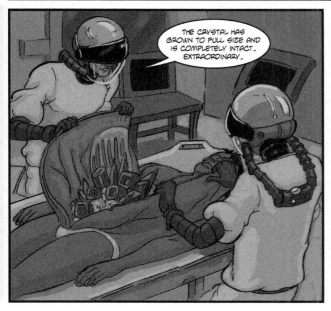

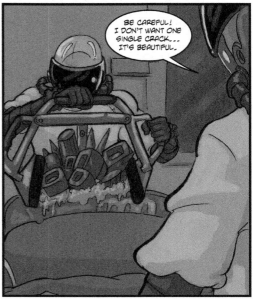

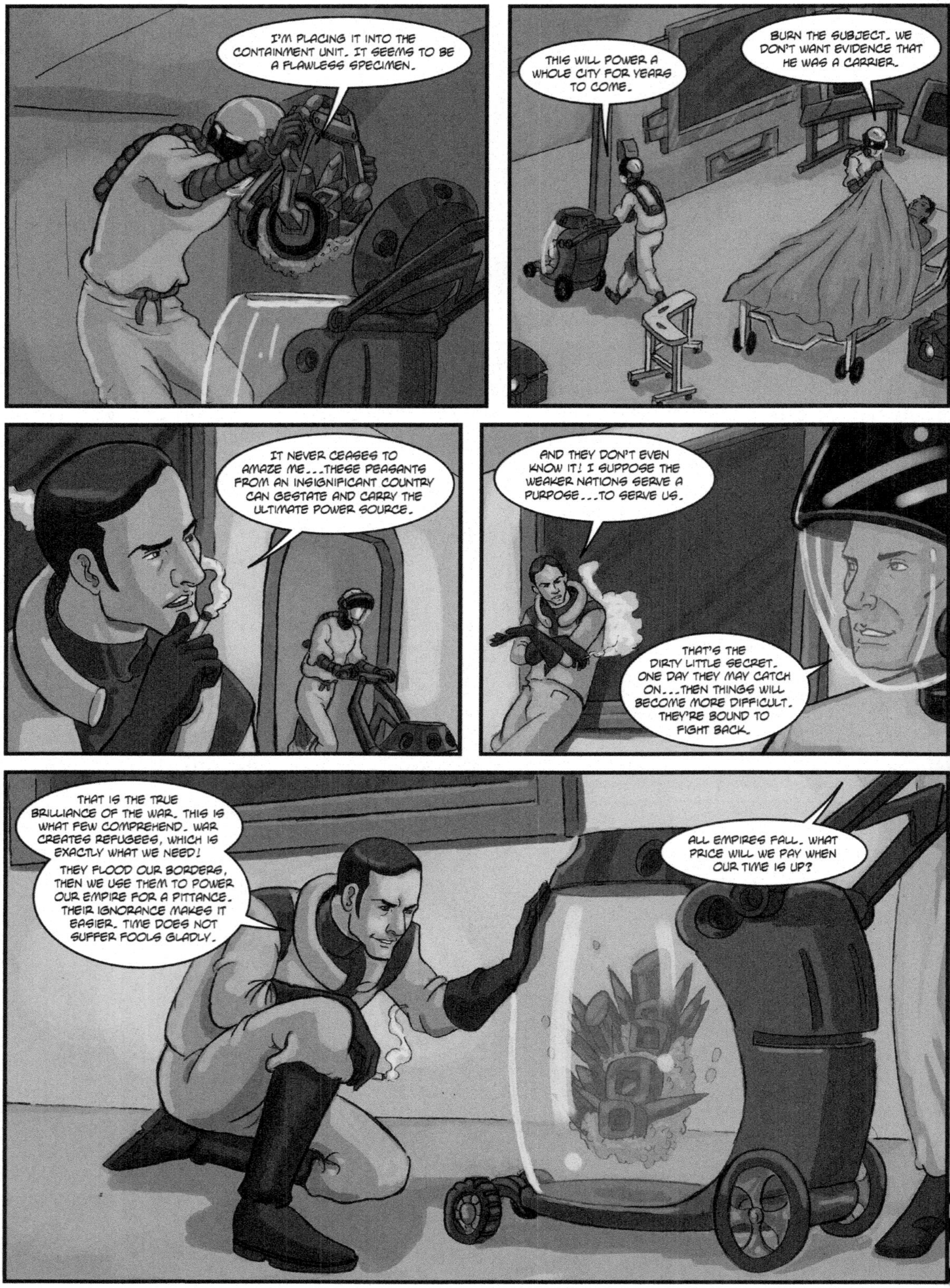
I'M PLACING IT INTO THE CONTAINMENT UNIT. IT SEEMS TO BE A FLAWLESS SPECIMEN.
THIS WILL POWER A WHOLE CITY FOR YEARS TO COME.
BURN THE SUBJECT. WE DON'T WANT EVIDENCE THAT HE WAS A CARRIER.
IT NEVER CEASES TO AMAZE ME...THESE PEASANTS FROM AN INSIGNIFICANT COUNTRY CAN GESTATE AND CARRY THE ULTIMATE POWER SOURCE.
AND THEY DON'T EVEN KNOW IT! I SUPPOSE THE WEAKER NATIONS SERVE A PURPOSE...TO SERVE US.
THAT'S THE DIRTY LITTLE SECRET. ONE DAY THEY MAY CATCH ON...THEN THINGS WILL BECOME MORE DIFFICULT. THEY'RE BOUND TO FIGHT BACK.
THAT IS THE TRUE BRILLIANCE OF THE WAR. THIS IS WHAT FEW COMPREHEND. WAR CREATES REFUGEES, WHICH IS EXACTLY WHAT WE NEED!
THEY FLOOD OUR BORDERS, THEN WE USE THEM TO POWER OUR EMPIRE FOR A PITTANCE. THEIR IGNORANCE MAKES IT EASIER. TIME DOES NOT SUFFER FOOLS GLADLY.
ALL EMPIRES FALL. WHAT PRICE WILL WE PAY WHEN OUR TIME IS UP?

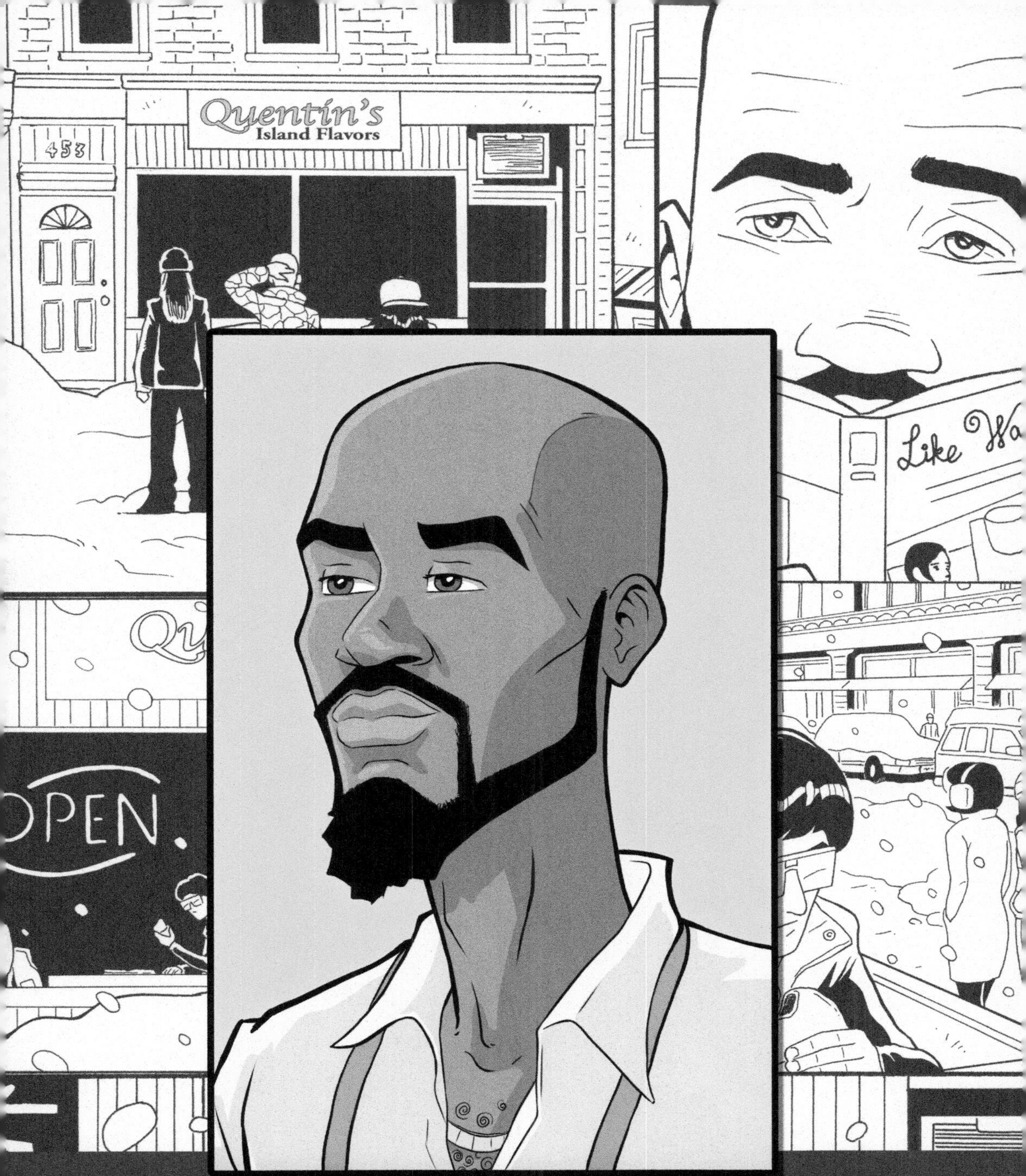
Quentin's
Island Flavors
453
OPEN

Coming In From the Cold
A SNOWDAZE Tale

STORY BY LEONARDO FAIERMAN
ART & LETTERS BY MARCUS KWAME ANDERSON

Leonardo Faierman, Writer

Buenos Aires / United States

Born in Buenos Aires but left at two years old. That was a weird day at school when I learned I'd never become president; had to settle for astronaut dreams. In the past I've published some poetry (I'm talking Kinko's), made some music, and slowly became a professional creative procrastinator with a fistful of unpaid bills. I'm 31 years of age now, paper-pusher extraordinaire, a sleeper-agent waiting for the time to strike. I've been wanting to write comics for over 20 years. This is it.

Marcus Kwame Anderson, Artist

Jamaica / United States

I was born in Kingston, Jamaica and moved to Albany, NY at an early age. I've been creating art for as long as I can remember. A black nerd long before it became somewhat en vogue, I grew up drawing comic characters and books. In high school I always had two things with me: a sketchbook and a Walkman. They were a lifeline that helped to keep me sane. That lanky teen grew up, had a family, became a teacher, poet, emcee, illustrator, and last, but certainly not least, co-creator of *Snow Daze*.

snowdazecomic.com

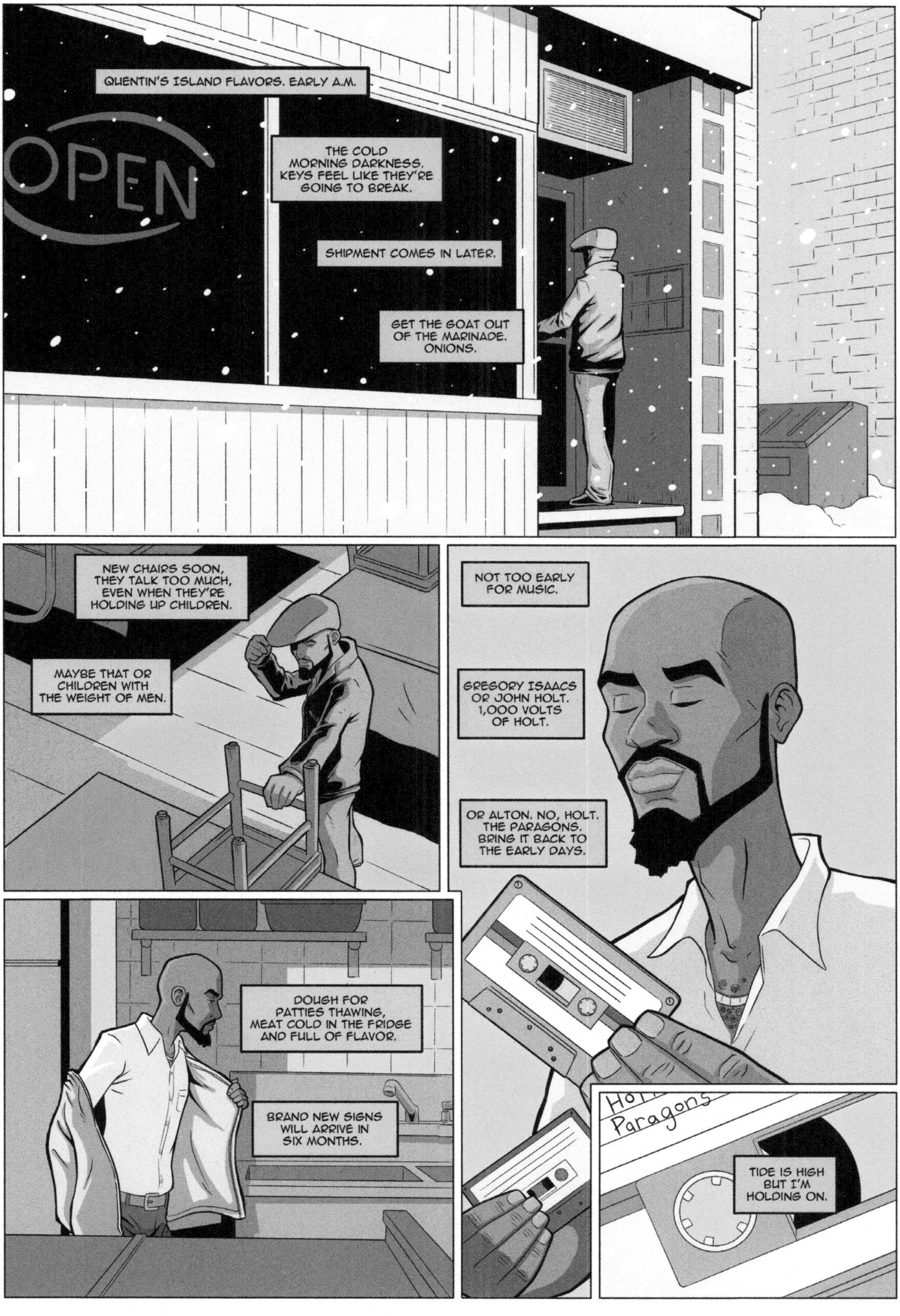
QUENTIN'S ISLAND FLAVORS. EARLY A.M.
OPEN
THE COLD MORNING DARKNESS. KEYS FEEL LIKE THEY'RE GOING TO BREAK.
SHIPMENT COMES IN LATER.
GET THE GOAT OUT OF THE MARINADE. ONIONS.
NEW CHAIRS SOON, THEY TALK TOO MUCH, EVEN WHEN THEY'RE HOLDING UP CHILDREN.
MAYBE THAT OR CHILDREN WITH THE WEIGHT OF MEN.
NOT TOO EARLY FOR MUSIC.
GREGORY ISAACS OR JOHN HOLT. 1,000 VOLTS OF HOLT.
OR ALTON. NO, HOLT. THE PARAGONS. BRING IT BACK TO THE EARLY DAYS.
DOUGH FOR PATTIES THAWING, MEAT COLD IN THE FRIDGE AND FULL OF FLAVOR.
BRAND NEW SIGNS WILL ARRIVE IN SIX MONTHS.
Paragons
TIDE IS HIGH BUT I'M HOLDING ON.

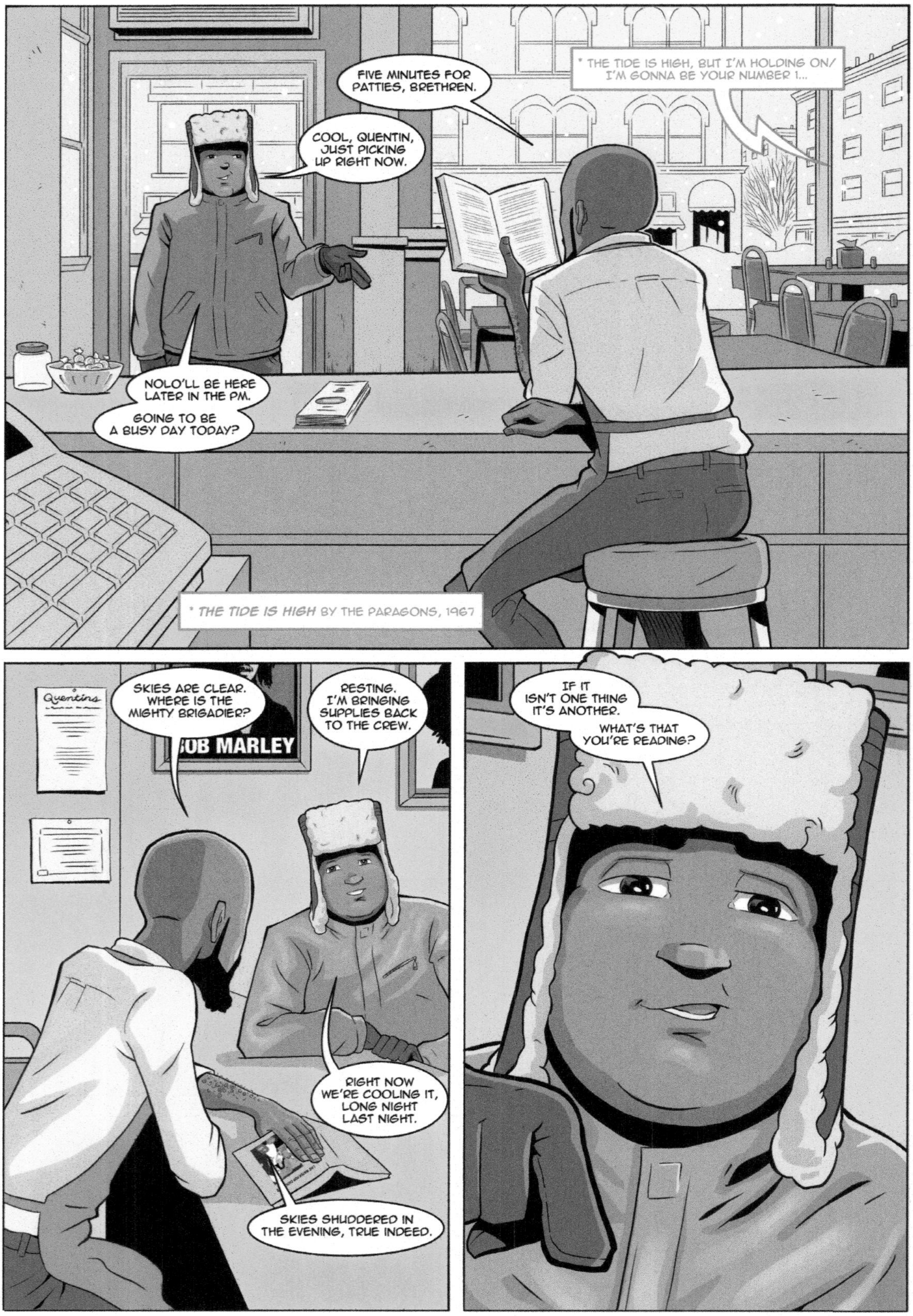
FIVE MINUTES FOR PATTIES, BRETHREN.
* THE TIDE IS HIGH, BUT I'M HOLDING ON/ I'M GONNA BE YOUR NUMBER 1...
COOL, QUENTIN, JUST PICKING UP RIGHT NOW.
NOLO'LL BE HERE LATER IN THE PM.
GOING TO BE A BUSY DAY TODAY?
* THE TIDE IS HIGH BY THE PARAGONS, 1967
Quentins
BOB MARLEY
SKIES ARE CLEAR. WHERE IS THE MIGHTY BRIGADIER?
RESTING. I'M BRINGING SUPPLIES BACK TO THE CREW.
RIGHT NOW WE'RE COOLING IT, LONG NIGHT LAST NIGHT.
SKIES SHUDDERED IN THE EVENING, TRUE INDEED.
IF IT ISN'T ONE THING IT'S ANOTHER.
WHAT'S THAT YOU'RE READING?

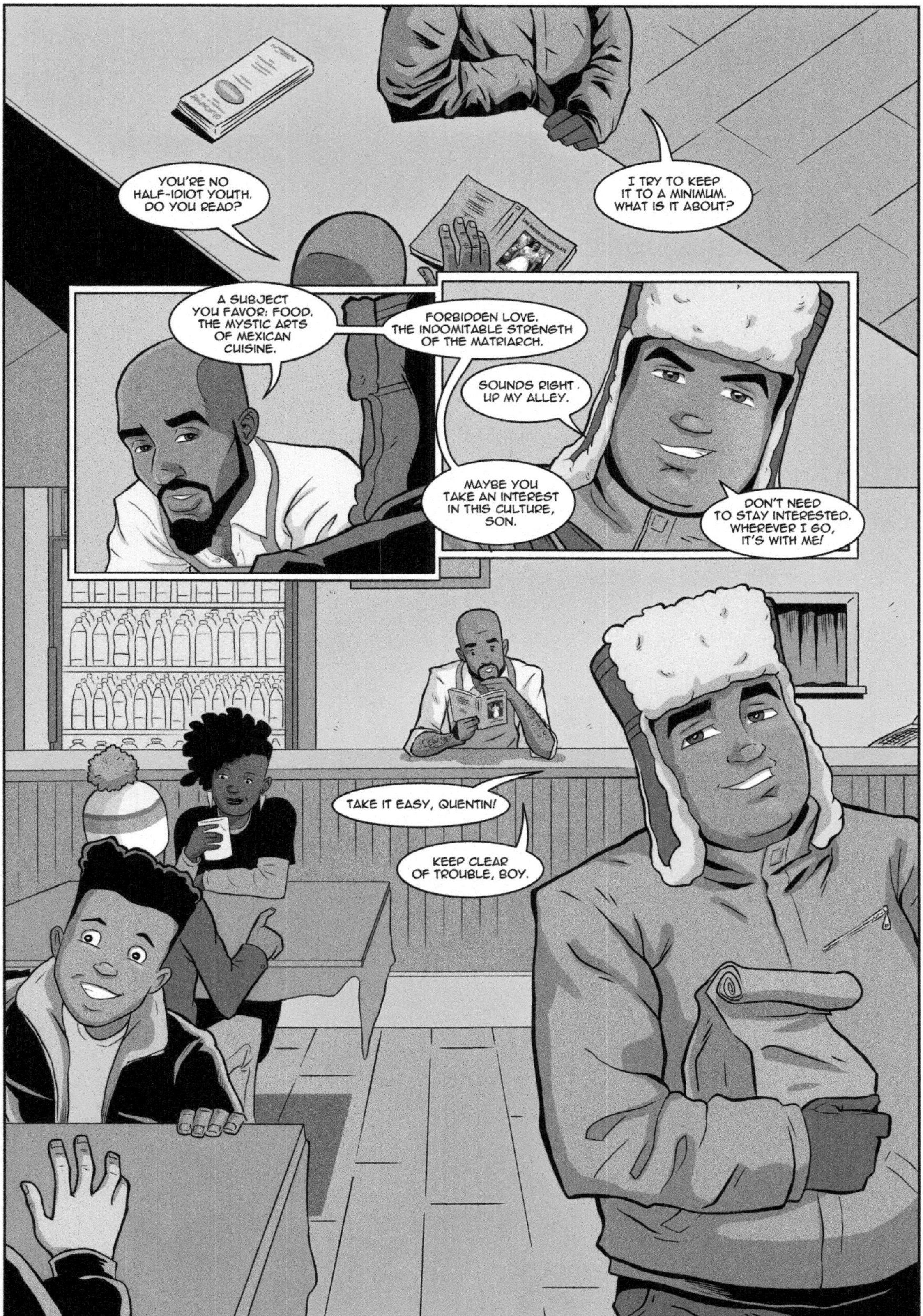
YOU'RE NO HALF-IDIOT YOUTH. DO YOU READ?
I TRY TO KEEP IT TO A MINIMUM. WHAT IS IT ABOUT?
A SUBJECT YOU FAVOR: FOOD. THE MYSTIC ARTS OF MEXICAN CUISINE.
FORBIDDEN LOVE. THE INDOMITABLE STRENGTH OF THE MATRIARCH.
SOUNDS RIGHT UP MY ALLEY.
MAYBE YOU TAKE AN INTEREST IN THIS CULTURE, SON.
DON'T NEED TO STAY INTERESTED. WHEREVER I GO, IT'S WITH ME!
TAKE IT EASY, QUENTIN!
KEEP CLEAR OF TROUBLE, BOY.

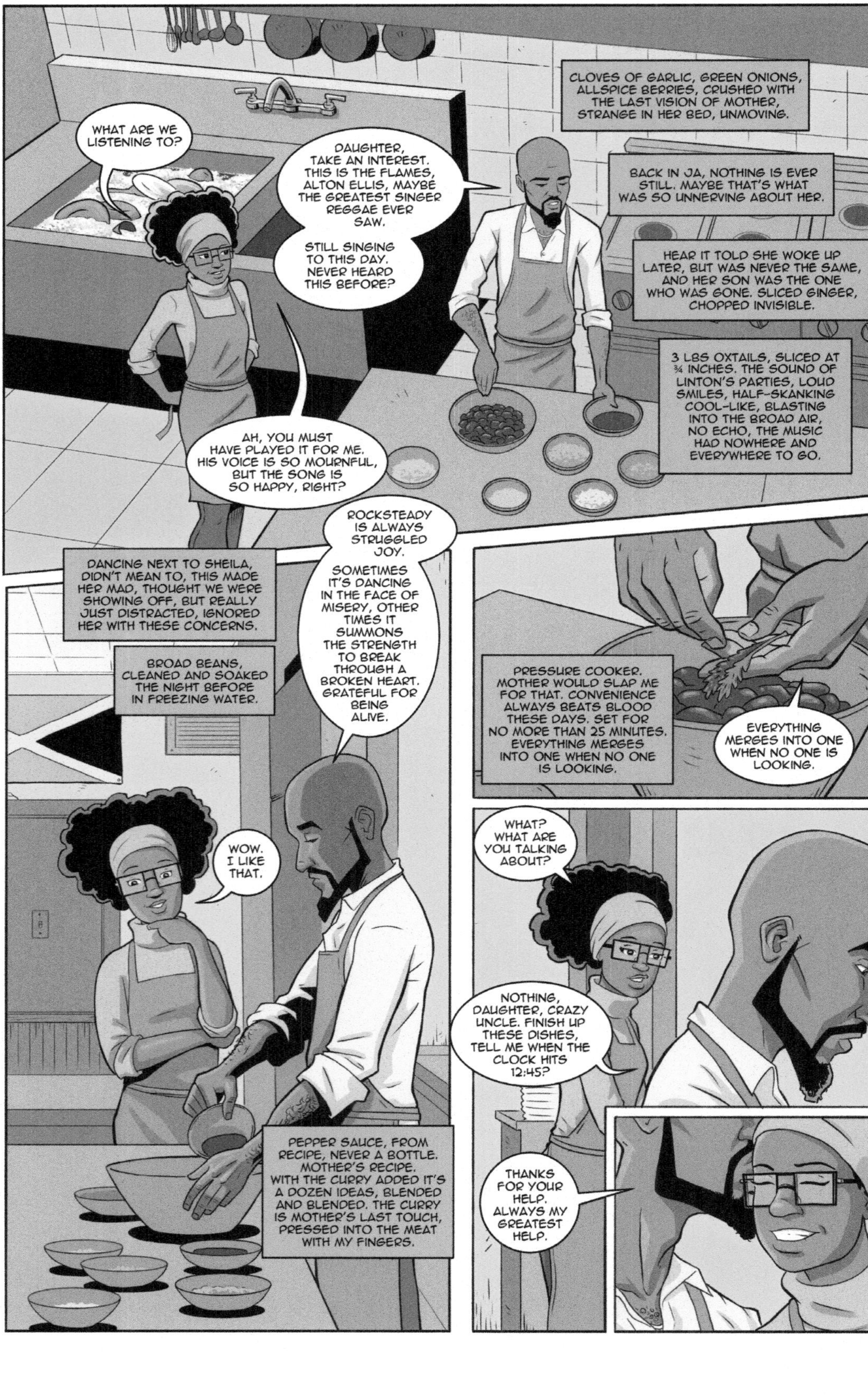
CLOVES OF GARLIC, GREEN ONIONS, ALLSPICE BERRIES, CRUSHED WITH THE LAST VISION OF MOTHER, STRANGE IN HER BED, UNMOVING.
WHAT ARE WE LISTENING TO?
DAUGHTER, TAKE AN INTEREST. THIS IS THE FLAMES, ALTON ELLIS, MAYBE THE GREATEST SINGER REGGAE EVER SAW.
STILL SINGING TO THIS DAY. NEVER HEARD THIS BEFORE?
BACK IN JA, NOTHING IS EVER STILL. MAYBE THAT'S WHAT WAS SO UNNERVING ABOUT HER.
HEAR IT TOLD SHE WOKE UP LATER, BUT WAS NEVER THE SAME, AND HER SON WAS THE ONE WHO WAS GONE. SLICED GINGER, CHOPPED INVISIBLE.
3 LBS OXTAILS, SLICED AT ¾ INCHES. THE SOUND OF LINTON'S PARTIES, LOUD SMILES, HALF-SKANKING COOL-LIKE, BLASTING INTO THE BROAD AIR, NO ECHO, THE MUSIC HAD NOWHERE AND EVERYWHERE TO GO.
AH, YOU MUST HAVE PLAYED IT FOR ME. HIS VOICE IS SO MOURNFUL, BUT THE SONG IS SO HAPPY, RIGHT?
DANCING NEXT TO SHEILA, DIDN'T MEAN TO, THIS MADE HER MAD, THOUGHT WE WERE SHOWING OFF, BUT REALLY JUST DISTRACTED, IGNORED HER WITH THESE CONCERNS.
BROAD BEANS, CLEANED AND SOAKED THE NIGHT BEFORE IN FREEZING WATER.
ROCKSTEADY IS ALWAYS STRUGGLED JOY.
SOMETIMES IT'S DANCING IN THE FACE OF MISERY, OTHER TIMES IT SUMMONS THE STRENGTH TO BREAK THROUGH A BROKEN HEART. GRATEFUL FOR BEING ALIVE.
WOW. I LIKE THAT.
PEPPER SAUCE, FROM RECIPE, NEVER A BOTTLE. MOTHER'S RECIPE. WITH THE CURRY ADDED IT'S A DOZEN IDEAS, BLENDED AND BLENDED. THE CURRY IS MOTHER'S LAST TOUCH, PRESSED INTO THE MEAT WITH MY FINGERS.
PRESSURE COOKER. MOTHER WOULD SLAP ME FOR THAT. CONVENIENCE ALWAYS BEATS BLOOD THESE DAYS. SET FOR NO MORE THAN 25 MINUTES. EVERYTHING MERGES INTO ONE WHEN NO ONE IS LOOKING.
EVERYTHING MERGES INTO ONE WHEN NO ONE IS LOOKING.
WHAT? WHAT ARE YOU TALKING ABOUT?
NOTHING, DAUGHTER, CRAZY UNCLE. FINISH UP THESE DISHES, TELL ME WHEN THE CLOCK HITS 12:45?
THANKS FOR YOUR HELP. ALWAYS MY GREATEST HELP.

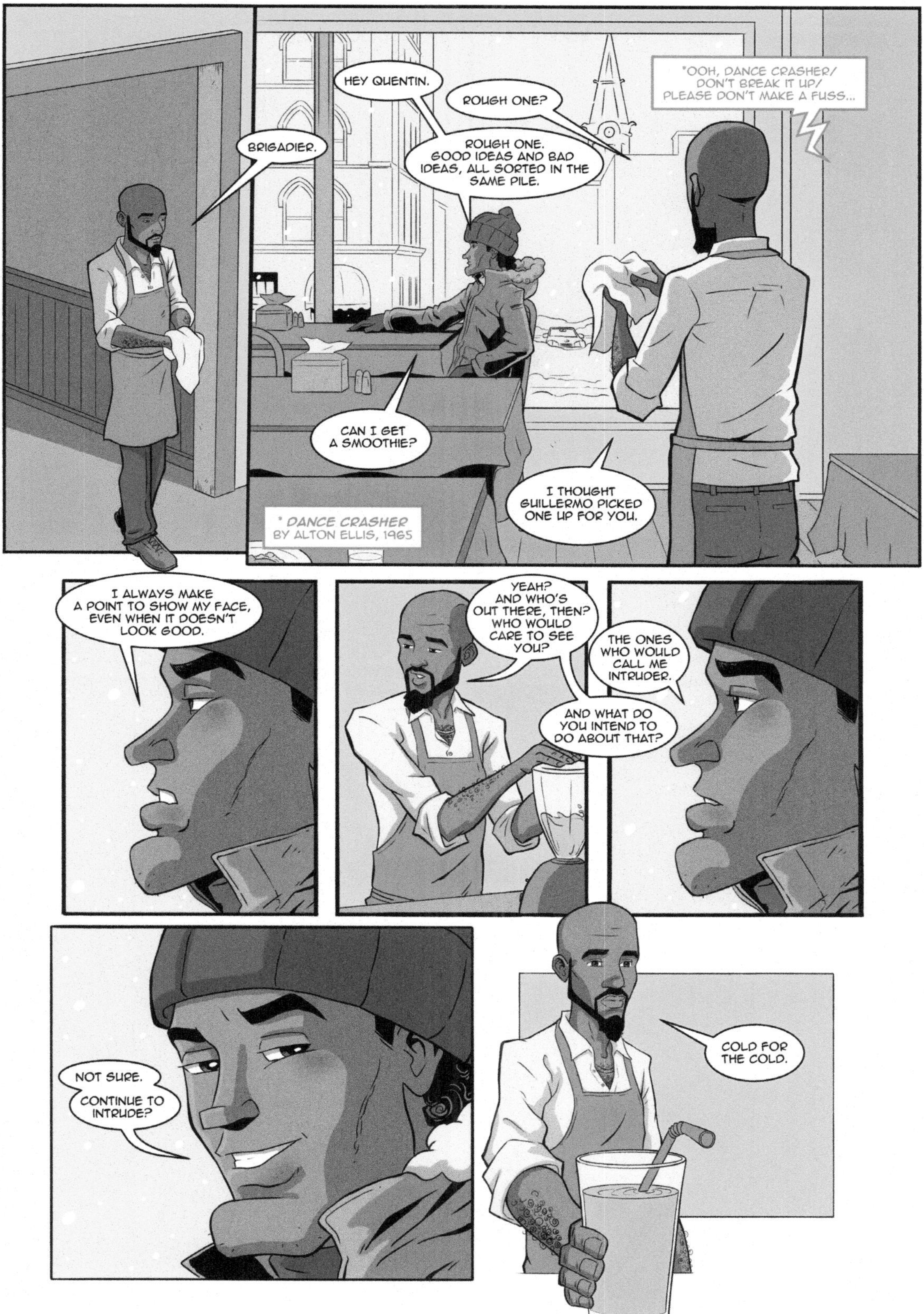
BRIGADIER.
HEY QUENTIN.
ROUGH ONE?
ROUGH ONE. GOOD IDEAS AND BAD IDEAS, ALL SORTED IN THE SAME PILE.
*OOH, DANCE CRASHER/ DON'T BREAK IT UP/ PLEASE DON'T MAKE A FUSS...
CAN I GET A SMOOTHIE?
I THOUGHT GUILLERMO PICKED ONE UP FOR YOU.
* DANCE CRASHER BY ALTON ELLIS, 1965
I ALWAYS MAKE A POINT TO SHOW MY FACE, EVEN WHEN IT DOESN'T LOOK GOOD.
YEAH? AND WHO'S OUT THERE, THEN? WHO WOULD CARE TO SEE YOU?
AND WHAT DO YOU INTEND TO DO ABOUT THAT?
THE ONES WHO WOULD CALL ME INTRUDER.
NOT SURE.
CONTINUE TO INTRUDE?
COLD FOR THE COLD.

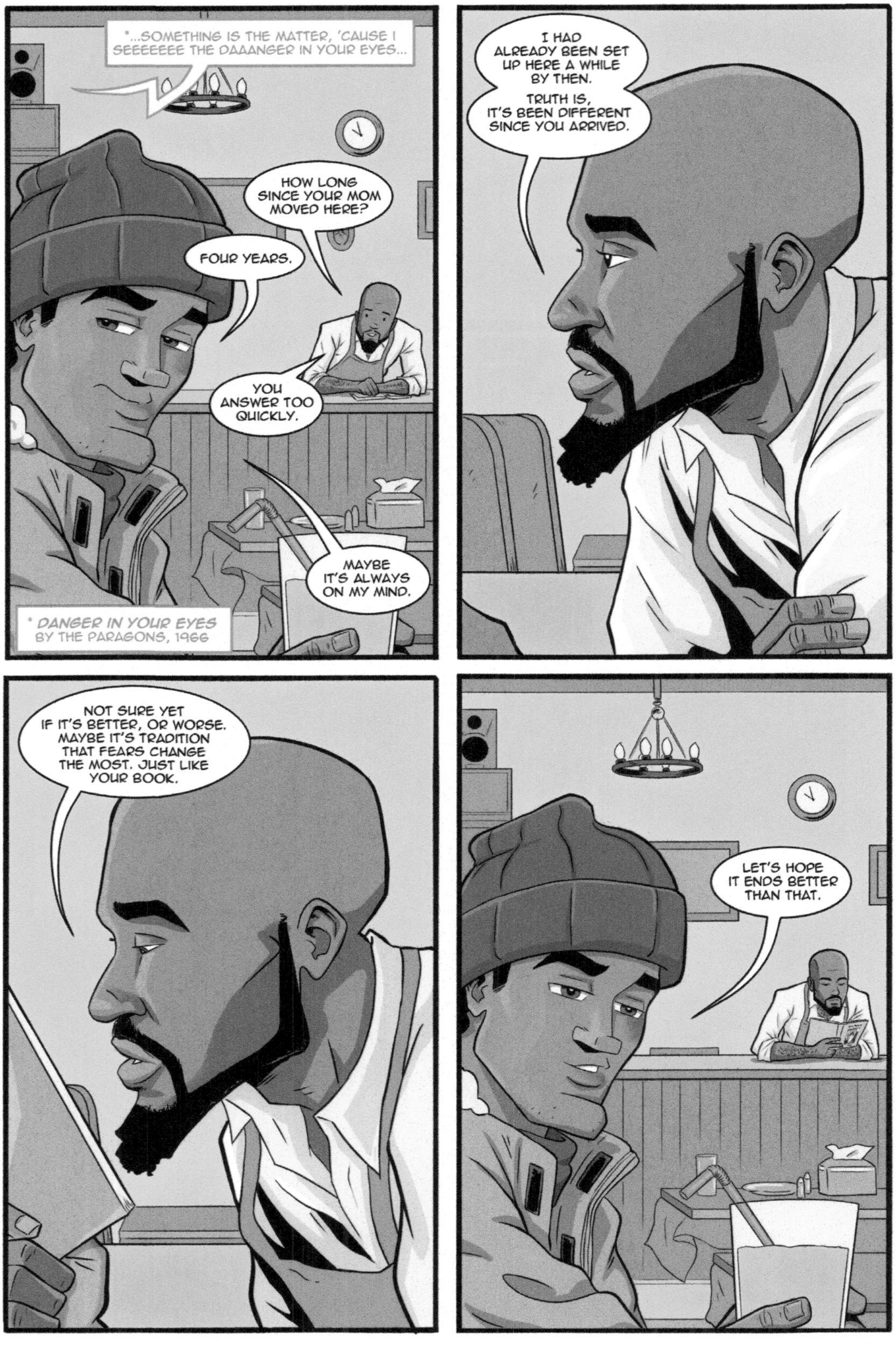
*...SOMETHING IS THE MATTER, 'CAUSE I SEEEEEEE THE DAAANGER IN YOUR EYES...
HOW LONG SINCE YOUR MOM MOVED HERE?
FOUR YEARS.
YOU ANSWER TOO QUICKLY.
MAYBE IT'S ALWAYS ON MY MIND.
* DANGER IN YOUR EYES BY THE PARAGONS, 1966
I HAD ALREADY BEEN SET UP HERE A WHILE BY THEN.
TRUTH IS, IT'S BEEN DIFFERENT SINCE YOU ARRIVED.
NOT SURE YET IF IT'S BETTER, OR WORSE. MAYBE IT'S TRADITION THAT FEARS CHANGE THE MOST. JUST LIKE YOUR BOOK.
LET'S HOPE IT ENDS BETTER THAN THAT.

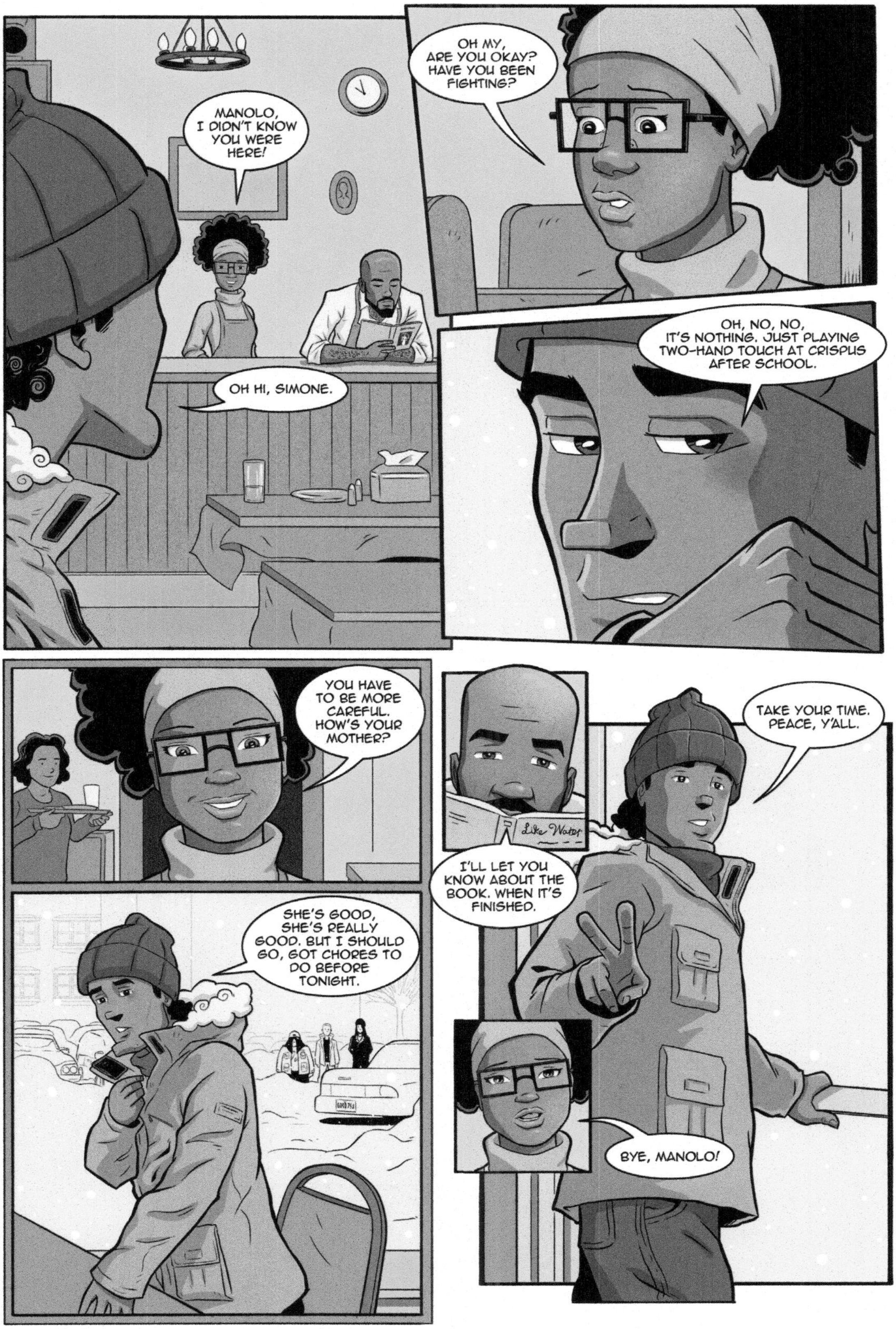
MANOLO, I DIDN'T KNOW YOU WERE HERE!
OH HI, SIMONE.
OH MY, ARE YOU OKAY? HAVE YOU BEEN FIGHTING?
OH, NO, NO, IT'S NOTHING. JUST PLAYING TWO-HAND TOUCH AT CRISPUS AFTER SCHOOL.
YOU HAVE TO BE MORE CAREFUL. HOW'S YOUR MOTHER?
SHE'S GOOD, SHE'S REALLY GOOD. BUT I SHOULD GO, GOT CHORES TO DO BEFORE TONIGHT.
Like Water
I'LL LET YOU KNOW ABOUT THE BOOK. WHEN IT'S FINISHED.
TAKE YOUR TIME. PEACE, Y'ALL.
BYE, MANOLO!

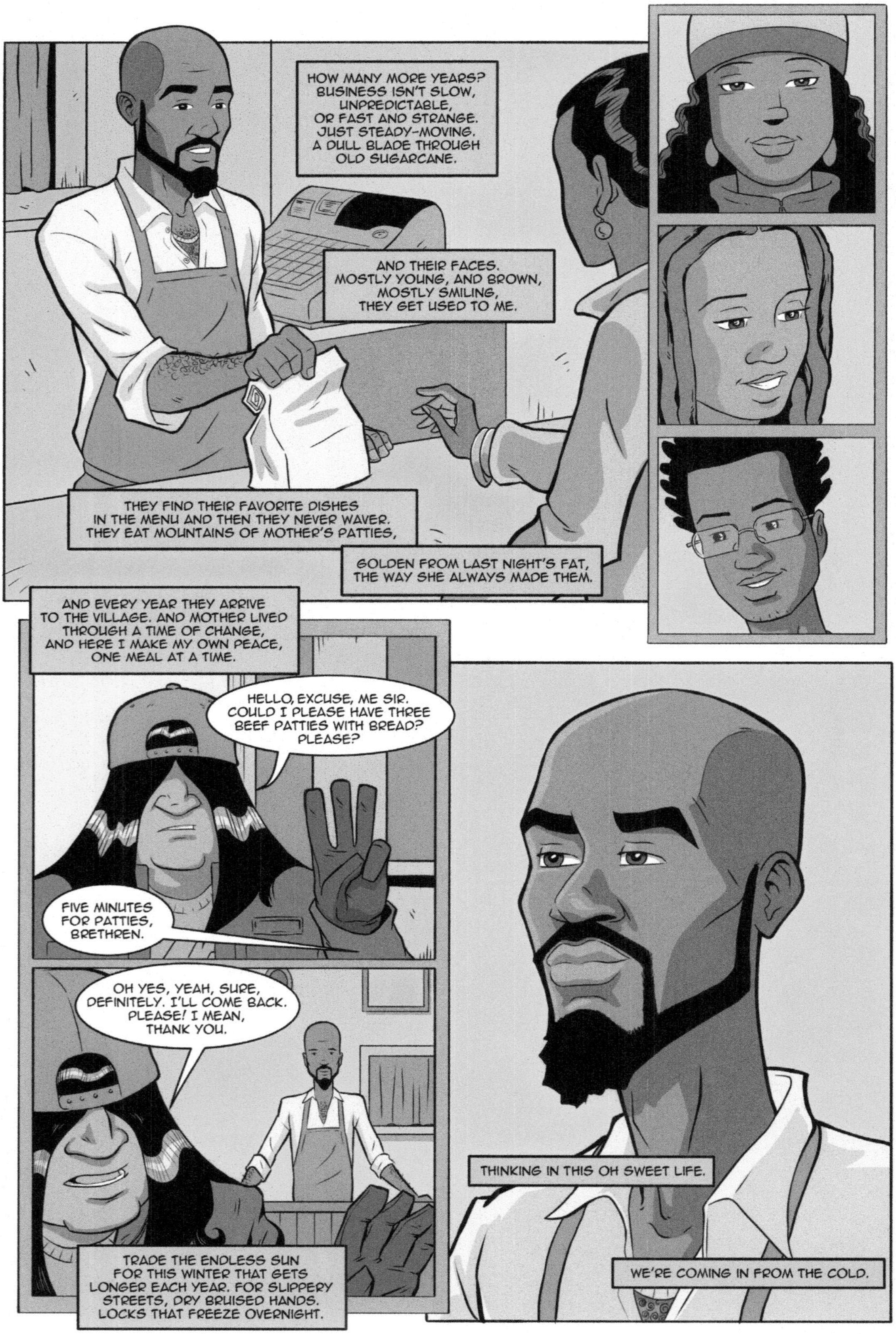

HOW MANY MORE YEARS? BUSINESS ISN'T SLOW, UNPREDICTABLE, OR FAST AND STRANGE. JUST STEADY-MOVING. A DULL BLADE THROUGH OLD SUGARCANE.
AND THEIR FACES. MOSTLY YOUNG, AND BROWN, MOSTLY SMILING, THEY GET USED TO ME.
THEY FIND THEIR FAVORITE DISHES IN THE MENU AND THEN THEY NEVER WAVER. THEY EAT MOUNTAINS OF MOTHER'S PATTIES,
GOLDEN FROM LAST NIGHT'S FAT, THE WAY SHE ALWAYS MADE THEM.
AND EVERY YEAR THEY ARRIVE TO THE VILLAGE. AND MOTHER LIVED THROUGH A TIME OF CHANGE, AND HERE I MAKE MY OWN PEACE, ONE MEAL AT A TIME.
HELLO, EXCUSE, ME SIR. COULD I PLEASE HAVE THREE BEEF PATTIES WITH BREAD? PLEASE?
FIVE MINUTES FOR PATTIES, BRETHREN.
OH YES, YEAH, SURE, DEFINITELY. I'LL COME BACK. PLEASE! I MEAN, THANK YOU.
TRADE THE ENDLESS SUN FOR THIS WINTER THAT GETS LONGER EACH YEAR. FOR SLIPPERY STREETS, DRY BRUISED HANDS. LOCKS THAT FREEZE OVERNIGHT.
THINKING IN THIS OH SWEET LIFE.
WE'RE COMING IN FROM THE COLD.

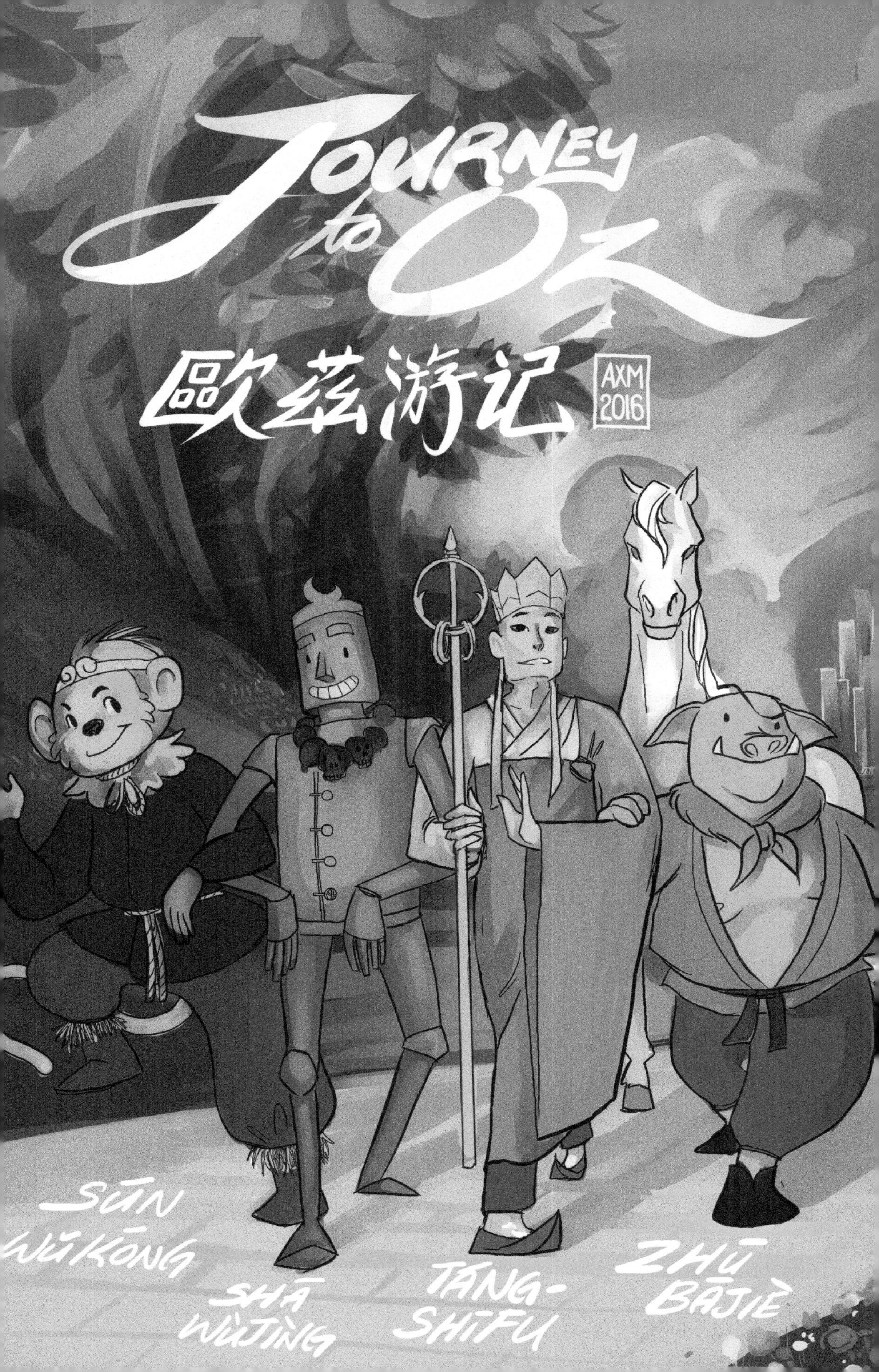
Journey to Oz
歐茲游记
AXM 2016
SŪN WÙKŌNG
SHĀ WÙJÌNG
TÁNG-SHĪFU
ZHŪ BĀJIÈ

Arianna Mao, Writer / Artist

China / Canada

Arianna Mao is a 1.5 generation Chinese immigrant currently living in beautiful Vancouver, Canada. She is fascinated by the idea of amalgamating, combining, and remixing different parts of her cultural background and heritage. More than that, because she lives in such a multicultural society, she is able to carefully craft her cultural experience, taking aspects and memories of her homeland and weaving it into the context of her surroundings.

She is a graduate of the Environmental Design program at University of British Columbia and is currently working as a drafter, painter, and illustrator. Current projects include short comics about topics as diverse as inexplicably falling in love with a best friend, superheroes, and exploring the unknown.

bellewether.tumblr.com

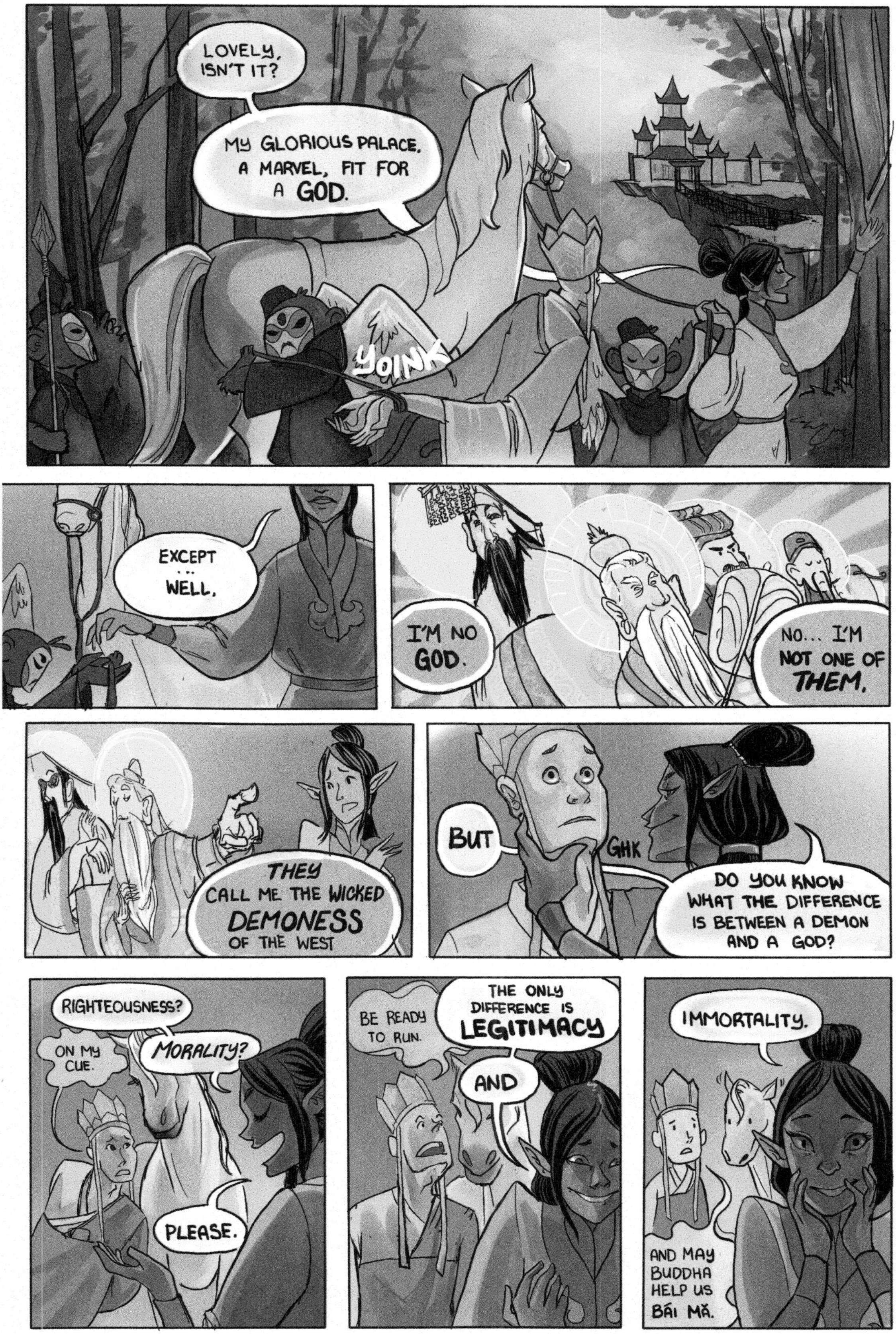
LOVELY, ISN'T IT?
MY GLORIOUS PALACE. A MARVEL, FIT FOR A GOD.
YOINK
EXCEPT ... WELL,
I'M NO GOD.
NO... I'M NOT ONE OF THEM,
THEY CALL ME THE WICKED DEMONESS OF THE WEST
BUT
GHK
DO YOU KNOW WHAT THE DIFFERENCE IS BETWEEN A DEMON AND A GOD?
RIGHTEOUSNESS?
ON MY CUE.
MORALITY?
PLEASE.
BE READY TO RUN.
THE ONLY DIFFERENCE IS LEGITIMACY
AND
IMMORTALITY.
AND MAY BUDDHA HELP US BÁI MǍ.

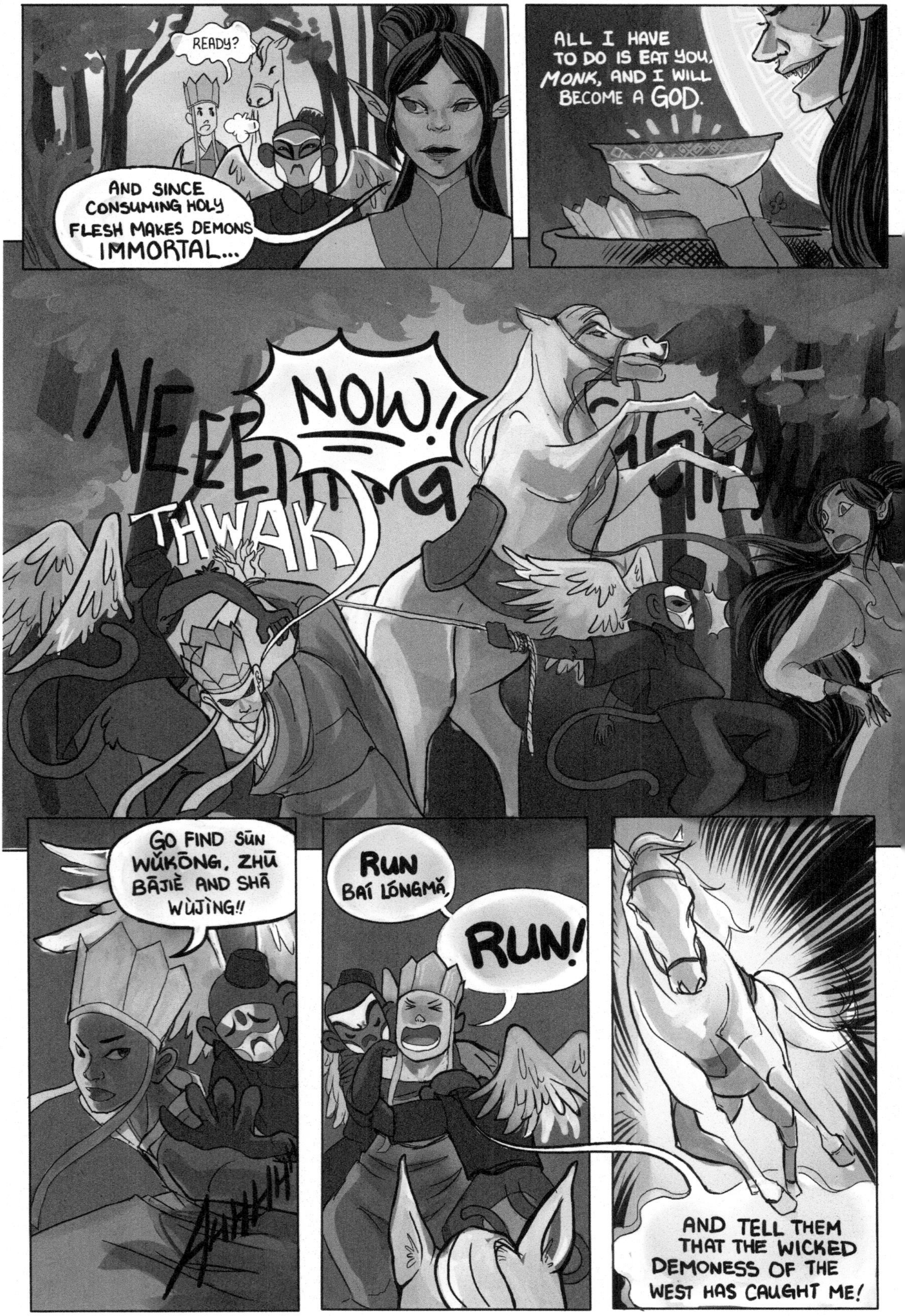
READY?
AND SINCE CONSUMING HOLY FLESH MAKES DEMONS IMMORTAL...
ALL I HAVE TO DO IS EAT YOU, MONK, AND I WILL BECOME A GOD.
NEEEIIIIIIIIGH
NOW!
THWAK
GO FIND SŪN WǓKŌNG, ZHŪ BĀJIÈ AND SHĀ WÙJÌNG!!
RUN BÁI LÓNGMǍ,
RUN!
AND TELL THEM THAT THE WICKED DEMONESS OF THE WEST HAS CAUGHT ME!

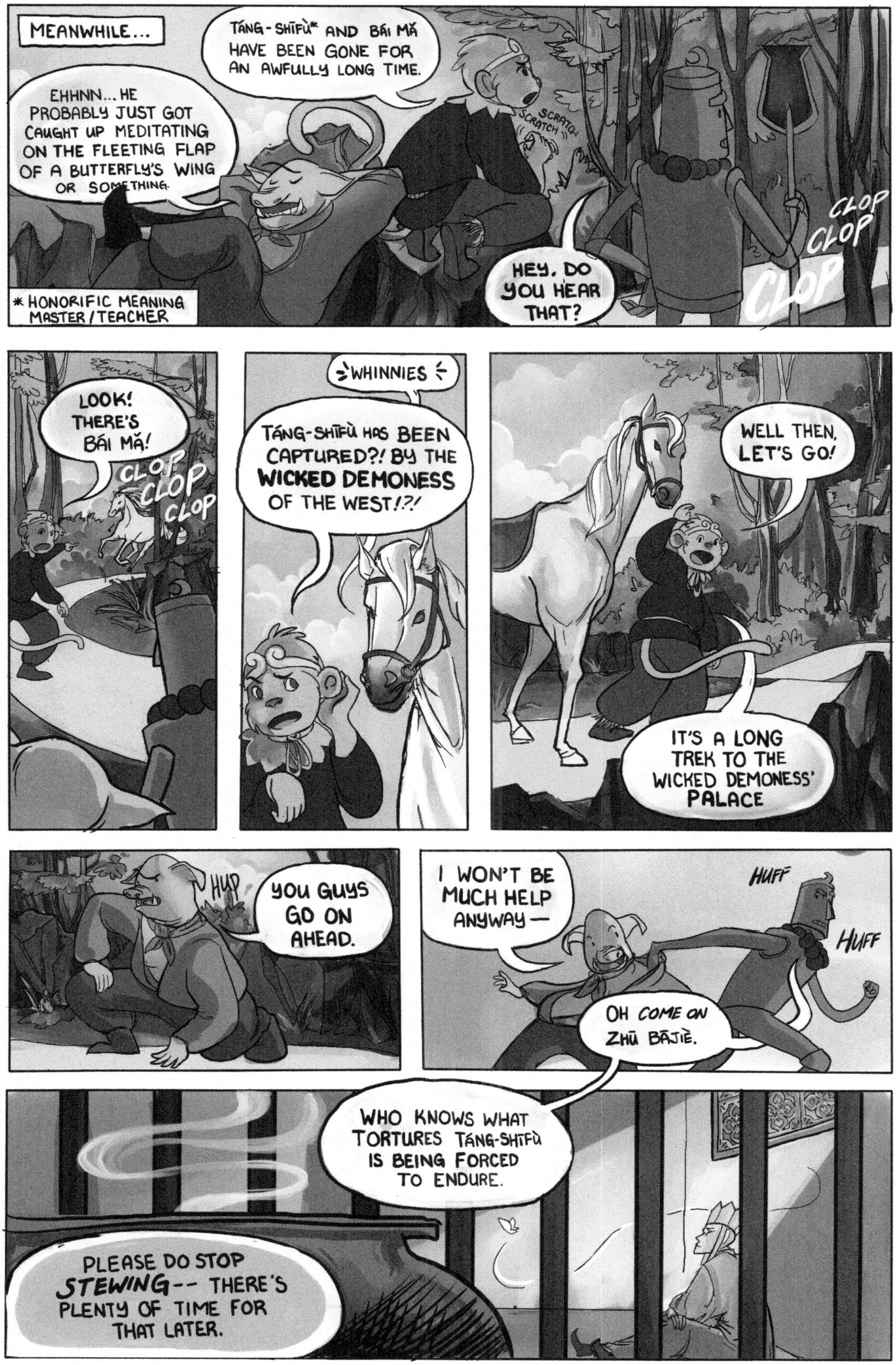

MEANWHILE...
TÁNG-SHĪFÙ* AND BÁI MǍ HAVE BEEN GONE FOR AN AWFULLY LONG TIME.
EHHNN... HE PROBABLY JUST GOT CAUGHT UP MEDITATING ON THE FLEETING FLAP OF A BUTTERFLY'S WING OR SOMETHING.
SCRATCH SCRATCH
HEY, DO YOU HEAR THAT?
CLOP CLOP CLOP
*HONORIFIC MEANING MASTER/TEACHER
LOOK! THERE'S BÁI MǍ!
CLOP CLOP CLOP
WHINNIES
TÁNG-SHĪFÙ HAS BEEN CAPTURED?! BY THE WICKED DEMONESS OF THE WEST!?!
WELL THEN, LET'S GO!
IT'S A LONG TREK TO THE WICKED DEMONESS' PALACE
HUP
YOU GUYS GO ON AHEAD.
I WON'T BE MUCH HELP ANYWAY—
HUFF
HUFF
OH COME ON ZHŪ BĀJIÈ.
WHO KNOWS WHAT TORTURES TÁNG-SHĪFÙ IS BEING FORCED TO ENDURE.
PLEASE DO STOP STEWING-- THERE'S PLENTY OF TIME FOR THAT LATER.

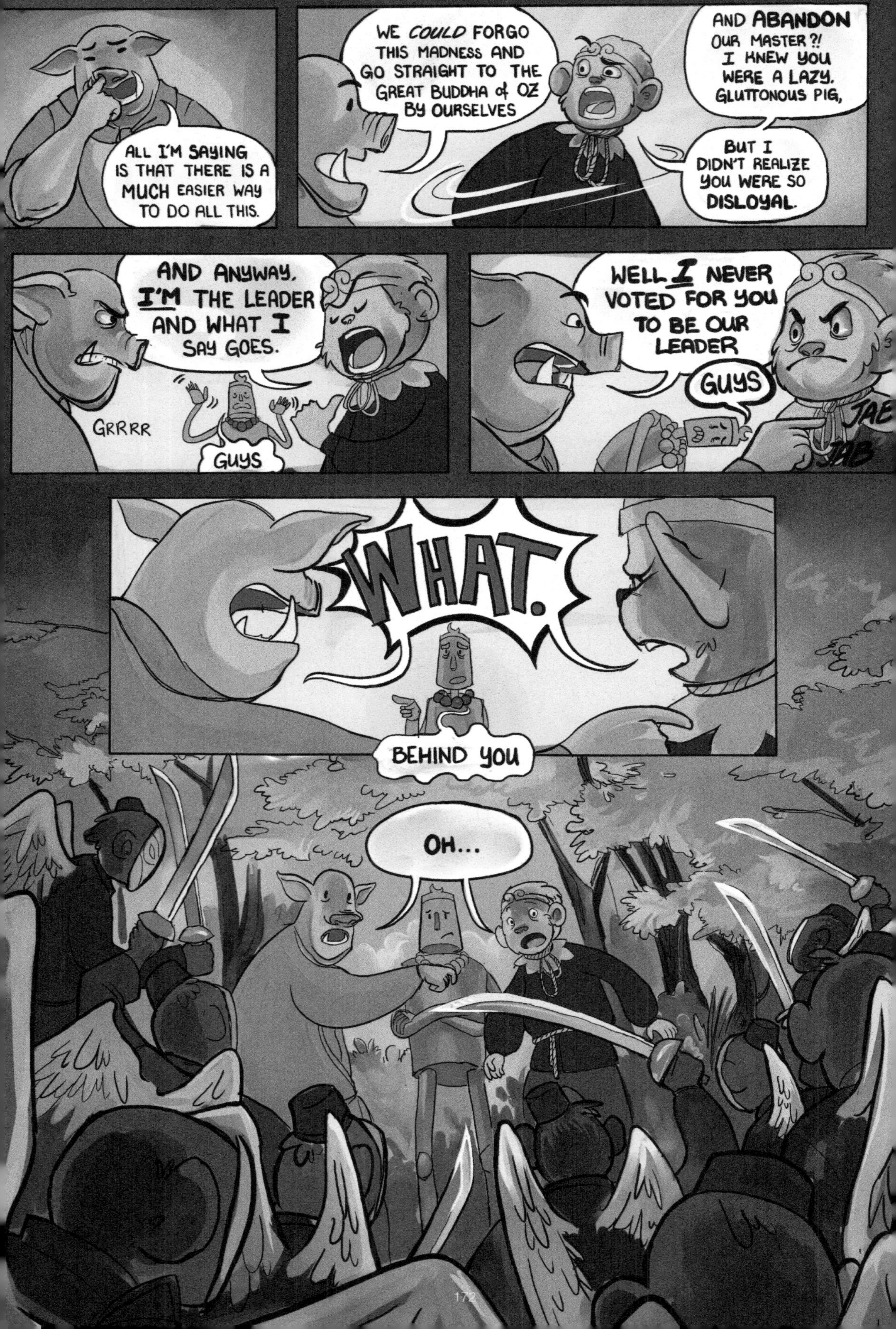
ALL I'M SAYING IS THAT THERE IS A MUCH EASIER WAY TO DO ALL THIS.
WE COULD FORGO THIS MADNESS AND GO STRAIGHT TO THE GREAT BUDDHA of OZ BY OURSELVES
AND ABANDON OUR MASTER?! I KNEW YOU WERE A LAZY, GLUTTONOUS PIG,
BUT I DIDN'T REALIZE YOU WERE SO DISLOYAL.
AND ANYWAY, I'M THE LEADER AND WHAT I SAY GOES.
GRRRR
GUYS
WELL I NEVER VOTED FOR YOU TO BE OUR LEADER
GUYS
JAB
JAB
WHAT.
BEHIND YOU
OH...

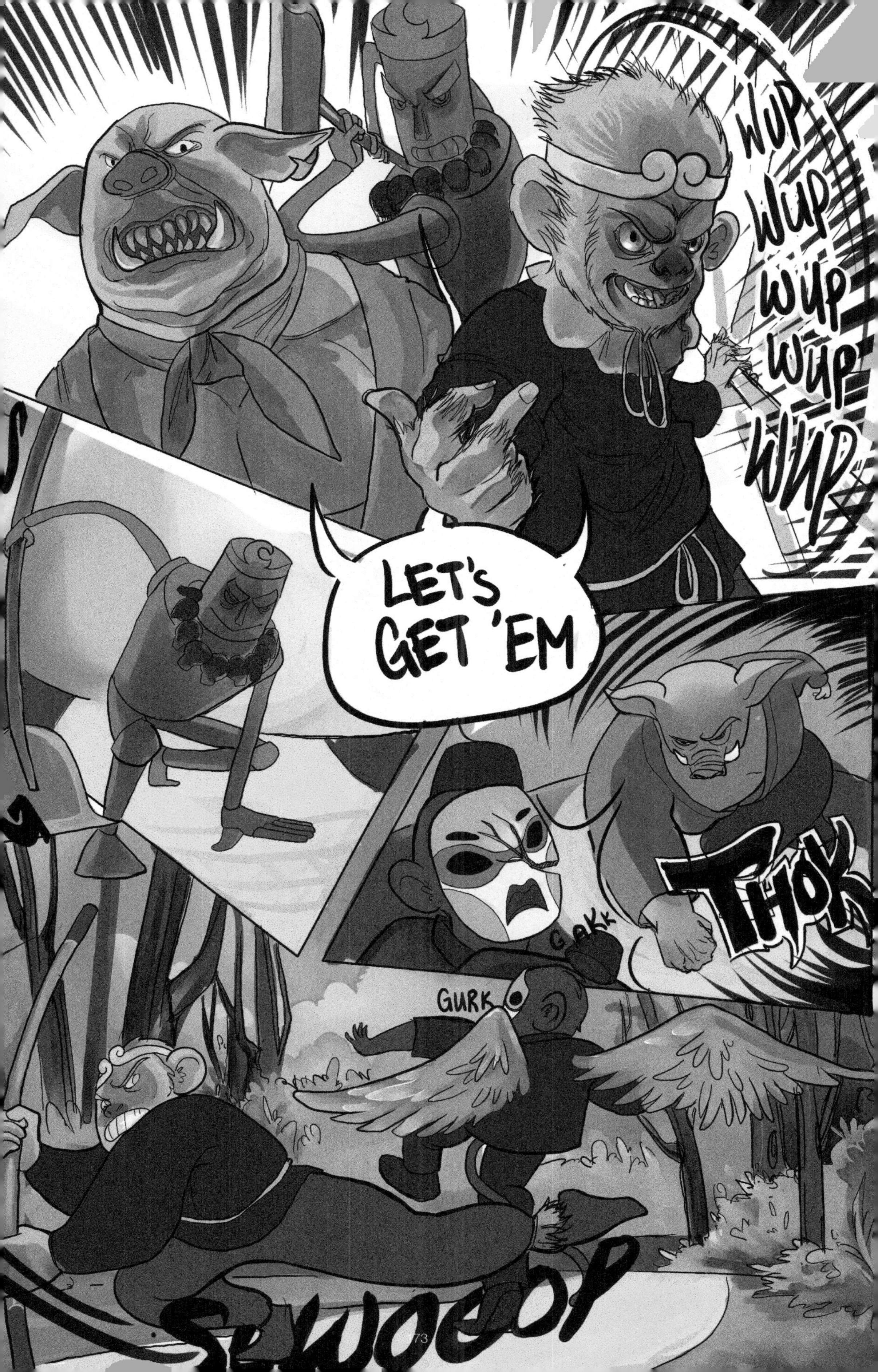

WUP WUP WUP WUP WUP
LET'S GET 'EM
THOK
GAKK
GURK
SWOOP

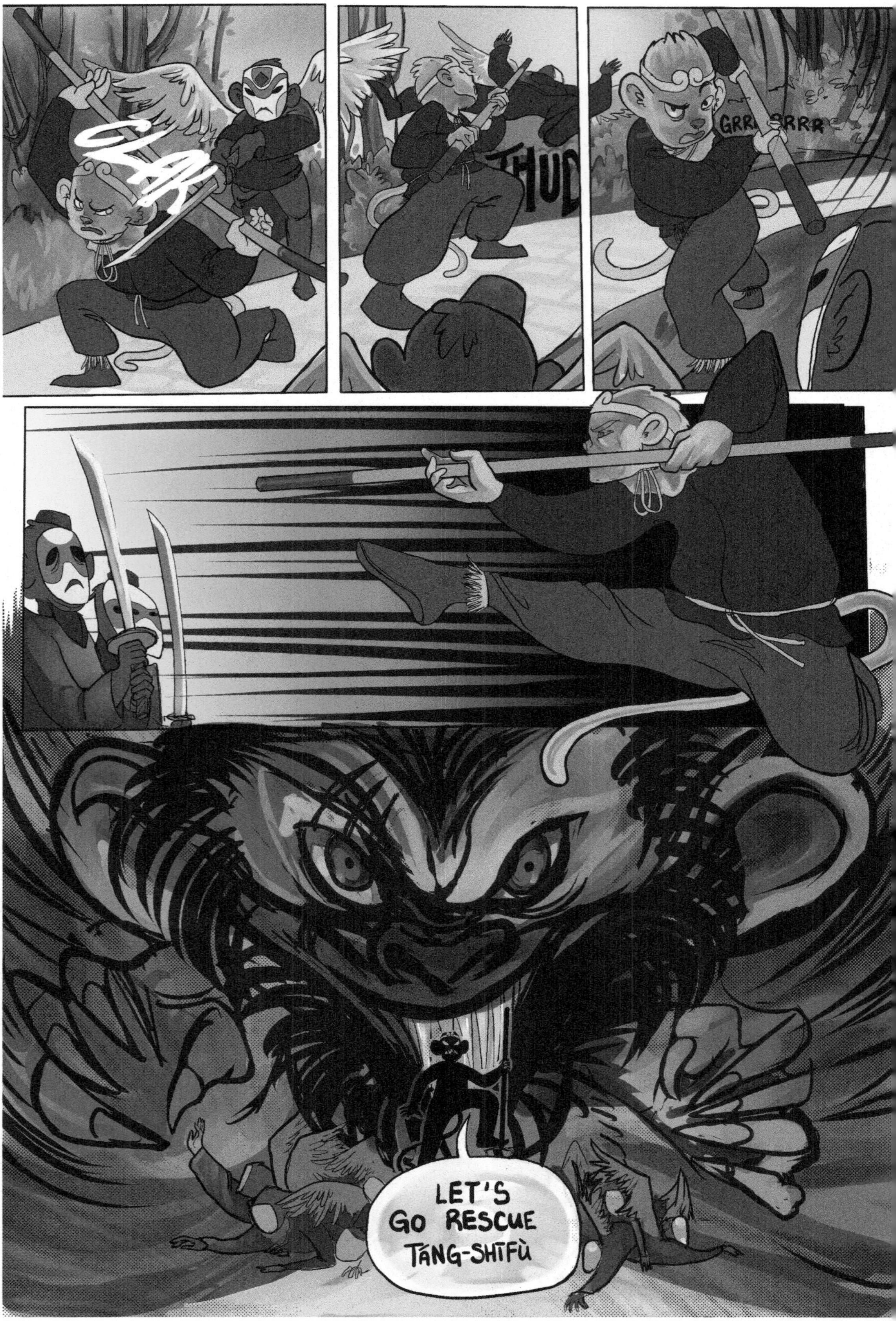
CLAK
THUD
GRRRRRRR
LET'S GO RESCUE TÁNG-SHĪFÙ

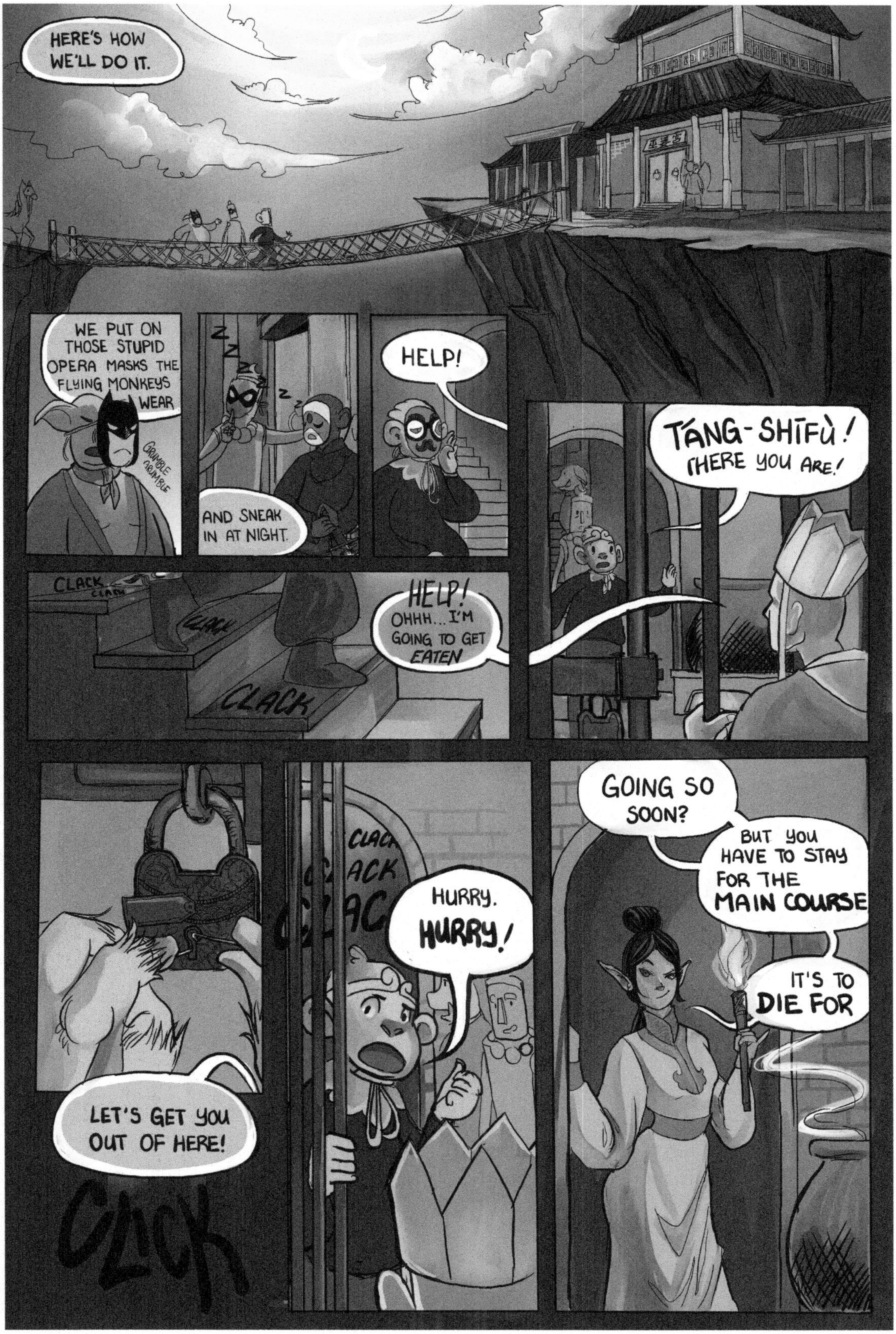
HERE'S HOW WE'LL DO IT.
WE PUT ON THOSE STUPID OPERA MASKS THE FLYING MONKEYS WEAR
GRUMBLE GRUMBLE
Z Z Z
AND SNEAK IN AT NIGHT.
HELP!
TÁNG-SHĪFÙ! THERE YOU ARE!
CLACK CLACK
CLACK
CLACK
HELP! OHHH... I'M GOING TO GET EATEN
LET'S GET YOU OUT OF HERE!
CLICK
CLACK CLACK CLACK
HURRY. HURRY!
GOING SO SOON?
BUT YOU HAVE TO STAY FOR THE MAIN COURSE
IT'S TO DIE FOR

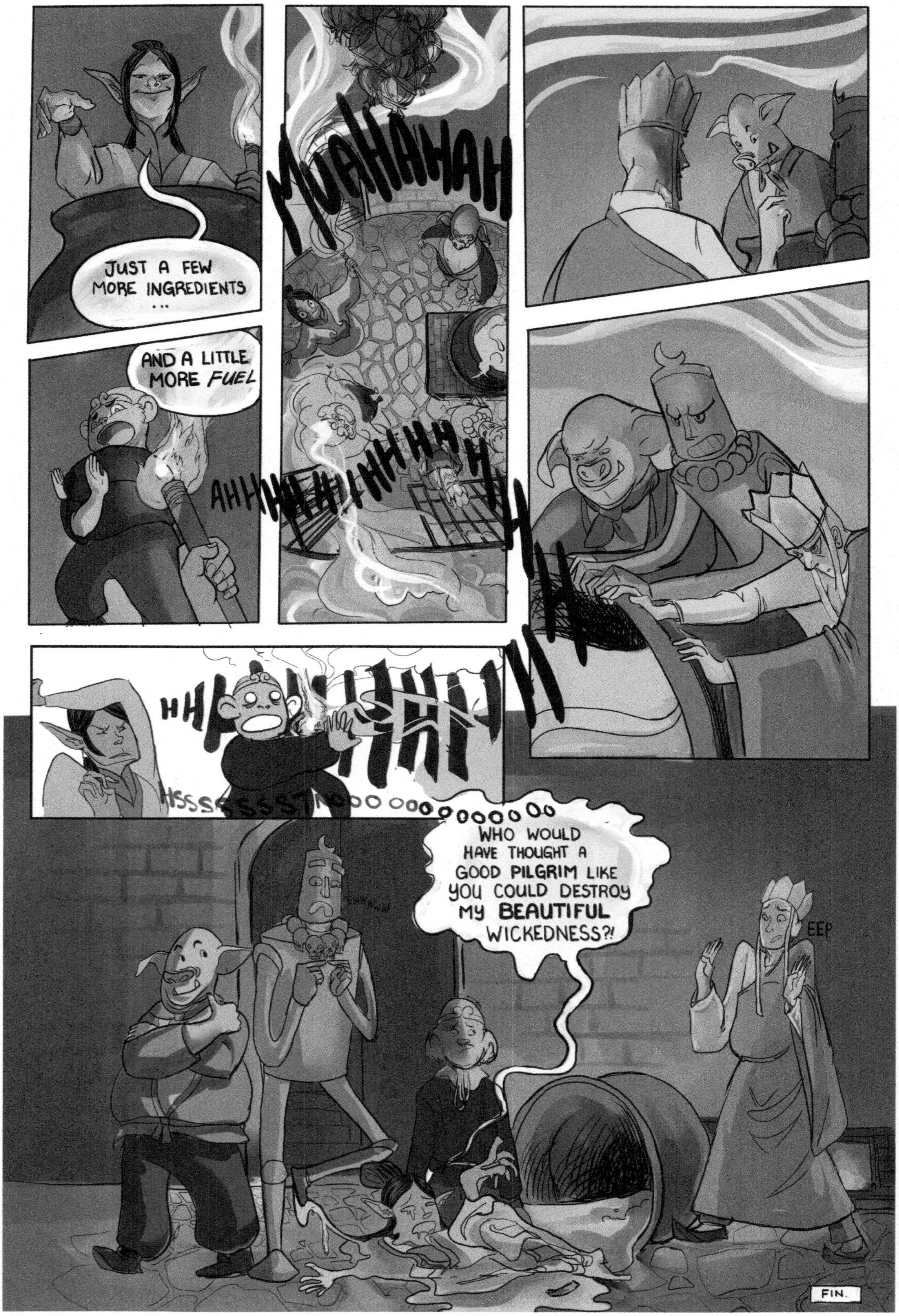
JUST A FEW MORE INGREDIENTS ...
AND A LITTLE MORE FUEL
MUAHAHAHAH
AHHHHHAHHHHHHHHHHHHHHHH
HHHHHHHHHHH
HSSSSSSSSTNOOO OOOOOOOOOOO
WHO WOULD HAVE THOUGHT A GOOD PILGRIM LIKE YOU COULD DESTROY MY BEAUTIFUL WICKEDNESS?!
EEP
FIN.

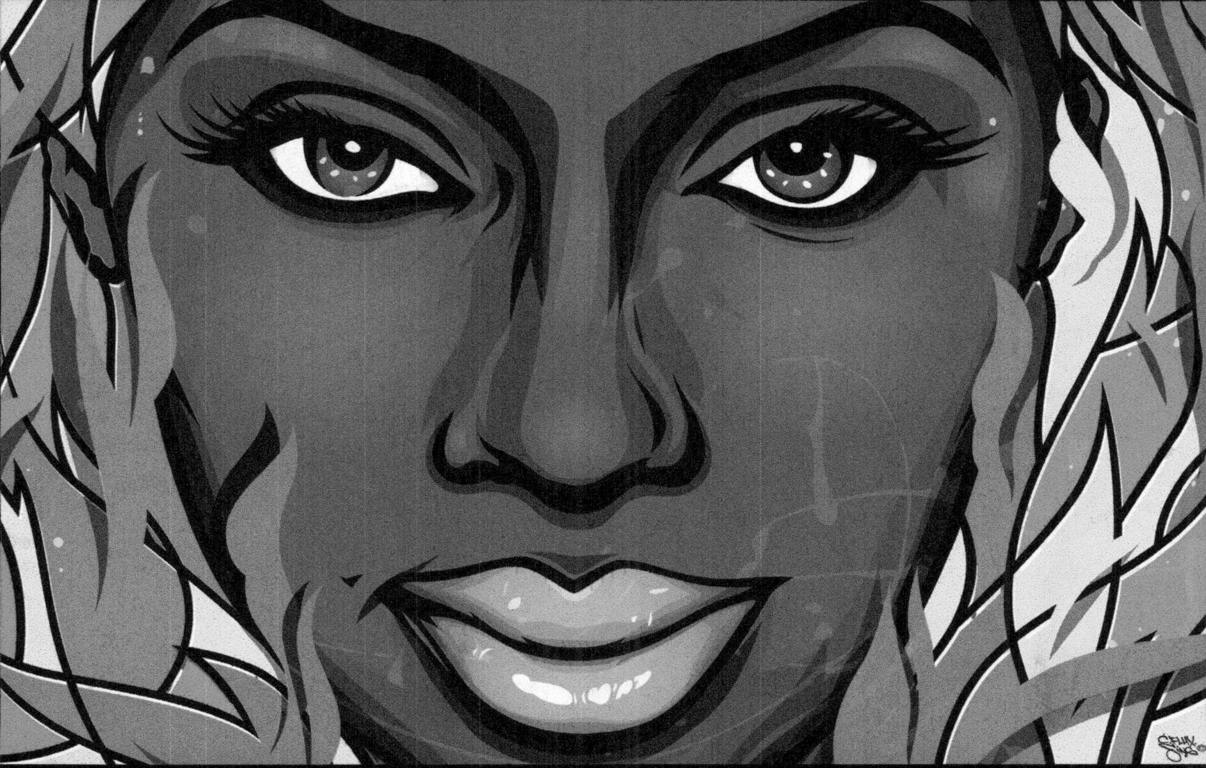

Craig "Flux" Singleton, Artist

United States

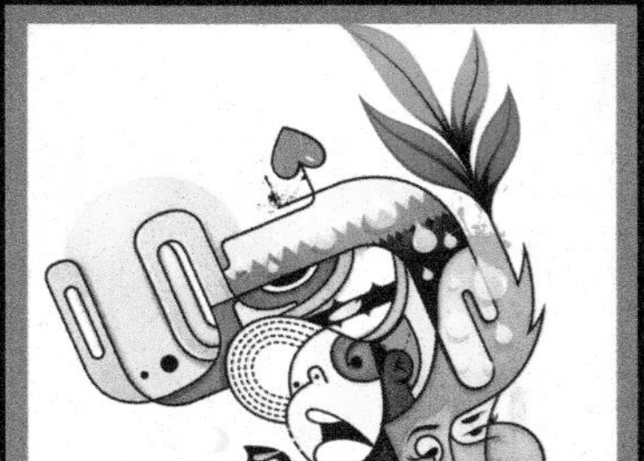
wonda

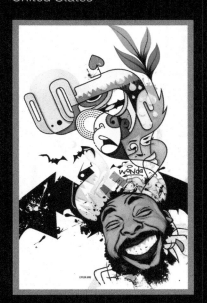

An import from Laurelton, New York, C. Flux Sing has made Atlanta his home for more than a decade. However, getting his just recognition as one of the city's most revered artists took patience. Currently, Georgia's capital is taking on a revolutionary stance by finally embracing art in all its facets; in particular, Sing's penchant for using vibrant color schemes which captivatingly tell a true story of the Black experience. Inspired by comic books, graffiti, abstract art, design, urban decay, and surrealism, Flux is driven to do something new that pushes the boundaries.

So whether it's heading a new branding project or adorning a wall with a vibrant mural promoting perseverance, C.Flux Sing will always have an audience who will appreciate art that comes from the heart.

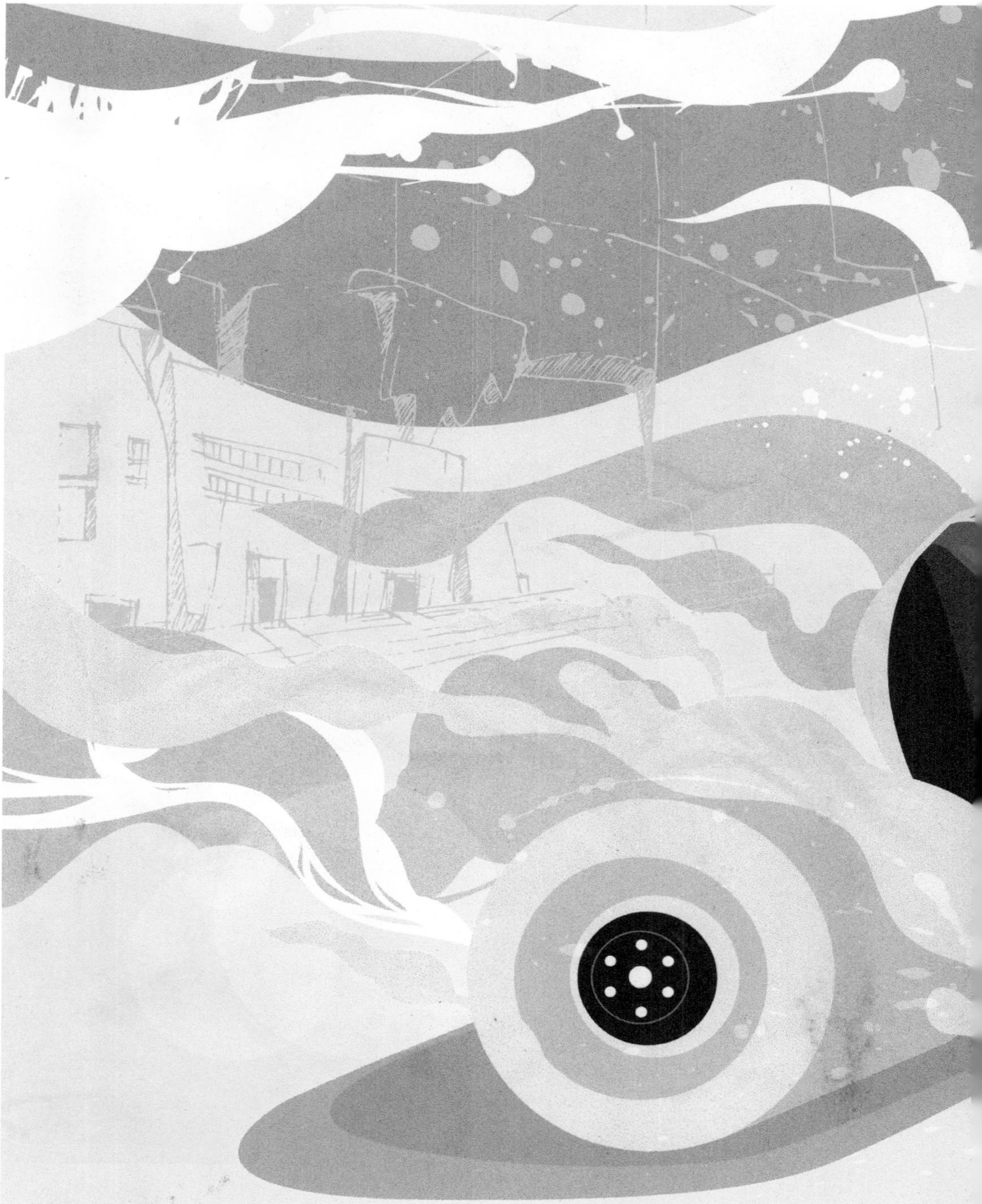

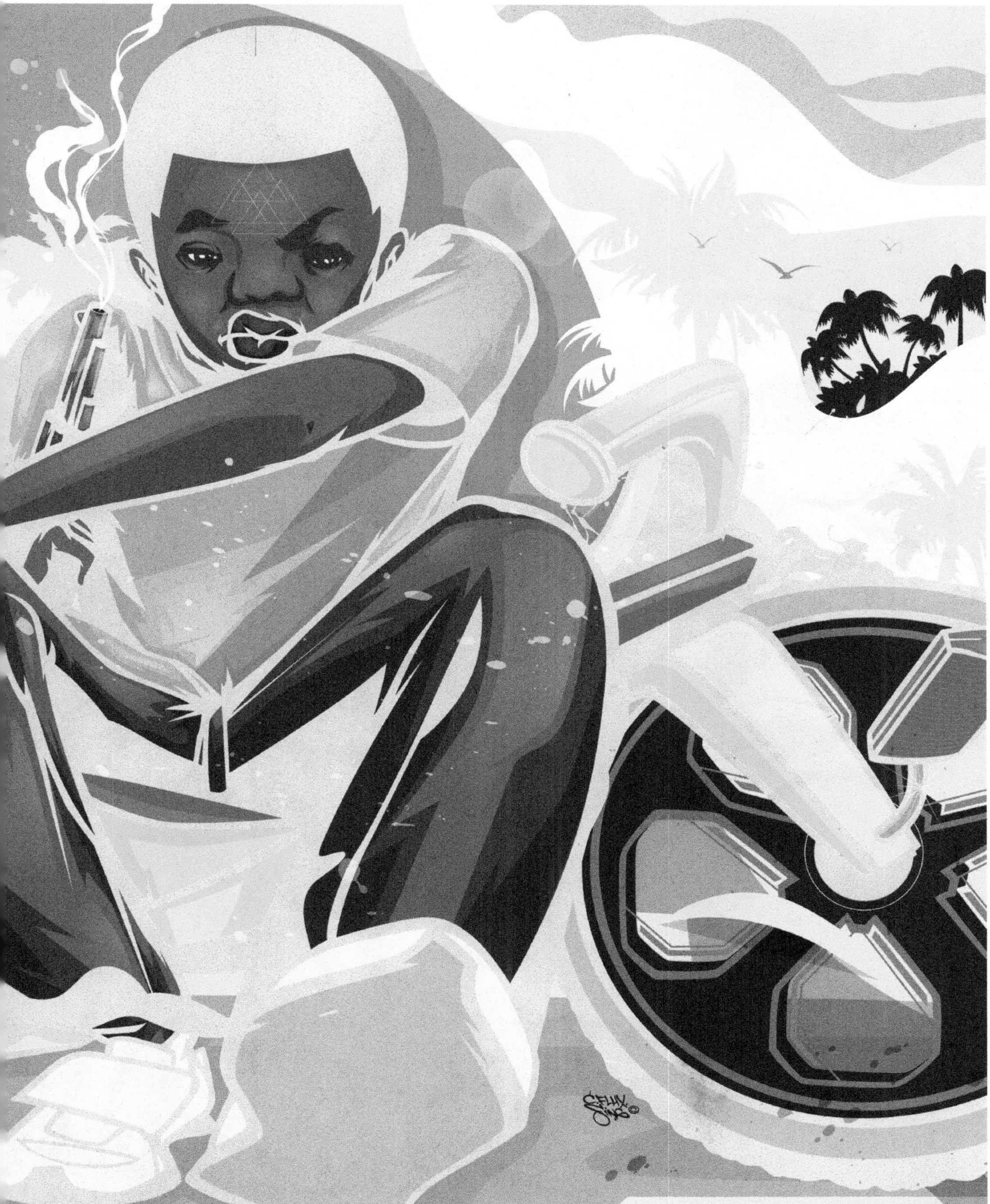

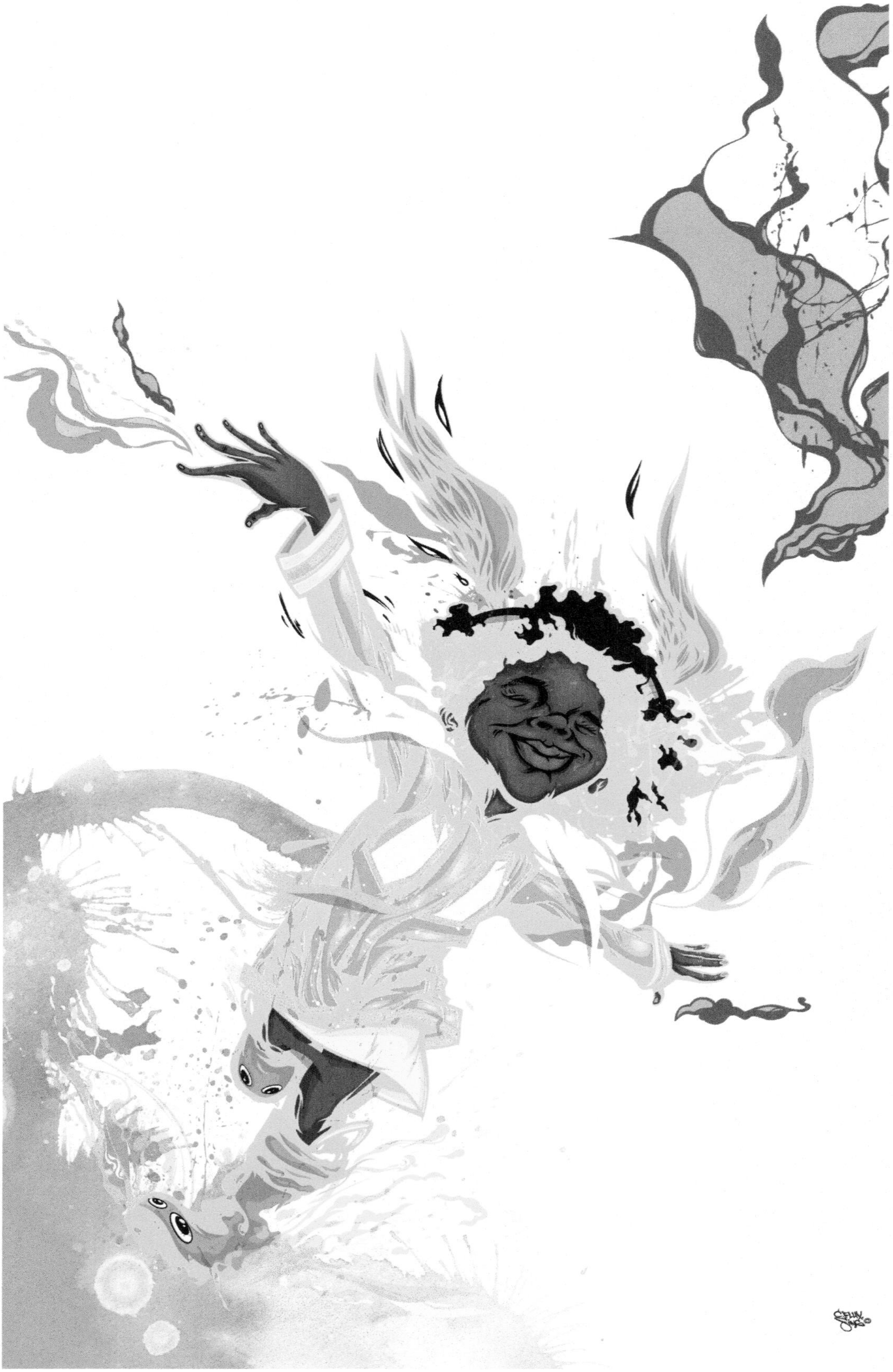

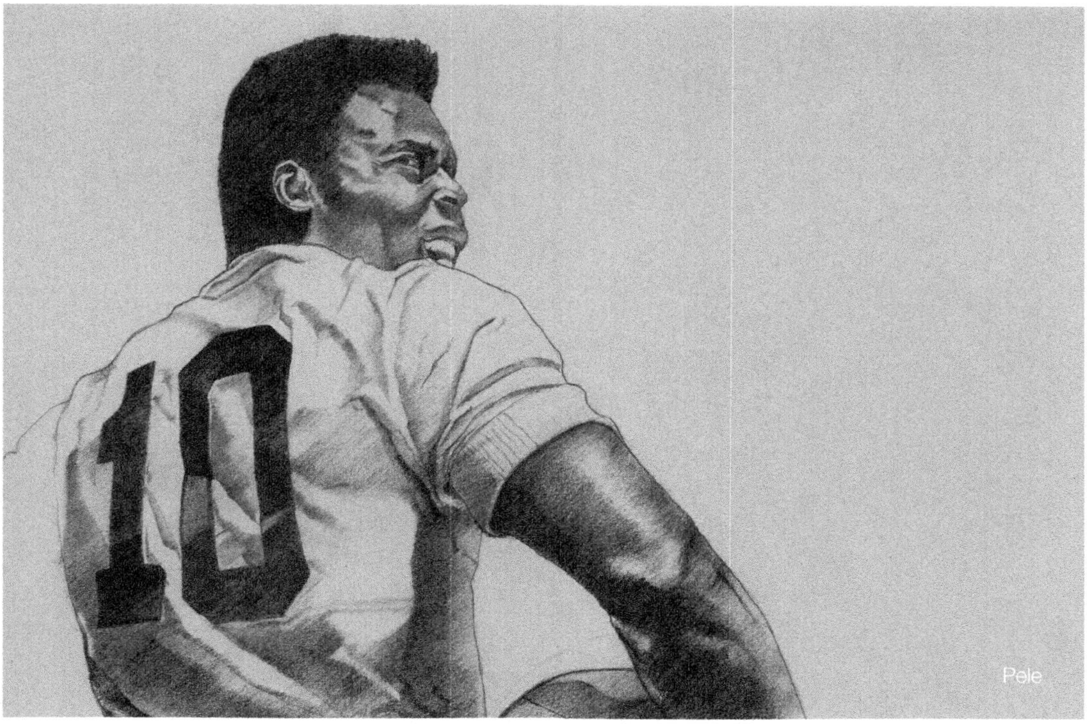
10
Pele

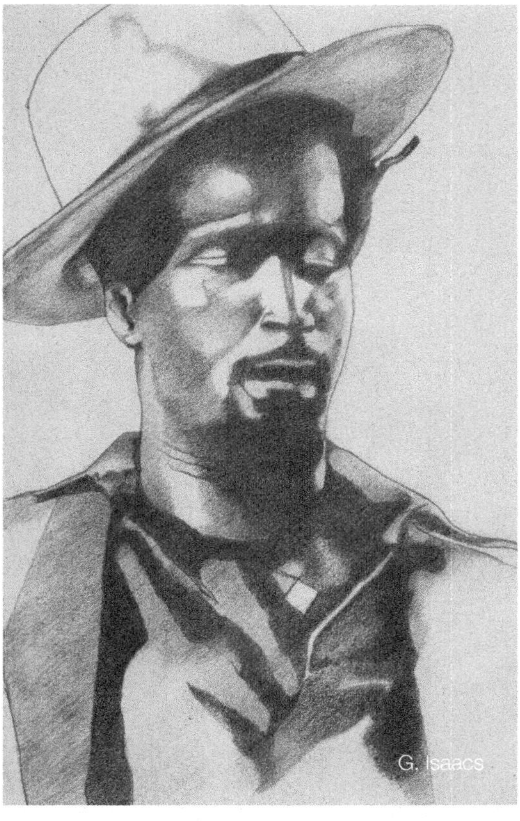
G. Isaacs

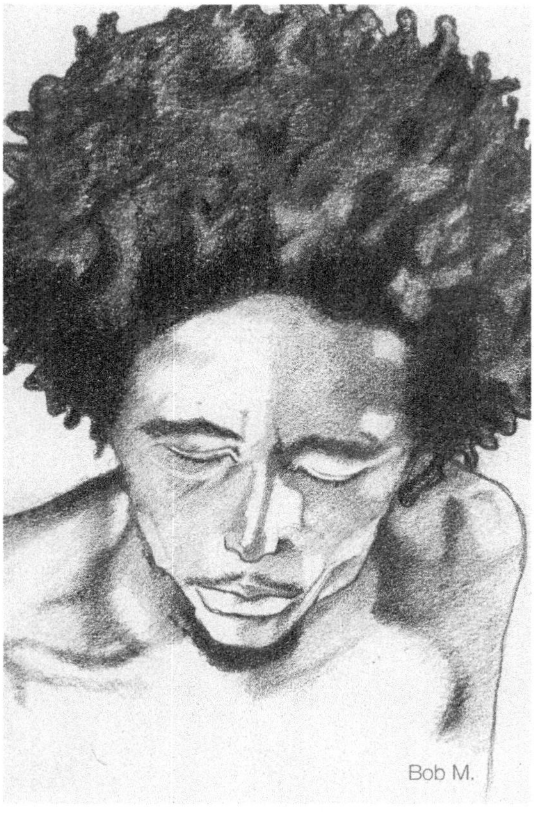
Bob M.

Dwane Maxwell
Jamaica / United States

Portrait Series

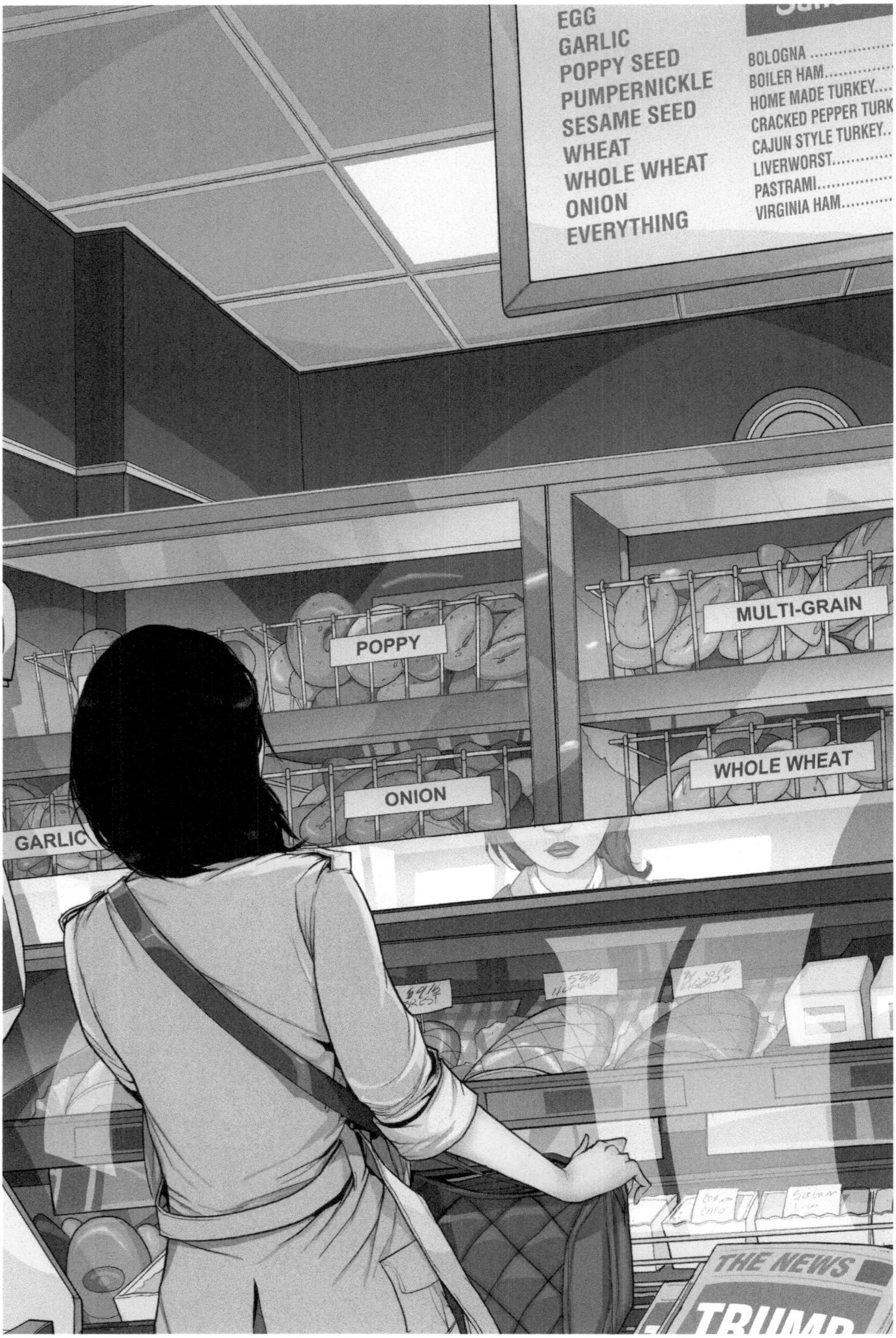
EGG
GARLIC
POPPY SEED
PUMPERNICKLE
SESAME SEED
WHEAT
WHOLE WHEAT
ONION
EVERYTHING
BOLOGNA
BOILER HAM
HOME MADE TURKEY
CAJUN STYLE TURKEY
LIVERWORST
PASTRAMI
VIRGINIA HAM
POPPY
MULTI-GRAIN
ONION
WHOLE WHEAT
GARLIC
THE NEWS

Jerome Walford
Jamaica / United States

Lip Service
forwardcomix.com

Going Postal: Redefined
by Jerome Walford

I rushed into the post office. The line was backed up, and customers were already breathing irritated sighs. The Chinese-American teller repeated her instructions, yet again, with a very pronounced accent. The elderly customer shook her head. She was probably in her 80s. Her head and shoulders were barely taller than the counter. The young man behind her approached, his arms covered with tattoos of skeletons and naked women. He offered a broad smile as he helped her figure out how to use the credit card terminal. He looked away while she entered her PIN. He walked away and groaned audibly but returned with a bigger smile than before. He soon realized she was having trouble mainly due to not speaking much English.

"Russian?" the tatted young man inquired of the customer line. A six-foot man in his forties approached, translated, and spoke with the woman's daughter on the phone.

After they sorted out the matter, the African-American supervisor came around from behind the glass to help the elderly woman reset the terminal and try again. The woman started to enter her PIN. The supervisor looked away.

As the woman shuffled to the exit, everyone returned to their place. The line progressed one space. We all breathed a contented sigh.

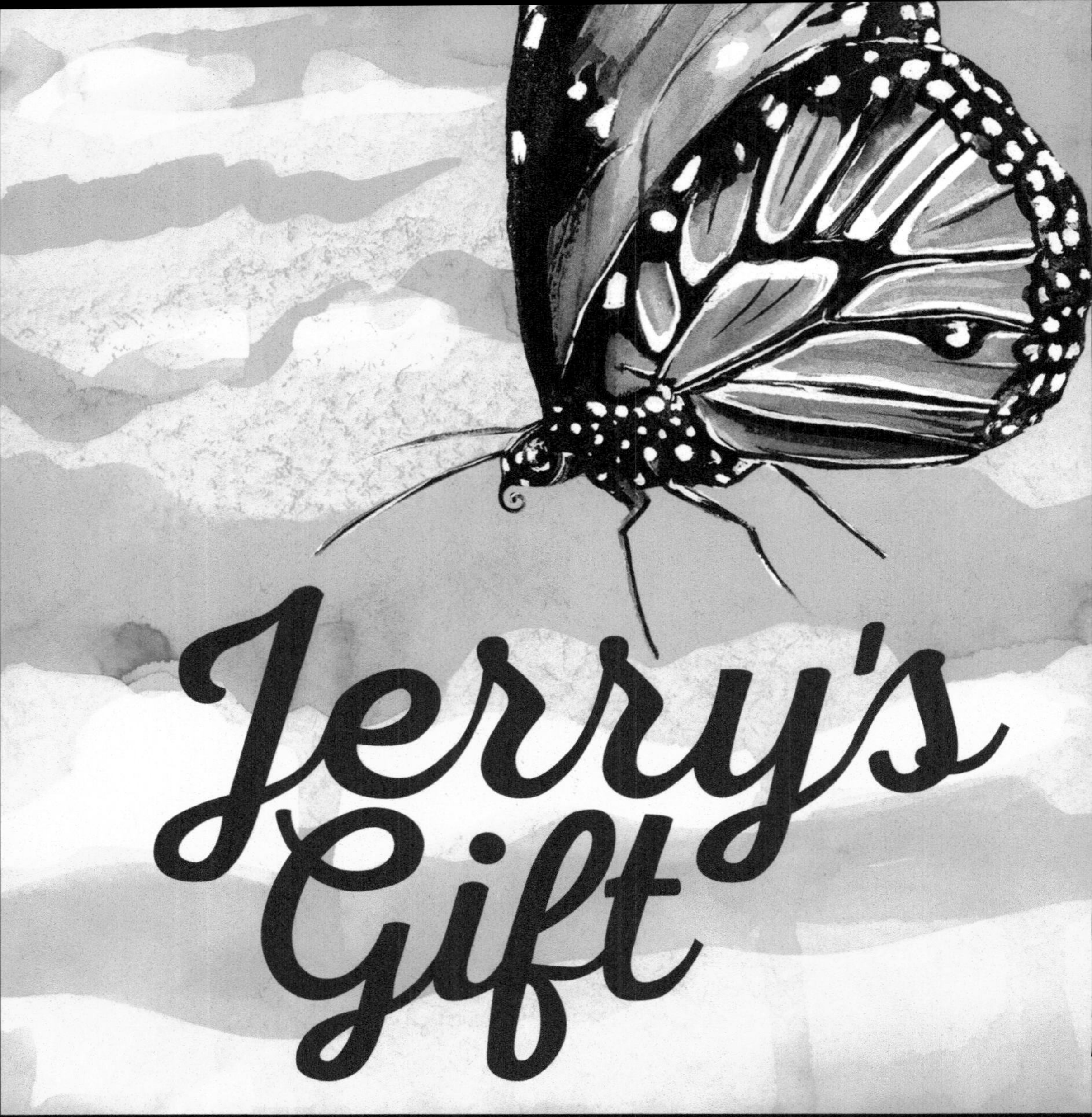
Jerry's Gift

Leah Yael Levy, Writer / Artist

Israel / United States

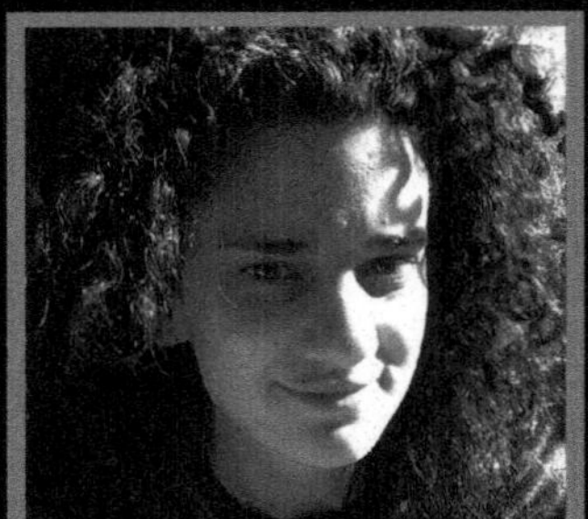

Born and raised in Moshav Beit Lechem Haglilit, in Israel. Currently based out of Oakland, CA. She first moved to New York City in 2002 to attend the Art Students League of New York, and later gained a BFA in Illustration from Parsons School of Design (2011). She is currently developing a graphic memoir for her thesis while working towards an MFA in Comics at California College of the Arts.

leahyaellevy.com

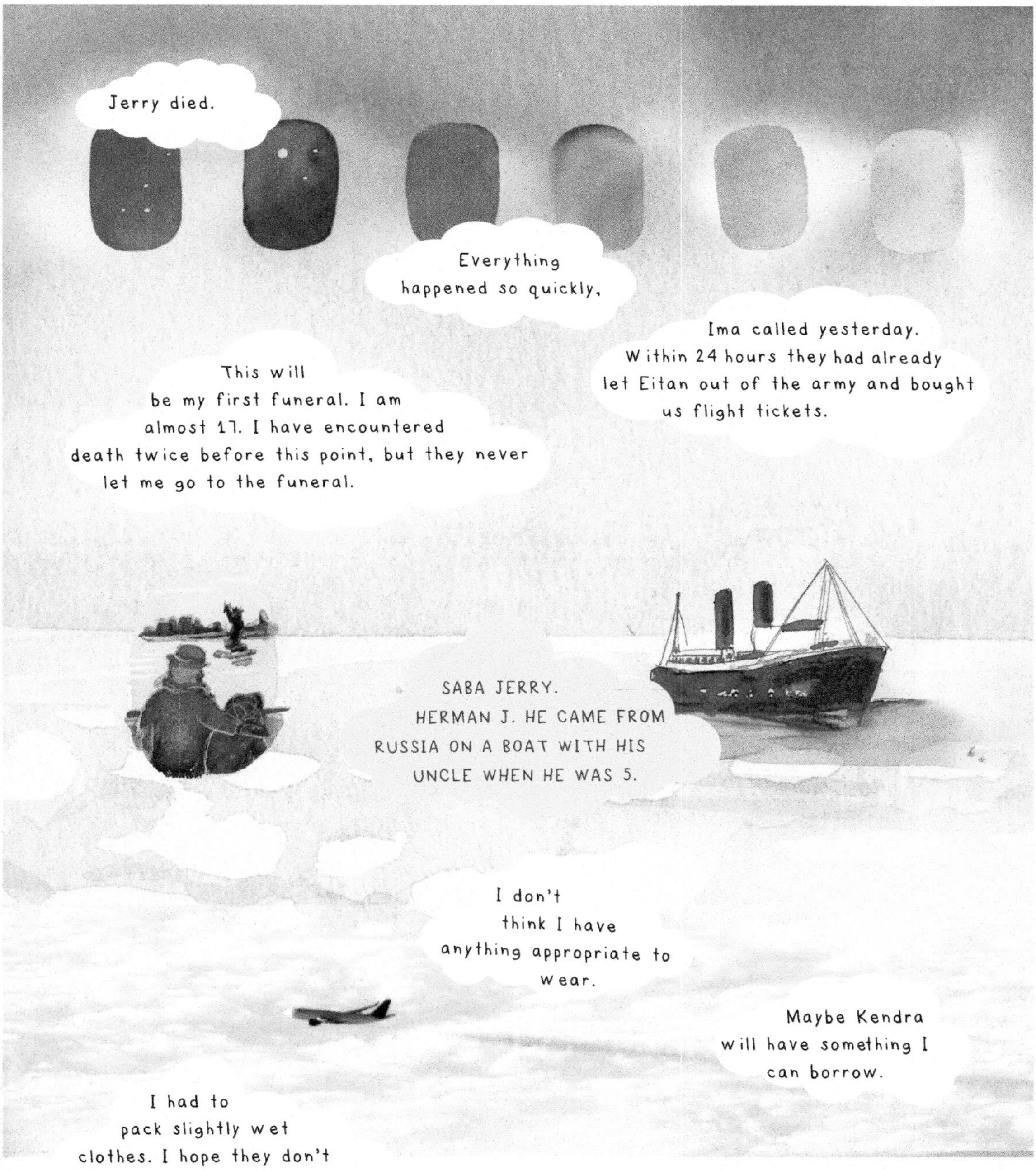
Jerry died.
Everything happened so quickly.
Ima called yesterday. Within 24 hours they had already let Eitan out of the army and bought us flight tickets.
This will be my first funeral. I am almost 17. I have encountered death twice before this point, but they never let me go to the funeral.
SABA JERRY. HERMAN J. HE CAME FROM RUSSIA ON A BOAT WITH HIS UNCLE WHEN HE WAS 5.
I don't think I have anything appropriate to wear.
Maybe Kendra will have something I can borrow.
I had to pack slightly wet clothes. I hope they don't stink by the time we get there..

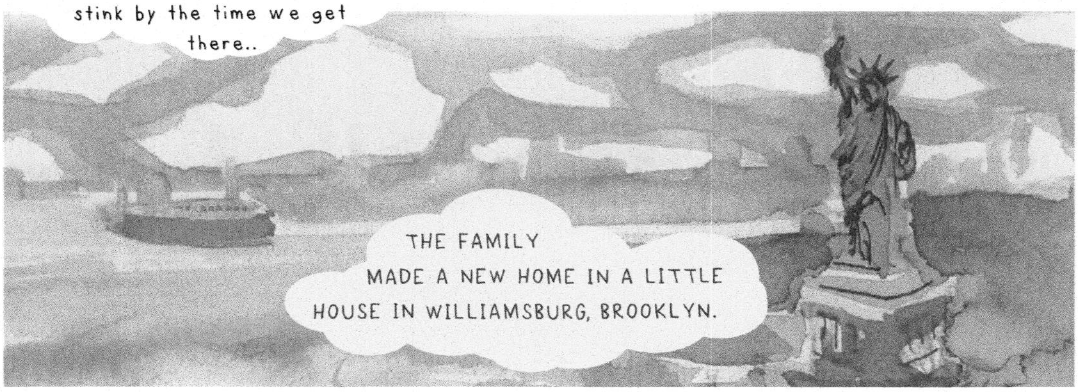
THE FAMILY MADE A NEW HOME IN A LITTLE HOUSE IN WILLIAMSBURG, BROOKLYN.

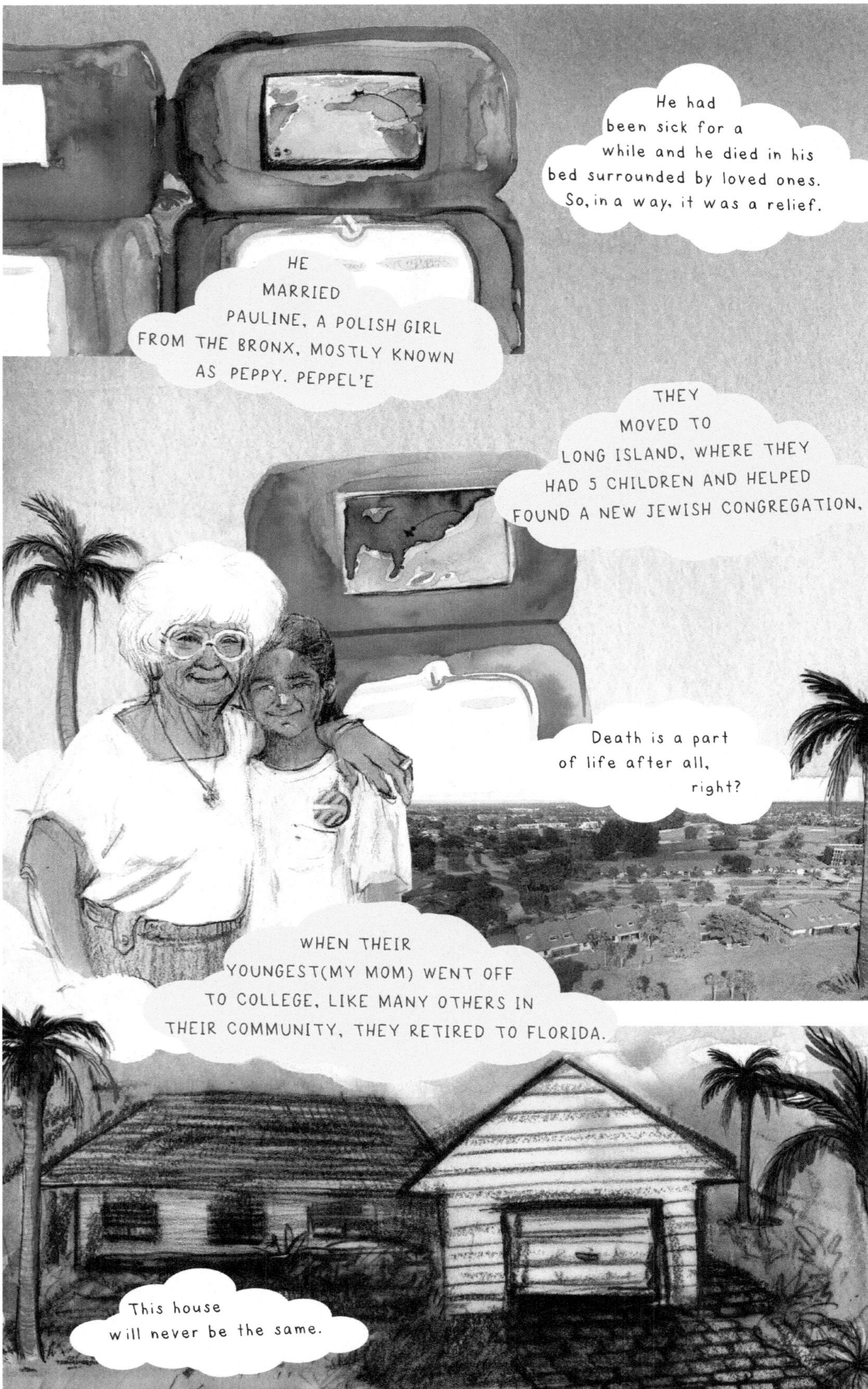
He had been sick for a while and he died in his bed surrounded by loved ones. So, in a way, it was a relief.
HE MARRIED PAULINE, A POLISH GIRL FROM THE BRONX, MOSTLY KNOWN AS PEPPY. PEPPEL'E
THEY MOVED TO LONG ISLAND, WHERE THEY HAD 5 CHILDREN AND HELPED FOUND A NEW JEWISH CONGREGATION.
Death is a part of life after all, right?
WHEN THEIR YOUNGEST(MY MOM) WENT OFF TO COLLEGE, LIKE MANY OTHERS IN THEIR COMMUNITY, THEY RETIRED TO FLORIDA.
This house will never be the same.

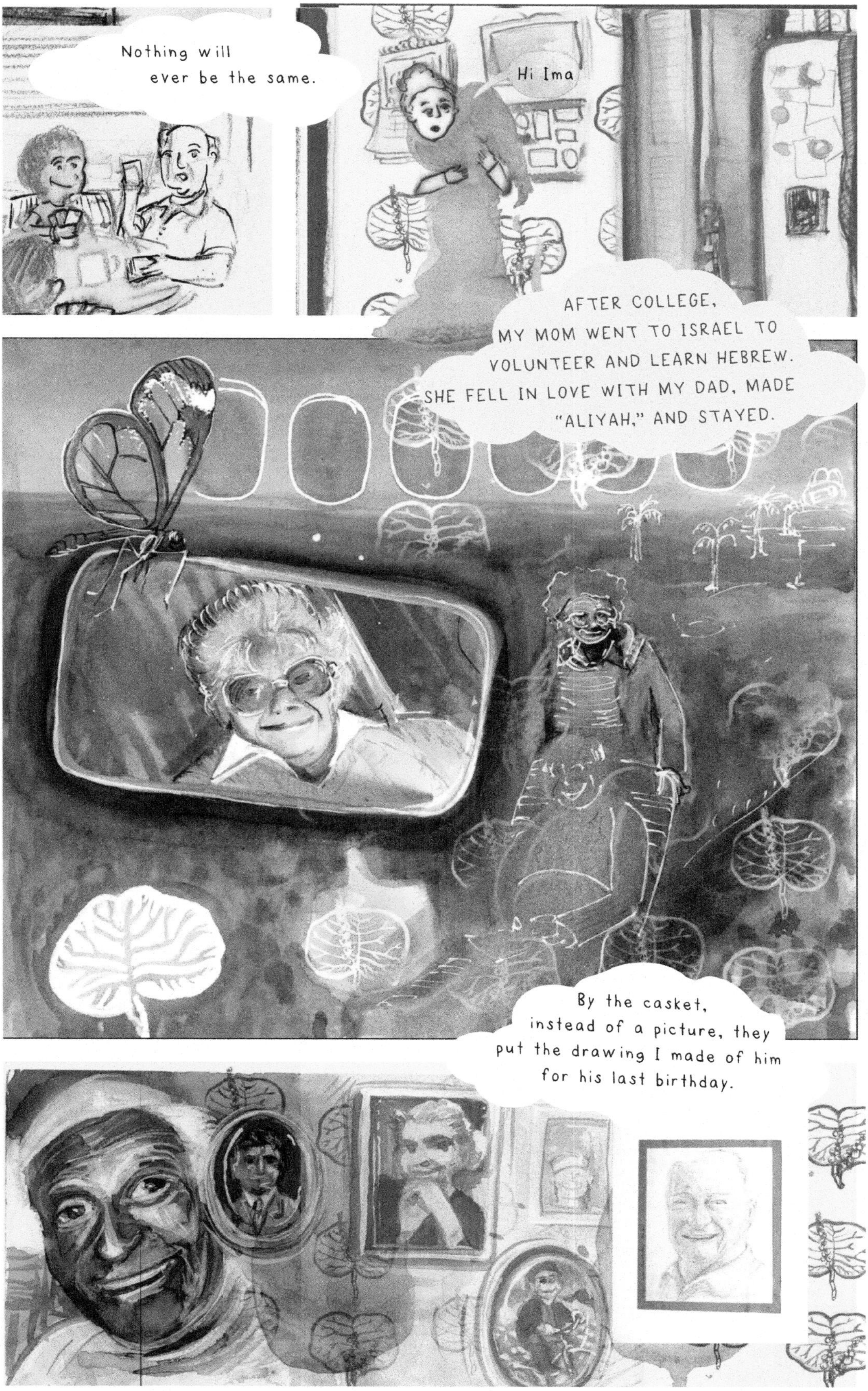

Nothing will ever be the same.
Hi Ima
AFTER COLLEGE, MY MOM WENT TO ISRAEL TO VOLUNTEER AND LEARN HEBREW. SHE FELL IN LOVE WITH MY DAD, MADE "ALIYAH," AND STAYED.
By the casket, instead of a picture, they put the drawing I made of him for his last birthday.

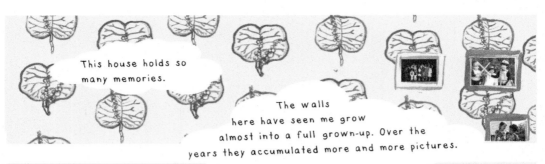

This house holds so many memories.

The walls here have seen me grow almost into a full grown-up. Over the years they accumulated more and more pictures.

אני רוצה מיץ תפוחים!

אבל אני לא יודעת א"ך!

תבקש' מסבתא, היא במסבח

-תג'די כבה

May I have some apple juice please?

I guess that's what happens when you have grand kids

And time....

Safta

Yes dear

May I have some apple juice, please?

Of course!

<THIS IS MY FIRST COMPLETE SENTENCE SPOKEN IN ENGLISH.>

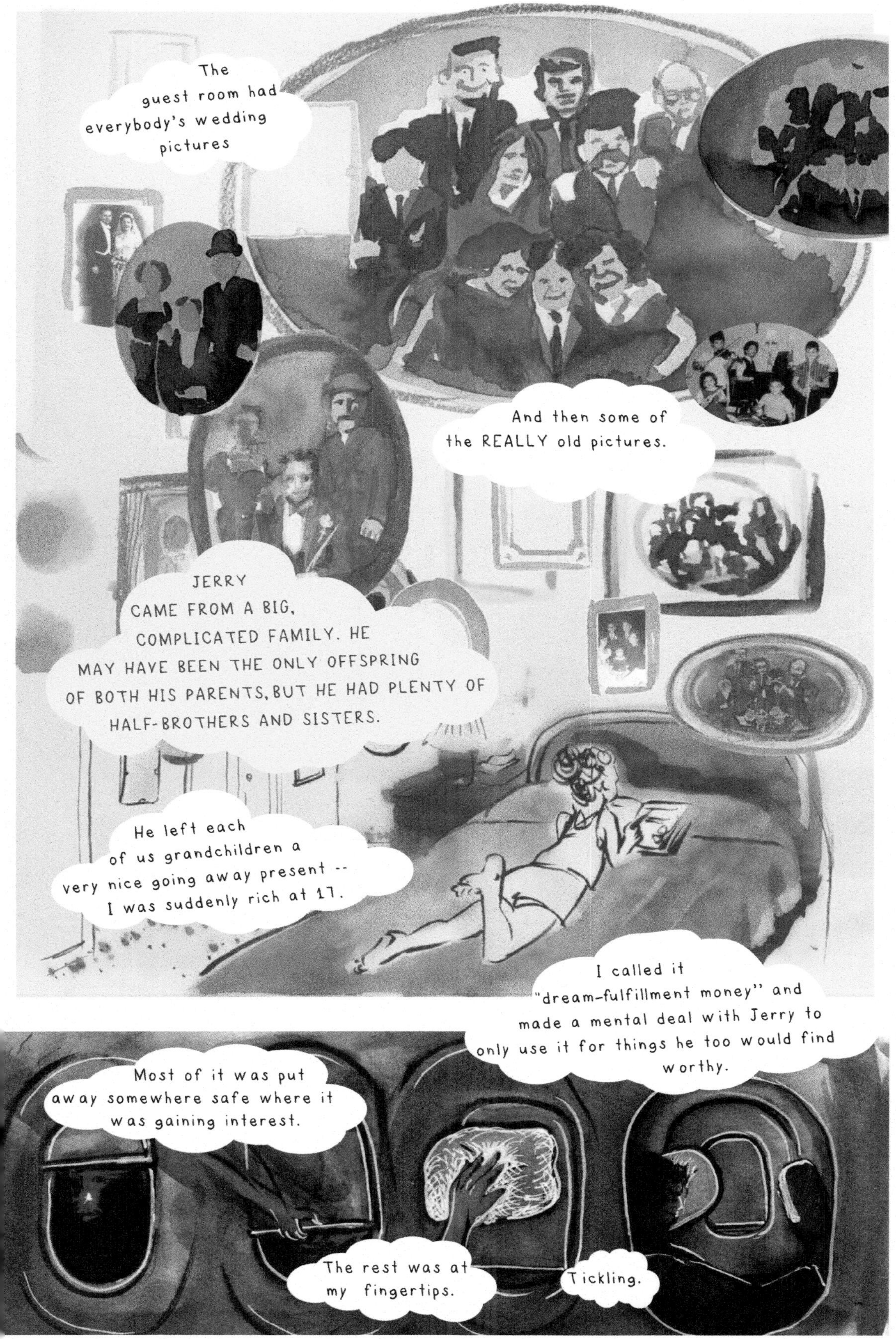
The guest room had everybody's wedding pictures
And then some of the REALLY old pictures.
JERRY CAME FROM A BIG, COMPLICATED FAMILY. HE MAY HAVE BEEN THE ONLY OFFSPRING OF BOTH HIS PARENTS, BUT HE HAD PLENTY OF HALF-BROTHERS AND SISTERS.
He left each of us grandchildren a very nice going away present -- I was suddenly rich at 17.
I called it "dream-fulfillment money" and made a mental deal with Jerry to only use it for things he too would find worthy.
Most of it was put away somewhere safe where it was gaining interest.
The rest was at my fingertips.
Tickling.

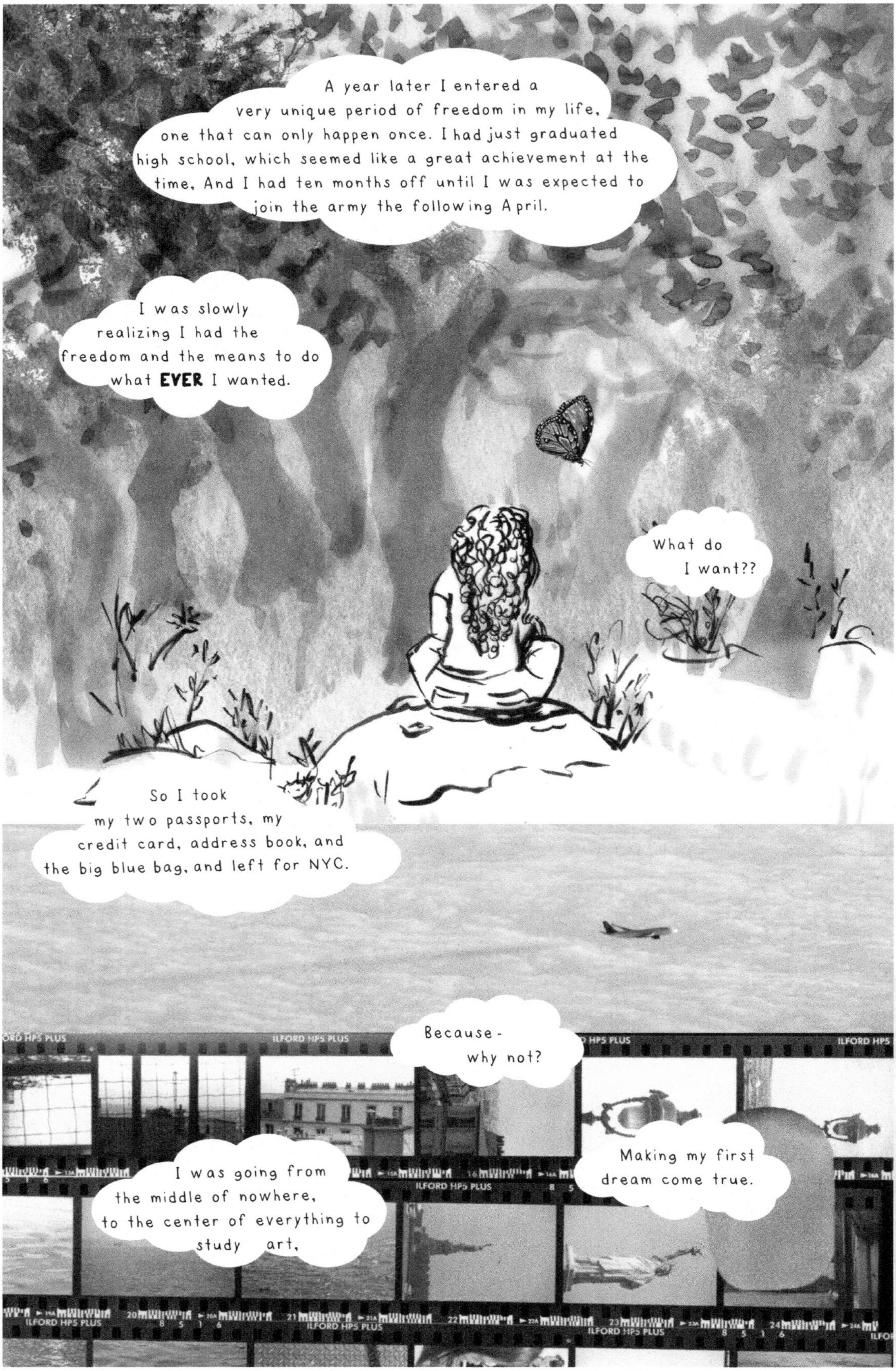
A year later I entered a very unique period of freedom in my life, one that can only happen once. I had just graduated high school, which seemed like a great achievement at the time. And I had ten months off until I was expected to join the army the following April.
I was slowly realizing I had the freedom and the means to do what **EVER** I wanted.
What do I want??
So I took my two passports, my credit card, address book, and the big blue bag, and left for NYC.
Because - why not?
I was going from the middle of nowhere, to the center of everything to study art,
Making my first dream come true.

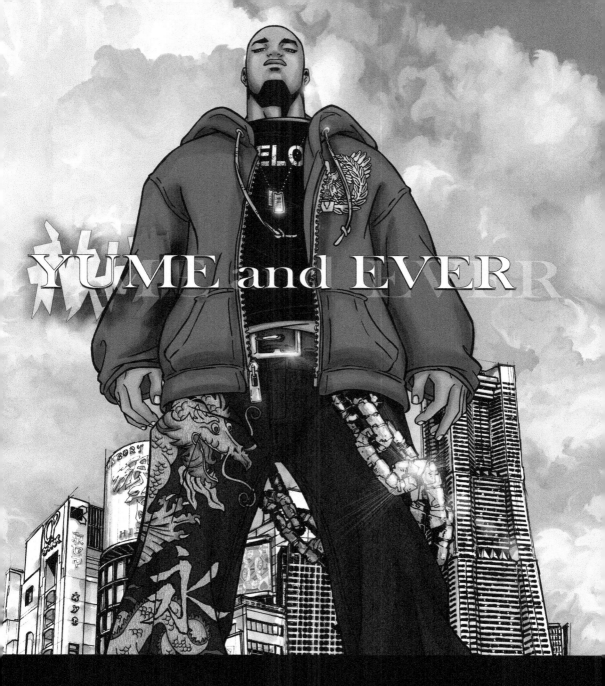

YUME and EVER

Alitha E. Martinez, Writer / Artist
United States

I've been a professional comic book artist for sixteen years, drawing for mainstream companies like Marvel and DC, Archie and Papercutz. I LOVE all things comics, art, and writing. Creativity is the most beautiful gift we've been afforded as humans. All I've ever wanted to do was to tell my own stories. In 2007 I established Ariotstorm Productions LLC / Peanut Butter Joe Studios to finally publish my own independent work. Enjoy this sample.

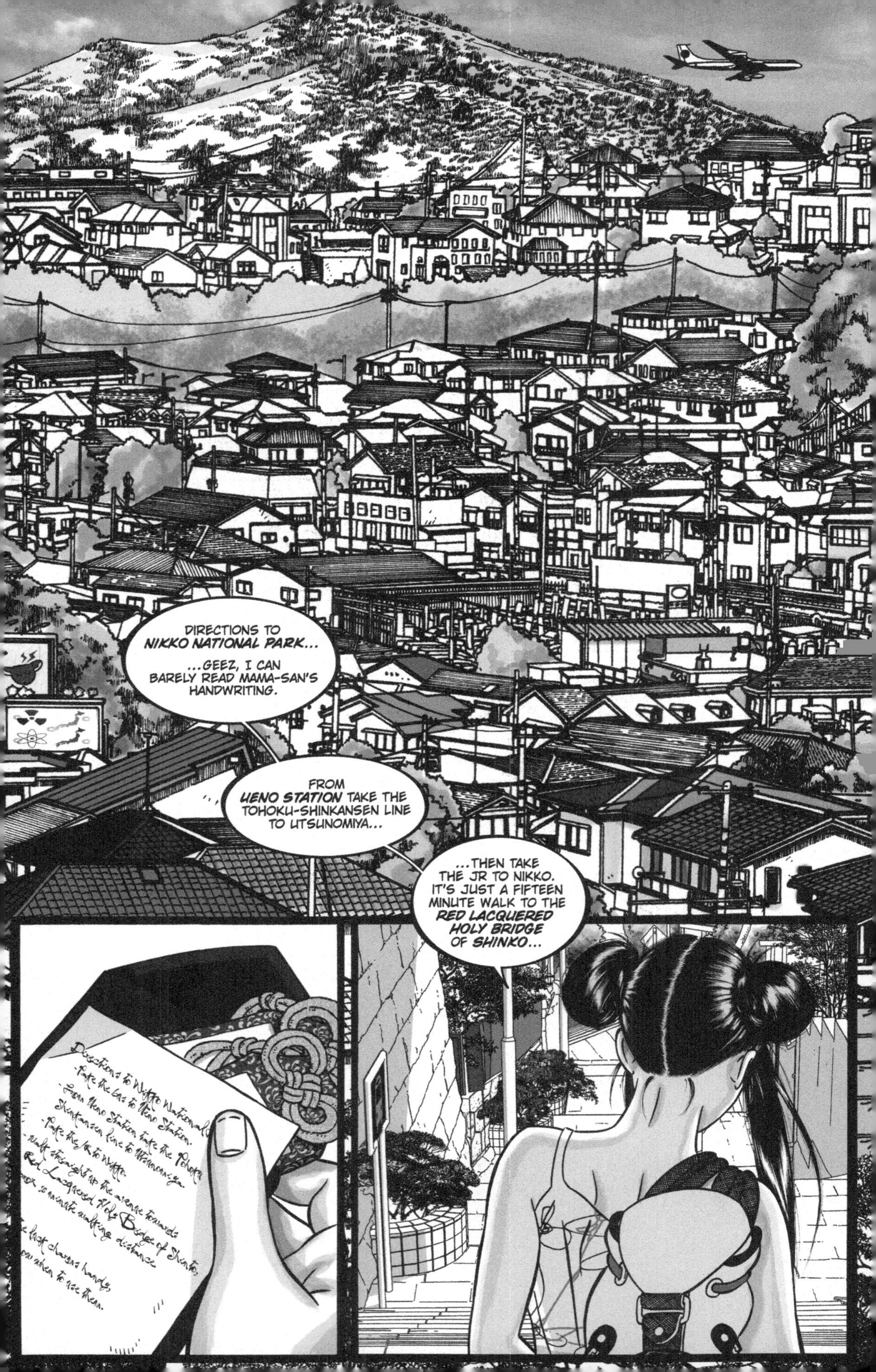
DIRECTIONS TO *NIKKO NATIONAL PARK*...
...GEEZ, I CAN BARELY READ MAMA-SAN'S HANDWRITING.
FROM *UENO STATION* TAKE THE TOHOKU-SHINKANSEN LINE TO UTSUNOMIYA...
...THEN TAKE THE JR TO NIKKO. IT'S JUST A FIFTEEN MINUTE WALK TO THE *RED LACQUERED HOLY BRIDGE* OF *SHINKO*...

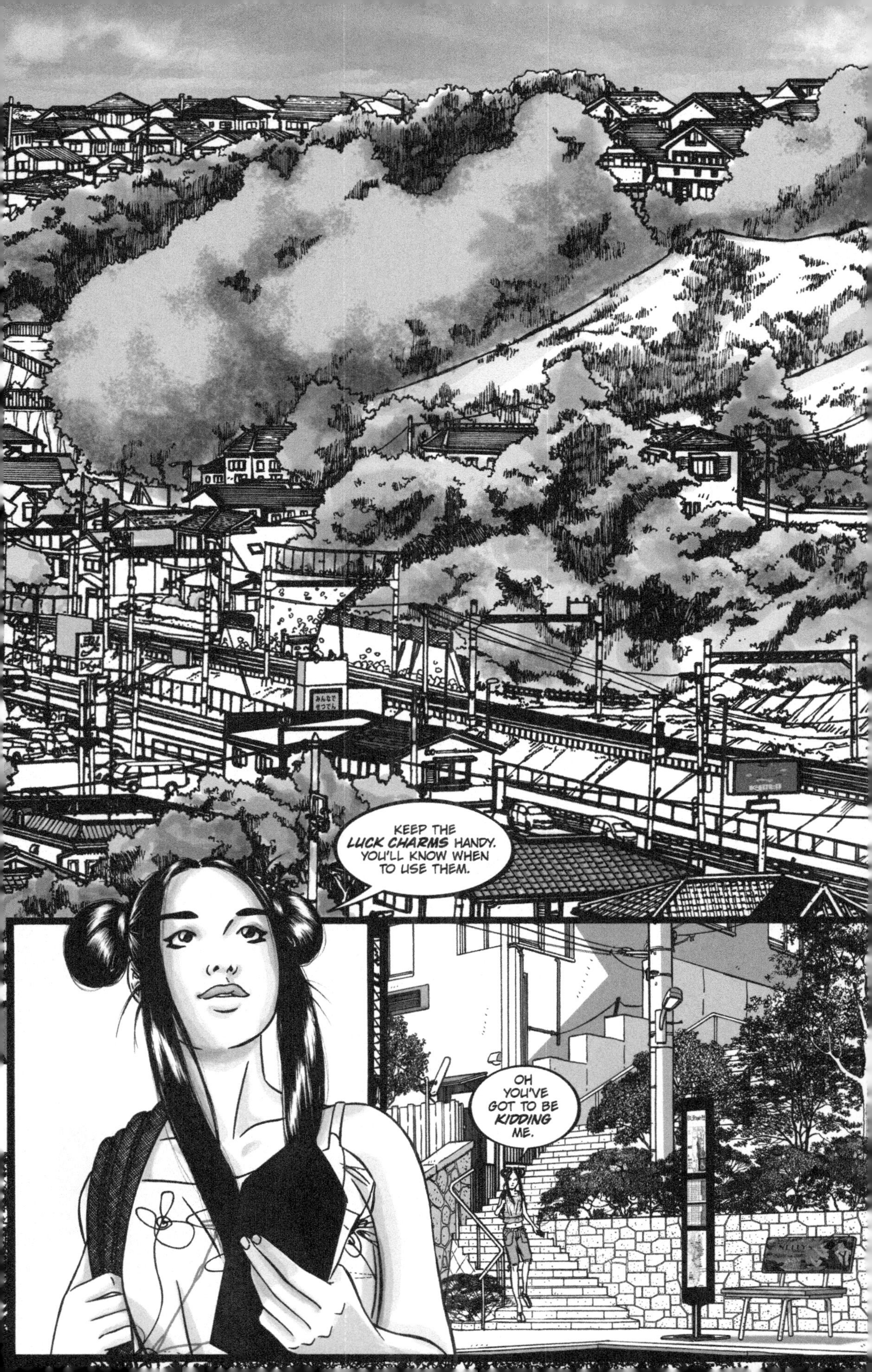
KEEP THE LUCK CHARMS HANDY. YOU'LL KNOW WHEN TO USE THEM.
OH YOU'VE GOT TO BE KIDDING ME.

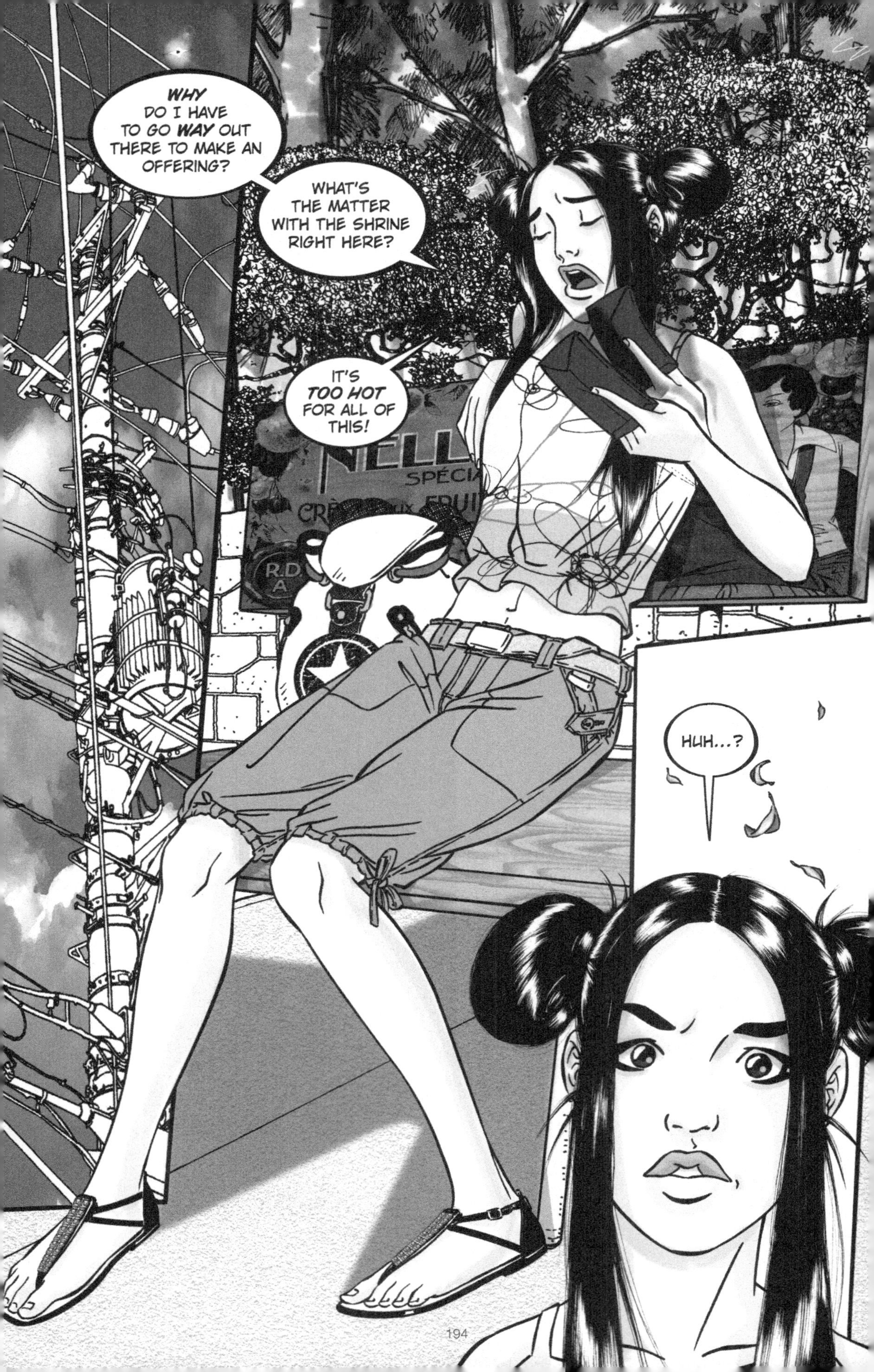

WHY DO I HAVE TO GO *WAY* OUT THERE TO MAKE AN OFFERING?
WHAT'S THE MATTER WITH THE SHRINE RIGHT HERE?
IT'S *TOO HOT* FOR ALL OF THIS!
SPÉCIA
R.D.
A
HUH...?

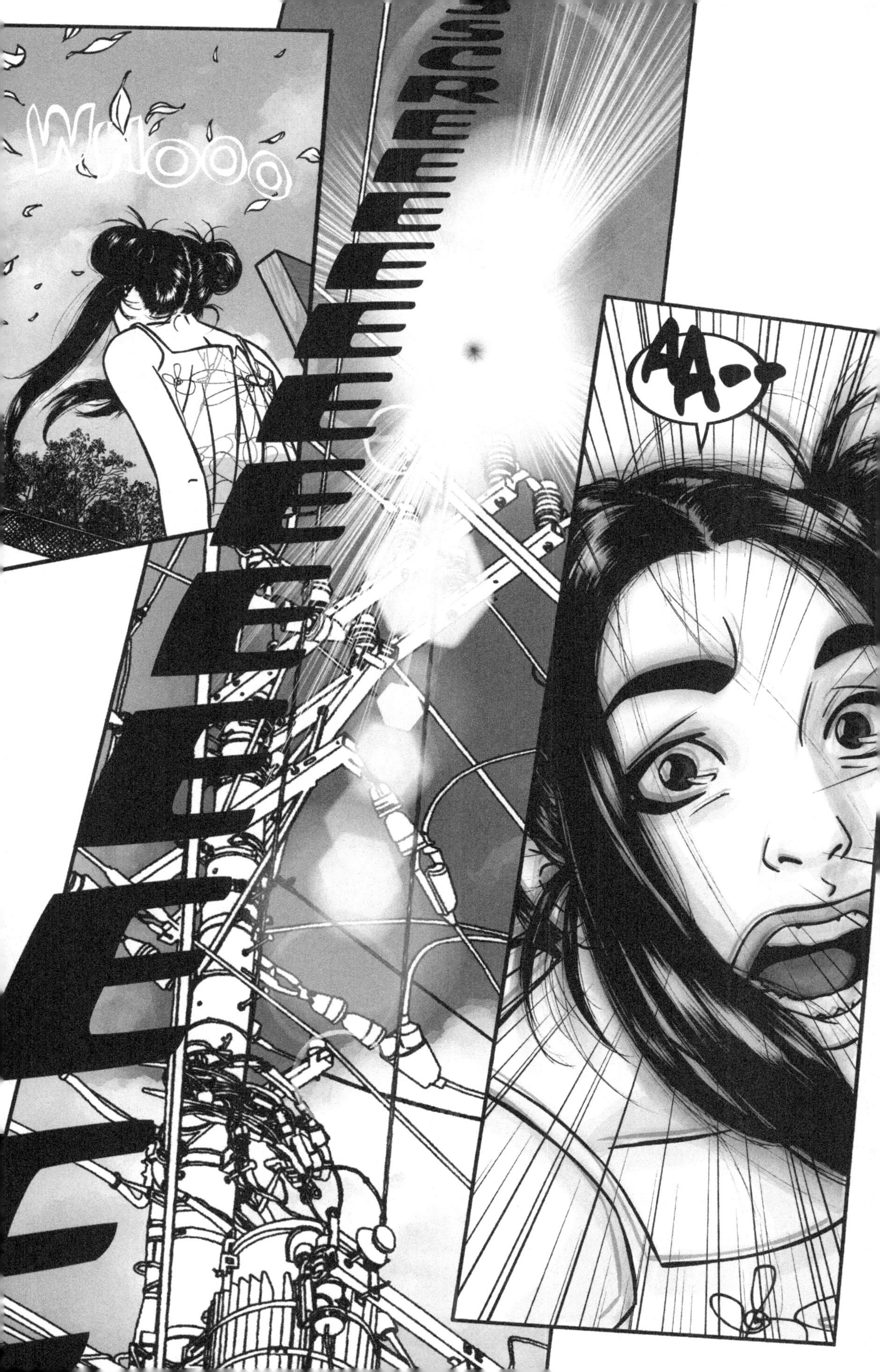
Whooo
SCREEEEEEEEEEEEEEE
AA--

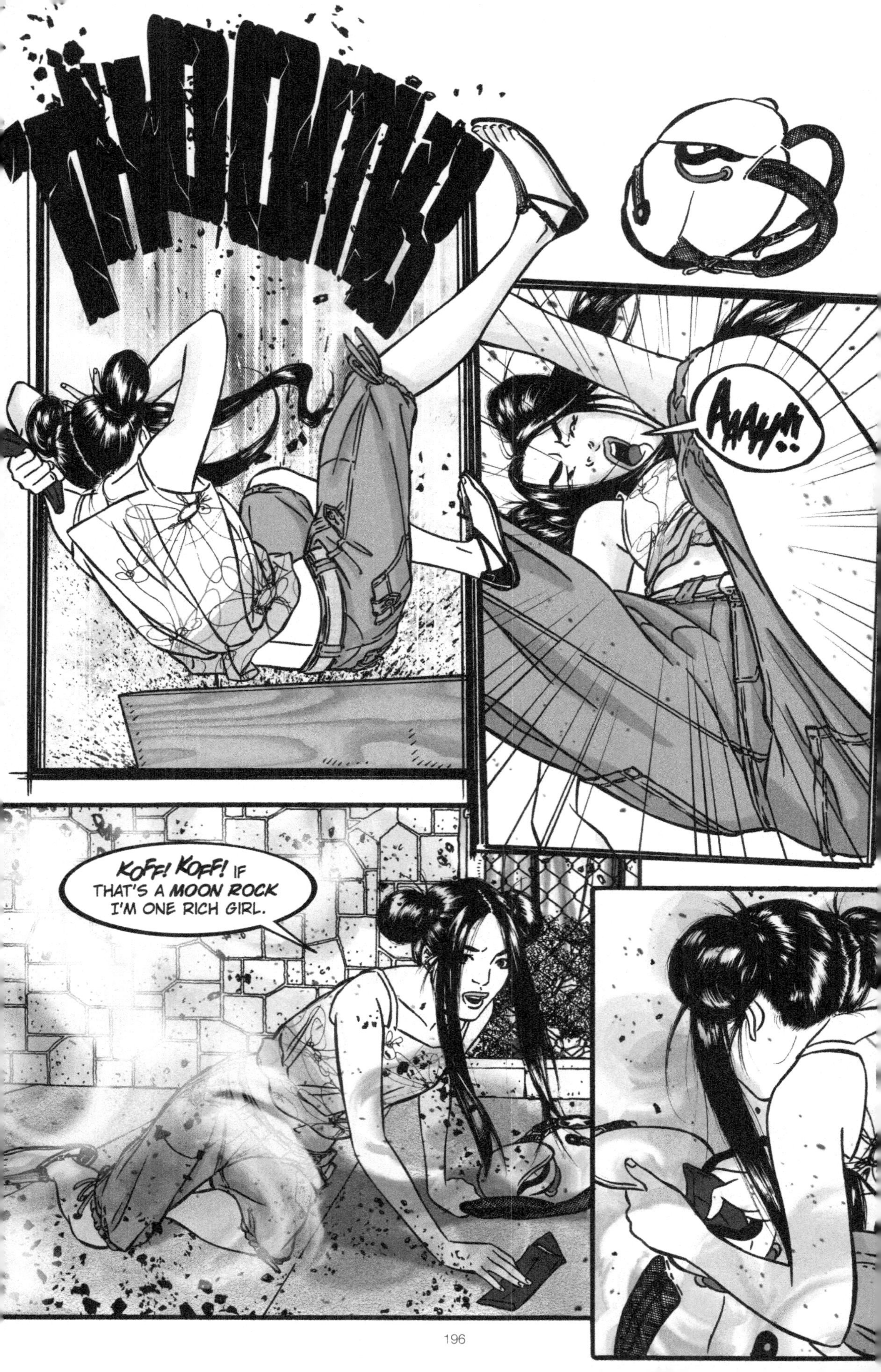
AAAH!!
KOFF! KOFF! IF THAT'S A MOON ROCK I'M ONE RICH GIRL.

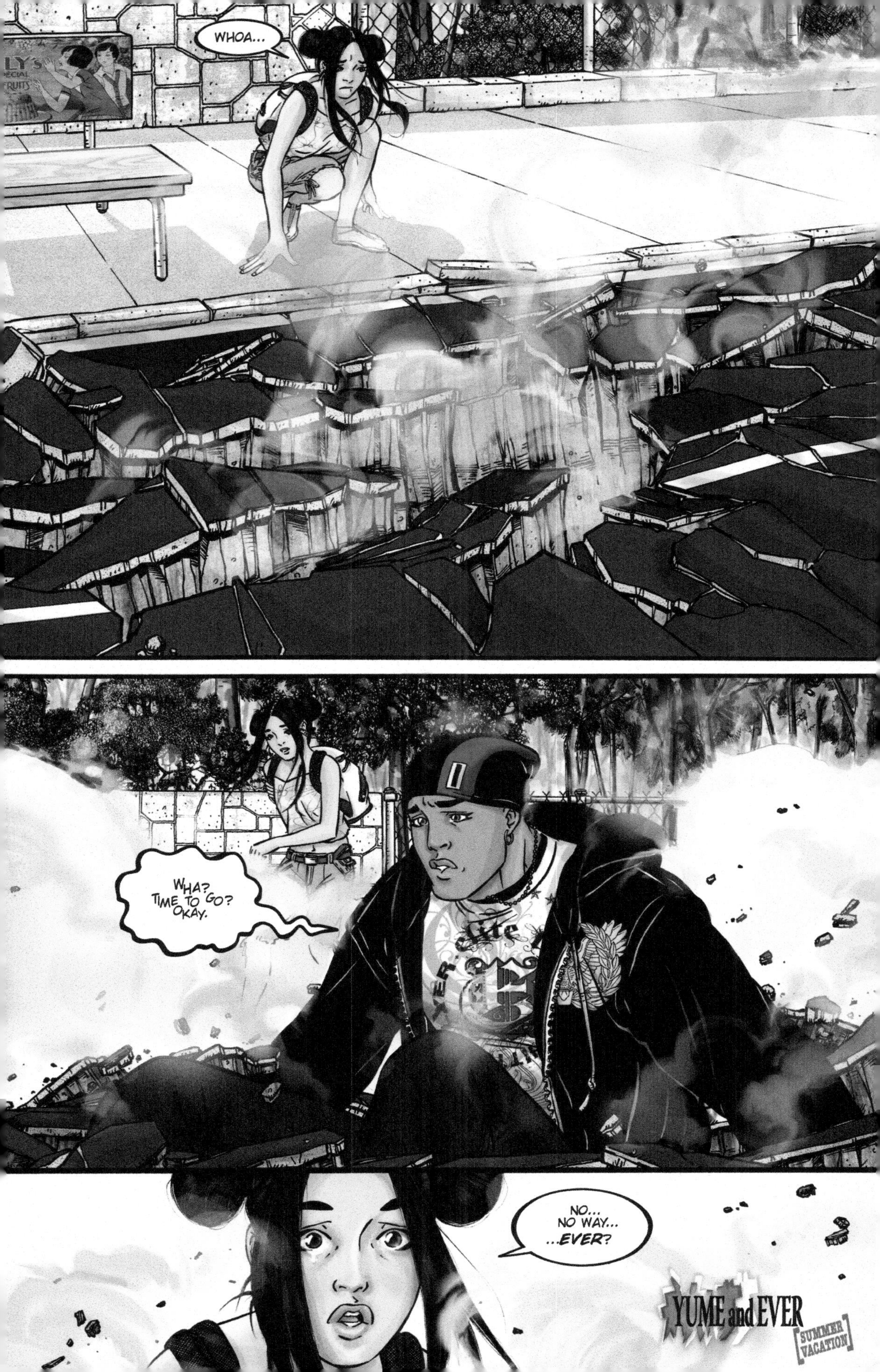
WHOA...
WHA? TIME TO GO? OKAY.
NO... NO WAY... ...EVER?
YUME and EVER
SUMMER VACATION

Paul Louise-Julie, Writer/Artist

United States / United Arab Emirates

Paul Louise-Julie is the creator, author, and artist behind the Egyptian werewolf graphic Novel Series, *The Pack*. Since its debut in March 2015, *The Pack* has become an indie hit, rising to #1 Bestseller five consecutive times on Kindle. Exclusively digital, all three issues can be found via iBooks, Kindle, Comixology, and Google Play. In December 2015, Louise-Julie announced plans for a shared universe published through his company, Midas Monkee. The first project is an African space opera titled *Yohance* and is set to drop this summer. By January 2016, it was announced that Midas Monkee's "Phase Two" will feature eight new titles - all inspired by African mythology. This shared universe will include comics, novels, art books, and children's books. Louise-Julie's goal is to reintroduce African mythology on a fantasy scale in a variety of genres and formats. Thus, reconnecting those of African descent, and by extension the world, with Africa's rich heritage. Paul currently lives in Dubai with his wife Canadace and their son, Sylvain.

The Pack
Knights of Nubia
Yohance

facebook.com/midasmonkee

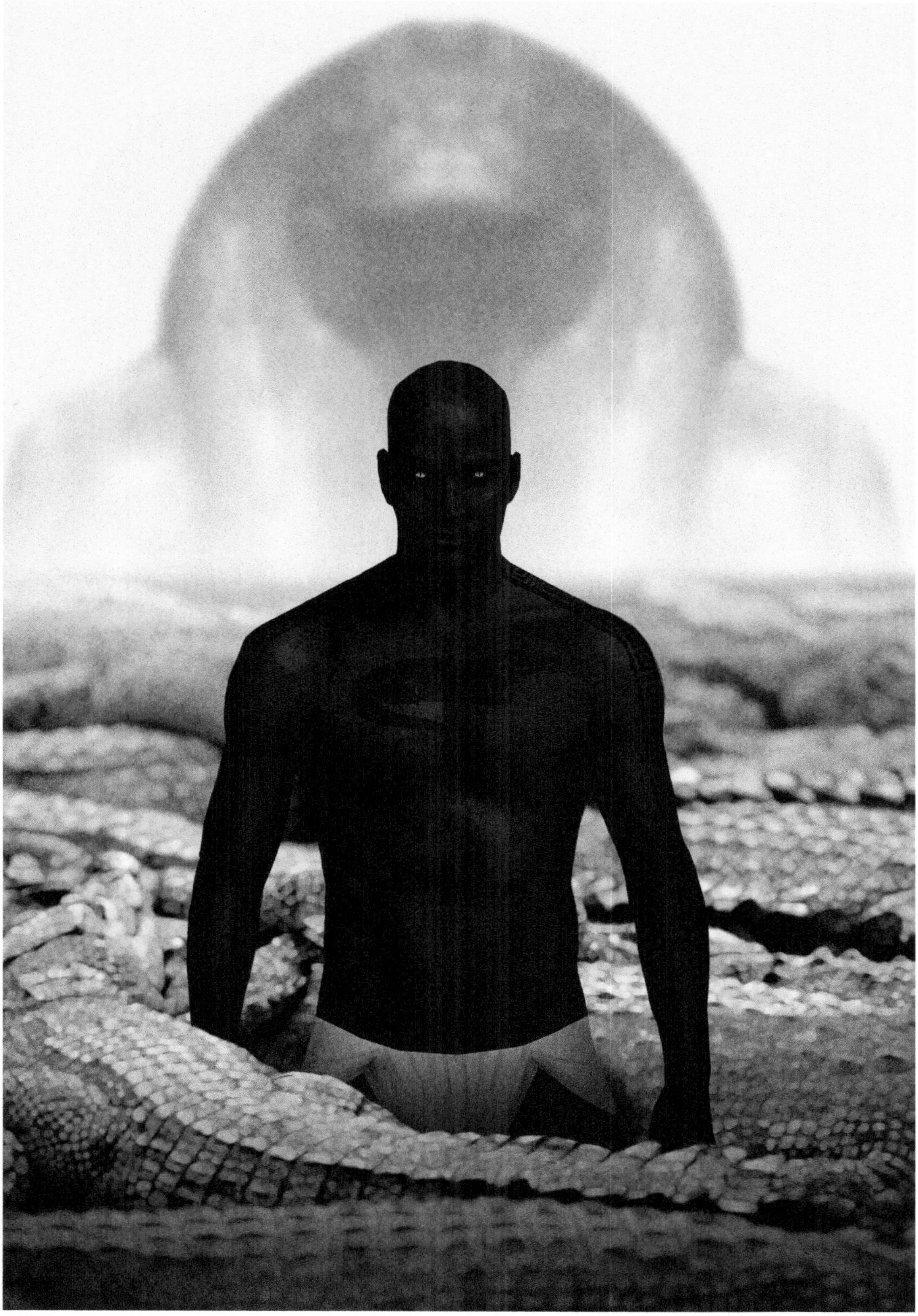

Paul Louise-Julie
United States / United Arab Emirates

The Pack - Son of Sobek
Egyptian Saga
A Midas Monkee Production

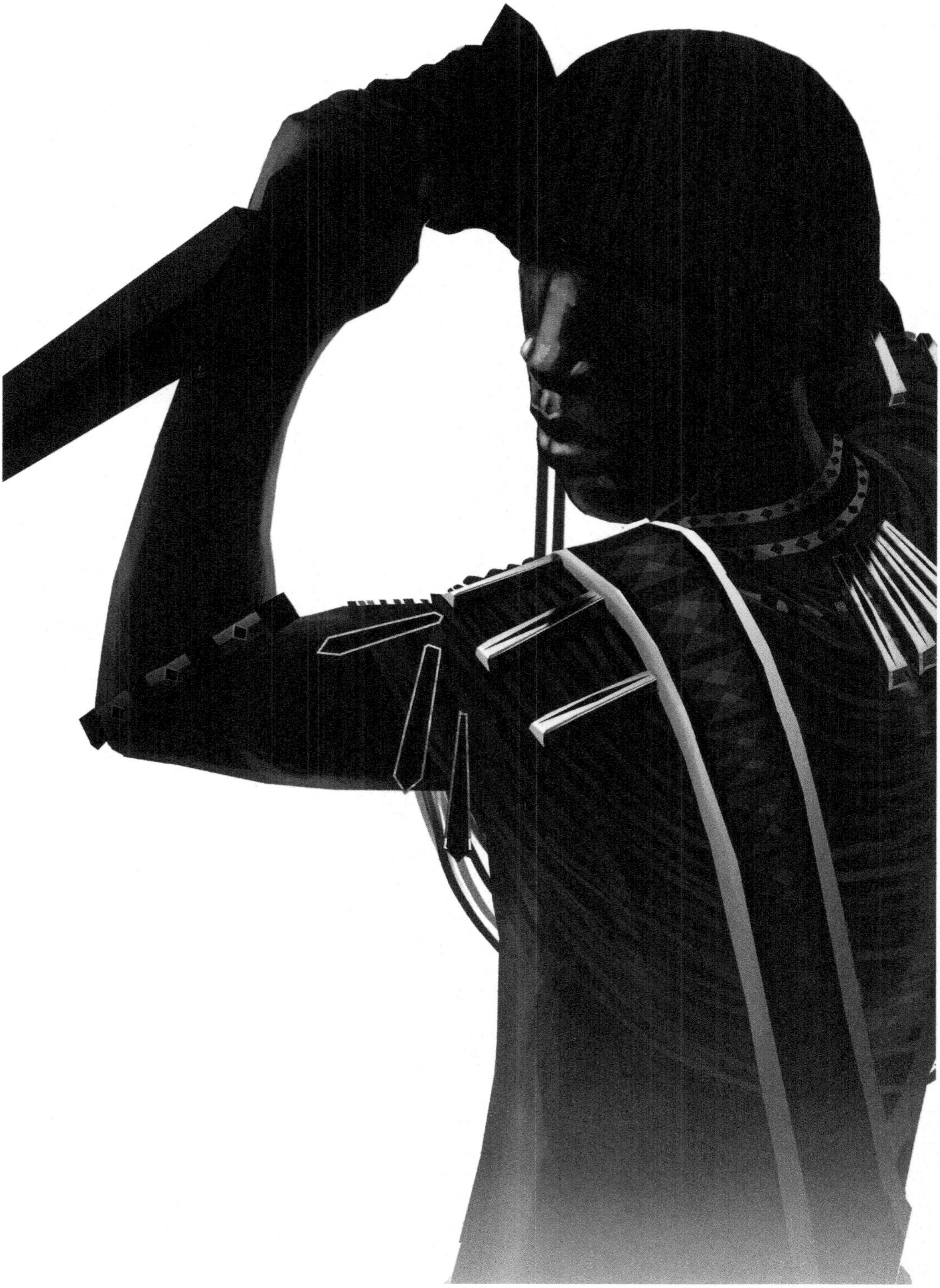

Paul Louise-Julie
United States / United Arab Emirates

Knights of Nubia
A Midas Monkee Production

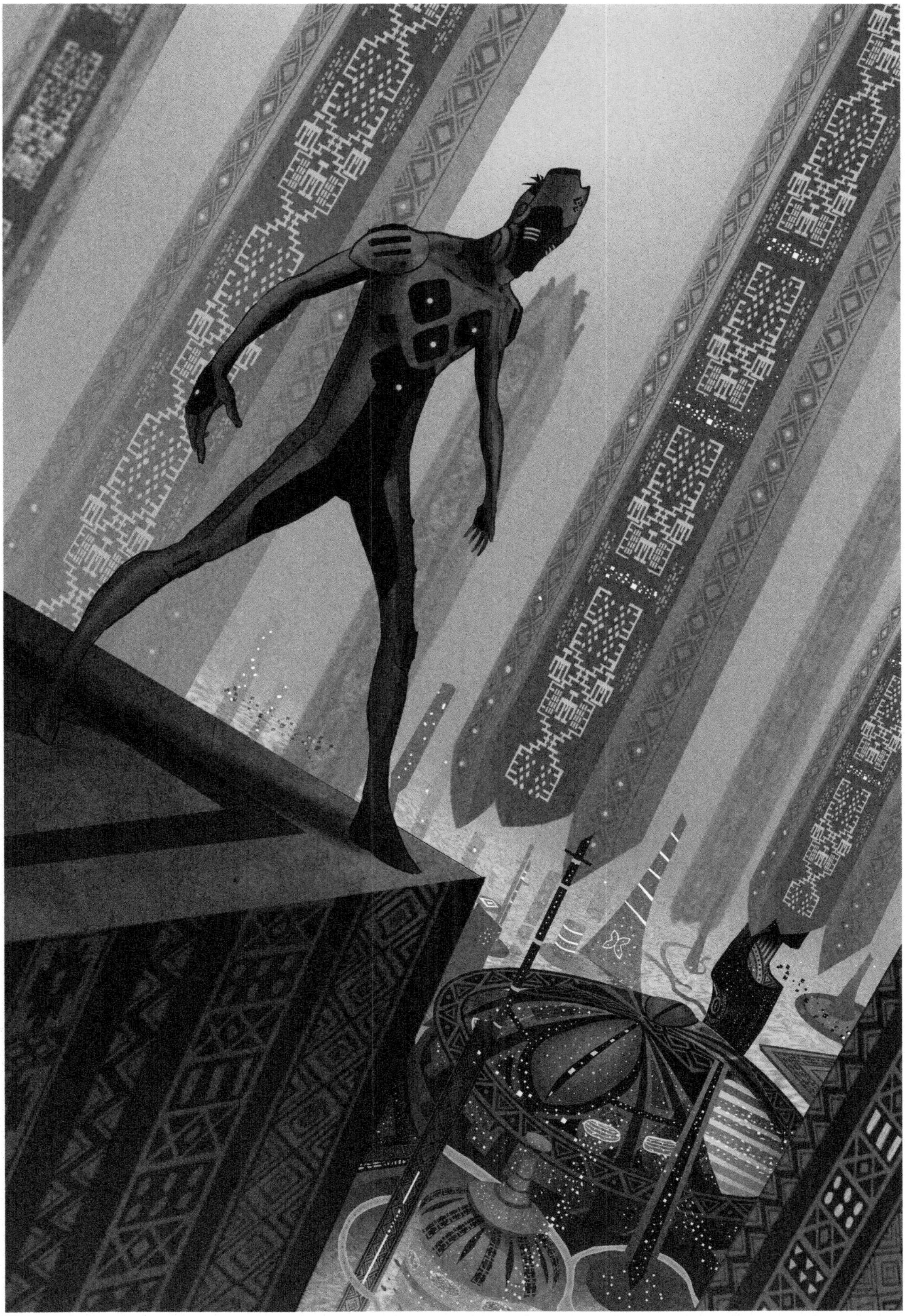

Paul Louise-Julie
United States / United Arab Emirates

Yohance
Part 2: The Ekangeni Crystal
A Midas Monkee Production

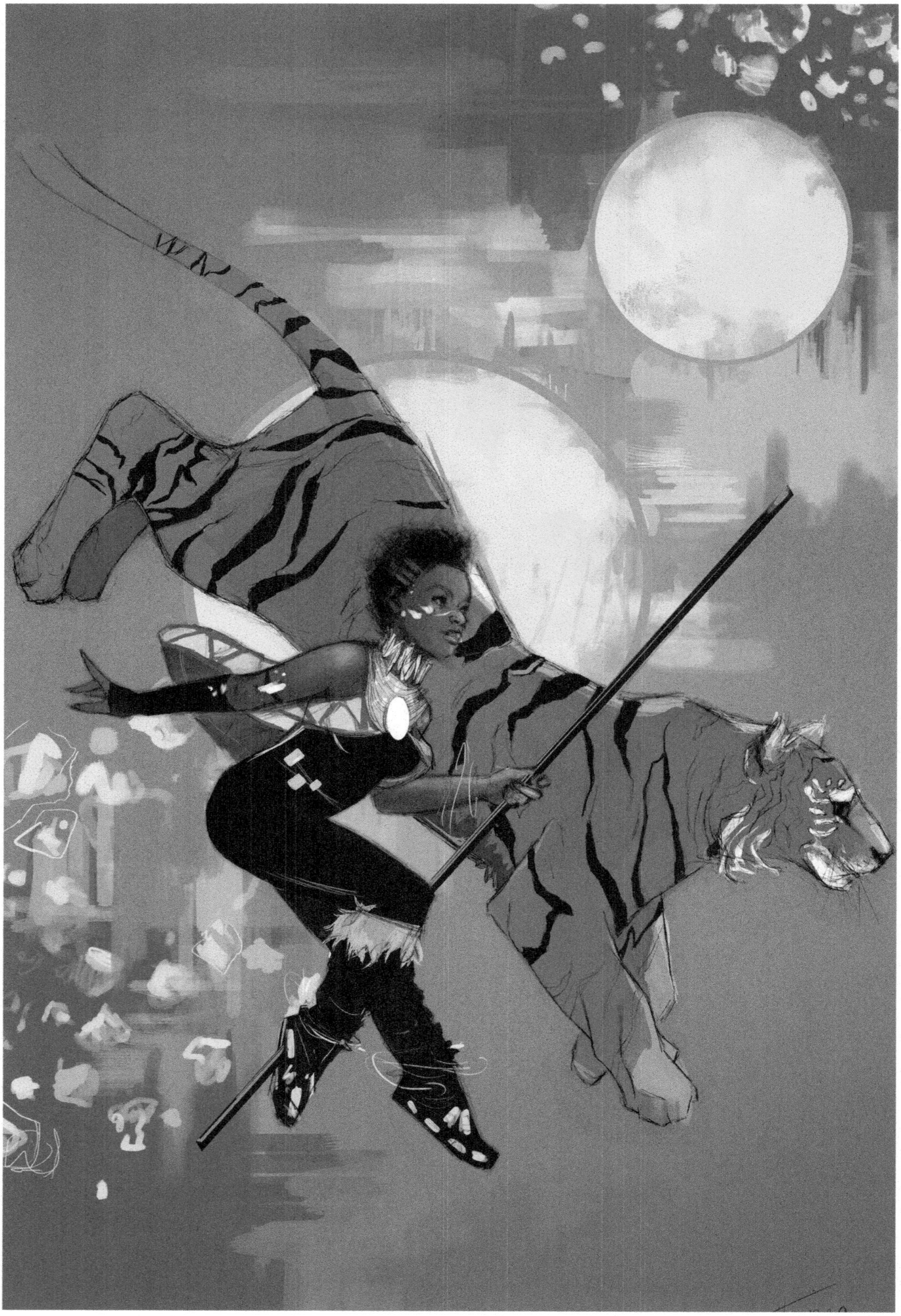

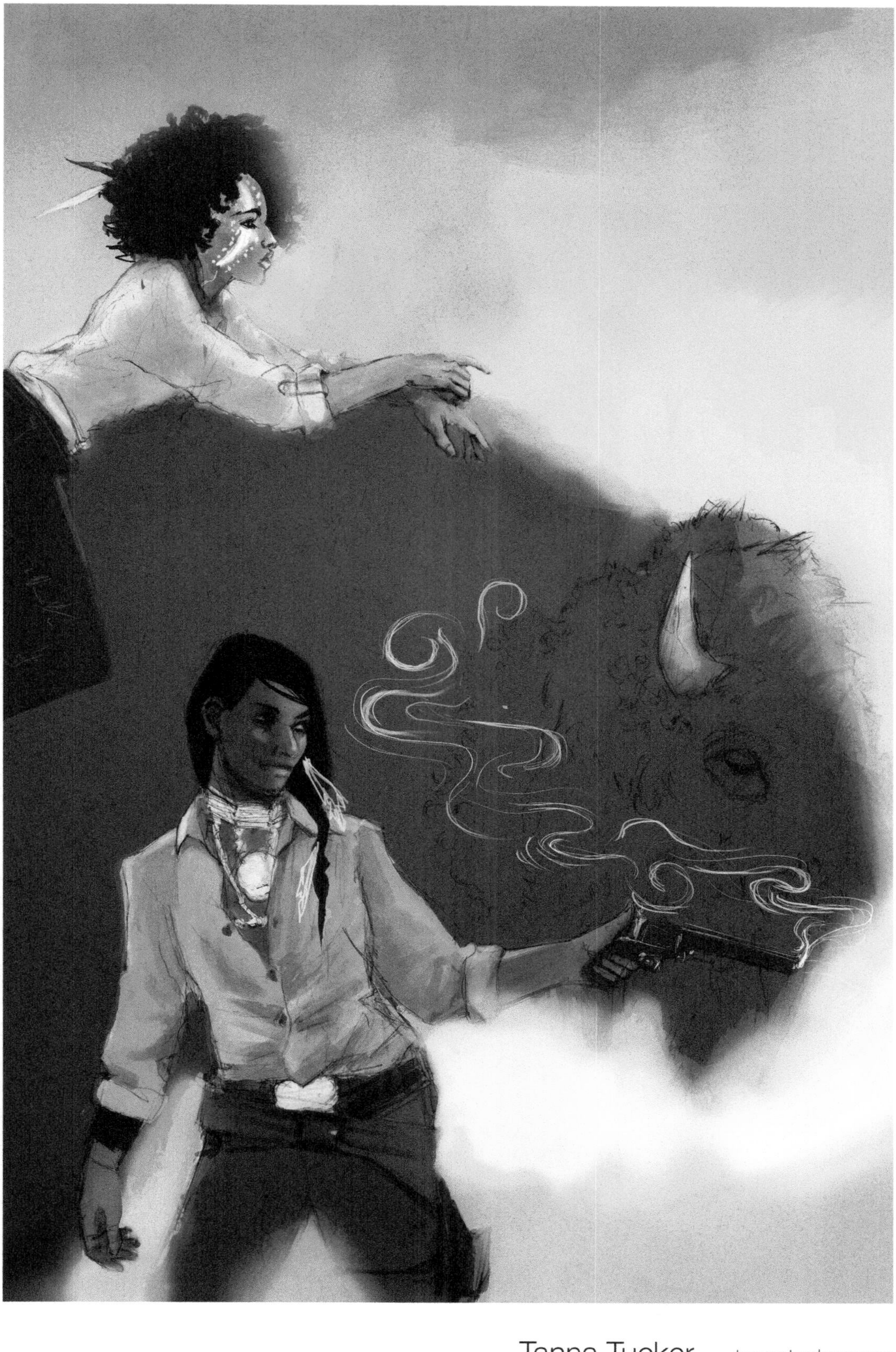

Tanna Tucker tannatucker.com
United States

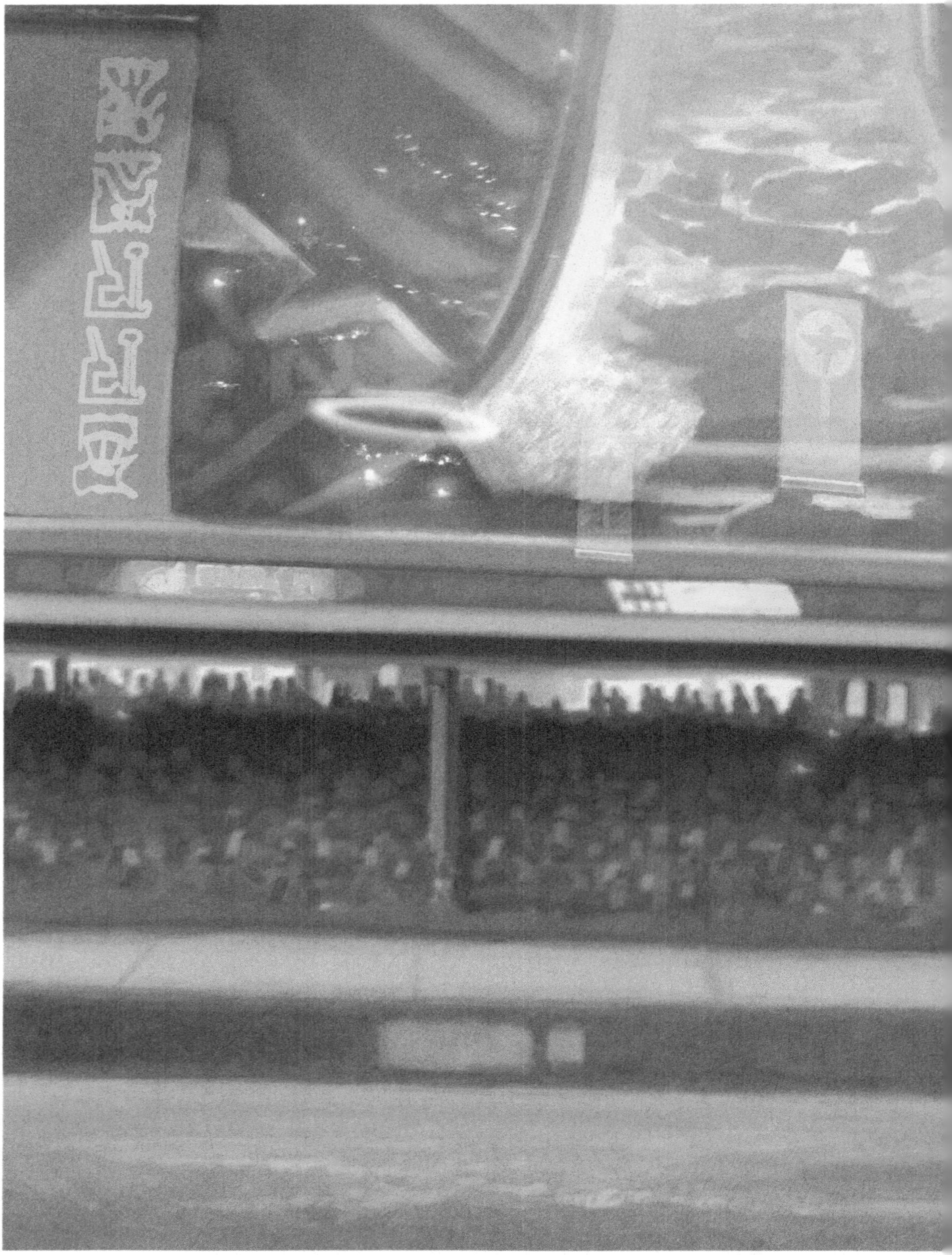

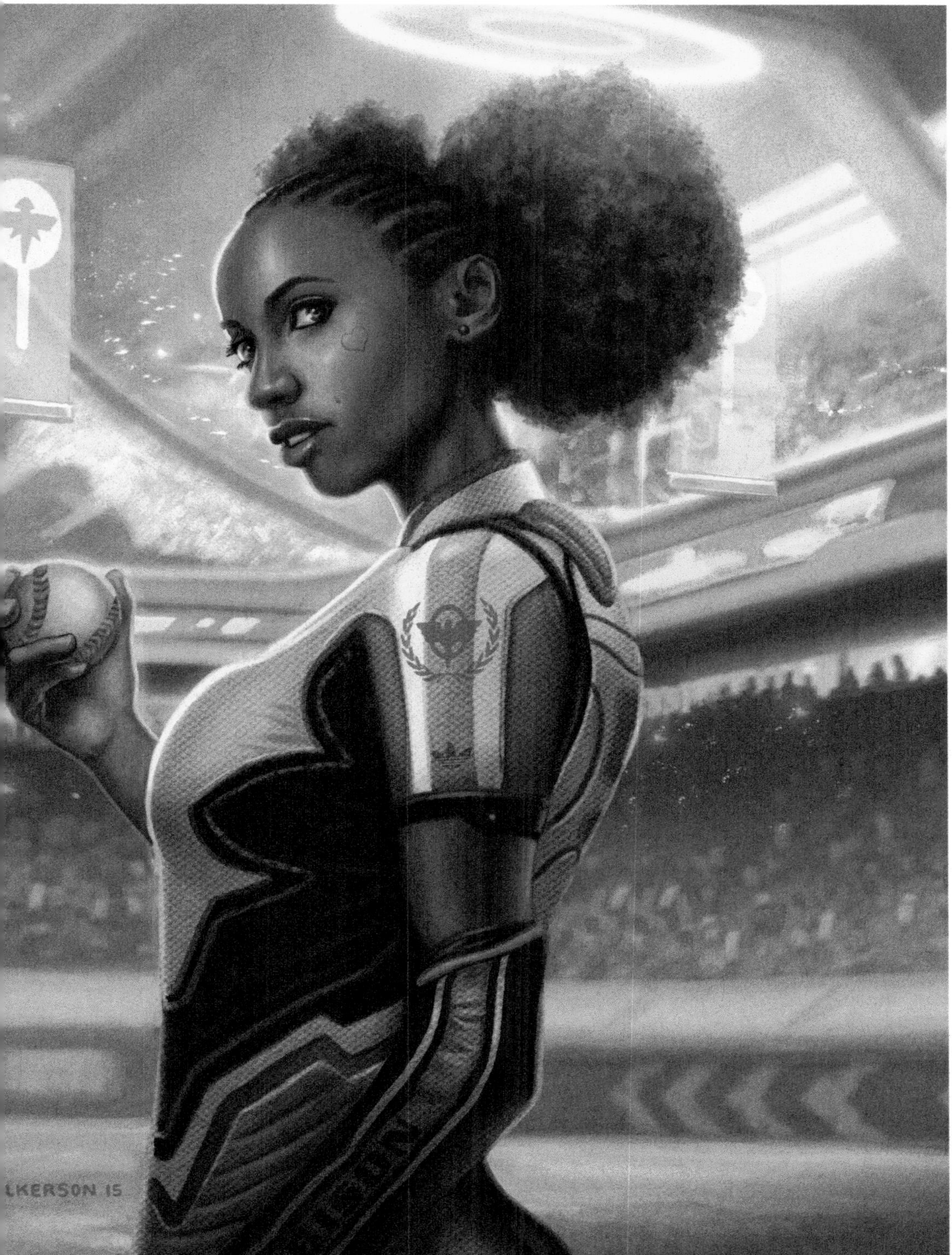
LKERSON 15

Eric Wilkerson
United States

Gemma Barrows Comes to Cooperstown
ericwilkersonart.com

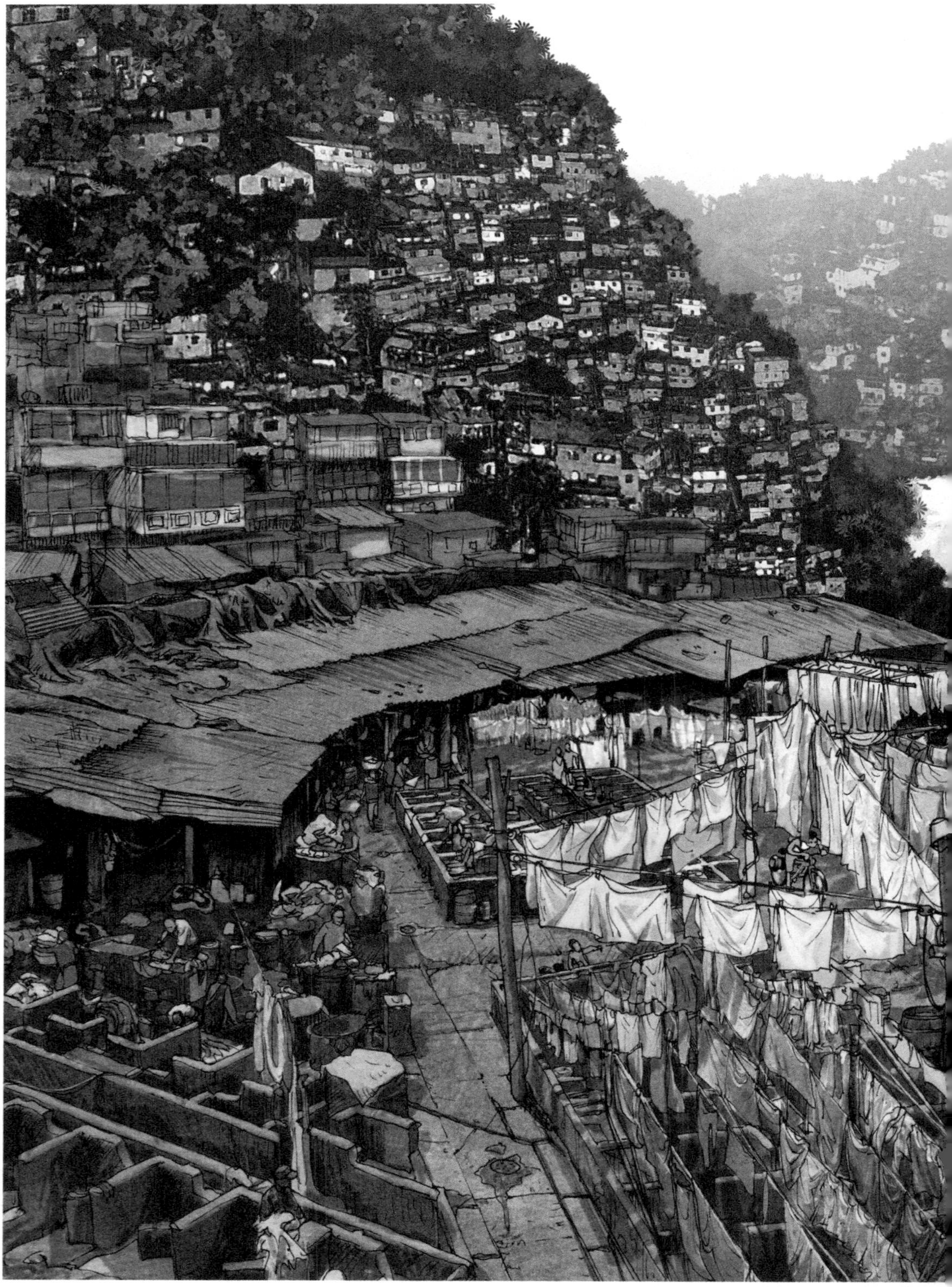

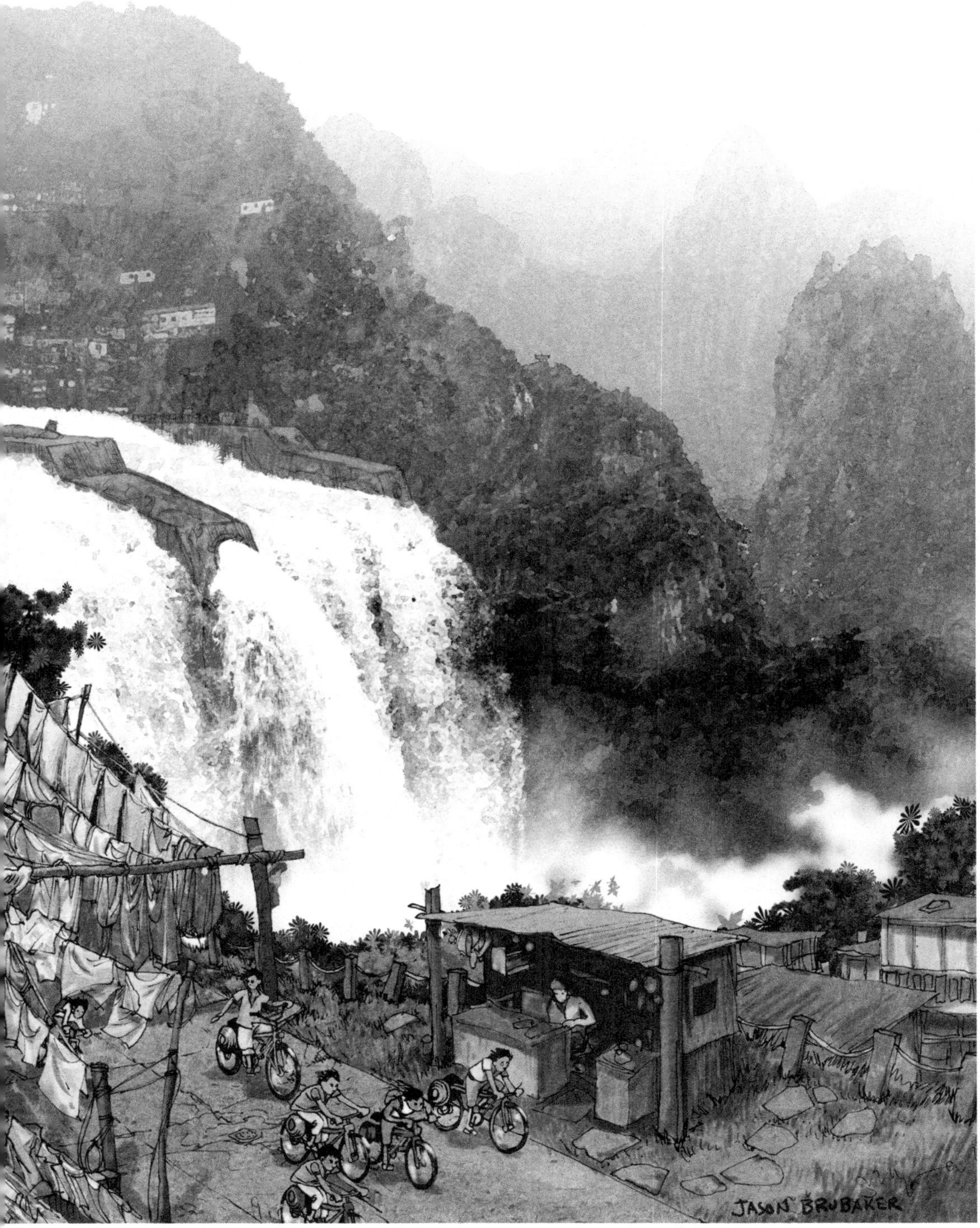
JASON BRUBAKER

Jason Brubaker
United States

Waterfall

Based on a story by John Lindauer

coffeetablecomics.com

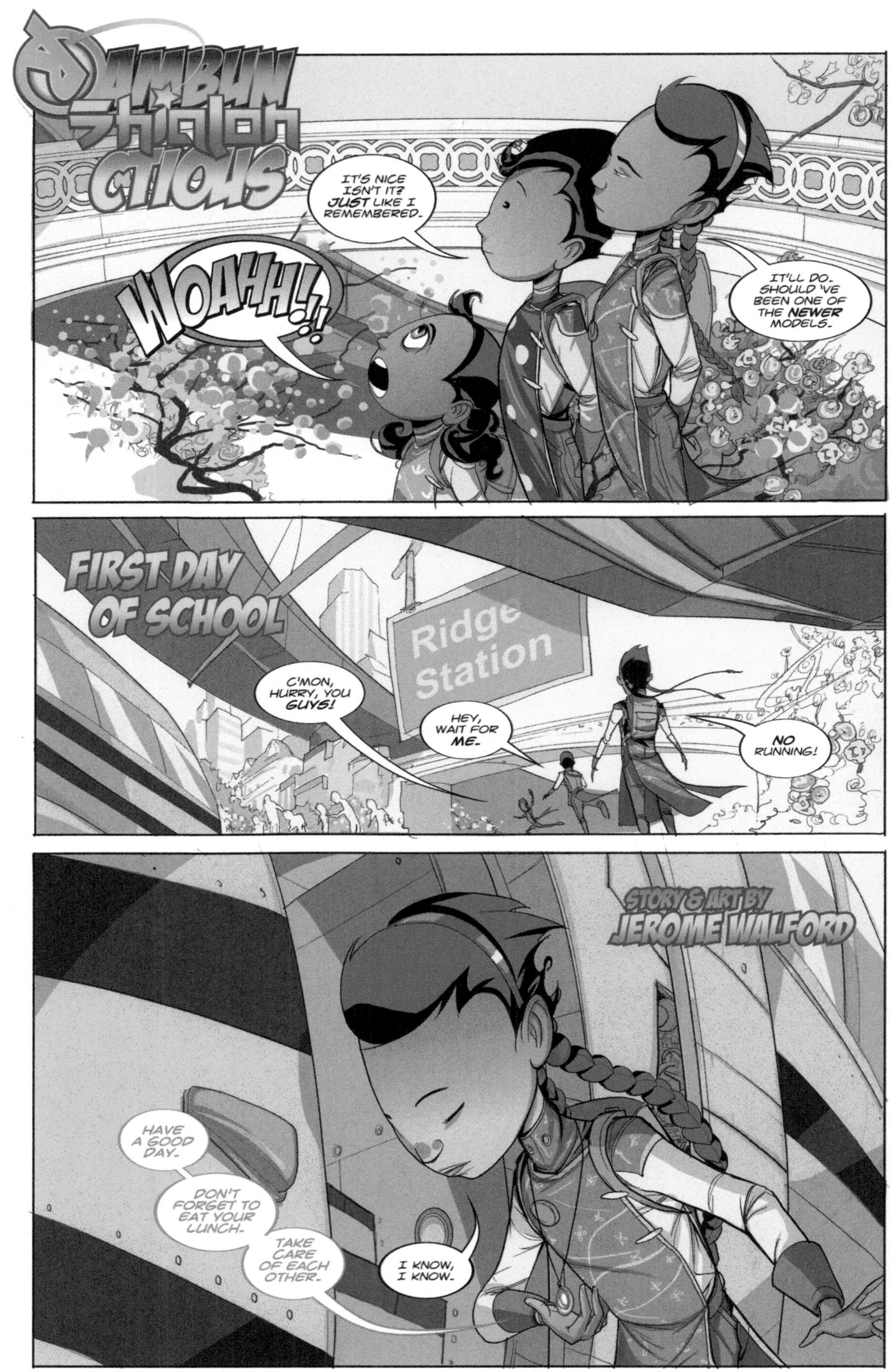
IT'S NICE ISN'T IT? JUST LIKE I REMEMBERED.
WOAHH!!
IT'LL DO. SHOULD 'VE BEEN ONE OF THE NEWER MODELS.
FIRST DAY OF SCHOOL
Ridge Station
C'MON, HURRY, YOU GUYS!
HEY, WAIT FOR ME.
NO RUNNING!
STORY & ART BY JEROME WALFORD
HAVE A GOOD DAY.
DON'T FORGET TO EAT YOUR LUNCH.
TAKE CARE OF EACH OTHER.
I KNOW, I KNOW.

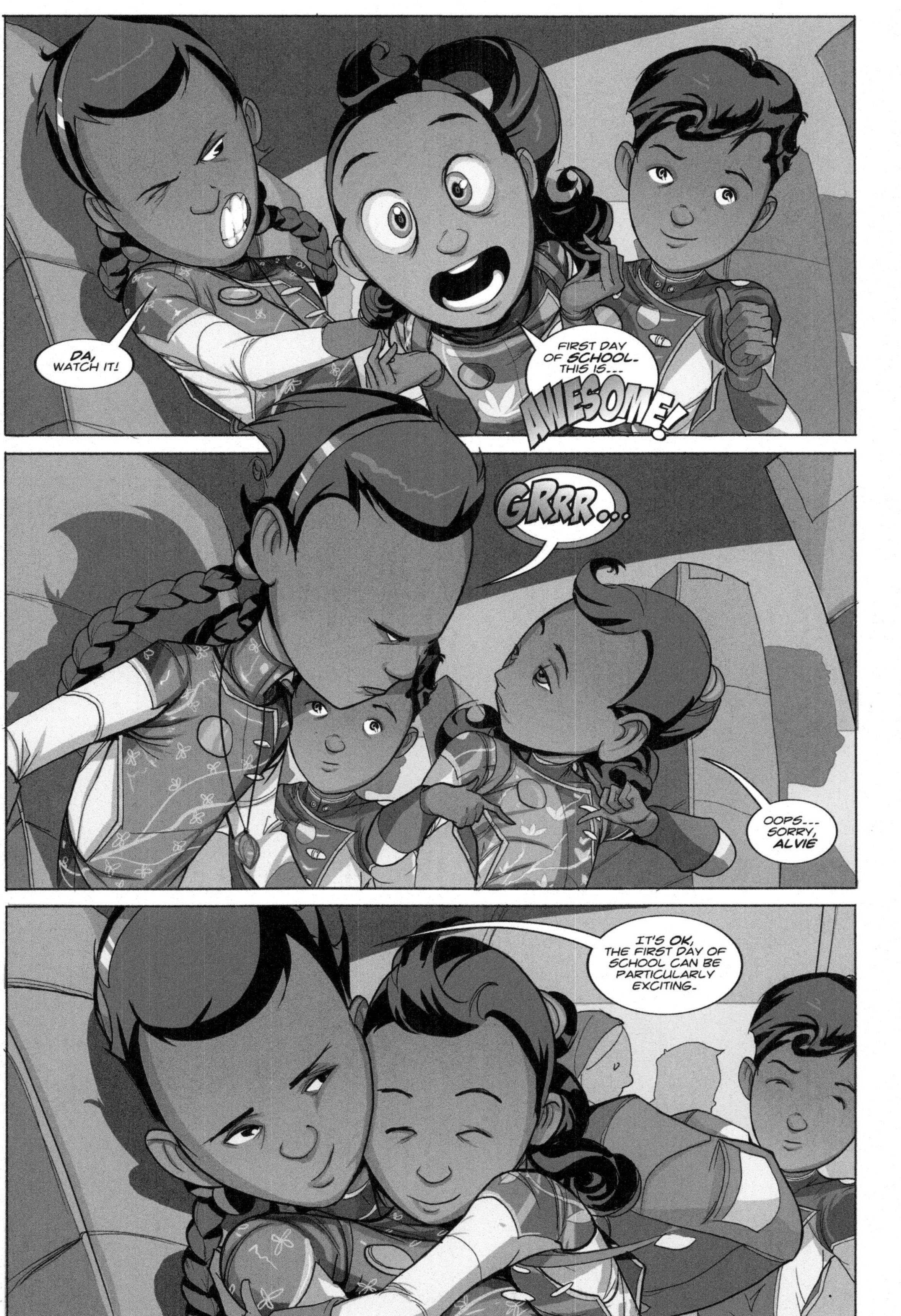
DA, WATCH IT!
FIRST DAY OF SCHOOL. THIS IS...
AWESOME!
GRRR...
OOPS... SORRY, ALVIE
IT'S OK, THE FIRST DAY OF SCHOOL CAN BE PARTICULARLY EXCITING.

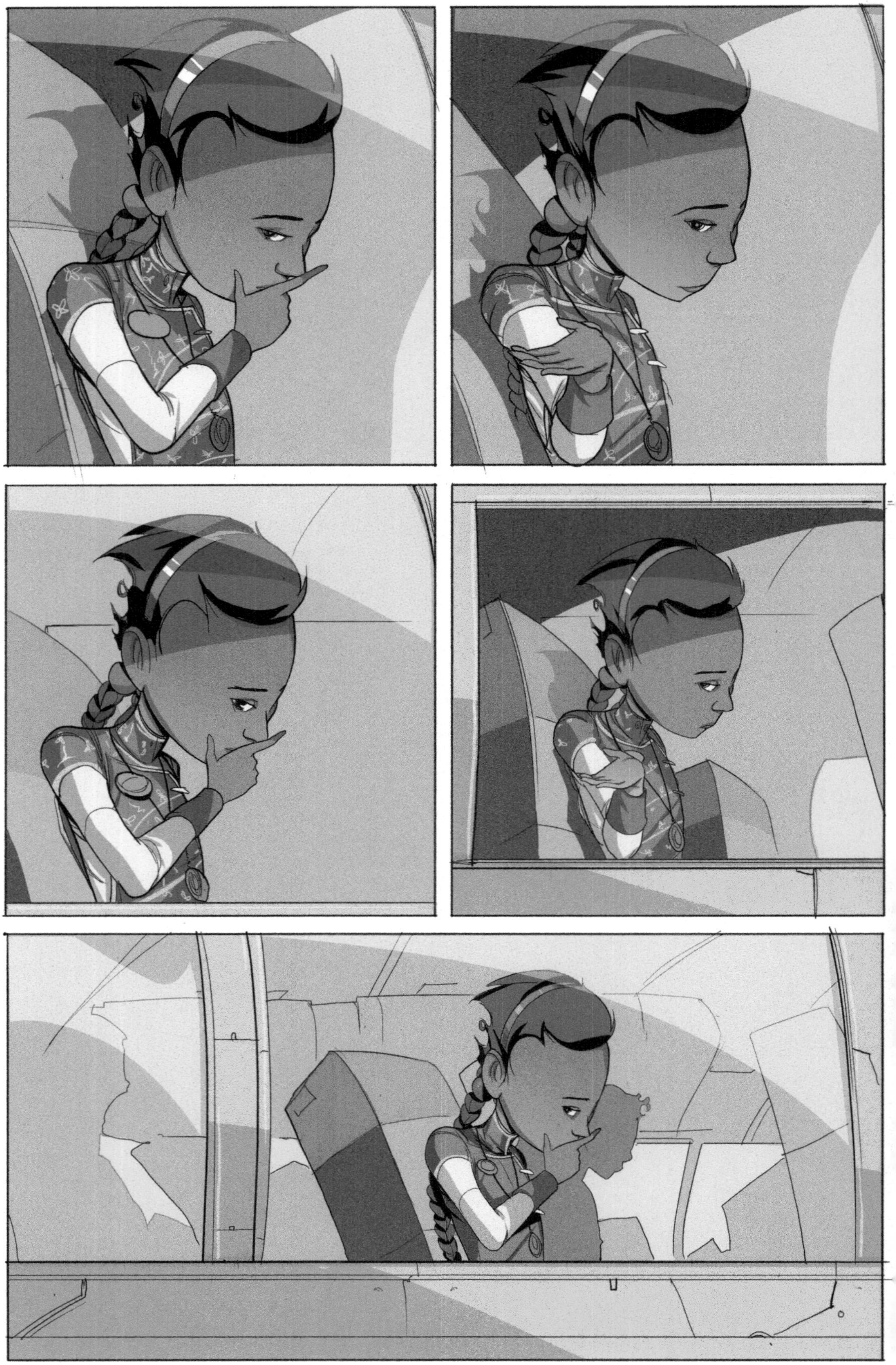

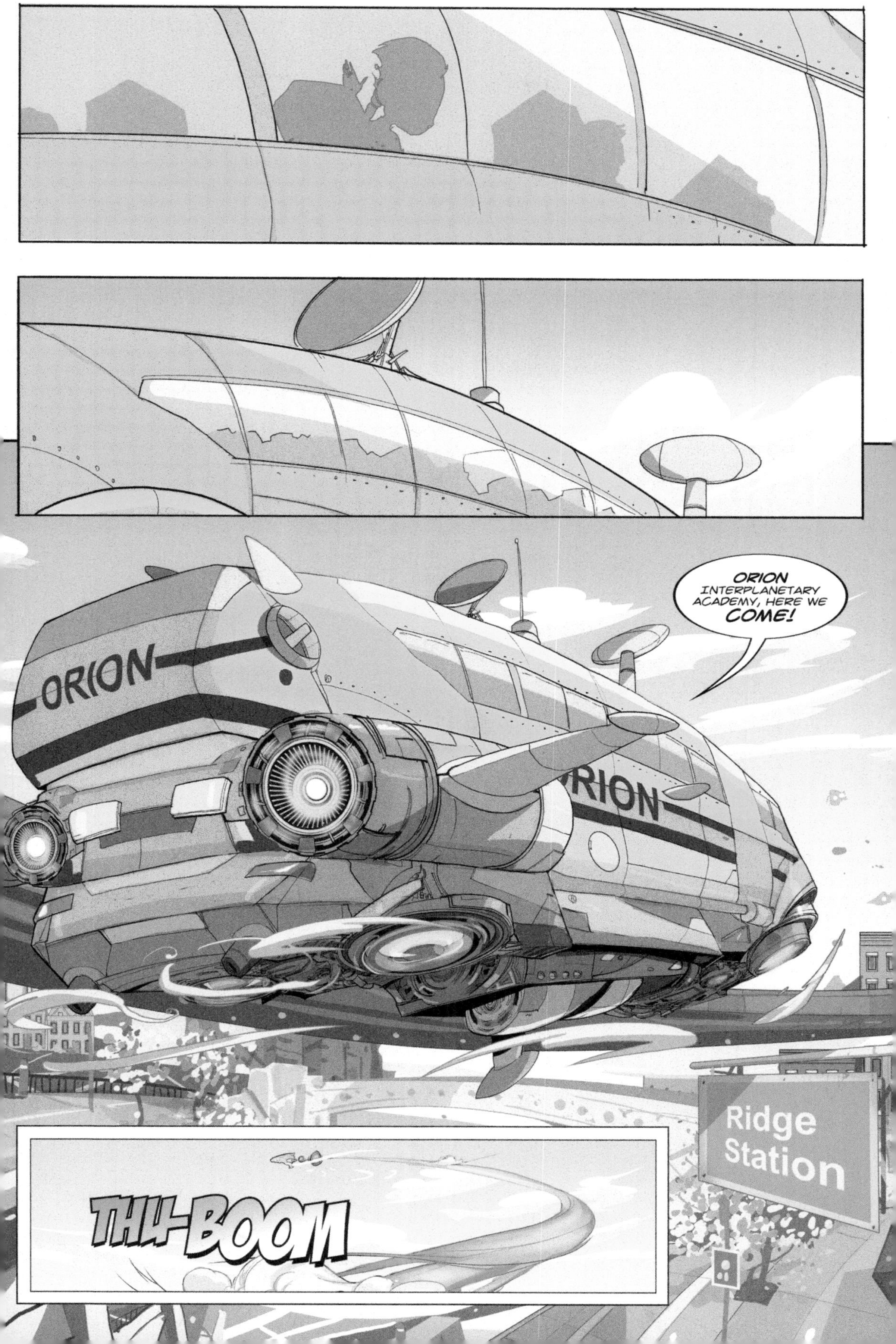
ORION
ORION INTERPLANETARY ACADEMY, HERE WE COME!
ORION
Ridge Station
THU-BOOM

Executive Producers

Jerome Walford

Amy Tan Walford

Jasmin King

Gary Stuart

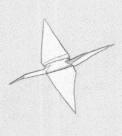

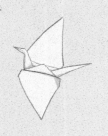

Producers

Marilyn Richard Glen
United States

Harrio
US / Korea / Qatar / Kuwait

Daniel Hom
United States

Sylvia and Thomas Hom
United States

Audrey S. Lee
United States

Aaron Taishoff
United States

Lyle Walford
United States

Production Team

Jerome Walford, Managing Editor
Maya Rock, Editor
Rebekah Griffin Greene, Editor

Special Thanks

Karama Horne, Social Media
Black Girl Nerds (BGN Network)
ComicAttack.net
Comicidal Podcast
AdrianhasIssues.com

Dedicated to all the parents who gave up the life they knew to give their children a chance at something better.

Dedicated to all the DREAMERS living life in the shadows.

Dedicated to refugees, escaping war and fear, making their way across foreign lands in search of a new place to call home.

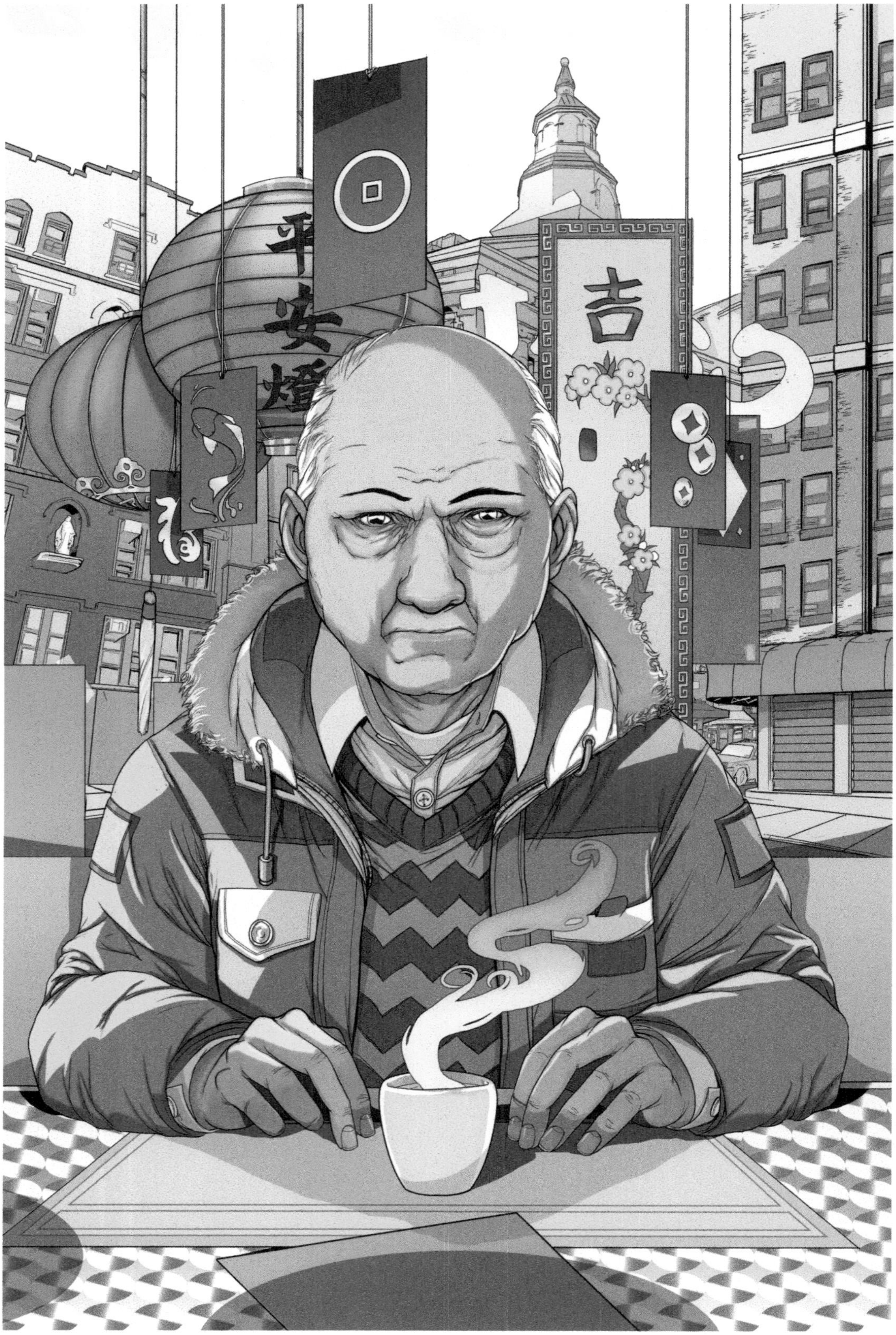
平安燈
吉

Jerome Walford
Jamaica / United States

Old Man & the Tea
forwardcomix.com

CPSIA information can be obtained at www.ICGtesting.com
Printed in the USA
BVOW05s2123160816

459246BV00004B/4/P